"This is a remarkably balanced overview of Reformation thought and of the context in which it emerged and developed. The discussed issues are so evenhandedly presented that the serious reader is moved to rethink his or her own position and the reasons for it. No less impressive is the author's contribution to the interconfessional and interreligious dialogue that involves critical judgment about where and on what matters the respective traditions need corrections. The result is a very readable book, appealing not only to students and scholars but also to general readers."

—Emidio Campi, *Professor Emeritus of Church History and former Director of the Institute for Swiss Reformation History, University of Zurich*

"Dr. Peterson has pursued an ambitious and challenging goal in this relatively compact volume. He seeks to clarify the legacy of the Reformation, specifically its impact on the Western world. Because of its introductory and summary nature and its significant engagement with current scholarship, particularly in German and English, this volume invites further exploration, evaluation, reinterpretation, and nuancing, even as it offers keen insights, draws important conclusions, and provides helpful perspectives. It can, therefore, serve as a useful scholarly resource, both in survey courses and in more advanced seminar settings."

—Kurt K. Hendel, *Bernard, Fischer, Westberg Distinguished Ministry Professor Emeritus of Reformation History, Lutheran School of Theology at Chicago*

"Paul Peterson's *Reformation in the Western World* is an ambitious and wide-ranging attempt to rethink the place of the Reformation in the grand narratives of the Western world. It takes on big themes, from tolerance and intolerance to capitalism, secularism, and the rise of modernism, and yet it never loses touch with the history or the spirit of the age, equally at home in the Reformation discussions of repentance and justification as in the theories of the modern day. Thoughtful, provocative, and based on broad scholarship, this book will encourage readers to think about the Reformation in new ways."

—C. Scott Dixon, *Senior Lecturer, The Queen's University of Belfast*

D0898621

REFORMATION
IN THE WESTERN WORLD
An Introduction

Paul Silas Peterson

BAYLOR UNIVERSITY PRESS

Unless otherwise stated, Scripture quotations are from the New Revised Standard Version Bible, copyright 1989, Division of Christian Education of the National Council of the Churches of Christ in the United States of America. Used by permission. All rights reserved.

Cover design: Daniel Benneworth-Gray
Cover art: Copper engraving by G. Eilers, 1868, which copies Wilhelm von Kaulbach's *The Age of the Reformation*, 1862–1866, a wall painting in the Staircase Hall of the Neues Museum, Berlin. The wall painting was destroyed during the Second World War.

This book has been catalogued by the Library of Congress with the ISBN 978-1-4813-0552-5.

Printed in the United States of America on acid-free paper.

For Lena and our children, Paul Richard and Maria Therese

Eternal life is grace given for grace out of mercy and compassion.

Andreas Bodenstein von Karlstadt (1486–1541)
Thesis 133 of his 151 Theses, which were posted
on Wittenberg's collegiate church door
on April 26, 1517

CONTENTS

CONTENTS

Preface

As I started the research for this book in the summer of 2013, my goal was to present the history of the Reformation and its influence on the Western world from an ecumenical perspective and with both the positive and the problematic dimensions. I am deeply indebted to many historians and theologians and would especially like to thank Volker Leppin for his many lectures and the occasional conversations over the years in Tübingen. His research has helped me understand the roots of the Reformation in the Middle Ages. I would also like to mention the ecumenical dialogue that I am participating in titled *Multiple Reformations? The Heidelberg–Notre Dame Colloquies on the Legacies of the Reformation* (2016–2018). At the first two conferences of this dialogue I had the opportunity to discuss many of the issues that are addressed in this book with a group of truly exceptional scholars, including Neil Arner, Matthew Ashley, Philip Benedict, John Betz, Euan Cameron, Emidio Campi, Simon Ditchfield, Scott Dixon, Johannes Eurich, Brad Gregory, Patrick Griffin, Peter Harrison, Hartmut Lehmann, Volker Leppin, Ute Lotz-Heumann, Friederike Nüssel, Wolfgang Schluchter, Jan Stievermann, Christoph Strohm, Klaus Tanner, Elliott Visconsi, Michael Welker, and Randall Zachman. I learned a great deal from all the conversations with these historians and theologians. Of course, I alone am responsible for any errors that might be contained in this book. I would also like to thank Donald K. McKim for his helpful suggestions and comments. A very special word of thanks is owed to Carey Newman, the director of Baylor University Press, for his interest in this book and his many helpful suggestions. This monograph would not have been possible without him and the many others at Baylor who have helped it along the way: David Aycock, Jordan Rowan Fannin, Karla Garrett, Jenny Hunt, Cade Jarrell, Amy Maddox, Miki Alexandra Caputo, and Diane Smith. I also wish to thank all the people who work at the wonderful libraries of the University of Tübingen (*pars pro toto*: Herr Franz Träger), the University of Heidelberg (Frau Karin Böttcher), and at Staupitz' old home, the Augustinian monastery on the Neckar in Tübingen (now called the Protestant Stift), especially Herr Ulrich Gebhardt. I am also grateful to Jamin Swenson for taking the time to proofread an early version of the manuscript. Finally, I would like to thank my most loving and brilliant wife and our children to whom this book is dedicated.

INTRODUCTION
The Good and the Bad of the Reformation

While Protestantism has become a predominately non-Western religion,[1] the debate about its relationship to the Western world has not stopped since a group of German historians, sociologists, and theologians started to think about it.[2] In terms of the cultural, social, and political impact, the Reformation was the most important event in the early modern period of the Western world. Initially, a group of pastorally motivated theologians wanted to improve—to reform—the church and society (Christendom). Above all, they challenged the theology behind the deeply problematic practice of the sale of divine grace (indulgences). As virtually everyone would affirm today, this desire to make things better was the "good" of the Reformation.

The theologically initiated reform was, however, quickly transformed into a political program. The theologians were just as involved in this as the princes. Together, and with popular support, they orchestrated reforms that reshaped the cultural, social, and political realms of human life. This "reforming" of Latin Christendom in the German territories quickly took on a life of its own as it spread to other parts of Europe. It was resisted and suppressed with intellectual, political, and military force by the Roman ecclesial authority structure and its political allies. From 1517 to 1545, "Protestantism seemed unstoppable and responses to it were largely haphazard."[3] Eventually, the moods of reform (which were far older than the Reformation) had an effect in Rome. Encouraged by Charles V, the emperor of the Holy Roman Empire, Pope Paul III then took action to reform the church himself. He commissioned a report that was later titled

"A Plan for the Improvement of the Church" (*Consilium de emendanda ecclesia*, 1536). It provided a very critical analysis of the situation and called for significant reforms.[4] It still took some time, however, before these ideas were implemented. After nearly three decades of resistance, real reform finally began in 1545 under the same pope. At the Council of Trent (1545–1563) the "Catholic reformers began to hit their stride and the leaders of the [Catholic] Church were forced to devise plans for genuine reform."[5] This also led to a new centralization of the Catholic Church and can thus be understood as the birth of Roman Catholicism as an alternative confessional identity to the politically backed Protestantism of the German territories.

The "bad" of the Reformation is seen in the violent rejections of the reforms and the violent implementation of the reforms. Not only did the Catholics and Protestants proceed to persecute and sometimes kill one another, the Protestants and the Catholics together persecuted and killed the Anabaptists. The confessional orders that emerged in the Reformation period, on both the Catholic and the Protestant sides, also implemented new disciplinary regimes that enforced the different confessional identities and radically polarized Christians. In the end, brothers and sisters of the same tradition of faith turned against one another and became violent enemies. Attempts at repairing the disunity started shortly after the reform movements took hold. Real progress toward this goal began, however, only in the second half of the twentieth century in the wake of the destruction of World War II. It is impossible to look back at the Reformation from a naive perspective today, as though it were entirely good or entirely evil. There is, rather, a need for a differentiated analysis of this event. The same must be said about the consequences of the Reformation.

The nature of the complex relationship between the Reformation and the modern Western world remains an important subject of debate. When thinking about this relationship, many questions immediately emerge, for example: How did the Reformation influence the Western world? Was the Reformation a positive or a negative event? Is the Reformation over, or is it still happening? Did the Reformation lead to democracy, capitalism, and secularism? What relationship did the Reformation have to political power? And how can the Reformation be remembered by both Catholics and Protestants today?

In the following pages, these questions and many others are answered from a historical and ecumenical-theological point of view. Following this, the status of ecumenism today and the issue of the Reformation itself in ecumenism are also analyzed. With a view to the commemoration of the Reformation, a handful of positive aspects of the Reformation are proposed that could be, I believe, positively commemorated by both Catholics and Protestants as valuable developments in the history of Christianity. These cannot be seen, of course, in isolation from the other problematic aspects of the history. The Reformation should be remembered in all its dimensions.

This book has seven chapters. In chapter 1 ("The Western World and the Reformation") the central terminology of this book is discussed. While many people have a general concept about the terms "the Western world" and "the Reformation," there is, in fact, a great deal of disagreement about what these terms actually signify. Both the term "the Western world" and the term "the Reformation" are analyzed from various perspectives. As will be shown, the Reformation can be understood in many different ways depending on the historical school of thought. In many of these different historical presentations, there is a "short Reformation" that always seems to find its way into the story. This short Reformation entails some of the most important events of the "long Reformation." The short version is introduced and analyzed. As will be shown, there are many conflicts of interpretation about the most important events of both the short and the long Reformation.

While the Reformers made many positive contributions to the Western world, they were also imperfect. Above all, they persecuted people who did not agree with them. In chapter 2 ("The Evils and Errors of the Reformers"), some of these problematic issues are addressed. The Reformers, and the Reformation as a whole, cannot be fully understood and honestly evaluated without the problematic and negatives sides of the history.

One of the big questions today concerning the Reformation is the degree to which it was a break with the traditions of the late Middle Ages. In chapter 3 ("Prehistory, Division, and Authority") an account of the long Reformation is presented. This shows how much the Reformation was dependent upon a history of reform movements in Western Christianity. In this chapter a few other big questions are addressed regarding the Reformation: How should the division of Christianity in the sixteenth century be understood? Did it turn "the church" into "the churches"? With this, how should the strong emphasis on the authority of the Scriptures in Protestant theology be understood? How much of this was a new development foreign to the history of Christian theology? As is argued here, in both of these cases there are points of continuity and discontinuity.

As the theological and ecclesial reform movements took hold in German lands, the political authorities (princes and magistrates) were deeply involved in this process. While the princes and magistrates did not develop the theological arguments for reform, they were often convinced of the truth of these arguments and supported the reforms with political power. In some cases, however, they used the movements to consolidate authority and influence in their territorial jurisdictions. In chapter 4 ("Political Power and Tolerance") this very problematic and complicated aspect of the Reformation is addressed. These ecclesial and political reforming movements often entailed an authoritarian and coercive dimension. In this context, the debate about the freedom of conscience and the separation of church and state became very important.

For over a century, historians and theologians have asked themselves how and why the Western world moved away from a church-influenced and nobility-controlled political order to a representative democratic system with the separation of church and state. Did this have to do with basic theological ideas (like the priesthood of all believers) and understandings of the church (ecclesiology)? Or was it more of a historical development that had to do with other things, such as the economy and a changing social order? Another question in this realm is, what role did religion play in the emergence of capitalism and secularism itself? Behind these specific questions is the broader question about the Reformation and modernity. Other issues come into play here as well, like the rise in literacy in the modern period, the liberation of suppressed groups (Jews, "heretics," women, etc.), the decline of belief in witches and evil spirits, and many others that are largely taken for granted today in the Western world. In chapter 5 ("Modernity, Democracy, Capitalism, and Secularism") these issues are addressed with a view to the academic debates regarding the Reformation's and Protestantism's influences on each of them.

A recurring theme that is found in theological, philosophical, and historical literature, one that also plays a role in cultural criticism and sociopolitical discourse, is the idea that the Western world is in decline. These decline narratives take many different forms. In some cases the Reformation plays an important role in these narratives. The issue of pluralism in society is often lamented in these narratives, and the Reformation is sometimes seen as the cause of the pluralism. Criticisms of multiculturalism and the growing influence of Islam in the Western world are often drawn into these histories. In chapter 6 ("The Western World Today") all of these issues are addressed. In addition to this, a positive interpretation of multiculturalism is provided that, at the same time, supports the goal of peaceful social integration. Furthermore, the discussion about Islam in the Western world is also addressed from a historical and contemporary perspective. Attention is drawn to reform movements in Islam and the challenging work of theological interpretation and reinterpretation of the Qur'an on the part of contemporary Islamic scholars. Through this process of theological interpretation, the Islamic religion can become a strong ally and supporter of the values of the Western world, such as the freedom of religion, democracy, and the equality of women. It will be demonstrated that there is a way of understanding the Western world that is open to multiculturalism and that is also optimistic about the future of Islam in the Western world. In many cases, the discussions about the Western world have often gone together with a criticism of multiculturalism and Islam. A different approach is taken in this book, one that is more realistic and pragmatic.

In chapter 7 ("The Reformation and Ecumenism"), the status of the Reformation in ecumenical theology and the hopes of the ecumenical movement are analyzed. At the outset, the current situation in ecumenism and its contemporary history are sketched out with a view to the historical context of the twentieth century. Some of the progress of the ecumenical movement is also introduced, for example, regarding one of the most important doctrinal issues of the Reformation: the doctrine of justification. With this, the current challenges and hopes of ecumenism are presented before offering a proposal for commemorating the Reformation from an ecumenical perspective. Finally, some of the theological rationale behind ecumenism is laid out. Here biblical sources, historical theological material, contemporary theology, and modern Catholic encyclicals are interpreted. In the conclusion, attention is drawn to the theology of love and reconciliation. Before turning to the issue of ecumenism in the final chapter, some background information about the part of the world that was most influenced by the Reformation shall be introduced below.

≪ 1 ≫

THE WESTERN WORLD AND THE REFORMATION

In the title of this book, the term "the Western world" (also called "the West" or "Western civilization") is used. This is because this book deals with the cultural, social, and political legacy of the Reformation in the modern Western world. There are two sides to this relationship. On the one hand, discussions about the Reformation often *look forward* to broader issues related to the historical legacy of the Reformation in the cultures of the West. On the other hand, discussions about the modern Western world often *look backward* to the Reformation (positively or negatively) as a defining event in the history of the West. In both cases there is a presumed relationship between the Reformation and the West. But what is the West?

The use of the terms "the Western world" or "the West" in this book is not intended to support ideas of cultural superiority, aggressive ideology, or friend/enemy distinctions. Furthermore, the West should not be understood as identical with Christianity, even though this part of the world was and continues to be deeply influenced by Christianity. The Christian faith is about following Christ, living in communion with other Christians in the life of the church, and serving the weak, vulnerable, and poor with a hope that transcends every border. By contrast, the Western World is a limited cultural, social, and political reality that collectively serves the interests and desires of its inhabitants. Christians cannot theoretically rule out the possibility that the West, or any other political order, could become an evil force that must be resisted.[1]

Our culture today is deeply connected with the history of the Reformation. Becoming familiar with the complicated legacy of the Reformation helps us to understand and respond to our contemporary religious, cultural, social, and political situation. In particular, it helps us to think more critically about how we should deal with the issue of religious difference in our societies today. This was a central issue in the Reformation and, in many regards, one of its most problematic aspects. Studying this history will help us to think critically about how we should deal with religious differences in our societies today. While the mistakes of past generations should be avoided, we can also learn from their greatest achievements. Studying the history of the Reformation and its legacy in the Western world also has a nonpragmatic dimension. We have inherited a religious and cultural heritage in the Western world that is, in many regards, truly exceptional. Thankfulness and humility are natural responses to great gifts of inheritance like this one. Of course, one can only be thankful for a gift if one knows what that gift actually is. For this reason, we must seek to understand and study the theology and the complex history of the Reformation, including its cultural effects in the Western world.

1.1 DEFINITIONS OF THE WESTERN WORLD

Etymologically, the English word "west" is of Germanic origin. This is used more often in everyday English than the term "occident" (also meaning "west"), which is of Latin origin. "Occident" derives from the Latin *occidens*, of *occidere* (to go down, setting [of the sun]), as used, for example, in early cartography: *partes occidentis* (areas of the west) or *partes orientis* (areas of the east). The word "west" is related to the Greek *hesperos, -a,* (evening, west), the Latin *vesper* (evening, west), and the old Germanic *westana* (ninth century onward).[2] In many European languages, the concept of the Occident or the West (*Abendland* in German; *Occident* in French) goes back many hundreds of years. The terms were originally more or less synonymous with "Christendom," but they eventually replaced it.

For most people today the general meaning of the term "the West" is immediately understood. Its precise definition is, however, usually not entirely clear. Of course a similar term, "Western Civilization," is commonly used in history classes in school curricula. This term signifies the same thing that the terms the "West" or the "Western world" signify. The terms "West" or "Western" are usually capitalized in the literature that addresses the concept because they refer to a cultural and political entity with a shared history and shared sense of identity (as conflicted as this may be). The general meaning of the term is familiar to many because it is often used in the media when reporting on world events and the response of the West or the Western world to these events. For this reason, it is often unfortunately associated exclusively with military actions, such as the NATO missions or geopolitical strategy.

The term "the West" is also related to the idea of the globalized "world community" in which there are dominant centers of power and influence in competition with one another. In this regard, NATO, the Cold War, and the emergence of the European Union have contributed significantly to the discourse about the West. This is, however, only one aspect of the reality of the modern Western world. Other aspects are its cultural makeup and historical origins, which are older than the twentieth century.

In this book, use of the term "the Western world" or "the West" designates those *religious traditions, institutions, cultures, and nations, including their contemporary shared values, that together emerged as the intellectual descendants and transformers of Latin Christendom.* This somewhat cumbersome description attempts to embrace two different aspects of the broader discourse on this subject: the language of historical origin (what "emerged") and the language of contemporary ideals (the "shared values"). The former signifies the continuity and historical roots of the West; the latter signifies the freely determined and continuously changing nature of Western culture. This description also emphasizes the importance of the Christian background of the West ("Latin Christendom"). The term "intellectual descendants" follows from the fact that the Western world and its intellectual traditions have spread across the world and are not the possession of the Western world. With this, it should not be forgotten that Judaism and, to a lesser degree, Islam were and are influential in the West. Furthermore, the fact that the West is in many ways the intellectual descendant of Latin Christendom does not mean, of course, that it is inherently bound to Christianity. In many cases, cultures and nations in the contemporary Western world have become more secular and less committed to the Christian religion.

One of the great stains of injustice and human brutality in the history of the Western world is seen in the treatment of the Jews. Jews have been persecuted throughout the history of the Western world. At the same time, Jewish religion and culture have been very influential in the formation of the Western intellectual and cultural tradition. The Christian kings of Europe in the Middle Ages imitated the rule of Solomon. The most learned humanist scholars of the European universities studied the

Hebrew language and sought to unlock the infinitely valuable wisdom of the Old Testament. Perhaps the best example of the mixture of these cultural traditions is to be found in the Sistine Chapel. There Jewish, Greco-Roman, and Christian themes and figures are interwoven with one another. Of course, it is a Christian chapel, and the work of art is a Christian presentation of the unity of these traditions. Nevertheless, in terms of religious history, the beauty of it has to do with the fact that it attempts to bring so much together. All the figures and themes from the pre-Christian era are given a place in the story. It does not present the history of Christianity as though it started with Jesus and the disciples. It is magnificent and compelling because the artists integrated the Jewish and Greco-Roman figures and themes.

The common core, mixture, overlap, and conflicting interpretation of Jewish and Christian traditions in the Western world is often referred to as the "Judeo-Christian tradition." Christianity became the state religion of the Roman Empire in the fourth century. From this point onward, more than any other religion, Christianity dominated Western cultural and intellectual tradition. In many regards this Christian intellectual tradition, even in the face of secularization, is still very influential today. Traditionally, terms like "Christian Occident" or "Christian West" were used to designate the Western world as a whole and to point out the fact that Christianity was the driving force behind its identity. Even today these terms are still used on occasion. This is, however, very problematic. It fails to recognize the other religious and intellectual traditions that have also contributed to the formation of the larger Western tradition. In the past Christians have often suppressed the Greco-Roman and, above all, the Jewish roots of the Christian faith. As a response to this, and in order to pay recognition to the Jewish roots of the faith, the term "Judeo-Christian" has become popular. It is, in fact, older than the twentieth century. The contemporary use of the term "Judeo-Christian tradition," as it is used to describe this mixing of traditions, is a way of acknowledging respectfully the Jewish presence and influence in Western culture. The term is, therefore, intended to be a gesture of recognition and honor. Rabbi Robert Gordis has addressed this term. In light of the fact that there are differences between Judaism and Christianity, he asks, "Is it still possible to speak in meaningful terms of a 'Judeo-Christian tradition'? I believe that the answer is in the affirmative. In the first instance, the historical fact that Christianity is rooted in Judaism is more than a fact of history."[3] Daniel R. Langton has also drawn attention to this theme. In response to the rejection of the term, he writes, "whether explicitly articulated or not, the idea of a shared body of Western attitudes, ideals, and values derived from a shared biblical tradition boasts a venerable pedigree and is undoubtedly woven into the very fabric of post-Enlightenment European culture."[4] In fact, one could also use the term "Greco-Roman-Judeo-Christian tradition" to pay tribute to the Greek and Roman influences that are also deeply interwoven in these shared Western attitudes, ideals, and values. In order to avoid these long compound adjectives, however, many simply use the term "Western tradition." These other adjectives are usually presumed in the term "Western," which implicitly acknowledges all of these religious and cultural influences.

Jews and Christians both regard the Hebrew Bible or the Old Testament as sacred scripture. This is the case even if it is arranged differently and understood differently in both traditions. The term "old" in Old Testament is to be understood in the sense of "first" and "honorable." The Christian Bible is certainly a Judeo-Christian book, but it is also more than this. It was written in Hebrew, Aramaic, and Greek. Furthermore, other languages also influenced it, such as ancient Semitic languages, Egyptian, Old Persian, and even Latin. The Egyptian, Mesopotamian, Canaanite, and Greek cultural worlds are all represented in the Bible. It is very much a multicultural book.

As is well known, despite this shared tradition of thought, Jews and Christians disagree with one another about how to interpret the major religious, philosophical, and moral questions that confront them. Similarly, Jews disagree with Jews, and Christians with Christians, regarding this same issue of interpretation. In all this disagreement, however, Jews and Christians are usually discussing a tradition that they share. Through their conflicting interpretations, furthermore, they are also contributing to the continual formation of their common heritage.

Although Christians learned so much from Jews throughout the history of Christianity, Christians nevertheless persecuted them on many occasions. Running parallel to the dark history of violence is, however, another history of competition and dynamic interrelationship. In this regard, Jews and Christians learned from one another and mutually contributed to the development of the cultural and intellectual tradition of Western civilization. The theology of rabbinic Judaism has influenced the theology of Christianity and vice versa. In this sense, the relationship between Judaism and Christianity can be understood as both a "mother-daughter" relationship and as a "sister-sister" relationship.

After the Holocaust (also called the Shoah, which is Hebrew for "the catastrophe") there has been a concerted effort to encourage cooperation and mutual respect between Jews and Christians. This has, in turn, strengthened the relationship between them. There is, of course, still a lot of work to be done in this regard. The work toward reconciliation goes together with the hope for a shared future of justice, peace, collaboration, and mutual respect. Today there are families, neighborhoods, religious communities, academic institutions, and working groups made up of both Jews and Christians. In some of these constellations there may not be a collective identity that can actually be described with a term like "Jewish-Christian"; yet in others there is indeed a common sense of identity that is, at the same time, both Jewish and Christian.

In recent history the term "Abrahamic traditions" has been developed to draw attention to the common religious history of Jews, Christians, and Muslims. While Abraham is understood differently in these traditions, all of them hold this figure in high regard. There is a growing body of literature showing how Islam influenced the Western world. Muslims contributed to the Western intellectual tradition in art and philosophical and religious thought. Although Muslims were expelled from Spain in 1492, the Islamic tradition of learning is visible in many areas. The most obvious example of this influence is Arabic numerals and Arabic terms in Western languages. The beautiful Islamic architecture in Spain is another classic example of the influence of Islamic culture in the Western world. Some Greek philosophical texts came to Europe in the Middle Ages through Muslim scholars. From a theological perspective, one of the most important examples of the influence of Islam in the Western world is found in the Middle Ages. Christian theologians of the Middle Ages drew upon and debated the Muslim philosophers Avicenna and Averroes. Muslim scholars also contributed to the field of natural science, mathematics, and astronomy. In these ways, Islam has contributed to Western culture.[5] Furthermore, other religious traditions and nonreligious people have also contributed to the Western intellectual tradition.

When asked where the dominant cultural, intellectual, financial, and geographical center of the West is to be found on a map today, most would probably respond by pointing to Western Europe and North America. With this, however, there is a robust periphery, including much of Eastern Europe and Latin America, as well as Australia, New Zealand, and Israel. There is no hard consensus about the geographical territory of the West. The above definition of the West emphasizes the historical origins, the religious background, and also the contemporary values of the West. The contemporary values may have emerged in the West, but they are in no way bound to it. Many cultures outside the West have adopted these values in part or in whole. One of the popular descriptions of the Western world today is a response to this phenomenon. In this sense, the idea of a "community of values" is often used to describe the West.

While a community of values transcends the map, a cultural value itself can nevertheless be mapped. In this sense, one way to map the West as a community of values is with the yearly Freedom of the Press report from the Freedom House (a nongovernmental organization based in the United States). In much of the literature on the West, the theme of freedom, and specifically freedom of the press, is often presented as one of the central values. In the report from 2015, all of Western Europe, North America, Australia, and New Zealand have a "free press." Japan also has a "free press." Mexico and most of Latin America, on the other hand, fall in the "not free" or only "partly free" categories (with most of Asia, the Middle East, and Africa). Uruguay and Chile are exceptions in Latin America, as they have a "free press." A good portion of southeastern Europe, including Greece and even Italy (the old center of Latin Christendom), also fall into the "partly free" category.

Other values can be mapped. Ronald Inglehart and Christian Welzel's cultural map of the world, for example, shows that there are basic similarities in values between Western Europe and the English-speaking countries of the world. These countries tend to value individual freedom and self-expression. Here again, Uruguay is plotted on the map much closer to western European countries and English-speaking countries than other South American countries.[6]

It is, of course, not only difficult to identify the West geographically, it is also difficult to describe the guiding principles that characterize it. Usually the term signifies a handful of cultural values that are generally shared. These values have been summarized in different ways. Heinrich August Winkler describes them as inalienable rights, the rule of law, representative democracy, and the separation of power.[7] These themes will be developed below in the discussion about soft consensus and pluralism in the modern Western world. Of course, these values can also be found outside the West in cultural enclaves within non-Western countries, as well as in many urban centers in Asia, the Middle East, Africa, and South America.

While some may claim that the West is a purely intellectual, nationalistic, or ideological construct, there are many reasons for holding that the term actually does signify something concrete. The term is often understood in the very limited sense within the historical polarity of the Cold War. This narrow view of the Western world overlooks, however, the shared history and cultural, philosophical, and religious traditions in those cultures that emerged from Latin Christendom and transformed it. The importance of the common Latin language can hardly be overemphasized in this regard.[8] The influence and cultural significance of the Enlightenment and the emphasis on the ideal of freedom are also key themes that are shared in the Western world.

Since it is difficult to plot the location of the West on the map, and since it is difficult to describe the shared values of the West, it is therefore not a surprise that the history of the West is quite complicated. There are many ways to narrate the history of the West. In most of the literature on the subject, however, the basic question as to whether there is a West is often presumed. There is a significant amount of literature that has addressed the theme of the Western world and its history.[9] The West has been presented in narratives that begin in antiquity (Heinrich August Winkler), in the Middle Ages Carolingian era (David Gress), in the Enlightenment (Michael Hochgeschwender), or even as late as the birth of NATO in 1948. It has been presented as a historical unity (Peter Rassow), as a sentiment of mediation and longing for the original cultural source (Rémi Brague), as a dynamic process of the interface of various cultures within the broader human community (William H. McNeill), as a universalizing process (John M. Headley), as a list of Six Killer Apps (Niall Ferguson; competition, science, property, modern medicine, consumerism, work ethic), as a biocultural phenomenon of an individual civilization (Oswald Spengler, similarly Arnold Toynbee), or as a sociological narrative of progressive rationalization, one which is embodied in the inner-worldly asceticism of Calvinist Protestantism (Max Weber).

The Reformation usually finds a place in the historical narratives of the Western world. This is why it has been necessary to start with a brief discussion of this term in its very complex semantic domain. There are also many critical narratives of modern Western culture that draw upon the story of the Reformation as a watershed point of its decline. In most every case, the legacy of the Reformation is a very important issue when it comes to addressing the modern Western world. But as we shall see, understanding the Reformation seems to be just as complicated as understanding the West.

1.2 THE REFORMATION IN HISTORICAL PRESENTATION

While there are many books on the Reformation, there does not seem to be a consensus about how the story of the Reformation should be told. In this section the complexity of the Reformation will be addressed in an attempt to formulate a differentiated analysis of its positive and problematic aspects.

Can we even speak of *the* Reformation? According to Thomas A. Brady Jr., the term "Reformation" should be used in the plural because it stands for "a complex set of transformations of Western Christianity—Protestant, Catholic, and others—during the sixteenth and seventeenth centuries."[10] While Brady is of course correct to point to this plurality of processes and movements of reform in the Reformation period, it is also possible to speak of this era as a whole and all these processes together as "the Reformation." This is very common in historical presentations. Euan Cameron, for example, provides a compelling argument for the unique historical significance of *the* Reformation: "The Reformation, the movement that divided European Christianity into Catholic and Protestant traditions, is unique." As he explains, "No other movement of religious protest or reform since antiquity has been so widespread or lasting in its effects, so deep and searching in its criticism of received wisdom, so destructive in what it abolished, or so fertile in what it created."[11]

It is also possible, with Thomas Kaufmann, to think of the Reformation as a *process*, a process of theological questioning, publishing controversy (e.g., in tracts, theological works, or satires, such as *Ecclus Dedolatus*), and transformative modification of the ecclesial order. This process was initiated by some, modified and supported by others, and resisted and rejected by still others. It was not and could not be contained in the ecclesial sphere, however, since it entailed political and legal ramifications that ultimately led to military conflicts.[12] Viewing the Reformation as a unified event or a singular historical epoch and a process of religious and political reform draws upon a broader philosophical question about history itself: Can history be broken into periods and viewed in distinct parts?

The difficulty of telling the story about the Reformation has to do with a very basic problem: How is this historical event to be located within the broader stories and epochs of human development and history? Is it to be seen as a specific period of history, or as a transitional event that inaugurated a new era? Jacques Le Goff has addressed this fundamental problem especially with view to the Renaissance. He holds that there is a certain necessity to see time in broad periodic shifts, for "breaking time into segments is something historians cannot help but do, no matter whether history is regarded as the study of the evolution of societies, or as a particular type of knowledge and teaching, or else as the unfolding of time itself." In all these cases, "periodization is more than a mere collection of chronological units. It contains also the idea of transition, of one thing turning into another; indeed, when change is sufficiently far-reaching in its effects, a new period represents a repudiation of the entire social order of the one preceding it."[13] As will be discussed below, the Reformation, as a major period of Western history, is perhaps best divided into two other categories: the long Reformation and the short Reformation.

Accounts of the Reformation usually take one of two major routes. One tends to present the Reformation from the sociopolitical context, as a social, cultural, economic, and political phenomenon; the other tends to present it from the theological and religious context, as a theological and religious phenomenon. Of course, these modes of narration are interrelated. Historically, the latter (concerned with theology and religion) was the dominant one. In the later nineteenth century, the former (concerned with society and politics) became more dominant. Nevertheless, both of these broad historical approaches continue to be practiced today.[14] Some historians have also successfully unified them.

When it comes to intellectual-historical accounts of the Reformation, there seem to be two dominant traditions. One tends to present the Reformation as prehistory to the early modern period and the Enlightenment, while the other presents it primarily as a series of consequences from late medieval religious, theological, and philosophical conflicts. One is oriented toward the prehistory, the other toward the historical legacy. The story of the Reformation can also be told as the formation of a new version of Western Christianity or, alternatively, as the development of Western Christianity as a whole. It can be described as the collection of a few common teachings and a relatively unified movement (or a few relatively unified movements) or as the fragmentary phenomena of many movements and many conflicting teachings without any points of orientation.

Theologically, it can be presented as a break with the traditions of Christianity or even described as the emergence of a new religion. Or one can provide an account of the Reformation as the rebirth of traditional theological positions held in historical Christianity against the corruptions of the late medieval ecclesial situation (as Pettegree remarks, it was "restoration not innovation").[15] The Reformation can be introduced as the product of great men who changed the course of history or as the consequence of a grand overarching zeitgeist that would have happened inevitably, with or without the major personalities. It can be presented as a "revolution of the common man," or, alternatively, the historian can focus on the transformation of the powerful, educated, and wealthy in the early modern period.[16] One can emphasize the sudden birth of a new confessional order based around cities or the slow transformation process on the countryside, where the Reformation was experienced as a "protracted affair" spreading over "several generations."[17]

Contemporary accounts of the Reformation have become very conscious of these different approaches to historiography and therefore usually try to merge these perspectives of inquiry into their presentations. In almost all the polarities that have been emphasized above, the middle way is to be preferred. The middle path of analysis affirms the truth in both perspectives and seeks to bring these viewpoints together. In this synthetic image of the history, the whole can be seen in the fullness of its complexity.[18]

All the historical accounts of the Reformation have to deal with the early sixteenth century. This short Reformation is embedded in another longer story of its prehistory and posthistory, often called the long Reformation. The short story will be addressed below, but first three major figures and their unique contributions to the reform movement will be addressed.

1.3 ANDREAS BODENSTEIN VON KARLSTADT'S 151 THESES

Virtually every historical account of the Reformation addresses a series of events that took place over the course of around fifteen years. For the sake of clarity, this series of events may be called the short Reformation. Every event in the short Reformation has a history of conflicting interpretation regarding the significance of these events.

The short Reformation would not have been possible without the long Reformation. The long Reformation is a story about a growing sense of autonomy north of the Alps in the Middle Ages, national resentment between the German territories and Italy and Rome, calls for reform in the church all over Christendom that go back to the Middle Ages, traditions of medieval mystical theology that internalized Christianity against trends of externalization (such as indulgences, relics, and pilgrimage), humanism and the intensification of learning and study of the Bible, the birth of many new universities across Europe in the later Middle Ages, the Western

Schism and double and triple rival popes (which threatened the legitimacy of the institution), and many other issues. Without this preparation, the short Reformation would not have been possible. The princes that supported the reforms (and thus ran the risk of imperial retaliation) were sometimes motivated by the new faith. They were, however, also making tactical political decisions that were justified given the changing cultural, social, and political situation.[19]

The most important point of departure for the short Reformation was certainly Pope Leo X's (1475–1521) proclamation of the "Peter's Indulgence" in 1515, which was issued to raise money for St. Peter's Basilica in Rome. Without this impetus from the pope, the Wittenberg theologians may have never come into conflict with the papal order in the way that they did. In the German lands, the most important person to advance this cause was the archbishop of Mainz, Albrecht von Brandenburg (1490–1545). His court theologians, and perhaps Johann Tetzel himself, wrote the *Instructio summaria* (Mainz edition, 1516; Magdeburg edition, 1517)—a handbook for selling the indulgences. It includes "threats to any who impeded preaching this indulgence, the invalidation of previous indulgences, the necessity for building St. Peter's in Rome, the promise of complete remission of all temporal penalties here and in purgatory" and a sliding scale of payment depending on one's standing.[20] Archbishop Albrecht's commissioner, Johann Tetzel (1465–1519), was heading up the work of preaching and selling indulgences. Although Tetzel was only one part of the larger system of the church-organized exploitation, he is often singled out as the key figure and branded the "holy thief." Much later, in 1541, Luther summarized what it was all about when he wrote, "Tetzel [. . .] sold grace for money."[21] It would have been more accurate to say that the papacy itself and much of the ecclesial hierarchy in Christendom were selling grace for money.

Elector Frederick did not allow Tetzel to sell indulgences in Electoral Saxony. For this reason, some people from the town of Wittenberg left the territory to purchase them elsewhere (in Eisleben, Halle, Zerbst, and Jüterbog). In response to the situation, Martin Luther (1483–1546), a friar of the Augustinian monastery and the preacher at the town church, St. Mary's, addressed the importance of true repentance and the dangers of the indulgences in his sermons. In a sermon in early 1517, for example, he called for an "inner repentance" (*poenitentia interior*).[22] Although Elector Frederick prohibited the sale of indulgences in Saxony, he was not opposed to the practice of indulgences in principle. In Wittenberg's collegiate church, he had his own collection of relics from which indulgences were issued. He probably did not want the competition from Tetzel to diminish his own profits.[23]

The criticism of the theology behind the indulgences continued in 1517 on a university platform. Encouraged by Johann von Staupitz, Andreas Bodenstein von Karlstadt (1486–1541) posted 151 theses on the collegiate church door in Wittenberg on April 26, 1517.[24] Karlstadt's theses were posted on the day before a special ecclesial event for the acquisition of indulgences. Karlstadt's theses were also issued without a formal disputation date and were addressed to a larger academic audience beyond Wittenberg. In this regard, Karlstadt was clearly trying to initiate a broad public dispute similar to the one Giovanni Pico della Mirandola initiated with his Nine Hundred Theses.[25]

Although Karlstadt did not mention the indulgences explicitly, his theses challenged the theology behind them and the very view of God and the Christian life that went along with them. Karlstadt was an important figure in the history of the Reformation. He was "Martin Luther's 'promotor,' and gave him his doctorate."[26] He also served as dean of the Wittenberg Faculty of Theology from 1512 onward for eight terms. He was known outside of Wittenberg because of his scholarly work in the field of scholastic theology. After completing a doctorate in theology in 1510 in Wittenberg, in May of 1516 he completed a doctorate in both civil and canon law in Rome. As doctor of theology and doctor of civil and canon law, archdeacon of the All Saints Collegiate Church, dean of the Faculty of Theology, and professor of theology, Karlstadt was among the most important and powerful people in Wittenberg.[27]

Early in his career, he was influenced by and promoted scholastic theology. After he returned from Rome, he went through a process of theological transformation. This began sometime in the fall of 1516 in academic discussions and debates at the Wittenberg faculty.[28] Following Staupitz and Luther, Karlstadt moved away from the opinion that scholastic theology (and especially the scholastic teachings about the freedom of the will, grace, and divine election) was in harmony with Augustine and the Scriptures. The new theology of grace, as promoted by Staupitz and Luther, emphasized Augustinian and Pauline theology, read through the lens of mysticism, as a corrective to the scholastic theology. Karlstadt eventually adopted this new approach. He probably read Staupitz' *Little Book on the Execution of Eternal Predestination* (1517) in the spring of 1517.[29] His conversion experience to this new theology is reflected in his 151 Theses from the spring of 1517. In these theses he strongly criticized scholastic theology. Soon after this he published an annotated edition of Augustine's *De spiritu et littera* in 1518.[30]

In his theses Karlstadt argued with total clarity that works have nothing to do with saving grace. He writes in his 151 Theses, "[24.] Grace is not preceded by good merits. [This thesis is asserted] against the common opinion." For "[38.] grace makes that God is called upon. [This thesis is asserted] against the common opinion." Further, "[81.] The sinner is justified without any sufficient preparation of suitability on his part. [This thesis is asserted] against almost everyone." Again, "[83.] Justification precedes, it does not follow, the doers of the law [i.e., justification comes first, before one can fulfill the law]." For "[85.] grace makes us lovers and doers of the law." Karlstadt clarified the teaching that would be so central to the theological reforms: "[88.] The human being is not justified by the [keeping of] rules for a virtuous life, [89.] not by the law of works, not by the letter, not by merits acquired by deeds [90.] but through faith in Jesus Christ, the Spirit, the law of faith and grace." This groundbreaking insight was not only relevant for the debate about indulgences. Karlstadt's theology had to do with a fundamental understanding of God's relationship to reality and our place in it: "[133.] Eternal life is grace given for grace out of mercy and compassion." In this way, Karlstadt can claim that "[138.] the just is therefore good and evil at the same time, a son of God and a son of the world." (Luther's way of expressing this through the phrase *simul peccator et iustus*, "simultaneously a sinner and a justified person."[31])

Karlstadt's final thesis is a call for more debate about the authority of the truth, the Scripture. This is precisely the same subject that his first theses also address:[32] "[151.] The fruitful authority of the truth [sc. the Scriptures] is understood better when it is debated more frequently; and this brings forth the true agreement that one conceals in clear speeches."[33] All these themes, and many more from Karlstadt's theses, are also found with Luther. Similar arguments can be found both in Luther's "Disputation against Scholastic Theology," which was defended by the student of theology Franz Günther on September 4, 1517, and in his Ninety-Five Theses from October 31, 1517.

Karlstadt's claims that "grace is not preceded by good merits," that man is not justified by "merits acquired by deeds," and that grace is "given for grace" all *implicitly* challenged indulgences, or at least a radical understanding of indulgences (as Tetzel was advancing). Everyone who could read Latin in Wittenberg (all the students, academics, and many of the citizens) would have understood the claim that grace was "given *for grace*" to be a direct challenge to the idea that grace was given *for money* or *for merits acquired by deeds* (including those that were "graced" by indulgences). While Karlstadt avoided direct conflict with the Catholic Church on this matter, his theology was an implicit challenge to it. Later, in his 370 Conclusions from 1518, he was also critical of indulgences.[34]

The specific emphasis on the unique authority of Scripture in theological debates, as asserted by Karlstadt in the first and last theses, was another key theological concept that became central to the Reformation. Another major issue in the background was the Christian's relationship to God. This was deeply interconnected with mysticism. The Reformation itself can be understood as the outworking of a specific mystical piety from the Middle Ages (especially from Johannes Tauler).[35] Karlstadt's theses were innovative in at least two ways: they asserted the unique authority of the Scriptures in theology (without rejecting the pope or tradition), and they asserted a theology of grace apart from works (which was related to the new mysticism). The content of the theses and the way that he posted them suggest that Karlstadt was promoting a reform agenda in Christendom.

Karlstadt was also the author of the first German propaganda tract of the Reformation ("Heaven and Hell Wagon") from the spring of 1519. On the top of the woodcut image is a wagon leading to heaven (through the cross); on the bottom is a wagon with scholastic theology, leading to hell. One of the sayings on the wagon to hell is "Our will makes good works [to become] substance." On the wagon to heaven, however, one reads, "Your will be done." The image is filled with short sayings about the simple gospel message on and around the wagon to heaven. False teachings, on the other hand, cover the wagon to hell. With tracts like this one, the basic gospel message, which was so central to the Reformation, was brought to the common people in a new anticlerical form. The sayings emphasize God's work in saving sinners, the mercy of God, and the inability of human beings to save themselves. The work of Christ on the cross is central in the image.

In Karlstadt's *Interpretation and Explanation* (1519),[36] he also promoted the gospel message to the common people.[37] From the spring of 1519 onward, Karlstadt had committed himself to the cause of the laity. He encouraged an understanding of the church as a church of the laity free from any priestly mediation of grace.[38] In this regard as well, Karlstadt was ahead of Luther. Luther arrived at this position months later, in the winter of 1519, as is seen in a letter to Spalatin.[39] The idea of the priesthood of all believers became a central concept in Luther's widely published "Address to Christian Nobility," written between June 7 and July 20, 1520.⁴⁰ The teaching about the priesthood of all believers enabled the transformation of the ecclesial and social order of Christendom. Luther taught that everyone who is baptized is a member of the priesthood. This enabled the nobility to hold a council as members of the church. While Karlstadt was reinterpreting the priesthood for the laity, Luther was reinterpreting it for both the laity and the nobility. Very soon after this, however, Luther rejected the idea of a congregationally led church, while Karlstadt continued to promote it.

Karlstadt's significance in the Reformation was also demonstrated in theological debates. At the Leipzig Debate in 1519, Karlstadt and Luther debated Johann Eck (1486–1543). In Luther's analysis, Karlstadt won the debate in Leipzig. Luther writes, "Eck and Karlstadt at first debated for seven days over the freedom of the will. With God's help Karlstadt advanced his arguments and explanations excellently and in great abundance from books which he had brought with him." He continues,

> Eck refused to debate unless the books were left at home. Andreas [Karlstadt] had used the books to demonstrate to Eck's face that he had correctly quoted the words of Scripture and the church fathers, that he had not done violence to them as Eck was now shown to have done. This marked the beginning of another uproar until at length it was decided to Eck's advantage that the books should be left at home. [. . .] Finally this deceitful man conceded everything that Karlstadt had asserted [. . .] boasting that he had led Karlstadt to his own way of thinking.⁴¹

Later in his letter to Spalatin, he remarked, "When I had concluded my part of the disputation, Eck debated once more with Karlstadt on new topics during the last three days, again making concessions in all points."⁴²

As mentioned above, Karlstadt's importance is seen in his early articulation of the unique authority of the Scriptures. In this he was actually ahead of Luther. Following the impulse of his 151 Theses, Karlstadt emphasized this authority in his 370 Conclusions from the spring or early summer of 1518. Thesis 1, for example, states, "A text of the Bible quoted by an ecclesiastical doctor is stronger and proves more than the saying of the one quoting it." Thesis 12 states, "The text of the Bible is to be preferred not only to one or several doctors of the church but even to the authority of the whole church."⁴³ This was a theoretical argument for Karlstadt. He was emphasizing a hierarchy of authority and not seeking to reject the papacy or tradition. Luther, by contrast, was still promoting the traditional medieval harmony model (between tradition and Scripture) in 1518. In 1519 at the Leipzig Debate, Luther asserted for the first time the unique authority of the Scriptures above tradition and thus endorsed the clear hierarchy of authorities and the contrast model that Karlstadt had developed.[44]

Karlstadt was also the first priest and university theologian to break the vow of celibacy and to marry (January 19, 1522). He was also the first to celebrate a Protestant church service (Christmas, December 25, 1521). He was also the first to push forward the reforms in Wittenberg and convince the city council to adopt the church reforms (January 24, 1521), which marked the implementation of the Reformation in actual church order. After returning from a short trip to Denmark in 1521, and while Luther was in the Wartburg, from 1521 onward, Karlstadt was the driving force of the Wittenberg Reformation. He was so influential among the laity that the university censured him as the reform movement went from a Reformation "from below" to one "from above."[45]

In all these regards, and especially because of the spring theses in 1517, Karlstadt was the first public leader of the short Reformation as it emerged in the provincial context of Electoral Saxony. This is the case even if Staupitz and Luther were the initial *theological* initiators. It is also the case even if Luther was the one to drive forward the conflict with Rome. In much of the secondary literature on the Reformation, Luther's dramatic confrontation with Rome (culminating in his excommunication) is often conflated with the actual implementation of the reforms. This misconstrues two distinct dimensions of the history. The conflict with Rome was certainly advanced by Luther; in the same regard, the actual reforming process in Wittenberg was initially advanced more by Karlstadt than anyone else, and, to a lesser degree, Gabriel Zwilling (especially in the monasteric context). In general, Karlstadt was also calling for more debate, for a scriptural foundation of theology, for a church of the laity, and for a new theology of grace. In this sense, he encouraged and implemented the reforming impulses that Staupitz and Luther theologically initiated.

1.4 MARTIN LUTHER'S NINETY-FIVE THESES

Luther established his new theological program—the mixture of Pauline theology, Augustinianism, and mystical theology—sometime in the mid-1510s, perhaps between 1513 and 1519.[46] His lectures on Romans in 1514 and 1515 were critical in this development. Following the publication of Archbishop Albrecht's *Instructio summaria*, Luther wrote his Ninety-Five

Theses. On October 31, 1517, he sent these theses with a letter to the bishop of Brandenburg and to the archbishop of Magdeburg and Mainz. In these correspondences he explicitly criticized the practice of indulgences. He called for the archbishop to recant his *Instructio* and asked him to instruct Tetzel to change his preaching.[47] In this regard, Luther went further than Karlstadt in his direct confrontation of ecclesial authority. Luther was building upon older criticisms of indulgences. While John Wycliffe's criticism of indulgences was condemned in 1415, there was still little official teaching about indulgences in 1517.[48] As a doctor of theology, Luther saw himself as authorized to debate this subject.[49] He challenged the indulgences with biblical-theological arguments that were rooted in pastoral concerns and a mystical piety.[50]

Did Luther actually post the Ninety-Five Theses on the collegiate church's door (All Saints) on October 31, 1517? The historical arguments are stronger on the "no" side in this debate.[51] The story emerged decades later as a plausible explanation of the events. At this time—when the story emerged—the history of the Reformation was being monumentalized. More importantly, the story seems to contradict Luther's own accounts of the event. Nevertheless, he most certainly sent a copy to Archbishop Albrecht. By the end of 1517, the Ninety-Five Theses had been published and distributed (after Luther shared them with others). Rather than publishing a German translation of the Latin theses, Luther published a German "Sermon on Indulgences and Grace" in March of 1518 that was distributed to a broad readership (and reprinted multiple times). There he attacks the position of the "new teachers":

> This is what I say: No one can defend the position with any passage from Scripture that God's righteousness desires or demands any punishment or satisfaction from sinners except for their heartfelt and true contrition or conversion alone—with the condition that from that moment on they bear the cross of Christ and practice the aforementioned works (but not as imposed by anyone). [. . .] I would like to hear who would prove the opposite [. . .] I say that even if this very day the Christian church decided and decreed that indulgences took away more than the works of satisfaction did, nevertheless it would still be a thousand times better that no Christian buy or desire indulgences but instead that they would rather do works and suffer punishment.[52]

Here in the spring of 1518, Luther seems to be breaking away from the old harmony model of the Middle Ages (which he was still formally endorsing). Luther's argument is made explicitly on the basis of Scripture. He refers to

Ezekiel 18:21; 33:14ff; Psalm 89:30-33; Luke 7:36-50; Mark 2:1-12; John 8:1-11. Rhetorically, Luther asked his readers to make a decision: follow the Scriptures or follow the "new teachers." This sermon, and especially this passage, is a good example of the theology that would come in the years ahead as Luther asserted with a growing tenacity the unique authority of Scripture against the "new teachers" and the papacy that supported them. As is clear from this passage, and so many more from the Reformation era, the Scriptures were the sole authority by which the Reformers could legitimately challenge Rome and the entire system of canon law.

With his Ninety-Five Theses before this publication, Luther challenged the theology of the indulgences explicitly. Like Karlstadt, Luther also emphasized the theme of divine grace. Thesis 62 reads, "The true treasure of the church is the most holy gospel of the glory and the grace of God."[53] The theses call for all of life to be drawn into a true repentance, an inward transformation. The criticism of the indulgences could go in many directions. A basic theology of grace and an emphasis on justification by faith was one of the major angles of attack, and perhaps the most fundamental attack. Another angle of attack was from the perspective of the poor. The reform of social issues was an important aspect of the pre-Reformation strivings for reform. This was central to the entire Reformation. Thesis 43 states, "Christians are to be taught that he who gives to the poor or lends to the needy does a better deed than he who buys indulgences."[54]

Luther showed opposition to the work of the pope in his Ninety-Five Theses. In this, he also went beyond Karlstadt. This opposition to the pope is embedded in rhetorical formulations. He essentially presents himself as defending the goodness of the pope and seems to put the blame on the lesser ecclesial authorities who were gathering the money through the indulgences. If one reads the theses closely, however, it is clear that Luther was actually accusing the pope of greed and insincerity. Indeed, Luther essentially claimed that the pope was not helping Christians but harming them. This deep resentment comes out in thesis 86 (where he pretends that he is simply repeating an opinion when in fact it is clearly Luther's own opinion): "Why does not the pope, whose wealth is today greater than the wealth of the richest Crassus, build this one basilica of St. Peter with his own money rather than with the money of poor believers?"[55] In his later "Explanation of the Ninety-Five Theses" he remarks on this thesis, "God grant that I lie in this matter, for this extortion of money cannot go on very long."[56] It is also present in thesis 89 of the Ninety-Five Theses:

"Since the pope seeks the salvation of souls rather than money by his indulgences, why does he suspend the indulgences and pardons previously granted when they have equal efficacy?"[57] Luther's challenge to the papal authority is also clearly felt in thesis 5: the "pope neither desires nor is able to remit any penalties except those imposed by his own authority or that of the canons."[58]

The same subtle challenge to papal authority comes out in thesis 6: "The pope cannot remit any guilt, except by declaring and showing that it has been remitted by God; or, to be sure, by remitting guilt in cases reserved to his judgment. If his right to grant remission in these cases were disregarded, the guilt would certainly remain unforgiven."[59] At the very end, Luther also directly challenges the theology that was being endorsed by Rome. There we read, "94. Christians should be exhorted to be diligent in following Christ, their Head, through penalties, death and hell. 95. And thus be confident of entering into heaven through many tribulations rather than through the false security of peace (Acts 14:22)."[60] The message is clear: The pope should be concerned with souls, not money. He should, furthermore, prepare the faithful to follow Christ in suffering, not give them false security. In these theses and in others, Luther makes it clear that he is challenging not only the practice of indulgences but also the very legitimacy of the work of the papacy itself. In Luther's mind, the pope did not really care about the "poor believers" whose money he was taking. As he says in thesis 50, "Christians are to be taught that if the pope knew the exactions of the indulgence preachers, he would rather that the basilica of St. Peter were burned to ashes than built up with the skin, flesh, and bones of his sheep."[61] Here again Luther pretends like the pope is innocent. Luther was, however, fully aware of the fact that the pope in Rome knew about the work of the indulgence preachers. In this regard, Luther's theses were in opposition not only to the teaching and practice of indulgences but also to the authority behind "Peter's Indulgence" of 1515: Pope Leo X. In short, Luther claimed that the pope's ministry was immoral and un-Christian, and this, understandably, put him into direct conflict with the ecclesial establishment.[62]

Luther's theses were correctly understood as an attack on the papacy. Archbishop Albrecht's view of Luther's theses and his letter is made clear in his own letter to his councillors in Mainz from December 13, 1517, where he calls Luther's work "poisonous error."[63] Very quickly the debate moved from being a debate about indulgences to one about papal authority. This was seen in Johann Tetzel's response to Luther in 1518.

Tetzel argued that "when anyone gives alms, prays, visits churches, undertakes pilgrimage, fasts, or does other good works that earn indulgences," these "indulgenced works are far better and more meritorious" than other works that were not "graced with indulgences."[64] Reflecting the opinion of Rome, Tetzel wrote, "For whoever buys an indulgence takes pity on his soul and makes himself well-pleasing to God thereby."[65] Indeed, "for the works that are graced with an indulgence are always better than the same ones accomplished with the same love but without an indulgence."[66] He goes on to argue that "the pope and the holy See, as well as the papal office, do not err in matters that concern the faith." Furthermore, to reject the teaching about indulgences is to reject the pope who has received "complete authority."[67]

Luther was thus branded a heretic for questioning the indulgences and, with them, papal authority.[68] By the spring of 1518, Rome had requested that Luther either revoke his claims or be expelled from the university and sent to Rome for a heresy trial.[69] Luther's conflict with Rome would escalate from this point onward, leading to the Heidelberg Disputation on April 26, 1518,[70] and the Leipzig Debate in the summer of 1519, where Luther openly claimed that the pope and the councils could err and that the authority of Scripture was supreme over these.

1.5 JOHANN VON STAUPITZ, THE LAST FORERUNNER

What—or who—was it, then, that pushed Karlstadt and Luther to challenge the theology behind the indulgences? Both Karlstadt's and Luther's chief influence was Johann von Staupitz (ca. 1468–1524) and his new interpretation of Augustine and the mystical theology of Johannes Tauler (1300–1361), a student of the mystical theologian Meister Eckhart (1260–1328).[71] Staupitz' mystical theology of grace and his emphasis on the Bible were essential to the prehistory of the short Reformation. Staupitz encouraged Luther to do a doctorate, and Luther may have even written his Ninety-Five Theses with Staupitz' approval.[72] Staupitz encouraged Karlstadt to publish his theses.

Staupitz, the tradition of humanism, the mysticism of Johannes Tauler, and the mystical work *Theologia Deutsch* were all very important for Luther's theological development.[73] Both Staupitz and Luther influenced Karlstadt in a similar shift toward a theology of grace in 1516 and 1517. While this mystical theological tradition was an essential part of the theological prehistory of the Reformation, the early theological agenda was also fundamentally biblical and practical in orientation.[74] This mixture of Augustinianism, mysticism, Pauline theology, and an emphasis on the Bible is found in both Karlstadt and Luther's theses.

Staupitz came from a noble family of the Motterwitz manor near Leisnig in Saxony. He was a friend of Elector Frederick and may have grown up with him. He studied in Cologne and Leipzig and later joined the Order of Hermits of St. Augustine sometime after 1489. In 1497 he went to Tübingen and in 1500 he acquired his doctorate in theology from the university there. At the same time he was prior of the Tübingen Augustinian monastery (today this is the Protestant Stift). In 1500 he became the prior of the Munich convent. He was then called to Wittenberg by Elector Frederick and became the first dean of the Faculty of Theology in Wittenberg (founded in 1502) and the professor of the Bible. In 1503 he became the representative of the general of the Augustinian Order in Germany and in the Netherlands. From this point onward he oversaw thirty convents, including Luther's in Erfurt.[75]

In 1512 Staupitz left this academic work behind to focus on practical ministry. His sermons in Nuremberg, Salzburg, and Munich were directed at a lay audience and, like his edifying pastoral Christian literature (written in German), show a stronger use of biblical themes rather than scholastic language. He became known as the tongue of the apostle Paul and the herald of the gospel by those who sympathized with his preaching and his message.[76] With his Augustinian-mystical-theological impulse, Staupitz emphasized that the entire path of human life leads to salvation exclusively on the basis of the mercy, love, and grace of God.[77] This is exemplified in the incarnation and in the suffering and death of Jesus, which connected God to human suffering. The sinner escapes his suffering through the grace of God. This happens when the Christian trusts wholly in God, loves God, and, at the same time, looks beyond his own strengths to redeem himself.[78]

It is not surprising that Luther later claimed, "I got everything from Dr. Staupitz."[79] This sentence is, as emphasized by Leppin, "correct biographically and theologically."[80] One might even claim that Luther was to become Staupitz' "protégé."[81] Staupitz supported Luther's career, taught him, counseled him, and was his friend.[82] As the debates about Luther and the Reformation began, he emphasized the mystical ideal of *Gelassenheit* (yieldedness, serenity) and avoided the conflict. He did not, however, distance himself from Luther.[83] He actually protected Luther from the order's Roman leadership and supported him at the questioning with Cajetan on October 13 and 14, 1518. Staupitz did, however, encourage

Luther to submit to the judgment of the church. He was probably one of the main reasons why Elector Frederick supported Luther, and, in this regard, the implementation of the reforms may not have been possible without Staupitz.[84]

Staupitz was thrown into a conflict of loyalty once Luther was condemned in 1521. Nevertheless, he neither broke off his relationship with Luther nor publicly distanced himself from him. He later joined the less strict Benedictine Order, which may have been his own way of enacting personal reform. Although he sympathized with the theological agenda of the Reformation, he did not join in the movement. He clearly saw the new emphasis on grace and the Bible as a confirmation of his own theology. In a letter to Luther from April 1, 1524, he presented himself as the *praecursor* (forerunner) of the new teaching. There he writes, "I once emerged as the forerunner of the holy evangelical teaching and hated the Babylonian captivity, as I still do."[85] The significance of these kinds of remarks cannot be overemphasized. This critical stance toward the situation in the church (which implied the need for reforms) was not only coming from young professors of theology but also from one of the most powerful figures in the Augustinian order north of the Alps.

With Staupitz' new mystical, Augustinian, biblical theology, which had a strong practical orientation, the old scholastic methods and problems appeared both meaningless and deeply problematic, not least because they were being used to support the theology of indulgences. Luther's turn to the subject of divine grace went together with his opposition to this scholastic theology. This opposition is identifiable from at least 1515 onward.[86] In the criticism of scholasticism as a system itself, Luther was far ahead of Karlstadt. Luther's criticism of the indulgences was closely related to this criticism of scholastic theology and his promotion of mystical Augustinianism.[87] The correlation between these two issues was already clear to him in 1517.[88] In his lectures on Romans in 1515 and 1516, for example, he "read Paul through the eyes of Augustine."[89] Luther's Augustinianism was, however, influenced by medieval mysticism. In his preface to the mystical work *Theologia Deutsch*, which he edited, he wrote,

> I wish to warn everyone who reads this book not to harm himself and become irritated by its simple German language or its unadorned and unassuming words, for this noble little book, poor and unadorned as it is in words and human wisdom, is the richer and more precious in art and divine wisdom. To boast with my old fool, no book except the Bible

and St. Augustine has come to my attention from which I have learned more about God, Christ, man, and all things.[90]

Luther also annotated sermons in 1516 from the mystical theologian Johannes Tauler. The emphasis on a mystical Augustinianism with a Pauline theology of divine grace in the articulation of the teaching about salvation was central to the initial emergence of the Reformation. Although these themes are older than 1515, when the "Peter's Indulgence" was issued, they were used in a new way to challenge the practice of indulgences after 1515. Much of the impetus for reform was therefore the basic pastoral concern for the people buying the indulgences. This practice seemed to conflict with the new theology; at the same time, this theology was itself developed and articulated to challenge this practice. In this regard, the practical and the theoretical dimensions of the reform movement went hand in hand.

The mystical theology is also found in Luther's "Disputation against Scholastic Theology" (disputed on September 4, 1517), where he addresses law and grace in theses 83–89. Thesis 84 reads, "The good law and that in which one lives is the love of God, spread abroad in our hearts by the Holy Spirit."[91] The idealized conception of the Christian life here is not one that is earned by striving in good works but one that is led inwardly from the Spirit. This emphasis on the inner working of the Spirit and the inner repentance of the Christian were both mystical and biblical (especially Pauline). Outward works, like seeking grace through indulgences, conflicted with this theology of inward grace.

Summarizing this approach to theology, Luther wrote in 1537, "The article of justification is master and prince, lord, ruler and judge of all kinds of teachings which preserves and directs all the church's teaching and straightens our conscience before God."[92] One of the most famous New Testament passages that teaches this doctrine is found in Galatians 2:16: "Yet we know that a person is justified not by the works of the law but through faith in Jesus Christ. And we have come to believe in Christ Jesus, so that we might be justified by faith in Christ, and not by doing the works of the law, because no one will be justified by the works of the law." While Paul, Karlstadt, and Luther were addressing different contexts, there is a common emphasis to be identified among them in the importance of faith and the centrality of divine grace for understanding salvation.

There is a major question that is debated at this point. Was the transformational process of religious and political reform that we today call the Reformation already at work in Karlstadt and Luther's theses? Or should these theses just be thought of as another academic debate of the late

Middle Ages that could have come and gone? Scott Hendrix writes, "In the famous theses of 1517, the last thing on Luther's mind was reform of the entire church."[93] While neither Karlstadt nor Luther could see what was coming, their theses were rooted in a reform theology of grace that went together with fundamental questions about authority. Especially Karlstadt asserted the authority of the Scriptures: "The Scripture teaches" (*scriptura docet*, thesis 25 from Karlstadt's 151 Theses). Luther also repeatedly asserted that "Christians are to be taught" (*Docendi sunt christiani*) in his theses (see theses 42–51).[94] In this regard, they were both attempting to initiate a debate about the legitimacy of prevailing teachings in the church. The theses were not academic exercises; they were manifestos of theological and ecclesial reform.

In Karlstadt's case, the theses specifically raised the issue of scriptural authority and addressed the theology of grace apart from works. Furthermore, Luther's first thesis (which was rooted in mystical theology) does not simply call for a reform of corrupt church practice in the tradition of late medieval church reform. It rather has a deeper reforming agenda: it calls for a reform of the very understanding of what it means to be a Christian. It asserts that the entire life of the Christian should be repentance. The same can be said of many of the other theses from Karlstadt and Luther. In Karlstadt's "Tract on the Supreme Virtue of Yieldedness" from 1520, this new sense of mystical interiority and trust in God is presented in its final consequences:

> Although God permits me to be beaten and ridiculed, boiled or roasted, broken on a wheel and torn to pieces, I know, nonetheless, that he is my God, that he is in control of my life and my suffering, and that he is my redeemer. Therefore, I will put my hope in him and cry unto him. And although he should kill and murder me (as Job says), I will hope in him, nonetheless. [. . .] I know that I must be yielded, and that I must let go of all creatures [. . .]. Everything within and around me must be yielded—everything that prevents body and soul to attain to the kingdom of God. May the gracious God grant that. Amen.[95]

This new thrust of theology is also seen in Luther's "Disputation against Scholastic Theology," where he directly confronted and rejected scholastic theology. Both Karlstadt and Luther were clearly advancing a new agenda of reform in the most fundamental issue of all: the basic understanding of what it meant to be a Christian. This was in direct conflict with the Aristotelian scholastic theology and with the exteriority of the practice of indulgences and other religious practices and rituals. Although these men did not want to institute a new church, there is a complex theological dynamic already at play in their theses that, once set in motion, could not be easily stopped.

While the division of the church did not follow a necessary course of development (and was thus contingent upon the specific actors who drove it forward and enabled it), the specific theological content of Karlstadt and Luther's theses from 1517 demanded fundamental reforms. Once these ideas began to move out of the monastery and university context, and once they were recognized as legitimate theological positions held by prominent professors of theology, conflict was sure to come—and it did.

1.6 THE "SHORT REFORMATION"

Following Pope Leo X's "Peter's Indulgence" of 1515, and Karlstadt and Luther's theses of 1517, the short Reformation unfolded quickly. After receiving Luther's letter and his theses, Archbishop Albrecht sent the theses to Rome. In the summer of 1518 a heresy investigation began. Luther was then invited to Rome for questioning. Because of Frederick the Wise's (elector of the empire and duke of Saxony, 1463–1525) intervention, the questioning was held in Augsburg with Cardinal Cajetan in October of 1518. Cajetan interrogated Luther about his understanding of the treasure of the church (the basis of the papal legitimization of the theology of the indulgences). Luther did not retract his rejection of the theology, as he held it to be unbiblical. With the support of Elector Frederick, Luther was then able to escape Cajetan's extradition request.[96] The conflict continued in the summer of 1519 at the Leipzig Debate between Johann Eck, on one side, and Karlstadt and Luther on the other. In these debates, as addressed above, Luther asserted that the Scriptures were the sole authority in doctrinal disputes, and he held that even the pope and councils could err. He also criticized the condemnation of Jan Hus' theology.

Another major part of the short Reformation is the publication of theological texts that called for reform. Luther's *Address to the Christian Nobility of the German Nation* was published in 1520. In this Luther called for the princes to embrace the reforms. He also provided a strong biblical theological argument for the reforms. He strongly challenged the Roman ecclesial order and emphasized the teaching about the priesthood of all believers. This teaching would become central in the agenda of the reform.

Luther was eventually condemned at the Imperial Diet of Worms in 1521. Elector Frederick then arranged for the controversial professor of his new university in Wittenberg to be taken to his Wartburg Castle in

Eisenach. From the beginning, the process of reform was supported and enabled by political authorities. This is one of the great paradoxes of the Reformation: the ecclesial reform would not have been possible without their protection.[97] The reforms in the 1520s in Wittenberg, for example, could have been stopped by Elector Frederick at any step along the way. While he did not promote the reforms explicitly, he and the city council of Wittenberg allowed them to be implemented. This is the other side of the story: sometimes the authorities were pushed to the reforms by their subjects. As Luther was in the Wartburg Castle in 1521 and 1522, the reforms of church order and liturgy were introduced in Wittenberg with Karlstadt and others in the fervor of a popular movement. Once Elector Frederick showed resistance to the process of reform in Wittenberg, however, Luther returned to Wittenberg in 1522 and took control of the reforming process.

After his return, Luther, the political authorities, and the university turned against Karlstadt, then censured his publications and sidelined him.[98] In this transition, the Reformation went from being a movement from the middle of society and from below to being one from above. Karlstadt then moved to Orlamünde in the south of Electoral Saxony and took a pastoral office in the country. If the inauguration of the Reformation is dated with the practical realization of the teaching about the priesthood of all believers and a true church organized by the laity, then the Reformation was first realized in Orlamünde in the summer of 1523. Here the laity started to elect their pastors, and Pastor Karlstadt began to dress like a peasant and work on his own farm. The archdeacon, faculty dean, professor and (double) doctor would then become known as Brother Andrew.[99] Similarly, one might point to the publication of the demands of the rebellious peasants in "The Twelve Articles of the Upper Swabian Peasants" in the spring of 1525, which called for the end of serfdom. These streams of the Reformation were taking the reforms very seriously.

Even with the condemnation of Luther in 1521, the processes of reform could not be stopped. From 1521 onward, reforms were implemented in Wittenberg. From 1523 onward, reforms were introduced in Strasbourg with Martin Bucer. In 1524 reforms were introduced in Zurich with Zwingli (following the breaking of the Lenten fast in 1522, the "Affair of the Sausages"). In 1524 the Peasants' Revolt began. The peasants and their supporters drew upon the theological ideas of reform and Luther's teaching about the priesthood of all believers. These revolts were suppressed in 1525 and 1526. The process of reform received official political establishment outside the Holy Roman Empire of the German Nation in 1527, when King Friedrich I of Denmark secured religious freedom for Danish Lutherans (Diet of Odense).

While the division of Europe's church was already well underway in the 1520s, at the Diet of Speyer in 1529, the Imperial Parliament (dominated by pro-Catholic representatives) decided that the 1521 edict against Luther should be enforced. A minority group in the parliament (made up of fourteen German towns and six princes) protested against the decision since they supported the Lutheran reforms. The term "Protestant" comes from this initial rejection of the edict. In their minority statement, they declared:

> We herewith protest and testify publicly before God [. . .] that we ourselves, our subjects and in behalf of all, each and every one, consider [the entire transaction] null and not binding; and we desire, in matters of religion [. . .] so to live, govern, and carry ourselves in our governments, [. . .] as we trust to answer it before God almighty and his Roman Imperial Majesty, our most gracious Lord.[100]

In the same year there was a revolt in the city of Lübeck as Protestants overthrew the city council and appointed a new chief official (burgomaster) of the city (Jürgen Wullenwever).[101] The persecution of the Anabaptists increased in the 1520s. The moderate Anabaptist Balthasar Hubmaier was burned at the stake on March 10, 1528, in the city of Vienna (after being driven out of Zurich). As the executioners rubbed gunpowder and sulfur into his beard, he said, "Oh salt me well, salt me well." He then asked those around to pray that God "will give me patience in this my suffering." His wife was drowned in the Danube three days later.[102] The Anabaptists rejected infant baptism and sought to purify the church. They separated themselves from the evil of the world and promoted a literal interpretation of Jesus' teaching. This led them to endorse pacifism and reject the coercion of the politically backed Reformers. The movement was very diverse. Some of their leaders were Balthasar Hubmaier, Menno Simons, Conrad Grebel, Hans Hut, Melchior Hoffman, and Jakob Hutter. Their teachings were summarized in the Schleitheim Confession of 1527. In 1534 Anabaptists managed to take control of Münster (Münster Rebellion) for a year. The leaders of this group of Anabaptists abandoned the teachings about peace and introduced polygamy before being overrun and executed in 1535. It was a truly exceptional case of Anabaptism, and it was not really representative of the bulk of their teachings or the sentiment of their movement.

In the theological narrative of the Reformation, the year 1530 is very significant. At the Diet of Augsburg in this year, the Protestants offered the Augsburg Confession as a summary of their teaching. It was written by Philip Melanchthon and based on previous summaries of Protestant theology. It asserted, above all, that the teachings of the Protestants were biblical and that they were in agreement with the early church.[103] Debates, responses, refutations, and unsuccessful negotiation followed between the Protestants and the Catholics. At one point Emperor Charles V declared that the Protestants had been refuted and demanded that they return to the Catholic faith. He claimed that he had to do this in his conscience "as Roman, Christian emperor, overlord, and guardian of the holy Christian church."[104] The only thing that could stop this imperial power was the power of the German princes.

Since the Imperial Parliament at Speyer ended in disagreement, and since Emperor Charles V did not accept the Augsburg Confession, the Protestants formed the Schmalkaldic League (1531–1547) to defend the reforms. If the beginning of the short Reformation is dated with Karlstadt's theses in April of 1517, the birth of the Schmalkaldic League in February of 1531 is probably the best date for its end. Following the League of Torgau (1526), it ensured that the reforms would be carried out and maintained within the empire. It protected the agenda of ecclesial reform against external military threat since all the members agreed to come to defense of one another if they were attacked for religious reasons.[105] This changed the political and religious map of the Holy Roman Empire.[106] What had started as a university debate had become a full-scale imperial conflict with military backing. In 1531 Luther wrote a "Warning to His Dear German People" calling for the Germans to reject the emperor's command to bring military force against the Protestants. Clearly, Luther and the other Protestants were willing to challenge political power if they were forced to give up the theological reforms.[107]

Attempts at reconciliation came very early in the history of the Reformation. At the colloquies in Worms and Regensburg (1540–1541), theologians tried to resolve the differences between the Protestants and the Catholics. The process of confessionalization was also quickly introduced. In 1541 John Calvin's *Ecclesiastical Ordinances* were adopted in Geneva, which led to a new disciplinary religious-political order. In 1545 the Catholic response to the events of the Reformation resulted in the Council of Trent. The Schmalkaldic War followed in 1546 and 1547. This brought a military defeat to the Protestants, but it was far too late. The reforms had taken hold all over northern Europe, both inside the empire and outside of it, and they could not be turned back. The conflict about the faith continued, and in 1555 the Peace of Augsburg was finally established. It allowed for the faith of the Augsburg Confession to be practiced in the territories of the Protestant authorities in the empire. While this was an endorsement of the Protestant theology, it brought about a new wave of confessional polarization in Europe.

The effects of the short Reformation were deep and far reaching in Western history. While the basic reform impulses were fundamentally positive developments in the history of Christianity, the violence that followed in the reforming process was a contradiction of the Christian teachings about love and long-suffering. It is therefore impossible to evaluate this historical development as either wholly positive or wholly negative. That which was to follow in the two centuries after the Reformation is well described by Diarmaid MacCulloch. Europe was "torn apart by deep disagreements about how human beings should exercise the power of God in the world, arguments even about what it was to be human. It was a process of extreme mental and physical violence."[108] It was also, however, a process that ultimately led to a new appreciation of the freedom of conscience. This happened as the practice of religious coercion was slowly recognized for what it was: futile, inhumane, and a contradiction of the gospel message itself. The Reformation was also a process that supported, in the long run, the movement toward egalitarianism. Of course, at the very heart of the reforming movements was the rediscovery of the theology of grace and the teaching that salvation comes by faith apart from works. In this sense, the Reformation entailed both positive and problematic dimensions. In the next chapter, some of these problematic aspects of the sixteenth-century reforms will be analyzed.

« 2 »

THE EVILS AND ERRORS
OF THE REFORMERS

In many regards, Martin Luther and the other major Reformers positively influenced Christianity. At the same time, however, other aspects of their work are far more complicated. These complicated and often problematic dimensions of their work cannot be easily separated from the overall picture of the Reformers or the Reformation as a whole.

More than anyone, the persona of Martin Luther was drawn into the center of the thematic planning of the 2017 celebrations of the five hundredth anniversary of the Reformation. While this is understandable, since he was a central figure of the Reformation, it is important to remember his and all of the other Reformers' complicated legacies. Of course, the Reformation as a whole cannot be reduced to one personality. It was a broad sociopolitical and cultural shift in early modern history that included thousands of key figures, groups, and institutions. Indeed, as the Reformation got going, Luther became "the Reformer on the edge of the Reformation."[1] Nevertheless, Luther's personality was still widely associated with the Reformation (in large part because of his many publications).[2] Both Luther's work and the initial history of the Reformation are infused with contradictory tensions that brought forth both positive and negative impulses. In the following section, some of these problematic sides of Luther and the other Reformers will be analyzed.

2.1 THE "RADICALS"

One of the very problematic aspects of the Reformation was the way in which the politically backed Reformers (like Luther, Zwingli, and Calvin) oppressed other Protestant groups. This started in the 1520s—right after Luther returned to Wittenberg from the Wartburg Castle (in his treatment of Karlstadt). These sidelined groups are often called the "radical Reformers." This refers to Karlstadt, the various groups of Anabaptists, the "Zwickau prophets," and other spiritualists and eschatological visionaries like Thomas Müntzer. The Peasants' Revolt (which was supported by many people who were not peasants) and the Anabaptist Münster Rebellion are two of the main reasons why the term "radical Reformation" is used—and in these cases it fits quite well.[3]

The "radicals" were the ones who spread the reform message across Europe in the 1520s. They were "driven by a fervent, impatient desire to see sweeping reforms made on the basis of religion. The radicals also insisted that Reformation meant much more than changes in devotional practices and ecclesiastical institutions; public life as a whole was urgently in need of Christianization."[4] Of course, all the Reformers (Luther, Bucer, and Zwingli included) wanted a christianization of society. Whereas the politically backed (magisterial) Reformers wanted to do this more slowly and in union with the political leaders, the radicals wanted to bring this about quickly, with or without—or even in opposition to—the political authorities. There was also a strong anticlericalism among many radicals (especially with Müntzer). The idea of "the common man" (*der gemeine Mann*) was central to this anticlericalism. This term "common man" was not a reference to the impoverished but to the "modestly propertied peasants and artisans who had no share in government." For the radicals, the common man could understand the gospel better than the corrupt priests and the ecclesial hierarchy. According to Müntzer, the clergy were responsible for the corruption of the faith and did not care about the deterioration of the church and society because they had a privileged status in the feudal order.[5] Luther also supported this sentiment in the early period.

The radicals had a vision of politics, society, and the church that was essentially built on principles of local autonomy and egalitarianism. Not the bishops or a higher church authority but the congregation itself should have control over the local church.[6] Sometimes they were actually patient with their demands. Müntzer and Hubmaier (at Waldshut) both rejected infant baptism in principle, but they nevertheless allowed parents to do this if they chose to. The radicals were, however, generally critical of the gradualist approach of introducing reforms. Many of the radicals saw this "as a pious hypocrisy contrived to conceal their subservience to secular authorities."[7]

As the Protestant faith spread, it often led to iconoclastic outbursts that went together with riotous groups who promoted anticlericalism and insurrectionist plans.[8] The princes, magistrates, and their theologians tried to stop this, as they did in Nuremberg (and many other localities) by controlling the preaching and printing. It was, however, impossible to control the passion of reform entirely. Even well after the reforms were introduced, there was, in fact, a great deal of plurality of religious belief. Regarding Bucer's Strasbourg, for example, the Jesuit Jacob Rabus would claim, "In poor Strasbourg you now have five or six sects among the common people. One fellow is an out-and-out Lutheran, the second a half-Lutheran, the third a Zwinglian, the fourth a Calvinist, the fifth a Schwenckfelder, the sixth an Anabaptist, and the seventh lot is purely epicurean."[9] As Brady remarks, the eighth group would have been, like Rabus, the remaining Catholics in the city. In many cases the magisterial Reformers never got the situation completely under control—despite having the help of the political authorities. In other words, the politically backed Reformers never entirely prevailed over the other groups.

In Luther's assessment, these Christians were "'fanatics [*Schwärmer*].' Restless, roaming spirits, separatists with no sense or feeling of responsibility for Church and society, disobedient to the temporal authorities and the Holy Scriptures."[10] It is, of course, a great irony in the history of the Reformation that the "fanatics" were the ones that introduced, for the first time, Protestant liturgies (Karlstadt), church services in the German language (Müntzer), and full-blown theories of religious tolerance (Sebastian Franck).[11] In much of the historical literature on the Reformation, the term "radical Reformation" is used to posit a third program of religious reform in the sixteenth century alongside the magisterial Protestants and the Catholics. In order to get to this three-part framework, however, one must unify the various groups (including the divided magisterial Protestants). This approach is problematic for the same reason that it is helpful: it simplifies the complexity of the early sixteenth-century religious landscape. In this framework the term "magisterial Reformers" (or "magisterial Reformation") is used to describe those Reformers who cooperated with the princes and civil magistrates, such as Luther (Electoral Saxony), Calvin (Geneva), Zwingli (Zurich), and Martin Bucer (Strasbourg).[12]

Of the various Reformers of the "Radical Reformation" (to use George Huntston Williams' term), in only "three or four instances" were they "misled into thinking that the regenerate magistrates from their own midst would prove more godly than Protestants and Catholics."[13] Apart from these few exceptions, all of them "denounced war and renounced all other forms of coercion except the ban, and sought to spread their version of the Christian life by missions, martyrdom, and philanthropy."[14] The "ban" was a nonviolent excommunication of deviant members from the ecclesial community. Generally, these groups advanced their reform agendas independently of the authorities and without political backing. Sometimes they rejected the political order; other times they were rejected by it. Some of them were more radical in their theology (like Müntzer), others were more moderate (like Karlstadt).

Early in the Reformation, many Anabaptist groups were seen as contemporary representatives of the heresy of Donatism. The Donatists of the fourth century promoted the idea of a pure church. They claimed that the efficacy of the sacraments depended upon the sanctity of the ministers. At the Diet of Speyer in 1529, a law was established (published on April 22) that condemned the Anabaptists and the Zwinglians. This received the approval of both the Catholics and the Protestants (Lutherans) at the Diet.[15] The Anabaptists were to be executed according to the law (which drew upon the condemnation of the Donatists in the ancient Justinian Code).[16] They were held to be heretical because they rejected the baptism of children and thus degraded the sacrament of baptism. The Zwinglians, on the other hand, seemed to be doing the same thing with the sacrament of Communion. The Lutherans and Zwinglians later met in Marburg in October of 1529 to reconcile their differences. While they did not come to a common understanding of Communion, they reached an agreement in their understanding of baptism.[17] Despite this agreement, they remained heretical in the eyes of the Lutherans. Luther himself held their teaching to be "fanatic."

While this term "radical Reformation" is used by many historians, there are three major problems with it.[18] Firstly, the term minimizes the common background and radicalness of all the Protestants in Latin Christendom and their joint rejection of the Roman papacy. Both the magisterial Reformers and the radical Reformers were protestants in the general sense of the term. Both groups shared the common background of Latin Christendom and both rejected—protested against—the Roman papacy and the political order that supported it. While some were more extreme than others, Luther, Zwingli, Karlstadt, Müntzer, and all the other Protestant Reformers were radical in that they were all calling the status quo into question. Luther, for example, was also radical in his opinions about the Jews (even for his day) and in his treatment of those who did not agree with him. Luther's "Address to the Christian Nobility" is clearly a radical work that called for fundamental reform. Luther was also radical in his view of the Catholic Mass and the pope. While some of the Protestants were more radical than others, all of them were radical.

Secondly, the attempt at designating one group of the Protestants as radical misconstrues the fundamental distinction between the two groups of Reformers. There were many disagreements about theology, church order, and sociopolitical issues among all the various Protestant groups. The Lutherans argued among the Lutherans while the Calvinists argued among the Calvinists. Even the Anabaptists argued among one another. Some Anabaptists thought that it was acceptable for Christians to be civil magistrates or to fight in wars, while others rejected this. The fundamental difference between the two groups (radical Reformers and magisterial Reformers) was not theology (which they all disagreed about). The fundamental difference between these two groups of Protestants was the status of their political backing. The sidelined independent radical Reformers had no political backing; the other group did.

A comparison between Zwingli and Caspar Schwenckfeld can illustrate this point. Zwingli had political support and endorsed a new theology of the sacraments according to which the bread and wine were to be understood symbolically and not in Luther's sense with the real presence of Jesus Christ. Since Zwingli maintained political backing for his program, he was not made a radical (even though this position was declared heretical at the Diet of Speyer of 1529 among the Lutherans). Today historians group Zwingli with the magisterial Reformers. Caspar Schwenckfeld, on the other hand, is put into the group of radicals. Initially, Schwenckfeld also had political backing from the Silesian nobility. Later he embraced a spiritualistic theology and, like Zwingli, reinterpreted the sacraments. Unlike Zwingli, however, Schwenckfeld eventually lost his political backing and went into exile in 1529. Theoretically, the nobility could have supported him and his new theology. If they had done this, it is possible that Schwenckfeld would today be put into the group of magisterial Reformers with Zwingli. On the other hand, if Zwingli had lost his political backing, it is possible that he would today be put into the group of radicals. This comparison shows how truly arbitrary these terms "radical" and "magisterial" really are. It also illustrates how the real distinction between these groups was political power in the first instance, and not theology.

For these reasons, a better conception of these two groups would be politically backed Protestants and nonpolitically backed Protestants, or politically backed and independent (in the sense of "no political backing") Reformers. Nevertheless, the term "radical Reformer" does seem appropriate for some of the cases. It is particularly appropriate when referring to events on the scale of the Peasants' Revolt and the Münster Rebellion, and some of the writings associated with these events.[19]

Thirdly, in common language today, the term "radical" has a negative connotation. This third argument is different from the first two, which are historical and analytical in nature. From our perspective today, the term "radical" conveys a value judgment about the independent Reformers. It suggests that they were abnormal, unusual, crazy, irrational, wrong, or even violent. Of course, the term "radical" does not have to be understood in this way. The historians that use the term do not intend to communicate these associations. In fact, the term can be understood positively.

Many of the ideas that usually fall into the independent Reformers' group are, by today's standards, not radical at all. Many of the independent Reformers simply wanted a more egalitarian church order (following the idea of the priesthood of all believers). This is normal today, not radical. Even the rebellious peasants of the Peasants' Revolt, who "incorporated the burghers of princely cities," do not seem so radical from our perspective today.[20] In the very popular "Twelve Articles of the Upper Swabian Peasants," published in the spring of 1525, the peasants (and the pastors and theologians that supported them) made a strong theological argument for the reform of the social order.[21] In their argument for freedom, they explicitly emphasized the point that *they did not want to overthrow every authority.* Rather they wanted to be set free from serfdom. They also emphasized the love of God and the love of neighbor while calling for the right to choose their own pastors. There is no call to arms in the articles. In the third article, which calls for freedom from serfdom, they declare,

> Third, until now it has been the custom for us to be regarded as a lord's personal property, which is deplorable since Christ redeemed us all with the shedding of his precious blood—the shepherd as well as the most highly placed, without exception. Thus, Scripture establishes that we are and will be free. (Isaiah 53, 1 Peter 1, 1 Corinthians 7.) Not that we want to be completely free, with no authority over us. God does not teach us

this. (Romans 13, Wisdom 6, 1 Peter 2.) We should live according to his commandments, not according to free, carnal whim. (Deuteronomy 6, Matthew 4.) Rather, we want to love God, acknowledge him as our lord in our neighbor, and we want to do everything gladly that God commanded us to do at the Last Supper (Luke 4 and 6). Although we should live according to his commandments, they do not teach us that we should not be obedient to authority, and not only to authority; rather we should humble ourselves before everyone. (Matthew 7, John 13, Romans 13.) They also show that we should gladly be obedient to our elected and established authorities (if established for us by God) in everything that is proper and Christian (Acts 5). Without a doubt, as true and just Christians, you will also gladly release us from serfdom, or show us from the gospel that we should be serfs.[22]

Other independents questioned Luther's doctrine of the sacraments, especially the teaching about the real presence of Christ in Communion. Today, however, many Christians (and many Christians in Lutheran churches) hold the symbolic view of the sacraments that Karlstadt and Zwingli endorsed. While these theological developments were considered radical in the sixteenth century, today they are normal. Other independents had spiritual visions and religious ideas that were, perhaps, out of the ordinary, but, again, so did Luther as he claimed to know about the demonic activity of his opponents and Satan's work in the "false brethren." Luther remarked, "I do not fear the external adversaries, for the church will not perish from the outside. But the internal evil, the false brethren [*falsi fratres*], they will do this. Judas had to betray Christ and the false prophets distorted the gospel."[23]

There were some, of course, who were radicals (in the usual sense of that word). The most famous of these was Thomas Müntzer. Unlike Karlstadt (who advised against this), Müntzer used religion to legitimize the Peasants' Revolt. At the same time, however, Luther himself used religion to justify the princes' brutal suppression of the peasants. These two things are not the same: one was actively promoting revolution, the other was reacting to the revolution. In both cases, however, religion was used to legitimize force.

Müntzer was born in Stolberg some miles west of Luther's birthplace, Eisleben. Although later, as a pastor, he supported the peasants in their fight against the nobility, the family name Müntzer was actually associated with the privileged urban class and the nobility in Stolberg.[24] He became a priest in Brunswick and, like Luther, was involved in the controversy about the indulgences. Like Luther, he was striving for purity in the church and was critical of the corruptions of the ecclesial order.[25] Müntzer went to Wittenberg in the fall of 1517. Later he was in Zwickau from August of 1520 to April of 1521. He then became a pastor in Allstedt, where he introduced reforms in 1523 and 1524. There he organized around five hundred people to resist a potential Catholic assault. He also encouraged the "rulers of Saxony to lead war against the godless."[26] Unlike Luther, Müntzer opposed feudal authority. He wanted the peasants to be freed and believed in an imminent apocalyptic coming of the kingdom of God, which would be egalitarian and communalist. He supported the Peasants' Revolt and in 1525 was captured, tortured, and executed. Luther thought that Müntzer was essentially Satan in the flesh, and he used all his power to stop him. He remarked regarding Müntzer's death in 1533, "I killed Müntzer, his death hangs around my neck. I did it because he wanted to kill my Christ."[27]

Another group of independent Reformers came from Zwickau, the "Zwickau-Prophets": Nicolaus Storch (a weaver), Thomas Drechsel (a blacksmith) and Markus Thomae (called Stübner, a former Wittenberg student who knew Melanchthon).[28] At the end of 1521, Nikolaus Hausmann, a pastor in Zwickau and a friend of Luther, moved the city council of Zwickau to oppose the group, and they were then driven out of the town. In December of 1521, they fled to Wittenberg, where they spread their ideas for a few days. At this time they met with Melanchthon. Melanchthon was actually impressed by them and may have come under their influence for a while.[29]

The Zwickau group saw themselves as a part of the reform movements and even referred to Luther.[30] They also rejected infant baptism (because infants lack faith) and claimed to have direct conversation with God and spiritual dreams. As a matter of fact, in 1520 Luther himself had referred to John 6:45 ("It is written in the prophets, 'And they shall all be taught by God.' Everyone who has heard and learned from the Father comes to me") on multiple occasions. He thus encouraged the idea that Christians can be taught by God directly.[31] The Zwickau group taught that the Spirit was the true teacher and not the Scriptures. They are reported to have taught, "Man must be taught by the Spirit alone. For if God had wanted man to be taught by scripture, he would have sent down the Bible to us from heaven."[32] Of course, on this specific issue there is no difference between the "prophets" and many modern-day liberal Protestants. The Zwickau group also had apocalyptic visions. This was common among many of the spiritualists. It had to do with the idea that "history had reached its 'harvest time,' and that God was about to intervene directly in the culmination of human affairs."[33]

While Luther was in the Wartburg Castle, he corresponded with Melanchthon about the Zwickau group in Wittenberg. Melanchthon actually asked Elector Frederick to release Luther from the Wartburg Castle in order for Luther to meet them.[34] In his correspondences about the Zwickau group, Luther came into contact with the idea of adult baptism for the first time. Luther rejected this theology by claiming that little children were already being baptized at the time of the apostles. Luther wrote to Melanchthon from Wartburg on January 15, 1522, "I have been waiting for Satan to attack this sensitive spot—but he decided not to make use of the papists. Now he is making efforts in and among us Evangelicals to produce the worst conceivable schism. May Christ quickly trample him under his feet."[35]

In his criticism of Müntzer in 1524, Luther asserted that he himself had the right to decide which doctrine was true and which was false since he had risked his life in the cause of the reform.[36] Luther saw Satan working in these "false brethren." Even after the brutal suppression of the Peasants' Revolt, Luther saw the Anabaptists as the "seeds of the Devil." In his letter to Philip I of Hesse from 1538, Luther tells the ruler that he should expel the Anabaptists from the Land of Hesse "with vigor" (*ernstlich*). He writes,

> It is not only my opinion but also my humble request that Your Princely Grace should expel them with vigor out of the land [Landgraviate of Hesse]. In spite of everything it [Anabaptism] remains the seeds of the Devil. [. . .] Your Princely Grace should not be concerned that once expelled from the land they will cause damage elsewhere. For elsewhere they will not have more space for activity; and even if they did, then those who hold office in the government and in the church there should take guard. For if I am concerned that the wolf who causes destruction in my stall could cause even more in other stalls, I cannot, for this reason, refrain from chasing him away. Each should guard his own stall.[37]

This citation is very helpful for understanding Luther's thinking. He sees the reform of the church taking place in a territorial framework, which he refers to as a "stall." He thinks of the church and the government cooperating with one another to implement the reforms and to discipline "with vigor" those who do not agree with the program. The princes—political powers with the threat of violent force behind them—were essential in Luther's understanding of church reform. Luther encouraged the powerful leader of the Landgraviate of Hesse to view the Anabaptists not as fellow Christians but rather as the "seeds of the Devil." Understandably, then, those who went on to persecute and murder the Anabaptists could call upon Luther in justification of their evil deeds. For Luther, even the Zwinglian Reformers (who also persecuted the Anabaptists) were driven by the devil in their theology. They were "fanatics" and were "blaspheming" the sacrament of the Lord's Supper by making it "mere bread and wine as a symbol or memorial sign."[38]

Luther managed to silence the opposition by excluding them, demonizing them, and explicitly encouraging political persecution of them. In this sense, Jörg Trelenberg is correct to point out that Luther "undoubtedly had a general, but also very concrete joint guilt in the violent suppression of deviant Anabaptism in the sixteenth century."[39] This is also expressed in Luther's handling of the German Peasants' Revolt. Luther encouraged the authorities to kill the rebellious peasants. Initially, he did not want this. Once the situation escalated, however, he called for the most brutal response from the princes against the peasants in *Against the Murdering and Robbing Hordes of Peasants* (1525).[40] Luther was not alone in suppressing groups that disagreed with him. Other politically backed Reformers also supported the persecution of the independent groups.[41] Luther bears a unique guilt in this, however, as he set a very important example for dealing with dissent at the outset of the short Reformation. In this way, the persecution in Wittenberg and in Saxony became a model for other Reformers.

While the politically backed Reformers tried to silence and demonize the independent Reformers, their versions of Christianity have flourished. There is some continuity that can still be identified between these groups from the sixteenth century and streams of theology and religious practice today. In terms of contemporary comparison, the theologies of Schwenckfeld and Sebastian Franck (another radical)[42] live on in modified form in contemporary liberal Protestant theology. The theologies of the Anabaptists and of Karlstadt are still strong in many evangelical and Anabaptist churches. The religious experiences and visions of the Zwickau group are also still alive in Pentecostalism.[43] Finally, the theology of Müntzer (if modified in some ways) is still found today among Christian socialists. Of course, the theologies of Luther, Zwingli, and Calvin also continue to thrive in the conservative-traditionalist wing of many contemporary Protestant churches. It must be acknowledged, however, that many of the contemporary liberal Protestant churches that officially bear their names, or stand in direct institutional-historical continuity with them, have actually abandoned much of the theology of the politically backed Reformers. This is especially the case with regard to the issue of persecution.

The story about the persecution of the independent Reformers has many dimensions. It is a story about the oppression of minority groups, the dangers of the unification of politics and religion, and the general need for tolerance. In another regard, however, it is also a story about the fundamental interpretive openness and ambiguity of theological and religious traditions. All these groups were providing new interpretations of the Christian faith. Only a few of them, however, were established with violence. This is, perhaps, one of the most problematic aspects of the history of the Reformation. As Harry Loewen has written, "Especially Lutheran Protestantism, to which the radicals had constantly appealed, has sinned against them most, for it failed to appreciate that they simply endeavoured to follow Luther's early reformation principles to their logical conclusion and live in accordance with the precepts of the gospel as they understood them."[44]

The lack of tolerance also contradicted a Christian teaching in the New Testament as outlined by Paul:

> Welcome those who are weak in faith, but not for the purpose of quarreling over opinions. Some believe in eating anything, while the weak eat only vegetables. Those who eat must not despise those who abstain, and those who abstain must not pass judgment on those who eat; for God has welcomed them. Who are you to pass judgment on servants of another? It is before their own lord that they stand or fall. And they will be upheld, for the Lord is able to make them stand. (Rom 14:1-4)

While Pauline theology was central to the Reformation, the full potential of this passage was often overlooked. Beyond this, the essence of the problem had to do with a foundational issue (which will be addressed in chap. 4): the idea that the church should use political power to make people better Christians and to suppress other versions of the faith to achieve this goal. Rather than letting the Spirit of God work, many of the politically backed Reformers tried to become like God and do the work of God. In this, they were the true radicals.

2.2 THE NATION

Luther's anti-Roman program of emancipation, which contributed to national identity and national thinking in the German lands, is something that has been addressed by many historians. German rhetoric of liberation was popular around 1500. Something like a mythologization of the Germans and their virtues is already found in Jakob Wimpfeling's *Germania* (1501) and in his *Epithoma rerum Germanicarum* (1505). According to Wimpfeling, the Germans did not get their greatest virtues from the Romans; they came from the Germans' own impetus.[45] At the time of the Reformation, national resentment between the Germans and Italy had dug in deep. As the sense of a unified German identity emerged, there was a "pronounced note of a more general German nationalism in the late medieval period, and it would prove crucial to the spread of the Reformation movement. In its origins it was aggressively xenophobic, directed at the Italians, the French, and above all the papacy."[46] The Reformation played into this tension and was, in part, also a result of it. The idea that Rome brought the German lands culture, religion, and imperial status (*translatio imperii*, "the transfer of the empire") was used to justify the demand for German payments to Rome.[47] This attitude emanating from Rome was, however, long despised by humanists north of the Alps before the conflict about the indulgences began in 1517.[48]

In his recent study of this theme, Caspar Hirschi, a contemporary Swiss German historian, claims that Luther explicitly promoted themes of national identity: "He set himself the task of reforming the German nation, not Christianity as a whole—despite his claim that his religious doctrine had universal validity. He combined anticlerical with anti-Italian polemics. He used a rhetoric of liberation, which carried little precise meaning for quite a while."[49] Luther did not, however, promote the national theme in the same way that the humanists did.[50] Hirschi argues that Luther's theology had a deeply negative account of humanity that went against some aspects of the humanists' account of the nation.

Luther did, however, address the various national characters (Scots, French, Italians, Germans, Jews, Turks, etc.) regularly in his writings. He often praised the German language as clear and straightforward, unlike Latin, which he called thin and meager. Hirschi writes,

> Luther's presentation of the German language as a raw instrument for plain speech served a key function in his self-promotion. It represented the qualities which he claimed for himself in contrast to the humanist masters of elegant Latin. Although a careful and gifted literary stylist himself, Luther liked to pretend that, as a writer and preacher, he did not care about rhetorics and style at all. His was a typical rhetoric of anti-rhetoric, a form of virtuoso speech that disguised and denied its virtuosity in order to appear as genuine and spontaneous expression.[51]

This kind of posturing helped Luther "build a long-lasting legacy as a true-bred German scholar—crude, blunt and thorough—exposing the humanist nationalists as dubious countrymen."[52] Luther's conflict with Erasmus was one of the first encounters between "religious fundamentalism" and nationalism. Hirschi claims that it is not anachronistic to use this term, fundamentalism, for Luther. He sees it as "both obvious and helpful—obvious, because he matches the criteria used today to label religious fundamentalists, and helpful because it clarifies his deep alienation from pre-Reformation culture and scholarship, particularly from Renaissance humanism."[53] Hirschi claims that Luther was an uncompromising biblical literalist preacher who had a dualistic view of the world as hanging between God and the devil. Such a theology or view of the world did not fit with the humanism of the sixteenth century or its ideas of nations. Only later, after this theology began to lose its grip in the nineteenth century, could modern nationalism emerge. As Hirschi writes, "Only when the political, economic and human cost of religious fundamentalism was becoming apparent and confessional confrontations were losing their inexorability could nationalism become truly powerful and popular."[54] This is an important point because it highlights the discontinuity between Luther and modern nationalism.

While Luther was no modern (post-Darwinian) nationalist, he was certainly a premodern nationalist. In many places in Luther's works, the theme of the "German nation" is emphasized. Luther wrote in his "To the Councilmen of All Cities of German Country" that he sought after "only the happiness and salvation of the whole of Germany."[55] In his "Warning to His Dear German People," Luther wrote, "I am not seeking my own benefit in this, but the salvation of you Germans."[56] In his preface to the mystical work *Theologia Deutsch* (1518), which he edited, he wrote,

> I thank God that I hear and find my God in the German tongue, whereas I, and they with me, previously did not find him either in the Latin, the Greek, or the Hebrew tongue. God grant that this little book will become better known. Then we shall find that German theologians are without a doubt the best theologians. Amen.[57]

This is clearly an example of early modern nationalism. This comes out in the sense of a German identity and language over against the "Latin, the Greek, or the Hebrew tongue." The nationalistic arrogance is also here in his claim that "German theologians" are "the best." These kinds of remarks from Luther certainly encouraged what would later become modern German nationalism.

In "To the Christian Nobility of the German Nation," Luther wrote, "Now that Italy is sucked dry, the Romanists are coming into Germany."[58] He continues his criticism: "How is it that we Germans must put up with such robbery and extortion of our good at the hands of the pope? If the kingdom of France has prevented it, why do we Germans let them make such fools and apes of us?"[59] He writes,

> Germany now gives much more to the pope at Rome than it used to give to the emperors in ancient times. [...] And we still go on wondering why princes and nobles, cities and endowments, land and people, grow poor. We ought to marvel that we have anything left to eat! Since we have now come to the heart of the matter, we will pause a little and let it be seen that the Germans are not quite such crass fools that they do not see or understand the sharp practices of the Romanists.[60]

While this is to be distinguished from the various nationalisms of the nineteenth and twentieth centuries, some of the themes are similar, such as the victim theme and the friend/enemy dichotomy.

Luther has often been drawn upon as the primal German hero of the German nation. In 1819 Johann Wolfgang von Goethe claimed that "the Germans first became one *Volk* through Luther."[61] One of the intellectual fathers of National Socialism, Houston Stewart Chamberlain, called Luther a "political hero" in 1934, in a book about Luther, the German race, and Hitler. He cited this famous line from Luther: "For my Germans I was born; them will I serve!"[62] Chamberlain goes on to cite another line from Luther, this one from his *Table Talk* from 1537 about a unified *Germania* under one political authority: "If Germany was under one lord, it would be invincible."[63] These remarks from Luther are examples of straightforward early modern nationalism that was used by modern nationalists. Heinrich Bornkamm, for example, could draw upon many citations from Luther to support *völkisch* thinking in the 1930s in Germany. His essay on this subject was originally published in 1933.[64]

The fact that so many German nationalists could find support for their agenda in Luther is not surprising. In many ways they were using him for their own unique causes. In others, however, there was certainly something in Luther, something that Luther himself encouraged, that they were drawing on. These are the points of contact or continuity between Luther and modern German nationalism. Of course, there are other examples of discontinuity. The most important difference is the rise of naturalistic and scientific ways of thinking about ethnicity in the nineteenth century. While there are some points of contact between Luther and modern German nationalism, modern nationalism of the nineteenth and twentieth centuries was also deeply influenced by Darwinian ideas and the political, cultural, and social struggle for a unified Germany in the nineteenth century.

Georg Wilhelm Friedrich Hegel (1770–1831) provided a nationalistic interpretation of the Reformation in the early nineteenth century. In his *Lectures on the History of Philosophy* one reads that "it was in the Lutheran Reformation that the great revolution appeared."[65] The basic idea is that of a progressive advance of history in the liberation of humanity toward the subjective consciousness of freedom itself. As he remarked in his *Lectures on the Philosophy of History*, "This is the essence of the Reformation: Man is in his very nature destined to be free."[66] The narrative then takes on a strong nationalistic tone:

> Here an important question solicits investigation:—why the Reformation was limited to certain nations, and why it did not permeate the whole Catholic world. The Reformation originated in Germany, and struck firm root only in the purely German nations; outside of Germany itself it established itself in Scandinavia and England. But the Romanic and Sclavonic nations kept decidedly aloof from it. Even South Germany has only partially adopted the Reformation—a fact which is consistent with the mingling of elements which is the general characteristic of its nationality.[67]

Hegel goes on to explain that both the "Sclavonic nations" and the "Romanic nations" ("Italy, Spain, Portugal, and in part France") "were not imbued with the Reformed doctrines." He argues that physical force may have played a role, yet "this alone would not be sufficient to explain the fact, for when the Spirit of a Nation craves anything no force can prevent its attaining the desired object: nor can it be said that these nations were deficient in culture; on the contrary, they were in advance of the Germans in this respect." Hegel goes on to explain that it had to do with "the fundamental character of these nations." This is the reason why "they did not adopt the Reformation." He then asks,

> But what is this peculiarity of character which hindered the attainment of Spiritual Freedom? We answer: the pure inwardness of the German Nation was the proper soil for the emancipation of Spirit; the Romanic nations, on the contrary, have maintained in the very depth of their soul—in their Spiritual Consciousness—the principle of *Disharmony*: they are a product of the fusion of Roman and German blood, and still retain the heterogeneity thence resulting.[68]

In this sense, there is a biological-cultural dimension to his philosophy of history: "The development and advance of Spirit from the time of Reformation onwards consist in this, that Spirit, having now gained the consciousness of its Freedom, through that process of mediation which takes place between man and God [. . .] now takes it up and follows it out in building up the edifice of secular relations." While "the Secular" was "formerly regarded as evil," with the Reformation a new age has come: "It is now perceived that Morality and Justice in the State are also divine and commanded by God, and that in point of substance there is nothing higher or more sacred."[69] This is then linked into the history of the rise of Prussia as a European power: "The Protestant Church increased and so perfected the stability of its political existence by the fact that one of the states which had adopted the principles of the Reformation raised itself to the position of an independent European power. This power was destined to start into a new life with Protestantism: *Prussia*."[70]

There is both truth and error in Hegel's thinking. The truth is that Protestantism did raise the status of the secular realm. This was made possible through the teaching about the priesthood of all believers. It was also made possible through the teaching that one could glorify God in work that was not sacred or ecclesial. It is also true that Protestantism greatly influenced the culture of Prussia. At the same time, however, other Enlightenment ideals were also very influential in Prussia.

The error in Hegel's thinking is the nationalistic and racial concepts. The theory that the Reformation had to do with some racial-ethnic character of the German peoples overlooks the true driving forces behind the Reformation: the ecclesial corruption with the practice of indulgences, the anti-Roman resentments, the new theologies of reform, the new mystical theologies, the growing power of territories and princes in the empire, the new universities (like the one in Wittenberg, which was founded in 1502), the increase in trade and communication, the printing press, the weakened legitimacy of the Roman papacy through the Western Schism, and many more issues that are addressed below. The claim that racial character was the reason for the Reformation is untenable. Hegel's racial theories come from the ideology of German nationalism in the nineteenth century (which was closely linked with German romanticism).

While the Reformation contributed to early modern nationalism, this was actually older than the Reformation. In this regard, the Reformation built upon and advanced older cultural, social, and political trajectories. Although there are points of discontinuity, the German nationalists of the nineteenth and twentieth centuries did not "create" a Luther out of nothing for their national agenda. They were rather building upon his early modern German nationalism. All of this was, of course, a rejection of the Christian teaching about the true Spirit of the Christian faith: "For in the one Spirit we were all baptized into one body—Jews or Greeks, slaves or free—and we were all made to drink of one Spirit" (1 Cor 12:13).

2.3 THE JEWS

One of the very problematic aspects of the Reformation is the fact that the reforming movements did not lead to a new positive relationship with the Jews but, in many cases, to a new promotion of anti-Jewish sentiment.[71] Many of the Reformers contributed to the anti-Jewish attitude and to the anti-Jewish theological arguments. In analysis of Martin Bucer's record on this matter, Martin Greschat holds that "Bucer must bear his share of blame for Christendom's calamitous sins against the Jewish people."[72] Calvin also contributed to this anti-Jewish attitude in Protestantism. His Bible commentaries have been very influential in the Christian tradition. In his commentary on Daniel, Calvin wrote, "I have had much conversation with many Jews: I have never seen either a drop of piety or a grain of truth or ingenuousness—nay, I have never found common sense in any Jew."[73] None of this, however, compares to the deplorable work of the mature Luther: *On the Jews and Their Lies* (1543).[74] Here Luther calls for the burning of synagogues, expulsion of the Jews, the confiscation of their books, and the destruction of Jewish homes. Karl Jaspers remarked regarding it, "What Hitler did, Luther advised, with the exception of direct murder in the gas chambers."[75]

Of course, in many ways Luther's ideas were typical of sixteenth-century Europe. Early on in the Reformation, Luther hoped that the Jews might convert to Christianity. Later, however, after they did not convert, he turned against them. Many other people at his time were also very critical of the Jews. In this sense, Luther was a child of his time (also with regard to his harsh criticism of the Turks). On the other hand, however, he was more radical in his attack on the Jews, a weak and vulnerable minority group. A Jewish response was even written against Luther that accused him of writing libels about them.[76] As Thomas Kaufmann remarks, "What separated Luther from the other essentially like-minded contemporaries was the excessiveness of his polemics, the offensiveness of his fighting spirit, so also the depth of his sense of mission and the intensity of an obsessive moral dilemma, as a prophet who once erred and later feels the need to be responsible for it and to speak out definitive and 'final words' about the Jews as stubborn enemies of Christ."[77]

Luther's arguments were being republished in the 1880s by authors who wanted to promote an anti-Semitic agenda. This was later drawn upon in the twentieth century:

> From the 1920s onwards, Lutheran theologians began to publish literature and florilegia affirming Luther's hatred against Jewish people. The "advice" to burn down synagogues, contained in his tract "On The Jews and Their Lies" (1543), was published several times before the so-called "Reichskristallnacht" on the 9th of November, 1938, during which Nazis destroyed Jewish property and synagogues.[78]

One of these new editions of *On the Jews and Their Lies* was reprinted by the National Socialists. On November 9 and 10, 1938, the November pogrom (*"Reichskristallnacht"*) provided an opportunity to carry out the German Reformer's old demands. After the synagogues were burned on that night in Germany, after the Jews were persecuted and many of them deported, the Protestant bishop Martin Sasse celebrated the madness, destruction, and rape and confirmed the sense of continuity with Luther. In the foreword (dated November 23, 1938) to his book *Martin Luther on the Jews: Away with Them!*, Sasse writes that "the power of the Jews in the economic field in the new Germany is finally broken"; "the divinely blessed struggle of the *Führer* for the full liberation of our *Volk* is crowned."[79]

There are many examples of the use and abuse of Luther in Nazi Germany.[80] In the post–World War II Nuremberg trials, Julius Streicher (1885–1946), a Nazi war criminal and editor of the radical anti-Semitic newspaper *Der Stürmer*, referenced Luther's *On the Jews and Their Lies* in defense of his anti-Semitism. Other theologians and church leaders also justified their anti-Semitism with reference to Luther.[81]

Already in 1941, William M. MacGovern drew the line "from Luther to Hitler" and sought to identify the "political philosophy" in a broad narrative.[82] While Protestants did tend to support the Nazis more than Catholics in the early 1930s,[83] Hitler (a Catholic) had far less to do with Luther than the rise of fascism in Italy and the German loss of World War I. Of course, Hitler and the Nazi ideology were helped by the longstanding tradition of German anti-Semitism and anti-Judaism, which Luther significantly encouraged. It is not a coincidence that there was a "Luther Renaissance" in German theology following World War I, in the context of rising nationalistic moods. Luther provided material for reflecting on themes related to national identity at a time when this was felt to be under threat.[84]

The anti-Jewish attitude that gained ground with many Reformers was in part caused by the long tradition of anti-Judaism in Christianity but also the new frustration that the Jews did not accept the gospel as it was preached in the new evangelical churches.[85] It is important to remember that the modern forms of anti-Semitism in the nineteenth and twentieth centuries were racist. This biological conception of anti-Semitism emerged after Darwinism. For Luther and the other Reformers, the anti-Jew attitude was not articulated in biological terms but in religious terms. The anti-Jew attitude in the Reformation, and especially in Luther's writings, was and remains a fundamental contradiction of the Christian teaching about loving one's neighbor: "You shall love your neighbor as yourself" (Mark 12:31). The work of reconciliation, which past generations have begun, can be taken up in new ways by coming generations.[86] In this regard, the reformation of the church is not finished; reforming the problems and repairing the broken relationships is a task for every generation.

2.4 WOMEN

One of the major questions in Reformation studies is whether the Reformation had a positive impact on the status of women. Many women contributed to the movements of reform.[87] In some regards, they also acquired a higher status because of the Reformation. English Puritans, for example, encouraged women to seek the conversion of their families, including their husbands.[88] This could be understood as raising the status of women over against their husbands. They were essentially being asked to assert autonomy in religious matters in their domestic relationship. The Anabaptists who took control of Münster, however, practiced polygamy and drew upon the Old Testament for its justification.[89] They believed in the propagation of children because, among other things, Christ would return once there were 144,000 true believers in the world. They were not only raising children, however. The reports of the interrogation of Anabaptist women suggest that they had memorized much of the Bible and were highly trained in theological arguments.[90]

Another issue in this field is the status of women in the sacred realm of the faith itself. With the Protestant rejection of the veneration of the saints, many sacred days that celebrated women saints were taken out of the calendar.[91] While convents and monasteries once provided many women with an alternative to marriage, the Reformation abolished this path of life.

These were usually closed in territories controlled by the Protestants. For some this must have been a liberation. Protestants championed family life, and many younger nuns embraced this with enthusiasm and married the new Protestant pastors (such as Katharina von Bora, who married Martin Luther).[92] For others, however, it was an unwanted transformation of their chosen way of life. Especially for many of the older nuns, it would have been difficult to adjust to the new form of life being imposed upon them.

According to Charlotte Methuen, Luther maintained that "women could not be appointed as preachers," although "in certain, limited circumstances women might be called to preach the gospel, not only in private but in public."[93] This limited role of women is also described by Robert W. Scribner: "Women's religious opportunities were undoubtedly narrowed by the Protestant Reformation, especially the religious space allowed to single women." He holds that "the only religious status available to women was that of the dutiful wife or daughter in the patriarchal household, the only role model that of the pastor's wife. Women were subjected to a new moralism which emphasized the need to discipline all disorderly elements."[94]

When it comes to Luther's actual view of women, there is a great deal of vulgarity. This vulgarity is found in many areas. He famously said, "I shit on the law of the pope and of the emperor, and on the law of the jurists as well."[95] His crudeness also comes out in his view of women.[96] Luther stated, "Men have broad chests and narrow hips; therefore they have wisdom. Women have narrow chests and broad hips. Women ought to be domestic; the creation reveals it, for they have broad backsides and hips, so that they should sit still."[97] He also remarked, "One finds many a stubborn wife like that who will not give in, and who cares not a whit whether her husband falls into the sin of unchastity ten times over. Here it is time for the husband to say, 'If you will not, another will; the maid will come if the wife will not.' "[98]

Luther believed that women were more inclined to witchcraft than men and (drawing upon Scripture) argued that witches should be killed: "women are more susceptible to those superstitions of Satan [. . .] If you should see such women, look away, for they have diabolical faces. Therefore, let them be killed."[99] He wrote, "It is commonly the nature of women to be timid and to be afraid of everything. This is why they busy themselves so much with witchcraft and superstition."[100] On more than one occasion, Luther also advised parents to drown their children if they were born disabled. He thought that they were the work of the devil.[101]

Responding to these dark sides of Luther, a recent book has drawn attention to "Luther without myth" by pointing to the "evil in the Reformer." Another recent book has claimed that "Luther can no longer be a role model."[102] Luther's view of women in these citations contradicted Paul, who wrote that "There is no longer Jew or Greek, there is no longer slave or free, there is no longer male and female; for all of you are one in Christ Jesus" (Gal 3:28). Luther also overlooked the fact that there are many women teachers and ministers mentioned in the Bible (Rom 16:1-3; Phil 4:2-3). Today, many Protestant churches have fully included women in the ministry. All of them have benefited enormously from this wise decision.

2.5 THE HIDDEN GOD

Luther's strong negation of reason, or, as he preferred to call it, "whore reason," and his emphasis on voluntarism are other disturbing aspects of his thought.[103] Luther was influenced by the philosophy of William of Ockham (ca. 1285-1347). In Ockham's thought, which influenced both Luther and Calvin, there is an emphasis on "the radical freedom of God and the inscrutability of the divine will." As Peter Harrison remarks about Luther and Calvin's voluntarism, "God does not command good acts— rather, certain acts are good because God commands them. [. . .] What is just and moral is to be understood in terms of the divine will, and not the reverse." The Reformation's criticism of good works comes into play here; that is, good works of human agents "derive their goodness not from any putative inherent worth, but because God chooses to regard them as meritorious."[104]

Some of this is also related to Luther's emphasis on the "hidden God" (*Deus absconditus*) of wrath, a view of God that corresponds to the "law" in the "law-gospel" paradigm. This theme has often been pushed to the extremes in interpretation. Theologians are sometimes forced to show how this paradigm does not lead to problematic views of God. When addressing the German Lutheran theologian Werner Elert's (1885–1954) strong emphasis on this theme, Matthew Becker asks, "Does not 'the *diastasis*' between God's wrath and mercy, between 'the hidden God' and the 'God revealed in Jesus,' between the law and the gospel, entail a schizophrenic God or, to put it differently, the return of the polytheistic heresy of Marcion?"[105] Of course, there are indeed some biblical passages that suggest that God is also hidden from us. For example, the psalmist writes, "How long, O Lord? Will you forget me forever? How long will you hide your face from me?" (Ps 13:1). Nevertheless, the theology of "the hidden

God" has also been drawn upon to come to some surprising conclusions. Reflecting on the contemporary significance of Luther's theology and the implications of the theology of "the hidden God," Oswald Bayer claims that "evil is imperceptibly mixed within the good."[106]

Luther's theological arguments for what seems to be a form of determinism is also a problematic area of the Protestant legacy. This goes back to older theological debates. In rejection of Thomas Aquinas' (ca. 1225–1274) understanding of divine providence, Ockham emphasized the divine will at the cost of secondary causes and equalized creation (*creatio*) and preservation (*conservatio*). God creates the world anew every moment.[107] Luther also affirmed this equalization: "We Christians know that with God to create and to preserve is the same."[108] This theology is related to Luther's claim in *On the Bondage of the Will* that "everything which happens" (*omnia quae fiunt*), although it may seem contingent to humanity, actually happens by view of the divine "by necessity and unchangeably" (*necessario et immutabiliter*).[109] John Calvin (1509–1564) also attests to this sole efficacy of God: "It is certain that not a drop of rain falls without the express command of God."[110] The theology of sole divine efficacy in these forms seems to minimize human responsibility and thus creates significant problems when it comes to addressing the problem of evil.

Others have argued for a rejection of this kind of determinism on grounds that are not theological. A recent study shows that encouraging a belief in determinism increases immoral behavior and that "doubting one's free will may undermine the sense of self as agent." Such a teaching may simply provide "the ultimate excuse to behave as one likes."[111] Naturally, Luther and Calvin did not intend to promote this kind of immoral behavior with their theology, even if some of the theological emphases on divine providence may be understood in this way. Both the Reformers emphasized that Christians should live in a way that is pleasing to God.

When it comes to the Protestant tradition of Reformed Calvinistic theology, the great issue that is discussed without end among theologians is the old doctrine of double predestination. This is one of the great theological legacies of Calvinist theology. Max Weber claimed that the doctrine of predestination in Calvinism was nothing less than dreadful: "In its extreme inhumanity this doctrine must above all have had one consequence for the life of a generation which surrendered to its magnificent consistency. That was a feeling of unprecedented inner *loneliness of the single individual*." Weber argued that the most important thing in life for people of the sixteenth century was the question about their eternal salvation. In this regard, a person "was forced to follow his own path alone to meet a destiny which had been decreed for him from eternity."[112] Not many theologians in the Reformed tradition today are willing to defend this doctrine in its classic form. Of course, many theologians have offered new interpretations of the teaching. This is because they know that the old doctrine that Calvin so passionately defended—that God decrees some to eternal damnation before they are even created[113]—fundamentally contradicts the teaching that "God is love" (1 John 4:8).

In order to follow Calvin's doctrine of predestination, one must abandon so much of the Bible. For example, 2 Samuel 14:14 teaches, "We must all die; we are like water spilled on the ground, which cannot be gathered up. But God will not take away a life; he will devise plans so as not to keep an outcast banished forever from his presence." This is the God of love of the Old Testament and the New Testament—the God who always finds a way to include the "outcast." It is, of course, an enormously challenging task to harmonize Calvin's claim that "all are not created on equal terms" with the dominant cultural, social, and political order of the modern Western world—a world that holds to precisely the opposite claim.[114] Calvin's claim that all are not created equal also contradicts the biblical tradition, which holds that every human being is created in the image of God (Gen 1:28).

The problematic legacy of the Reformation, as seen in the doctrine of double predestination, and in the many other issues addressed above, makes it impossible to view the Reformation as a wholly positive development in the history of Christianity. There were, however, positive aspects of the Reformation, such as the teaching about reform, divine grace, and the priesthood of all believers. The Reformation must be remembered with all these contradictory dimensions, otherwise it is only partially understood. In order to understand the Reformation fully, one must also become familiar with the prehistory of reform—the long Reformation.

≪ 3 ≫

PREHISTORY, DIVISION,
AND AUTHORITY

How was it possible that after over a millennium of history, Latin Christendom could be torn asunder and divided into two rival religious and political factions in little over a decade? While the history of the Middle Ages was shaped by conflict, tension, and plurality, the divisions that emerged were usually overcome and unity was restored (as was the case in the Western Schism of the late fourteenth and early fifteenth centuries). With the Reformation of the early sixteenth century, however, the split would become permanent. The easy answer to this question is, the structural conditions that enabled the tense unity of the Middle Ages changed in the early modern period. As a consequence, the old Rome-centered order simply could not maintain its authority in the expanding and transforming Europe. While this forward-looking analysis is certainly correct, there is another story about the collapse of papal power and the division of Christendom, one that finds the answer in the past.

Old debates about the reform of Christendom, which go back centuries before the time of the Protestant Reformation, prepared the way for Jan Hus and the Wittenberg revolt. The medieval conflict about the authority of the pope and churchwide councils, and the deterioration of the legitimacy of an older theological style—Aristotelian scholasticism (which went together with the rise of nominalism in the thirteenth century)—made it possible for Karlstadt and Luther (following other theologians from Tübingen and Erfurt) to reassert scriptural authority as the basis of doctrine. The short Reformation would have never happened without this long process of cultural transformation. There were also many other developments that contributed to the prehistory of the reforms in social, economic, and political realms. These will be addressed below before evaluating the division of Christendom from a broad historical perspective. Finally, the foundational question about authority in the church will be analyzed in historical and theological perspective. From the beginning, the short Reformation was a debate about the nature of authority. As will be shown, the emphasis on scriptural authority among the Reformers was not a new theology but rather the reassertion of a classic position in Christian theology.

3.1 PRE-REFORMATION STRIVINGS FOR REFORM

The Reformation is sometimes presented as an arbitrary break from the relative harmony of the pre-Reformation era. This idea is found among some of the authors of German romanticism (such as Novalis and Friedrich Schlegel). It is sometimes brought into play when criticizing the level of pluralism in contemporary Western culture. The Reformation is presented as inaugurating modern pluralism in that it divided the ancient spiritual unity of Christendom and led to a multiplicity of false teachings. A few questions emerge immediately in face of this "untenable axiom of discontinuity," as Oberman calls it.[1] Was the Reformation indeed an arbitrary break from the traditions of the late Middle Ages? And can one speak of a harmonious spiritual unity in the pre-Reformation era? In this section, the first question will be addressed. As will be argued, the striving for reform in the Reformation of the sixteenth century was not something new but rather a continuation and transformation of reform movements in the long Reformation.[2] In the next section, the second question will be addressed. There it will be argued that the pre-Reformation era was not a harmonious spiritual unity.

The claim that the Reformation was an unanticipated break from the pre-Reformation era overlooks the reform impulse before 1517. Many historians have pointed to the pre-Reformation attempts at reforming the church. Euan Cameron writes, "Whatever the people of Europe may have thought about *religion* around the year 1500, they clearly did not think that all was well with the *Church*."[3] Of course, as Cameron also emphasizes, this is not to suggest that everyone wanted to reform the church. Many people were happy with it, including its theologies, and old rituals. Many others, however, sought to reform the church. Anne Hudson has called one of these movements, the Wycliffite movement, "the Premature Reformation."[4] In the pre-Reformation era there was a widely held criticism of hierarchical clericalism. The theology of the church itself was already disputed by Berengar of Tours (d. 1088) when he questioned the doctrine of transubstantiation in the eleventh century. In the twelfth century, Peter Waldo (d. 1217) and the company of Waldensians criticized indulgences, gave away their wealth, ignored warnings from ecclesial authority, translated parts of the Bible into the common language, and preached without papal approval.[5] The Waldensians were excommunicated and persecuted well into the twentieth century. Francis of Assisi (ca. 1180–1226) also exemplified an alternative spirituality in the Middle Ages. He imitated Christ and embraced poverty in his denial of worldly power.

Writing about the thirteenth century, Charles Taylor also addresses the concerted effort of Latin Christendom to promote a new devotion and religious practice in all of society. While the "start of the movement can be identified at various moments," a good date would be 1215, the year of the Fourth Lateran Council. This made confession universal, and there was "something like an 'internal crusade' from the thirteenth century on, mainly carried by the preaching of the mendicant orders."[6] He goes on to address the Dominicans in this context and claims that "the new spirituality had an individuating side." This had to do with reforming the moral life and mending human relations. With this, however, came "a new individuality."[7] A shift can be seen toward "more personal religious life" and a new desire to pray and read the Bible.[8] With the new piety came also a new discussion about the authority of theology and the church.

In *Defensor pacis* (1324), Marsilius of Padua (ca. 1290–1343) conceptualized, following Dante Alighieri's *De monarchia* (1312–1313?), a theoretical separation of secular and ecclesial power in distinct realms of sovereignty.[9] The unique authority of Scripture was also rediscovered in the Middle Ages. This went together with discussions about the limitations of the papacy. For example, William of Ockham wrote that if a "question" arises "between pope and emperor or other Catholics about power that the pope asserts belongs to him by divine law, the emperor and his subjects will not be able to argue chiefly from imperial law, or the pope chiefly from canon law; they both must in the end go back to the sacred Scriptures, which neither, if he wishes to be regarded as a Catholic, will presume to deny."[10] This rediscovery of the unique status of the Scriptures (above the pope, councils, or canon law), which became more popular in the fourteenth and fifteenth centuries, would ultimately enable the later challenge to papal authority in the early sixteenth century. A major forerunner in this regard was John Wycliffe (ca. 1330–1384); he translated the Bible into English with some of his assistants. Both Wycliffe and Jan Hus (ca. 1370–1415) were promoting new reform traditions in the Middle Ages by challenging ecclesial authorities and emphasizing the authority of the Bible. Tetzel repeatedly compared Luther's "heresy" to both of these figures.

Some of the theologians of the later Middle Ages were also rethinking the nature of the Christian's relationship with God. This would become very important in Wittenberg. The mysticism of Meister Eckhart (ca. 1260–1327), which was rejected by the ecclesial hierarchy, is an example of this new approach to theology, one that was concerned with the religious experience of the believer. His student, Johannes Tauler, was widely read among the Wittenberg group. Another mystical author, identified as a "priest and warden" of the Teutonic Order in Frankfurt, wrote a very influential book in the late fourteenth century called *Theologia Deutsch*, a work that Luther would later praise and edit. It also contributed to the reorientation of theology in the late Middle Ages. More than any author of the Middle Ages, Thomas à Kempis (ca. 1380–1471) influenced the new spirituality of the late Middle Ages. His *The Imitation of Christ* (*De Imitatione Christi*, early fifteenth century) is still widely read today. This book encouraged the new devotional impulse of pietistic discipleship, Christian interiority, and spiritual reflection in the pre-Reformation period. It inaugurated the "new devotion," the *devotio moderna*, as it would be called.

The methodological emphasis on source research—*ad fontes* (to the sources)—in the Renaissance and in humanism can hardly be overlooked when considering the long Reformation. The academic sensibilities of humanism, the general attitude itself, played an important role in the prehistory of the Reformation. The time had come to rediscover the classical texts and to apply a new critical scholarship that went beyond the provincial opinions of ecclesial authorities. This is seen, for example, in Desiderius Erasmus of Rotterdam (1466/69–1536) and Johannes Reuchlin (1455–1522).[11] Indeed, the origins of modern critical scholarship are found in humanism. Many of the authors of the Reformation also emphasized the importance of the Bible in theology in contrast to the medieval traditions of scholasticism. They too were going "back to the sources" in their strong focus on the Scriptures. The English theologian and Bible translator William Tyndale (1491–1536) is a very good example of this symbiosis of humanism and Protestantism. In his translation of the Bible, for example, Tyndale used his new linguistic skills to challenge the tradition. He went so far as to translate the Greek word *ekklesia* not with "church" but rather with "congregation."[12] Naturally, this also reflected his conviction that the true sense of *ekklesia* was the priesthood of all believers.

When thinking about the strivings for reform in the late Middle Ages, one should also consider the church hierarchy at this time. In terms of ecclesial issues, the double and triple claims to the papal office of the late Middle Ages (the "Western Schism," 1378–1417) had a critical destabilizing effect on the legitimacy of the old order. The fall of Constantinople in 1453 also added to the sense of instability in the Latin West: "Westerners, above all humanists, viewed the fall of Constantinople not merely as a Greek loss but as a blow to Christendom, Europe, and Western Culture."[13] The Dominican Girolamo Savonarola (1452–1498) also contributed to the unsettling mood. As the de facto leader of Florence, he criticized corruption and launched a campaign for the renewal of morals. He resisted Roman authority and was eventually excommunicated by Pope Alexander VI and executed. Savonarola was later praised by Luther.

With all this in the background, there were also many calls for reform throughout Christendom before 1500. One of the popular expressions was *reformatio in capite et in membris* (reformation in the head and in the members). Emidio Campi, professor emeritus of church history at the Theological Faculty of the University of Zurich and director of the Institute for Swiss Reformation History, has shown how the strivings for reform were a major theme in the pre-Reformation era. He rightly argues that the Reformation should be understood in its broad character, including the developments not only in Germany but also in many other parts of Europe. He writes,

> The Reform Movement, in fact, reached beyond the sphere of Monasticism, and beginning in the eleventh century, embraced religious movements among the laity such as the Albigenses, Cathars, and Waldensians. Especially the latter considered the Constantinian turn to be the ruin of Christianity, and they consequently sought to renew the church from the inside out, in order to lead it back to an apostolic life.[14]

The sense of a decline of the church was a common theme in the late Middle Ages. This was drawn upon by various streams of theology and ecclesiastical-political works.[15] As the idea of ecclesial decline became more plausible, the calls for reformation grew louder.[16] In 1170 Pope Alexander III called for an *emendatio ecclesiae in capite et in membris* (improvement of the church in the head and in the members).[17] Similar calls were made by Pope Innocent III in his bull from 1231, where he addressed a *reformatio universalis ecclesiae* (reformation of the universal church).[18] Luther was linking up to this tradition of reform, and transforming it, when he remarked in 1518 that the church "needs a reformation, but this is not something for one person, the pope, also not many cardinals, [...] but rather for the entire world, or more correctly, for God alone. The time for such a reformation is known only by him who created time."[19] While there are differences between the understandings of reformation in the Middle Ages with the popes and cardinals, and Luther's understanding in the early sixteenth century, Luther was clearly building upon and transforming this older tradition of reform rhetoric. For these reasons the sixteenth-century Wittenberg Reformation is best understood as a part of a larger development of reform in the later Middle Ages.[20] It is therefore best to think of the Reformation as comprising "several movements" that were "nurtured not by a single, but by a variety of impulses." In this sense, the Reformation may be understood as a broad "European phenomenon." The roots go "back hundreds of years" and exemplify what may be called the "Long Reformation."[21] Indeed, there was already a cultural divide between the German lands and Italy in the fifteenth century. For many people north of the Alps, and for many of the princes and kings of Europe (who were all seeking more power), the papacy had lost significant legitimacy by 1500. The conflict about indulgences came at a time when the movements toward reform were already well known and widespread.[22]

Once one begins to see the contours of this long prehistory, the Reformation is made much more understandable. In many regards, it was a necessary reform for which a great deal of preparation had already been done, sometimes with the cost of human life. Much of the reform movements in the long Reformation were resisted. In this sense, the Wittenberg reform can be understood as a response to the stagnation of a century of ecclesial reform.[23] The old reform movements that sought to transform and improve the papal ecclesial structures and the churches would finally be replaced with a new reform movement that fundamentally challenged the authority systems of the papal order and the very understanding of the Christian's relationship to God as it had been reflected in the practice of indulgences.

The Hussitism after Hus' execution was also central to the prehistory of the Wittenberg Reformation.[24] In the fifteenth century, the University of Prague was a center for reform movements with Hus. The forerunners of Hussitism can be found in the Bohemian *devotio moderna* and in other developments in central-eastern Europe, in Bohemia and Moravia (roughly the Czech Republic today). The Hussites' calls to reform show that the energies of reform were developing long before the sixteenth-century Reformation. This can be illustrated with the issue of the separation between the laity and the clergy.

Luther's emphasis on the priesthood of all believers (in his appeal to the German nobility in the summer of 1520) was a very central aspect of the Reformation. Luther seems to have advanced a tradition of interpretation already found with Johannes Tauler. Tauler held that devotion was the central issue that makes one a priest (man or woman), and not the church's consecration. Luther developed this critique of the priesthood by claiming that it is baptism that is the deciding issue.[25] The significance of this claim cannot be overemphasized.

The movement toward this perspective can also be seen before this in the Hussites' Four Articles of Prague at the beginning of July in 1420. These four articles exemplify some of the core themes of Hussitism. The first article demanded that there should be freedom to preach the word of God—that is, that the interpretation and declaration of the teachings of the Scriptures was not only for priests but for all believers. This was a radical shift of authority from the ecclesial hierarchy to all Christians. The second article demanded that the laity be given Communion in both bread and wine (Utraquism). The third article called for the church to give up its worldly power and return to the ideal of poverty. This granted the nobility extensive influence, similar to the Lutheran Reformation a century later. The fourth article called for the punishment of public sins regardless of the class of the sinner.[26]

The Hussites also established an alternative ecclesial system with the help of the nobility in the fifteenth century. While the moderate Bohemian Hussites eventually won the day (with the help of Catholics) over the radical Taborite Hussites, and while all the original demands of the Four Articles of Prague were not brought to realization, the Council of Basil of 1433 granted the Hussites the right to administer Communion in both forms. There was thus something like a nobility-supported reformation in fifteenth-century Bohemia. Knowledge of this controversy spread across Christendom and encouraged pre-Reformation theologians that were faithful to the Rome-centered order, like the pre-1517 Luther, to criticize it (as Luther did before his open conflict with Rome). The shockwaves of the Hussite Wars were felt across Europe. They were certainly a part of the prehistory of the massive reform that came a century later in the 1520s north of Bohemia.[27] Movement toward an ideal of a more egalitarian church did not start in the sixteenth century but long before this, as is seen with Hus and the Hussites.

Hus and the Hussites are also important for other reasons. The figure of Hus played a key role in the early sixteenth-century Reformation.[28] This is because opponents of Luther often associated him with Hus and the Hussites, even from the beginning of the conflict about the indulgences. Up to 1521 Luther was intensively engaged in the study of Hus' teachings and his life. Although it is rarely mentioned, Luther also had some contacts in Bohemia with whom he corresponded. The Reformation contributed to the propagation of Hus' work. Information about his trial was spread around Christendom as the stakes of the conflict with the Wittenberg theologian were raised. Luther even saw Hus as a forerunner of the reform. He also drew upon Hus' theological work *De ecclesia*. In this treatise on the church, Hus had been influenced by the theology of John Wycliffe. Luther was also aware of the Hussites' criticism of the church. In his lecture on Romans in 1516–1517 Luther rejected some of the Hussites' practices and theology. Although he saw the Hussites as heretics before 1517, in the midst of Luther's own conflict with the ecclesial authority, Hus would become a role model for him. A transition in his understanding of Hus began in 1518. By 1519 and 1520, Luther had adopted precisely the same criticism of the church as the Hussites.

In 1519 and 1520, and thereafter, many themes from the Hussites were adopted by the Reformers, such as the demand that the Lord's Supper be administered to the laity in both bread and wine, the criticism of the doctrine of transubstantiation, the emphasis on scriptural authority, the criticism of clerical corruption and power, and the demand for equal standing for all regardless of the political or social position in issues of justice and with regard to the punishment of crime. Hus and the Hussites therefore played an important role as examples. This is also the case in the self-presentation of the Reformation in the early Reformation period, especially in 1519 and 1520. It was widely known that Hus was executed. This itself made the associations of Luther with Hus possible in the early period of the short Reformation.

These associations of Luther with Hus are attested to in various sources. On July 24, 1519, Johann Eck, a professor of theology at Ingolstadt who was involved in Luther's condemnation and who debated Karlstadt and Luther in Leipzig, wrote a letter to Jakob Hochstraten (1460–1527) regarding Luther's remarks at the Leipzig Debate in 1519. He states, "Regarding the Articles of Bohemia he [Luther] said that some of the articles which were damned at the Council of Constance were very Christian and evangelical. He frightened many by this audacious error."[29] In the same letter, Eck wrote, "On the day of Saint Peter [June 29, 1519] in the disputation hall, Luther gave a very erroneous Hussite sermon in the absence of the prince."[30] Later, in 1520, in Luther's address "To the Christian Nobility," he acknowledged that "an injustice was done" to Hus and that "his books and doctrines were unjustly condemned."[31] Shortly after this, Müntzer also supported Hus in his "Protest about the Conditions of the Bohemians" ("Prague Protest," 1521). There he calls Hus "the precious and holy fighter."[32] In these ways Hus was in the middle of the short Reformation.[33]

The short Reformation also had a prehistory in movements of social reform from the late Middle Ages. After the Reformation began to take shape, in many cities and towns the churches introduced new financial collections to support the poor. As the mendicant orders (those religious orders that relied upon charity) were banished from many Reformation lands, the monetary support that they once received was often transferred to these new collections. A good example of the theological arguments that were behind these reforms is found in Karlstadt's tract "On the Removal of Images and That There Should Be No Beggars among Christians" (1522).[34] The rejection of begging was also taken up into the Augsburg Confession (1530). It teaches that true perfection is to "fear God" and "to have great faith and to trust that for Christ's sake we have a gracious God" and also to be "diligent in the performance of good works for others and to attend to our calling. True perfection and true service of God consist of these things and not of celibacy, mendicancy [begging], or humble attire."[35]

The reform of the church went together with the reform of the social order. The Reformers rejected the begging orders and begging itself and called upon Christians to do good works diligently. They strove for a "good order" of society. This is not to suggest that the Reformation was simply a social reform movement. As Campi has shown, Luther's interest in reforming the church was not because life was somehow uniquely difficult. Luther wanted to reform the church because he strove for the purity of doctrine in accordance with the Scriptures. The legitimate reformation, in Luther's opinion, was one that was reverently listening to the truth of the Scriptures.[36] At the same time, however, Luther's criticism of the extortion of the poor was a strong theme in his Ninety-Five Theses. Karlstadt and Luther saw themselves as reforming both church and society.[37]

While the Reformers wrote a great deal about ecclesial corruption, there are also some surprising remarks from the popes at this time. Pope

Adrian VI (1522–1523) went so far as to acknowledge that the corrupt ecclesial hierarchy ultimately enabled the Reformation. Shortly after the Reformation had come into full swing, he openly acknowledged the fault of the Catholic Church in bringing about the "persecution" of the Reformation. The following text was read at the Diet of Nuremberg on January 3, 1523. Before this, it was addressed to the pope's nuncio, Francesco Chieregati, on November 25, 1522. The pope gave Chieregati instructions regarding what he should say at the diet. In the statement Pope Adrian VI claims,

> Additionally, you should say that God allows this persecution [*persecucionem*, sc. the Reformation] of His church because of the sin of man, especially of the priests and superiors of the Church. [. . .] We know that there has been in this Holy See for some years many horrible abuses in spiritual matters and offenses against the divine commandments, indeed, that everything had actually become perverted. So it is no wonder if the disease [*aegritudo*] spread itself out from the head to the members [*a capite in membra*], that is, from the popes to the lower church leaders [*a summis pontificibus in alios inferiores prelatos*].[38]

Indeed, even the pope thought that a "disease" had spread through the church before the Reformation. One of the old questions of church historians is, If Rome had accepted and encouraged the reforming process in the early sixteenth century, could the old Rome-centered papal system have been preserved and the split in Western Christendom prevented? Karl Fink wrote that Rome "prevented the reform and got the Reformation for it."[39] This may be true; on the other hand, however, even if Rome did not prevent the reform, it is entirely plausible that the old Rome-centered order could not have been saved. The political tensions that stood behind the Reformation in the early sixteenth century would have continued even if the Wittenberg theologians did not promote their new Augustinian theology and criticize the indulgences.

The Reformation can be understood as the emergence of a new interpretation of Christianity that was, at the same time, a rediscovery of ancient Christian teachings—in this sense it was a renaissance or revival of the faith. It was enabled by multiple cultural, social, economic, and political developments. Theologically, and in terms of the ecclesial nature of the movement, it was indebted to medieval mysticism, biblical theology, a Pauline theology of grace and faith, and also some pastoral concerns and egalitarian impulses. These various new streams of theology acquired legitimacy not only among the princes but also among the common people. The revival of the faith, which was critical of the Rome-backed indulgences, was understandably rejected by Rome. As the Roman authorities saw it, Rome had long invested its wealth and administrative power into the evangelization of the German lands. They could not now be expected to heed to an unknown theologian at the new provincial university in Saxony.[40]

Latin Christendom did not have to split simply because of a revival of the faith. Under the right circumstances, it would have been possible for this revival to continue to exist within the Rome-centered ecclesial order of Christendom. If the Roman authorities had realized what they were dealing with, they probably would have responded differently. As is often the case in great events of world history, the people at the steering wheel (in this case, above all, the pope, some bishops, priests, and university professors) simply did not see what was coming. The excommunication of Luther was certainly a great error on the part of the pope and in terms of political calculation. They could have eliminated the sale of indulgences in the region around Wittenberg and introduced a series of measures to seek reconciliation with the Faculty of Theology in Wittenberg. They could have even advanced Luther to a higher position in the church hierarchy. Theoretically, it would have been possible to stop the Wittenberg Reformation, but the ecclesial authorities were either poorly advised or unwilling to take the necessary steps.

The Wittenberg Reformation is made more understandable when the corruption of the church at the beginning of the sixteenth century is grasped. The various reform movements before 1517 and the many other external issues that contributed to the spread of the reforms are also important aspects of what is rightly called the long Reformation. In this sense, the Reformation was not an arbitrary break from Rome. It was deeply connected to old reform movements and many other issues from the fifteenth and early sixteenth centuries that ultimately enabled the split in Latin Christendom to take place.

3.2 PRE-REFORMATION PLURALIZATION

The Reformation is sometimes presented as the impetus of pluralization and fragmentation in the Latin West. Johann Eck argued in his *Enchiridion* that when "the authority of the councils is taken away, everything in the church will be unclear, doubtful, unresolved and uncertain."[41] According to the contemporary form of this argument, before the Reformation Christendom was a relatively harmonious social and religious order. After the Reformation, however, this social and religious order was fragmented and set on a track toward pluralization and ultimately relativism.[42] One of the problems with this theory is that it overlooks the many signs of pluralization in the pre-Reformation era. In this section the cultural, social, and political dimensions of this pluralization will be analyzed.

When looking at European history from 1250 to 1500, we see an era characterized by "revolutionary economic and social restructuring." Remarkable things happened in culture, society, and politics in a relatively short amount of time, especially when compared to previous epochs.[43] While it is true that the Western Church was a "highly organized religious community,"[44] there was also a variety of conflicting intellectual, social, and economic impulses at work within this community. One example of this is the establishment of the many new universities in the Middle Ages. These are evidence of a growing self-consciousness of new centers of power. As the prestige and authority of various smaller regions within Renaissance Europe grew, these regions, led by princes or kings, established their own universities, which, in turn, created new centers of intellectual discourse and debate. With the emergence of these universities in the fourteenth and fifteenth centuries, the intellectual landscape was diversified, and the level of competition between the universities increased. The Paris-Oxford monopoly on theology, for example, was broken after 1347.[45]

The pluralization in the late Middle Ages was advanced by the expansion of mobility, trade, and communication.[46] For example, the institution of early modern horseback-driven postal communication was established in the pre-Reformation period. The continental route of communication linked together Antwerp, Brussels, Augsburg, Innsbruck, Venice, Rome, and Naples.[47] One of the main reasons for the new expansion of knowledge and opinion in early modern Europe was the transformation of the medium of knowledge itself. There was an explosion in the production of books between the twelfth and the fifteenth centuries. Later, with the new movable type printing press, the emergence of early modern communication contributed to the spread of information in the cities, the exchange of critical opinions, and the pluralization and internationalization of debate.

The social orders were not left untouched in the dynamic process of pluralization. The decentralization of power structures in the Latin West was a major issue in this process. In this regard, the Latin West is often compared to the Christian East. In the East there was an alternative tendency toward "Caesaropapism," as Max Weber argued. This is the unification of religious and political power.[48] In the Latin West, by comparison, religion and politics were officially separated. Furthermore, a robust and influential urban middle class (to use today's terminology) developed around the castles in the Middle Ages (the burghers, the bourgeoisie, the citizens). The pre-Reformation epoch was marked by a divergence between the higher nobility and the lower nobility and the establishment of a social hierarchy in the cities. The introduction of these points of distinction in the Middle Ages has been interpreted as a result of the relative openness of society toward those who were climbing the social ladder.[49]

All these examples indicate that European pre-Reformation urban society was not a static monolith or a harmonious unity. It was rather in a dynamic process of social transformation and diversification. The points of distinction in the nobility also reflect the establishment of local authorities and jurisdictions that were essential for the realization of the Reformation. In the later Middle Ages, various smaller political entities were continually struggling for power and influence against larger political entities and other equals. This was the case not only for the many imperial cities but also for smaller principalities, grand duchies, and duchies. The political competition on multiple levels led to innovation, growth, pluralization, and self-differentiation. Culture, the arts, and education all benefited from this competition, which was built upon and enabled by the autonomy of various political entities.[50] The movement toward representative political order also began in the Middle Ages: "In most of the states of Christian Europe there was, from the late twelfth century, a move from the non-representative meetings of kings and great subjects to a more representative institution."[51] In fact, the impetus probably came from the ecclesial realm, where the principle of representative assembly was long established. This process of political and social transformation ultimately led to the formation of Europe's nation-states in the early modern period.[52] All these examples of pluralization are older than the Reformation. Some of the related theological and ecclesial issues have already been addressed above. In these we also see a clear sense of competition and, in many cases, a striving for reform. There were also many theological and philosophical disputes that were carried out between the thirteenth and the fifteenth centuries (such as the rise of nominalism). These disputes reflect a dynamic context of intellectual and ecclesial pluralization.

When considering the diversity of pre-Reformation Christendom, many historians tend to focus on the intellectual, political, and economic issues at work in society. With these, it is also important to consider the lives of normal people around 1500. The vast majority of people (ca. 95 percent) were illiterate at this time. They usually died around the age of forty years old, although some did make it into their sixties and seventies. Around 90 percent of Europe's population lived in the countryside. The peasants usually worked on small farms and lived in villages. They were, above all else, concerned about their basic subsistence. They usually paid some of their earnings to the landlords, who provided protection. This basic framework, the feudal order, was the normal way of life around 1500. Most of these people were not concerned about academic theology, and it had little direct influence on their lives. The Christian religion was, however, very important for peasants and commoners. Through it they could come into contact with a benevolent God. They could receive blessings for their everyday life and a sense of protection.[53] This protection was important to the agrarian culture of farmers and peasants who were so dependent and vulnerable. The religion also provided an ideal moral ethos, which the priests and monks exemplified. It also provided a means for social transformation. Aided by pastors and theologians who supported them, the commoners and peasants could also generate strong biblical-theological arguments to challenge the feudal institution. Among the peasants and the "common man" (*der gemeine Mann*), a new theologically legitimized anticlerical attitude emerged in the later Middle Ages that flowed into the Reformation and ultimately transformed feudal society.

Given the great difference between the peasants and commoners, on the one hand, and the priests and theologians, on the other, was there even a common religion?[54] It is probably best to think of the faith on two levels: "a formalistic, external one for ordinary people and an ethical, spiritual one for the educated."[55] In fact, a major feature of the prehistory of the Reformation is the changing relationship between the clergy and the laity. This would be fully realized in the teaching about the priesthood of all believers. Even before the short Reformation got going, these two classes of people were becoming more similar. The clergy were acquiring property and participating more and more in the market, while the laity were going through a process of clericalization by learning to read and write, and by learning to understand law and to think about theological matters. "As the differences between them lessened, relations between them became more competitive and less complementary than they earlier had been."[56] Another consequence of this was the changing status of the clergy. As they became worldlier, they eventually lost legitimacy in the eyes of the laity. As Brady explains, "These changes belong to the prehistory of the Protestant reformers' desire to redraw the boundaries between clergy and laity by mobilizing the laity and demonizing the old clergy."[57]

The rising authority of the papacy in the later Middle Ages is an important counterimage to the growing diversity of Christendom. The pope was at the top of the ecclesial hierarchy at the beginning of the sixteenth century, but the key leading figures in the church were actually the urban bishops. The shift toward medieval papal absolutism began in the eleventh century.[58] Pope Gregory VII (pope from 1073 to 1085) sought to increase the powers of the papacy dramatically. His work on papal power from 1075 (*Dictatus papae*) became an "unrivaled symbol of a papacy whose claim to sovereign power caused it, practically speaking, to appear as a replacement for Christ." Indeed, "the underlying tone of the entire document emerges in the statement that the pope alone can do everything in the Church; without him, nothing can be validly or legally done; there appear to be absolutely no limits to papal authority."[59] This tradition would reach its pinnacle in the claim of Pope Boniface VIII in his bull *Unam sanctam* (1302) that obedience to the Roman pontiff was necessary for salvation itself. The Catholic theologian Hans Küng has described the Gregorian reform "from above" as giving the church a "centralist-absolutist papacy," a "clericalist juridicism," and "obligatory celibacy for the clergy." He argues, "In reality, throughout its first millennium, the Church got along quite well without the monarchist-absolutist papacy that we now take for granted."[60] While the pope was seeking to establish his absolute dominance in the church, most people lived within the confines of the feudal order and had little or no knowledge of the pope.

The social-historical presentations of the Reformation, which are concerned with the vast majority of the population of Christendom around 1500, present not a harmonious unity but a world filled with tensions, everyday fears, and power struggles. From this perspective, "medieval Christianity remained more chaotic than united."[61] It is, however, not only the social histories of the peasants and commoners that paint a diverse picture. At many levels of Latin Christendom in the late Middle Ages, there are dramatic examples of pluralization, tension, and development. Leppin writes that the church of the Middle Ages had a "through and through heterogeneous appearance."[62] While the Reformation would certainly become an important impulse for further pluralization in the Latin West, there were many other forces—in book production, communication, education, social hierarchies, and economic and political life—that were pushing toward a more pluralistic order long before 1500.[63]

3.3 THE CHURCH AND THE CHURCHES

One of the old criticisms of the Reformation is the claim that it divided the (one) church into the (many) churches. The Reformation most certainly entailed the division of Christendom—but how is this division to be evaluated? When one looks out onto the thousands of different Christian denominations, and when one imagines all the heartache and conflict that went along with the thousands of church divisions, it is easy to regret the entire process of ecclesial separation. In this, one might look to the Reformation as the beginning of all the division: the great fall from grace. The problem with this theory is that there are many other divisions to be found before the Reformation. To point this out is not to minimize the significance of the division of Latin Christendom in the Reformation. It is rather to put this division into perspective. As the document "Reformation 1517–2017: Ecumenical Perspectives" from the Ecumenical Working Group of Protestant and Catholic Theologians affirms, "The Reformation originally did not intend to divide Western Christendom."[64] While divisions did follow from the Reformation, there were already many other divisions in Western Christendom, and in Christianity as a whole.

One of the great divisions can be seen in the wars against the Hussites in the fifteenth century or the persecutions of the various reform groups from the Middle Ages, such as the Waldensians. Even to claim that the fall from grace happened in 1054 with the schism between the Eastern and Western churches would be too late. It would even be inaccurate to claim that "the church" became "the churches" in the fifth century, when the oriental orthodox churches (or churches of the first three councils) could not agree with the formulations of the Council of Chalcedon in 451. Four hundred years before Chalcedon, in the New Testament, we already see theological disputes and evidence of different churches all worshiping Jesus Christ as their Lord and Savior.[65] While there is "the church" in the strict theological sense of the "invisible church," there was never "the church" in the sense of a universal Christian community that agreed entirely on the answers to the most important questions in matters of faith and Christian practice.

Even the first community around Jesus was marked by reported divisions and betrayal. Against Peter, Jesus said, "Get behind me, Satan!" (Matt 16:23). Judas is also reported to have said to the chief priests and the elders, "I have sinned by betraying innocent blood" (Matt 27:4). Paul also records this in his letter to the Galatians: "But when Cephas came to Antioch, I opposed him to his face, because he stood self-condemned" (Gal 2:11). While Paul was himself in quarrels with Peter, he later lamented the same thing in other congregations. One of the most famous examples of this is found in Paul's letter to the Corinthians: "For it has been reported to me by Chloe's people that there are quarrels among you, my brothers and sisters. What I mean is that each of you says, 'I belong to Paul,' or 'I belong to Apollos,' or 'I belong to Cephas,' or 'I belong to Christ.'" (1 Cor 1:11-12). The lamenting of ecclesial division and the theological countering of it (in calls to love one another) are also found in the Johannine literature, reflecting Jesus' original message (John 13:34-25; 17:20-23; 1 John 3:10-11; 4:7-21; 2 John 1:5-6). In all these cases, the call to unity and the call to love one another may also be understood as a natural response to the actual lived reality of quarrelling divisions within the ancient church.

One of the driving forces of the Enlightenment was the desire to overcome the plurality of Christianity with a pure form of religion. This was, however, essentially a rejection of the inherent plurality of the faith. Gotthold Ephraim Lessing, for example, brings this to expression when he writes that "the Christian religion is so uncertain and ambiguous, that there is scarcely a single passage which, in all the history of the world, has been interpreted in the same way by two men."[66] Lessing's solution, which became the solution for many of the figures of the Enlightenment, was to focus on reason alone. He called this "the Christianity of Reason." This approach is radical, however, in that it seeks to abolish the inner tensions, plurality, and diversity of the faith. Radical forms of fundamentalism also attempt to do away with the inner tensions and plurality of the faith. They seek to posit a pure form of the religion (based not on reason but on the Bible) and then attempt to abolish all ambiguity. Rather than these views of unity, what is needed is a new discovery of the beauty of this plurality of meaning in the one Christian faith. Such a conception of church unity can spring from a generous orthodoxy that sees unity not in terms of sameness but rather in terms of interconnected parts of the whole.

The Jesuit theologian Roger Haight presents "seven areas of tension" that were "intrinsic to the constitution of the early church." He sees the early church as characterized by a "principle of subsidiarity," which means that "the whole church should not assume responsibility for that which can be accomplished on a 'lower' or more local level. The principle preserves an integral whole church as a union of churches."[67] Such a "principle of subsidiarity" is a theological inroad to ecclesial unity today. (This is addressed further in chap. 7.)

3.4 SCRIPTURE, TRADITION, AND THE MAGISTERIUM

What is the highest authority in matters of faith? Most Protestant Reformers held that the Scripture stood above the pope, councils, or tradition in authority. Because of this strong emphasis on scriptural authority, the Reformation is sometimes presented as promoting a new teaching about scriptural authority that was, as the argument goes, actually foreign to the history of Christian theology.[68] This criticism of the Reformation is related to the issue discussed above regarding the divisions among Christians. The supposedly new emphasis on scriptural authority is made responsible for enabling and encouraging the divisions among Christians because it relocated the locus of authority in the Bible (which can be interpreted by anyone) outside of the authority structure of the ecclesial hierarchy (the magisterium). But was the Reformation emphasis on scriptural authority really a new teaching? Furthermore, is it not the case that the modern Catholic Church also affirms the unique authority of the Scriptures? In this section it will be argued that the emphasis on scriptural authority in the Reformation was actually not a new teaching unique to the Reformation but a faithful continuation and rediscovery of the ancient theological tradition in Christianity. Some of the background to this issue and contemporary Catholic teaching on the Scriptures will also be analyzed. Finally, new Protestant understandings of the papacy will be addressed. Before moving to these issues, however, some of the background to this debate about authority and the Scriptures shall be addressed.

The authors of the New Testament set an example for all later Christian theologians by referring to the Old Testament as their authority in theological disputes. The most important passage that established this authority is 2 Timothy 3:16-17: "All scripture is inspired by God [adjective θεόπνευστος; Vulgate: *divinitus inspirata*, lit., 'divinely inspired'] and is useful for teaching, for reproof, for correction, and for training in righteousness, so that everyone who belongs to God may be proficient, equipped for every good work." Already in the New Testament, furthermore, we see that Paul's letters were receiving a unique status of authority. Second Peter 3:15-16 states, "And regard the patience of our Lord as salvation. So also our beloved brother Paul wrote to you according to the wisdom given him, speaking of this as he does in all his letters.

There are some things in them hard to understand, which the ignorant and unstable twist to their own destruction, as they do the other scriptures." Here Paul's letters are clearly being drawn into the semantic field of the "other Scriptures." At this time they were already integrated into Christian church services just like the Old Testament.

As the theological tradition emerged in the early church, the idea of the "rule of faith" took shape. This was a short summary of the Christian teaching drawn from the Scriptures. It was handed down from one generation to the next and became known as "tradition"— that is, literally, the thing that was "handed down" or "handed over," the "handover" (*traditio*). Of course, the biblical canon had not yet been formed at this time. Nevertheless, the gospels, the Pauline epistles, and other letters of the New Testament were widely recognized as apostolic and thus understood to be "holy writings." The term "rule of faith" is found with Irenaeus, bishop of Lyons (ca. 135–ca. 200), in his work *Against Heresies*, which was written from around 175 to 200.[69] The rule of faith and the tradition it stood for was a second confirming instance of that which was already found in the Scriptures. When it came to describing a heretic, Irenaeus asserted that the "heretics follow neither Scripture nor tradition."[70] The order of words is important here: neither *Scripture* (which was the foundation of the tradition) nor tradition (which summarizes and communicates the Scripture). The same thing is found in Tertullian's (ca. 160–220) *Prescription against Heretics* (*De praescriptione haereticorum*), which was written around 200. He also uses the term "rule of faith" (*regula fidei*) to name a brief list of biblical teachings drawn from various biblical Scriptures:

> Now, with regard to this rule of faith [*regula fidei*] . . . the belief that there is one only God, and that He is none other than the Creator of the world, who produced all things out of nothing through His own Word, first of all sent forth; that this Word is called His Son, and, under the name of God, was seen "in diverse manners" by the patriarchs, heard at all times in the prophets, at last brought down by the Spirit and Power of the Father into the Virgin Mary, was made flesh in her womb, and, being born of her, went forth as Jesus Christ; thenceforth He preached the new law and the new promise of the kingdom of heaven, worked miracles; having been crucified, He rose again the third day; (then) having ascended into the heavens, He sat at the right hand of the Father; sent instead of Himself the Power of the Holy Ghost to lead such as believe; will come with glory to take the saints to the enjoyment of everlasting life and of the heavenly promises, and to condemn the

> wicked to everlasting fire, after the resurrection of both these classes
> shall have happened, together with the restoration of their flesh.[71]

This is typical of the church fathers. It is simply a summary of the
Bible. Following the apostles themselves (see Paul's short summary in
1 Cor 15:1-5), the fathers saw it as necessary to summarize the faith into
brief statements in order to communicate it to the new members of the
faith and to the youth. This summary was drawn from various passages
in the Bible. It was not understood to be autonomous of the Scriptures;
it was rather understood to be a faithful summary of the Scriptures. The
same thinking is behind the creedal statements of Christianity that were
developed in the centuries that followed. In all these cases, it has to do
with a summary of the biblical teaching. No one, or virtually no one,
thought that they were establishing a new tradition as an alternative to
the scriptural tradition. No one thought that they were doing anything
other than summarizing the biblical teachings that were the doctrinal
foundation of the faith. This is the presumption that goes unstated
precisely because it was so foundational that it did not need to be stated.
No one thought that any teacher or group of bishops had the authority
to override the Scriptures since the Scriptures were understood to be of
direct apostolic authority. This understanding of the unique authority of
the Scriptures is the dominant position in the history of theology. While
there were many disagreements about how to interpret them, virtually
no one claimed that there was another authority above the Scriptures.
Augustine, for example, explicitly emphasized the high status of the
Scriptures in this sense. He wrote,

> But who can fail to be aware that the sacred canon of Scripture, both
> of the Old and New Testament, is confined within its own limits, and
> that it stands so absolutely in a superior position to all later letters of the
> bishops, that about it we can hold no manner of doubt or disputation
> whether what is confessedly contained in it is right and true; but that
> all the letters of bishops which have been written, or are being written,
> since the closing of the canon, are liable to be refuted if there be anything
> contained in them which strays from the truth.[72]

The unique authority of the Scriptures was a very dangerous issue for
people in high positions in the church. The Bible could always be used to
challenge their authority and tradition itself. The attempt to harmonize
these different realms of authority was a major challenge in the history
of theology. One of the classic conceptions of the relationship between

tradition and the Scriptures was developed by Vincent of Lérins (d. ca. 445). In the most important passage of all his works, he writes,

> We must, the Lord helping, fortify our own belief in two ways; first, by the authority of the Divine Law [sc. Scriptures], and then, by the tradition of the Catholic Church. [. . .] Since the canon of Scripture is complete, and sufficient of itself for everything, and more than sufficient, what need is there to join with it the authority of the Church's interpretation? For this reason,—because, owing to the depth of Holy Scripture, all do not accept it in one and the same sense, but one understands its words in one way, another in another; so that it seems to be capable of as many interpretations as there are interpreters. [. . .] Therefore, it is very necessary, on account of so great intricacies of such various error, that the rule for the right understanding of the prophets and apostles should be framed in accordance with the standard of Ecclesiastical and Catholic interpretation. Moreover, in the Catholic Church itself, all possible care must be taken, that we hold that faith which has been believed everywhere, always, by all [*quod ubique, quod semper, quod ab omnibus creditum est*]. For that is truly and in the strictest sense "Catholic," which, as the name itself and the reason of the thing declare, comprehends all universally. This rule we shall observe if we follow universality, antiquity, consent [*universitas, antiquitas, consensio*].[73]

While this work, and this passage itself, would only become influential in the sixteenth century (and then especially in the nineteenth century), the theological ideas here are a good example of the emerging conception of the relationship between the Scriptures, tradition, and the ecclesial authorities in the Middle Ages. According to Vincent's theology, specific instances of authority, the interpreters, are to take on a role of mediation. They are to ensure that the interpretation is "framed in accordance with the standard of Ecclesiastical and Catholic interpretation." Vincent's argument was developed to guard against heresies. His theology has been interpreted in different ways. In a very problematic line of interpretation, Vincent's interpreters take the place of the Scriptures as the ultimate authority because they are the ones who determine what the Scriptures teach. This is actually what happened in the Middle Ages, and especially with the papal authoritarianism of the later Middle Ages.

Vincent's theology can be understood in a different way, however. The Gallic monk-priest was certainly not arguing for an instance of absolute authority that dictates, by virtue of its own authority, "the right understanding of the prophets and apostles." He is not saying that the Scriptures are in contradiction with one another and that they need someone simply to make a decision about what is right. He is also not saying that the "authority of the church's interpretation" is above the Scriptures. Nor is he saying that the "authority of the church's interpretation" is infallible.

In light of contradicting teachings, the assignment of the interpreters is to provide a right understanding of the Scriptures, not to determine the faith by declaration. For Vincent, the authority of the interpreters was *derivative*. This is why he specifies his understanding of the universal faith as that faith that has "been believed everywhere, always, by all." It is not a faith that the interpreters constructively determine, dictate, or establish, but rather the faith that accords to the triad of universality, antiquity, and consent. The implied argument here is that the very interpretations that they provide are to be themselves in harmony with the Scriptures and the universally accepted teachings of Christianity as reflected, for example, in the earliest creeds. The qualifier of consent suggests that Vincent wanted to emphasize that which was shared and agreed upon, that which was held in unison among Christians. With these three qualifiers, Vincent set a very high standard for the interpreters that carefully limited their jurisdiction. In all this, Vincent presumed that the Scriptures themselves are the authority that is interpreted. The interpreters are not the final authority. The interpreters only have authority by virtue of their interpretation of the Scriptures and by virtue of their adherence to the Scriptures and to the three qualifiers. This is why the Scriptures are named first before the tradition. As he writes, "first, by the authority of the Divine Law [Scriptures], and then, by the Tradition of the Catholic Church."

One might extrapolate upon the systematic framework of the theology here by suggesting that the interpreters are on the third level of authority below the tradition, which is the second level. Both the tradition and the contemporary interpreters are, however, below the Scriptures, which constitutes the first level of authority in matters of Christian faith. Furthermore, on this third level, the interpreters were restrained by the three qualifiers. After all this, Vincent reminds his readers that "all possible care must be taken that we hold that faith." This remark shows a slight sense of skepticism toward the interpreters. He reminds them to be careful because, as one may presume, it is apparently possible to err in these matters.

Correctly interpreted, Vincent's position can be understood to entail a balance of power and a carefully constructed system of checks and balances that strictly regulate the exercise of scriptural interpretation.

This theology was corrupted in the Middle Ages as the ecclesial institution put itself in the place of the Scriptures and asserted absolute authority. In doing this it decoupled itself from the corrective framework of scriptural authority and eliminated the separation of power in ecclesial theological disputes. It became the correcting and determining instance of authority above Scripture rather than being the corrected and determined instance of interpretation under Scripture. As will be addressed below, this view of "church over Scripture" became a major issue in the Reformation.

Another dimension of the debates about authority in the pre-Reformation era was the status of the councils. The authority of church councils grew in the Middle Ages, especially in the thirteenth, fourteenth, and fifteenth centuries. The Fourth Lateran Council (1215) marked a new stage in this development of conciliar power. The rise of conciliar power was always met with a challenge from the papacy. The authority of the council was, however, strengthened in the Western Schism (1378–1417) as multiple bishops claimed to be the pope of the church. With the resolution of the schism, the tension between the papacy and the council continued.

In the Middle Ages, the idea became popular that the centralized authority structure of the church was the only legitimate interpreter of the Scriptures. This went together with the idea that the laity should not even have access to the Bible. There are many examples of this in the Middle Ages. In 1210 the archbishop of Sens, Pierre de Corbeil, and others issued the following command in an edict: "We command concerning books of theological nature written in Romance [Old French], that they shall be handed over to the diocesan bishops [. . .] and that all their possessors shall be regarded as heretical."[74] The Council of Toulouse (1229), under Pope Gregory IX, prohibited the laity from using the Bible, indeed even the possession of it:

> Lay people shall not have books of Scripture, except the psalter and the divine office: and they shall not have these books in the vulgar tongue. Moreover we prohibit that lay people should be permitted to have books of the Old or New Testament, except perchance any should wish from devotion to have a psalter, or a breviary for the divine office, or the hours of the blessed Virgin: but we strictly forbid their having even the aforesaid books translated into the vulgar tongue.[75]

A general prohibition was offered by the Dominican chapter general in 1242 in Bologna: "Neither shall any brother for the future translate sermons, or collations, or other holy scriptures."[76] Chapter 36 of the provincial council of 1246 for Narbonne, at Béziers, held that certain officials "shall see that it is rigorously carried out that theological books shall not be kept, either by the laity in Latin, or by them or by clerks in the vulgar tongue."[77] The document goes on to address the penalties for violations. There are many examples of prohibitions in the Middle Ages. Some of these even called for the translations to be burned by the bishops. If one did not turn in his Bible eight days after its publication, he would be, whether lay or cleric, held suspect of heresy.[78]

The countermovement against this authoritarianism began in the Middle Ages. Wycliffe, for example, wanted to move the Scriptures into the hands of the laity. Both Wycliffe and Hus emphasized the priority of the Scriptures above ecclesial authorities in matters of faith. Hus held the Scriptures to be the final court of appeal in theological issues.[79] While the tradition was important, when it or any other authority contradicted the Scripture, the Scripture stands. As Thomas A. Fudge explains this principle in Hussite theology, "When the Bible was juxtaposed to the exclusive claims of popes or bishops, primacy was consistently given to the former."[80]

On July 6, 1415, at the Council of Constance (at the end of the three-popes crisis), Hus was condemned by the church leadership and handed over to the authorities to be burned to death. Refusing to recant his teachings, and moments before they lit the fire, he said, "And in that truth of the Gospel that I wrote, taught, and preached in accordance with the sayings and expositions of the holy doctors, I am willing gladly to die today."[81] As this remark and many others from his work show, Hus saw himself as promoting the Christian faith in harmony with the Scriptures and tradition. He did not see himself as abandoning the true Christian tradition.

Both Wycliffe and Hus contributed to the reestablishment of the unique status of Scripture in the Middle Ages. They were also evidence of the fact that the authorities in the church could not entirely control the reform movements. This conflict over authority—the authority of the pope, of the council, of Scripture, and of the right to interpret Scripture—continued in the late Middle Ages leading up to the Reformation. "It became evident in the later Middle Ages and more urgently in the early sixteenth century," as Gillian R. Evans writes, "that something was wrong with both the doctrine and the practice of authority in the Church in the West."[82]

One of the dominant positions in this debate about authority in the church was the idea that the bishops and the popes, canon law, the handed-down theological tradition, and the confessional statements from the ancient councils, were, on the whole, in harmony with the Scriptures. For many reasons, this traditional viewpoint started to appear less plausible in the later Middle Ages. In the fourteenth and fifteenth centuries, theologians started to systematically analyze the differences between scriptural teachings and the other teachings of the tradition, canon law, councils, and the popes. A good example of this before the Reformation is found in Wessel Gansfort (1419–1489). He was called the "Master of Contradiction" in an originally pejorative sense. In his writings he emphasized "semantic clarity and methodological reasoning," as was typical of the new theology of the later Middle Ages.[83] The rediscovery of scriptural authority was thus influenced by the decline of Aristotelian scholasticism in the late Middle Ages and the rise of nominalism.[84] In the late 1480s (probably in 1489), only a few decades before the short Reformation began, Gansfort wrote to Jacob Hoeck in a response to Hoeck's criticism:

> Your warning that the authority of the pope should mean more to me than reason is distasteful to me. [. . .] You warn me that in these matters the authority of the pope should not merely take the place of reason but should be above it. But what is that "reason" of mine, if not Scripture? The will of the pope and the authority of Scripture have not been established on an equal footing so that the will of the pope is to be measured by the truth of Scripture and vice versa.[85]

The theological thinking here was not new in the history of Christianity, but it was revolutionary in the ecclesial context of the late Middle Ages. The early church fathers were also convinced of the unique authority of the Scriptures.[86] They did not have, however, an absolutist pope that was challenging the unique authority of Scripture. In this regard, the situation of the late Middle Ages is unique. In the debate about authority, the status of the Scriptures was being rediscovered.

The Reformation further challenged the optimism of the older perspective of harmony (between the Scripture, tradition, and the ecclesial authorities). More and more it became clear that the ecclesial authorities and their teachings were not in fundamental harmony with the Scriptures. The official ecclesial endorsement of the questionable teaching about indulgences significantly damaged the legitimacy and plausibility of the older harmony model. In this regard, the Reformation marks the beginning of a new phase in the conflict about authority in the church.

Drawing upon this medieval tradition of scriptural authority, Staupitz influenced both Luther and Karlstadt. Luther also encountered this emphasis on the Bible while he was in Erfurt with Jodocus Trutfetter.[87] The reestablishment of scriptural authority can already be seen in Karlstadt's 151 Theses from the spring of 1517. The first four theses read, "[1.] The statements of the holy fathers [church fathers] are not to be rejected [2.] unless they have been corrected or retracted [by them]. [3.] If they [the statements] differ from one another, one should not choose what is simply pleasing [4.] but rather that [statement] which is more greatly supported by the divine testimonies [*divinis testimoniis*, the Scriptures] or reason [*ratione*]."[88] Karlstadt's final thesis also returned to this issue of authority: "[151] The fruitful authority of the truth [sc. the Scriptures] is understood better when it is debated more frequently; and this brings forth the true agreement that one conceals in clear speeches."[89]

In these theses from the spring of 1517, Karlstadt strongly encouraged the rediscovery of the classic theological position regarding the unique authority of the Scriptures. While he did not call for a rejection of the teachings of the "holy fathers" (the church fathers), he highlighted the unique status of the Scriptures. The right teaching, the legitimate one, is the one that "is more greatly supported" by the Scriptures. Karlstadt did not reject the papacy in principle; he rather emphasized that it was subordinate to the Scriptures. In his 370 Conclusions from the spring or early summer of 1518, thesis 348 reads, "If the Roman pontiff were inclined to destroy what the apostles and prophets taught, he would be clearly shown not to be giving a judgment, but rather to be erring."[90]

The Roman response to Luther's criticism of indulgences in his Ninety-Five Theses came from the papal court theologian Sylvester Prierias (1456–1523). The debate then went directly to the question of authority. Prierias claimed, "Whoever does not hold to the teaching of the Roman church and the pope as an infallible rule of faith from which the Holy Scripture also derives its power and authority: he is a heretic."[91] Johann Eck had a similar view. Eck argued that "the power of the church" is "above scripture" (*potestas ecclesiae super scriptura*), for "scripture is not authentic without the the church's authority" (*scriptura non est authentica sine authoritate ecclesiae*).[92] At Luther's hearing with Cajetan on October 13, 1518, in Augsburg, Luther cited Galatians 1:8 and argued, like Karlstadt, that "the pope is not above, but under the word of God."[93] Like Karlstadt, and Hus before them, Luther did not intend to reject the authority of the doctrinal tradition or the church fathers. When these matters come into conflict with one another, however, the Scripture stands.[94]

At the first day of the debate in Leipzig, Karlstadt claimed, "We desire to assert or to teach *nothing without* [*nihil sine*] these [Holy Scriptures]."[95] In this, Karlstadt was clearly asserting the unique authority of the Scriptures in matters of Christian faith. That principle of theology that is expressed *positively* in *sola scriptura* is here expressed *negatively* in Karlstadt's *nihil sine*. At the Leipzig debate, Karlstadt endorsed the "exclusivity of the Scriptures" with regard to binding theological matters.[96] The meaning of this was clear to those who heard it: the final authority is the Scriptures, not the pope or any other authority. In the theses that Luther drafted for the Leipzig Debate, thesis 13 states, "The very feeble decrees of the Roman pontiffs which have appeared in the last four hundred years prove that the Roman church is superior to all others. Against them stand the history of eleven hundred years, the text of divine Scripture, and the decree of the Council of Nicaea, the most sacred of all councils."[97]

In the course of the Leipzig Debate with Eck, Luther's own position became clear: popes and councils can err; the ultimate authority in theology is the Scriptures. He also defended Hus, who was condemned as a heretic by the Council of Constance. It was at the Leipzig Debate that it became clear to Luther that only those arguments that emerge from the Scriptures themselves could be "mandatory," while the authority of the church fathers and councils had only a "supportive and referential function."[98] The *form* of these arguments was new (since it was only possible in the ecclesial situation of the late Middle Ages); the *content*, however, was ancient: the Scriptures have a unique authority in doctrinal issues that stands above the tradition and church authorities. In this regard, the Reformation simply reasserted the classic position in Christian theology.

After the debate in 1519 (which entailed a fundamental break with Rome in terms of the content of Luther's arguments), Luther began to draw the pope into the semantic field of the antichrist. He did this because Eck ascribed to the pope such a centrality in matters of faith that it contradicted the gospel.[99] The focus on the unique status of the Scriptures is also seen later in Luther's work in 1520. After the publication of the papal bull *Exsurge Domine*, which threatened to excommunicate Luther, Luther's books were burned in some cities, such as Louvain, Cologne, and Mainz (and perhaps Leipzig and Merseburg). On December 10, 1520, the Wittenberg theologians responded in kind and burned the papal bull, canon law, and some scholastic works. Luther then wrote "Why the Books of the Pope and His Disciples Have Been Burned by Martin Luther" (1520). He drew upon canon law and papal decrees in his rejection of the theology. The very first reason he gave was, "The pope and his men are not bound to be subject and obedient to God's command." The fourth reason was, "The pope and his see are not bound to be subject to Christian councils and decrees."[100] The tenth reason: "No one on earth can judge the pope. Also, no one can judge his decision. Rather, he is supposed to judge all people on earth."[101] The fifteenth reason: "The pope has the power to make laws for the Christian church." The eighteenth reason: "He has forbidden marriage to the whole priesthood."[102] And, perhaps the most important, reasons twenty-eight, twenty-nine, and thirty: "He makes his useless laws equal to the gospels and to Holy Scripture, as he repeatedly indicates in the decretal."[103] "The pope has the power to interpret and to teach Holy Scripture according to his will and allow no one to interpret it otherwise than he wants."[104] "The pope does not derive authentic existence, strength, and dignity from Scripture, but Scripture from him, which is one of the main articles."[105]

In all these regards, the issue of authority was the driving issue. Luther emphasized that the papacy is under the Scripture and not above the Scripture. This is also expressed in Luther's "Defense and Explanation of All the Articles" from March of 1521. There Luther claimed that the pope held that "man's teachings is more important than God's word, and the pope is higher than God."[106] Against this Luther claimed, "When anything contrary to Scripture is decreed in a council, we ought to believe Scripture rather than the council. Scripture is our court of appeal and bulwark."[107] He adds, "Has it come to this in Christendom that we must hear that God and his Word must yield to the pope and his law? The time has come to suffer a hundred deaths instead!"[108]

At the Diet of Worms on April 18, 1521, Luther proclaimed before the ecclesial authorities and Emperor Charles V (Luther was almost forty years old at this time, while the Emperor was only twenty),

> Unless I am convinced by the testimony of the Scriptures or by clear reason (for I do not trust either in the Pope or in councils alone, since it is well known that they have often erred and contradicted themselves), I am bound by the Scriptures I have quoted and my conscience is captive to the Word of God. I cannot and will not recant anything, since it is neither safe nor right to go against conscience. . . . May God help me. Amen.[109]

In this statement Luther was actually affirming an old position in debates of theology. With Luther, academic (university) theology had won the day over monastic theology. Luther sides with the academic school and claims that Christian teaching had to be based on both the authority of Scriptures and reason.[110] While Charles V did condemn Luther as a heretic, his reasoning was not based on faithful submission to Pope Leo X. He acted out of a concern for religious traditionalism in an attempt to maintain the legacy of his aristocratic dynasty. There are actually some remarks from him recorded before Worms that show his sympathy for Luther.[111]

The Diet of Worms had a significant influence on Luther's own development. This truly dramatic experience of conflict with the emperor and the ecclesial authorities encouraged Luther to see that temporal authority could not and should not try to dictate matters of the conscience.[112] Christopher Spehr holds that this event in Worms was a key moment in "world history" (*Weltgeschichte*).[113] While it is important to remember the significance of this event, it is also important to remember the legacy of Hus here. Luther's refusal to bow to the authorities and recant his teachings was a grand insinuation of Hus. At this point Luther's enemies had been associating him with Hus for over three years. Like Hus, the Wittenberg Reformers wanted to reaffirm the unique authority of Scripture.

In many ways the Reformers could refer to tradition to support their emphasis on scriptural authority. While the humanist fascination with the original sources contributed to the Protestant admiration of the text, the emphasis on scriptural authority was not a departure from the classic theological tradition but a reaffirmation of it. In the classic tradition, the Scriptures are the supreme authority in doctrinal disputes. This teaching was taken up into the new Protestant confessions. This was emphasized strongly in the First Helvetic Confession (1536), which described the Scriptures as *Verbum Dei* (the word of God) and the *perfectissima et antiquissima Philosophia* (most perfect and ancient philosophy). It was also summarized in the *Epitome of the Formula of Concord* (1577), which holds that Scripture is the *iudex, norma et regula* (judge, norm, and rule) of Christian doctrine. Virtually all the church fathers held to a similarly high view of Scripture as the revealed word of God and the final norm of doctrine.

This understanding of the unique status of the Bible has also been widely acknowledged in the modern Catholic Church, for example at the Second Vatican Council. In the council's *Dogmatic Constitution on Divine Revelation, Dei verbum*, the teaching office is presented as subordinate to the word of God, to Scriptures: "This Magisterium [teaching office] is not superior to the Word of God, but is its servant [*non supra verbum Dei, sed eidem ministrat*]."[114] Scripture and tradition flow "from the same divine wellspring [*ex eadem divina scaturigine*]" and "in a certain way merge into a unity [*in unum*] and tend toward the same end [*in eundem finem*]."[115] Although the authority of the Scriptures is clearly acknowledged to be above the teaching office, a qualification is made in order to distance this modern Catholic position from the Reformation traditions: "It is not from Sacred Scripture alone [*non per solam Sacram Scripturam*] that the Church draws her certainty about everything which has been revealed. Therefore both sacred tradition and Sacred Scripture are to be accepted and venerated with the same sense of loyalty and reverence [*pari pietatis affectu ac reverentia*]."[116] As the Latin text shows, the authors were thinking about the idea of *sola scriptura* here and, in harmony with the Council of Trent, sought to distance the Catholic position from this teaching. A qualification is also added in the next paragraph. The "task of authentically interpreting the word of God, whether written or handed on, has been entrusted exclusively [or, 'alone'] to the living teaching office [*soli vivo Ecclesiae Magisterio*] of the Church."[117]

This document attempts to affirm the unique authority of Scripture (and thereby acknowledge the truth of the Hussite and later Protestant emphasis on the authority of the Scripture) and, at the same time, preserve a position for the magisterium in the interpretation of the Scriptures. These statements are some of the distant echoes from the pre-Reformation and Reformation debate about the authority of Scriptures. The initial groundbreaking statement cited above was even taken into the Catechism of the Catholic Church: "This Magisterium is not superior to the Word of God, but is its servant. It teaches only what has been handed on to it. At the divine command and with the help of the Holy Spirit, it listens to this devotedly, guards it with dedication and expounds it faithfully. All that it proposes for belief as being divinely revealed is drawn from this single deposit of faith."[118]

While the Catholic Church maintains a significant role for the magisterium, the modern qualifications clearly emphasize the primacy of the Scripture. The teaching office is always to be understood as *non supra*. The magisterium is "not above" the Scriptures, it is under them. Pope Paul VI wrote, "The truth about God, about man and his mysterious destiny, about the world; the difficult truth that we seek in the Word of God and of which, we repeat, we are neither the masters nor the owners, but the depositaries, the heralds and the servants."[119] He clearly positions human authority, and thereby his authority as pope, under the authority of the Scriptures. Pope John Paul II also affirmed in *Ut unum sint* (1995) that he does his work "with a clear sense" of his "own human frailty."[120] He also addressed "disagreements in matters of faith" among Christians and the importance of the "conscience":

> Above all, these disagreements should be faced in a sincere spirit of fraternal charity, of respect for the demands of one's own conscience and of the conscience of the other party, with profound humility and love for the truth. The examination of such disagreements has two essential points of reference: Sacred Scripture and the great Tradition of the Church. Catholics have the help of the Church's living Magisterium [*Catholicis Magisterium semper vitale succurrit Ecclesiae*].[121]

Indeed, all Christians—and not only Catholics—can consult the magisterium for help in their deliberations about what the Scriptures teach and the "great Tradition" preserves. Pope Francis' encyclical *Lumen fidei* (2013) states "the magisterium always speaks in obedience to the prior word on which faith is based; it is reliable because of its trust in the word [*quoniam Verbo committitur*, lit., 'because it is committed to the Word'] which it hears, preserves and expounds."[122] So also Avery Cardinal Dulles has acknowledged that although tradition is a "Spirit-governed transmission of the gospel," when it comes down to brass tacks, "particular traditions are subject to critical scrutiny."[123] It seems that the modern Catholic Church has essentially affirmed that which Karlstadt claimed in thesis 348 of his 370 Conclusions from the spring or early summer of 1518, and that which Luther held in the fall of 1518: the pope, and every other authority, is *non super, sed sub verbo Dei* (not above, but under the word of God).

This unique authority of the Scriptures was also affirmed in the third document ("Your Word is Truth") of the Evangelicals and Catholics Together, an ecumenical working group of Evangelical Protestant and Roman Catholic Christians. They confirmed the following statement:

> Together we affirm that Scripture is the divinely inspired and uniquely authoritative written revelation of God; as such it is normative for the teaching and life of the Church. We also affirm that tradition, rightly understood as the proper reflection of biblical teaching, is the faithful transmission of the truth of the gospel from generation to generation through the power of the Holy Spirit. As Evangelicals and Catholics fully committed to our respective heritages, we affirm together the

coinherence of Scripture and tradition: tradition is not a second source of revelation alongside the Bible but must ever be corrected and informed by it, and Scripture itself is not understood in a vacuum apart from the historical existence and life of the community of faith.[124]

This document also contains specific remarks from the Evangelical theologians rejecting an understanding of *sola scriptura* as *nuda scriptura* (naked scripture), which, as they hold, "disregards the Holy Spirit's work in guiding the witness of the people of God to scriptural truths," and, as they add, encourages subjectivist interpretations. The specific remarks from the Catholics on this issue emphasize that tradition is not "an addition to Holy Scripture or a parallel and independent source of authoritative teaching."[125] Modern Protestants have also sought to recognize the importance of tradition, although usually adding careful qualification. For example, Daniel J. Treier writes in his essay on this matter, "contrary to popular misconceptions of *nuda scriptura*, tradition plays a vital role when understanding God's revelation via Scripture, but the role is 'ministerial' rather than magisterial."[126]

A convergence of Catholics and Protestants is found in many areas of the theological discussion. The famous German Protestant theologian Wolfhart Pannenberg, for example, has even proposed a way to recognize the bishop of Rome. He holds that the bishop of Rome may be understood as leading a ministry for the unity of Christianity as a whole. He writes,

> It is a fact of Christian history that with the end of the primitive Jerusalem church the church of Rome became the historical center of Christianity. If any Christian bishop can speak for the whole church in situations when this may be needed, it will be primarily the bishop of Rome. In spite of all the bitter controversies resulting from chronic misuse of the authority of Rome in power politics, there is here no realistic alternative. The general public no less than most of the churches of the Christian world are aware of this today. We ought freely to admit the fact of the primacy of the Roman Church and its bishop in Christianity. Not the fact itself so much as the way of describing it is the point at issue, along with the question of the implied rights.[127]

Pannenberg emphasizes the primacy of the gospel in all things but goes on to claim that the "Lutheran Reformation never rules out in principle a ministry to protect Christian unity on the universal level of Christianity as a whole."[128] As he points out, Luther turned against the pope because he saw him as heretical. Yet today the modern Catholic Church has removed these objections and clearly positioned the office under the Scriptures. As

Pannenberg specified, the holder of this office should not be called the "head" of the church, because only Jesus Christ has this designation in the New Testament (1 Cor 11:3-4; Eph 1:22; Col 1:18). It would be "sufficient" if the office were "a sign of the unity of all Christianity, not a cause and sign of its divisions."[129] The same theology is found with the American theologian Robert W. Jenson. After developing a "*communio* ecclesiology," he writes, "the ecclesiology just sketched obviously suggests the necessity of a pastor of the one universal church, a shepherd of *its* unity. One ought not to adopt the *communio* ecclesiology without considering this."[130] Pope Francis has also encouraged a new spirit of reform regarding the papacy. He writes, "The papacy and the central structures of the universal Church also need to hear the call to pastoral conversion. [. . .] Excessive centralization, rather than proving helpful, complicates the Church's life and her missionary outreach."[131]

For a new interpretation of the papacy as a representative ministry of ecclesial unity, it would be best if the office was held by three people (made up of men and women) at the same time. This would reflect the fact that in Christian theology the ultimate sense of unity is understood in triadic plurality. The officeholders would also have to be democratically elected by representatives of all of Christianity for a fixed term of service. They would also have to be held under conciliar oversight and understood, in every sense, as *non super, sed sub verbo Dei*. Furthermore, as the Spirit of God is omnipresent, a residence in Rome could not be a necessary condition for this office. On the contrary, a place with the poor would be preferred, rather than a place with grand buildings and signs of worldly wealth and power.

What does all this suggest? The reservoirs of shared material in both traditions have provided room for broad agreement about the unique authority of Scripture. Many Catholics and Protestants endorse—with minor qualifications—the essence of the teaching that the forerunners of the Reformation and the later Reformers of the sixteenth century emphasized: the teaching office is *non supra* and "tradition is not a second source of revelation alongside the Bible." There are, of course, differences in understanding, but a general agreement about the unique authority of Scriptures is shared.[132]

The rediscovery of the unique authority of the Scriptures by many theologians in the late Middle Ages (such as Wycliffe, Hus, and Gansfort) and then later with the Wittenberg theologians was one of the things used to challenge the coercion of otherwise absolute human authority. The unique standing of scriptural authority in doctrinal issues, *sola scriptura* (Scripture alone)—which is often mentioned in relationship to the other "alones" (*solus Christus, sola fide, sola gratia*)[133]—was reasserted in the dispute with the ecclesial authorities about the legitimacy of the church's selling of grace for money (indulgences). In this regard, the emphasis on scriptural authority had the function of limiting the reach of human power and challenging the status of unquestioned tradition. The emphasis on the authority of Scripture worked as a controlling instance on human authority.

This shift from the control of *human authority* to *textual authority* is analogous to the basic principles of modern Western democracies: the separation of powers and the limitation of human rulers through the rule of law. In the Reformation it was the rule of the Scriptures that had to be brought against the pope and his theologians. This was the only possible source of religious authority that could be legitimately asserted against them. When the pope and the leaders of the church of the late Middle Ages officially endorsed the scandalous sale of grace for money in order to finance a prestigious building project, the necessary response was to challenge their endorsement. When this challenge was rejected, the next step was to challenge their authority altogether. In this process of reform, the original standard of Christian theology was returned to its proper place. Scripture alone was to be the final authority, not the pope, a council, or any teacher. All secondary instances of authority were to be understood as derivative authorities, *non super, sed sub verbo Dei* (not above, but under the word of God), for "the will of the pope and the authority of Scripture have not been established on an equal footing."[134]

« 4 »

POLITICAL POWER AND TOLERANCE

One of the most problematic and, indeed, deadly issues in the history of the Reformation was the unification of religious and political power. This happened on both the Protestant and the Catholic sides. It turned back the tradition of the Middle Ages in which the ecclesial authority structure had a semiautonomous standing over against the magistrates, princes, kings, and emperors. In the new territorially organized religious-political regimes, the ecclesial order was entirely interconnected with and dependent on the local territorial political authority. A new culture of disciplinary consolidation emerged at this time as the religious and political authorities jointly policed the legal, social, religious, and educational institutions of a given territory from above. The intolerance of the Protestants and Catholics toward one another, and toward dissenting groups in their territories, set the stage for the emergence of modern liberalism, which elevated the rights of the individual (freedom of conscience), separated the church from the state, and advanced the countermovement of tolerance. This story has often been told as a negative decline-and-fall narrative in which secularism extracted "oppressive religion" from the public sphere. This negative account is, however, historically inaccurate. It was not secular theorists who called for this liberalization but Christians, who were acting out of compassion and Christian love. This historical development toward religious freedom does not begin in the eighteenth and nineteenth centuries, but already in the early sixteenth century at the outset of the Reformation.

4.1 THE "CITY OF GOD" AND THE "EARTHLY CITY"

With the Reformation, princes often became miniature popes, or supreme bishops (*summus episcopus*), in their territories.[1] The result was a virtual unification of political and religious authority. The political authorities, magistrates, and princes did not force this agenda on the Reformers. In many regards the Reformers supported this new fusion of the church and the state.[2] Of course, there is a long history of collaboration between the church and the state in the Middle Ages and before.

Drawing upon the ancient teaching of Jeremiah, early Christians sought to contribute to the social and political order in which they lived. In the prophecy of Jeremiah, the Lord told those in exile to "seek the welfare of the city where I have sent you into exile, and pray to the Lord on its behalf, for in its welfare you will find your welfare" (Jer 29:7). Running parallel to this impulse of religiously motivated collaboration and identification with the political and social order is the counterimpulse of tension and distinction. This distinction, which is found throughout the Western tradition, comes out most strongly in the story of Moses and Pharaoh, as the Israelites were liberated from slavery in Egypt (Exod 1–15). God told Moses, "I will send you to Pharaoh to bring my people, the Israelites, out of Egypt" (Exod 3:10). Antigone's response to Creon in Sophocles' tragedy *Antigone* is another good example of this moment of separation. There she remarks that the decrees of man are not "strong enough to have power to overrule [. . .] the unwritten and unfailing ordinances of the gods. For these have life, not simply today and yesterday, but forever."[3]

These two impulses are also found in those New Testament passages that were central to the history of Christian political thought. One of these records the words of Christ: "Give therefore to the emperor the things that are the emperor's, and to God the things that are God's." (Matt 22:21). With this, the famous Pauline admonition is "Let every person be subject to the governing authorities; for there is no authority except from God, and those authorities that exist have been instituted by God" (Rom 13:1). That verse from Paul is often understood with the Petrine qualification: "But Peter and the apostles answered, 'We must obey God rather than any human authority.'" (Acts 5:29). In these passages one finds both the impulse toward collaboration and identification and the other impulse of tension, distinction, and separation.

This dynamic of identification and distinction continued through the history of Christianity in late antiquity and in the Middle Ages. In 313, under Constantine, Christianity went from being a *religio illicita* (a forbidden religion) to a *religio licita* (a permitted religion). In 380, under Theodosius, Christianity was then effectively made the religion of the Roman Empire. Before this, however, there were many elite Romans participating in the Christian religion. There is evidence of this already in the first century.[4] In this context the two impulses of identification and distinction were made explicit again with Augustine (354–430) and the paradigm of the "city of God" and the "earthly city," one ruled by the love of God, the other ruled by the love of self.[5]

Even Augustine, however, was willing to advance the city of God with the coercion of the earthly city. He encouraged the imperial government to suppress the Donatists and even wrote *On the Correction of the Donatists* (417) to justify this. In defense of such coercion, he "mixed the pragmatic and the theological" and suggested that "God himself was coercive, compelling humans through grace."[6] Augustine pointed to a verse in the New Testament to support his cause: "Then the master said to the slave, 'Go out into the roads and lanes, and compel people to come in, so that my house may be filled'" (Luke 14:23). He was so concerned with Christian unity that he endorsed the persecution of those who seemed to be dividing Christianity. As Augustine wrote, "Consider what treatment they deserve at the hands of the Christian powers of the world, who are the enemies of Christian unity throughout the world."[7]

The suppression of the Donatists echoed through Western history. It provided every ruler with the necessary legitimacy for suppressing deviant groups. Charlemagne (d. 814) is another example of pre-Reformation religious coercion. He forced the Saxons to convert to Christianity. As is recorded in the *Annals*, he ordered the execution (decapitation) of at least 4,500 Saxons on a single day in 782 in his campaign of christianization.[8] The suppression of the Donatists and the forced conversion of the Saxons are two horrific examples of political power being used in an attempt to advance the cause of the church. In the end, both of these cases actually did just the opposite. As the church supported the use of coercion for its own cause, it abandoned its identification with the city of God and contradicted the very core teachings of the faith. In these stories the impulse of identification with the political order is strong, while the counterimpulse of distinction is weak or nonexistent.

For much of the Middle Ages, however, the impulse of distinction was the dominant one. This is expressed in the tense power struggle between the political and ecclesial authorities. Pope Gelasius I, pope from 492 to 496, remarked in his letter to the Emperor Anastasius, "Two there are, august Emperor, by which this world is ruled: the consecrated authority of priests and the royal power. Of these the priests have the greater responsibility in that they will have to give account before God's judgment seat for those who have been kings of men."[9] The Investiture Controversy was another key historical moment in the development of the principle of separation. It was a conflict about the right of appointment, especially regarding high offices in the church. It was resolved with the Concordat of Worms in 1122, which granted the ecclesial authorities "all investiture in ring and staff" (in their sacred function) while retaining some rights for the emperor in the appointment of some bishops and abbots "by the scepter" (in their secular function as rulers).[10] This division of the ecclesial and political realms was characteristic of the Middle Ages. By contrast, the Reformation brought a new consolidation of power and a new emphasis on the identification of the ecclesial with the political realms.

4.2 POLITICAL POWER IN THE CHURCH

The unification of ecclesial and political power in the Reformation had its theological point of departure in Luther's address "To the Christian Nobility of the German Nation Concerning the Reform of the Christian Estate" (1520). The princes did not need a theological argument to legitimate their power grab in ecclesial matters. They had already exerted great influence over the churches in their territories before the Reformation. If they wanted such an argument, however, they got it with Luther. James Atkinson has rightly called this work "one of the most significant documents produced by the Protestant Reformation."[11] Luther's call to reform drew upon and crystallized ideas that were long fermenting before 1517. It also laid the groundwork for much of what was to come. If there is any document from the first years of the Reformation that exemplifies the many areas in the church that were in need of reform, it is this short work. Luther makes many arguments, but his concern is focused on corruption in Christendom. He addresses greed, wealth, false teachings, disorder, injustice, corrupt finances, and a corrupt political order. He also criticizes the resistance to reform, the problems of waste, vanity, and theological errors, and the rejection of the teachings of the Scriptures. After reading it one immediately has the sense that the driving force behind the Reformation was a response to corruption in the context of early sixteenth-century German resentment against the "Romanists."

The emphasis on the priesthood of all believers, above all else, underlies the logic of Luther's strategy of reform.

One of the most problematic aspects of the Reformation is clearly expressed in this work: the near unification of ecclesial and political power. In his address Luther uses the analogy of "Three Walls" that had insulated the Roman authority from reform. He attacked these with theological criticisms.[12] Luther claimed that his main agenda was "to help the German nation to be free and Christian again after the wretched, heathenish, and unchristian rule of the pope."[13] This criticism of the Roman papacy was central to Luther's concern. The first wall was the idea of a spiritual estate (consisting of pope, bishops, priests, and monks) that insulated the church authorities from reform. He argued that "those who exercise secular authority" are baptized just like all Christians.[14] For this reason, "we must regard their office as one which has a proper and useful place in the Christian community."[15]

From there he went on to assert that between the "religious" and "secular," there is "no true, basic difference," for all Christians are in the same "spiritual estate."[16] Luther rejected the claim that the "spiritual estate" was above "temporal power." He even held that the latter may punish the former. He argued that the temporal authority has been "ordained by God to punish the wicked and protect the good" and that it should do its duty in the whole Christian body, even if this leads to punishing the pope. The temporal power "should be left free to perform its office in the whole body of Christendom without restriction and without respect to persons, whether it affects pope, bishop, priests, monks, nuns, or anyone else."[17] Here Luther rejects the idea that the clergy had a special standing that would exempt them from civil authority.

The Reformation ultimately eliminated the special status of clergy. Before the Reformation they had a protected status when it came to a trial of criminal behavior. In this case they were tried under special ecclesial jurisdiction, the *privilegium fori* (privilege of the court of jurisdiction).[18] Even before the Reformation, however, in some parts of Europe the clergy would have also been subject to secular courts—for example, in serious crimes. This was one of the controversial matters in the Middle Ages that was debated between secular and religious authorities. King Henry II, for example, tried to institute a policy in 1164 that would let criminal clergy be summoned to a secular court. They were to be handed over to an ecclesial court, stripped of their clerical status, then returned to the secular court to be executed. But this was rejected by Pope Alexander III.

There is evidence that clergy disregarded the law in the Middle Ages in Paris and took advantage of their status: "Youthful students and masters enjoying the *priviligia canonis* and *fori* as members of the clergy were known for their brawling and rioting, as well as for committing more violent crimes. Their protected status encouraged aggressive behavior."[19] The desire for equality under the law was also a part of the Hussite Reformation. Today no one is making the argument that we should return to the old order in which clergy are not tried under the same law as all citizens and political leaders when it comes to criminal behavior. In this regard, the modern Western world has essentially affirmed this aspect of the Reformation.[20] With the elimination of the "First Wall" there was to be only one priesthood: all who were baptized. This was the "radical" Luther of the early Reformation. Both Karlstadt and Luther promoted this principle of egalitarianism, which was closely related to other anticlerical sentiments in the early sixteenth century.[21]

The "Second Wall," which he rejects, is the idea that the pope has a unique authority with regard to the interpretation of the Scriptures. Luther argued, "The Romanists must admit that there are among us good Christians who have the true faith, spirit, understanding, word, and mind of Christ."[22] This sentence brings out the driving force of the entire Reformation: not only bishops and popes can become theologians; everyone can. Peasants drew upon this sense of egalitarianism and teaching about the priesthood of all believers when they asserted their equality as redeemed Christians and demanded freedom from serfdom. They argued that "Christ redeemed us all [. . .] the shepherd as well as the most highly placed [. . .] Scripture establishes that we are and will be free."[23] In Luther's argument, he then emphasizes that all Christians are priests and that there is one faith that they have, one gospel and one sacrament (baptism). He thus argues that all Christians have the power "to test and judge what is right or wrong in matters of the faith."[24]

The "Third Wall" was the idea that "the pope alone has the right to call or confirm a council."[25] To this Luther claimed that if the "First Wall" is torn down, and the "Second Wall" taken away, this "Third Wall" necessarily falls with the others. As evidence of the need to correct the pope when he is in error, he cites Matthew 18:15-17. Here Jesus teaches:

> "If another member of the church sins against you, go and point out the fault when the two of you are alone. If the member listens to you, you have regained that one. But if you are not listened to, take one or two others along with you, so that every word may be confirmed by the

evidence of two or three witnesses. If the member refuses to listen to them, tell it to the church; and if the offender refuses to listen even to the church, let such a one be to you as a Gentile and a tax collector."

The significance of the Bible in the Reformation cannot be overemphasized. The presumption that one could simply cite a Bible verse and thereby legitimately call the entire sociopolitical order into question followed from the belief that the Bible was the word of God. Following Wycliffe and Hus, virtually all of the Reformers of the sixteenth century drew upon this unique authority of Scripture to legitimate their reform.[26]

Luther also argued that the Scriptures do not teach that the pope alone has the exclusive power to call and confirm church councils. He claims that if the pope is in error, a free council must be held to correct him. He states that in this case the "temporal authorities" should call the council, "especially since they are also fellow-Christians, fellow-priests, fellow-members of the spiritual estate, fellow-lords over all things."[27] Willingly or unwillingly, in this argument (which builds on the conception of the priesthood of all believers) Luther inaugurated the unification of ecclesial and political authority in the Protestant territories. Later in the same work he could therefore claim that "all festivals should be abolished, and Sunday alone retained."[28] He holds that they "are abused by drinking, gambling, loafing, and all manner of sin."[29] Luther pleads with the nobility that the festivals should be abolished regardless of who instituted them, even if the pope is behind them. He then makes another argument that brings together spiritual and political power. He states that "every town, council, or governing authority not only has the right [. . .] to abolish what is opposed to God and injurious to men's bodies and souls, but indeed is bound at the risk of the salvation of its souls to fight it."[30] The same sense comes up earlier in his address when he writes that "the Christian nobility should set itself against the pope as against a common enemy and destroyer of Christendom for the salvation of the poor souls who perish because of this tyranny."[31] These examples show how much power Luther gave the nobility in spiritual things. He was asking them to become pastors of their territories, and that is precisely what happened.

Examples can be found before 1517 of secular authorities who were in competition with papal authority and bishops for influence in the churches and who considered the church in their territories to be not only under their influence but also under their authority (such as Herzog Georg von Sachsen).[32] The fifteenth-century Hussite Reformation in Bohemia and Moravia was another exception to the medieval tradition of separation. It was a forerunner for the Lutheran Reformation in that the nobility, with broad popular support, also exercised authority over the ecclesial realm. Nevertheless, up until the Reformation, the church was relatively successful in maintaining a semiautonomous status as a unique divine instance of spiritual authority in the *civitas terrena* (earthly city). Of course, the actual ownership of ecclesial properties was an area of occasional confusion in the Middle Ages. Some of these properties were even listed in records as being owned by Jesus Christ.[33]

With Luther's "Address to the Christian Nobility," he provided an interpretation of the priesthood of all believers that allowed for the nobility to participate in the management of the church. Luther did not invite them to see themselves as equal members of the church. He rather invited the nobility to exercise their political power to care for the souls of their subjects. Once the ecclesial authority structures were reorganized in the Reformation, this essentially enabled the princes to control the church. On the whole, Christendom went from being a social order that was controlled by the *superterritorial* church and the territorial state (with *more* power struggle between them) to being one that was controlled by a *territorial* church and a territorial state (with *less* power struggle). What started as a reform movement from below (or, more correctly, from the middle) became a Reformation from above.

4.3 THE REFORMATION "FROM ABOVE"

The initial reform movements in Wittenberg from October of 1521 to March of 1522, which are often referred to as the "Wittenberg Movement,"[34] were driven forward by university theologians, priests, and common people. Later, however, under Luther's influence, the reform came under the control of the prince. This historical development in Wittenberg became a standard model for many of the reform movements in Europe in the early sixteenth century.

The Wittenberg movement is evidence of the fact that the Reformation was a university and student phenomenon.[35] University theologians, priests and friars, students, and numerous common people started to demand the implementation of the reforms that the academic theologians had been discussing and debating. In terms of sacramental practices, the Reformation movement in Wittenberg began on September 29, 1521, when Philip Melanchthon, professor of Greek at the University of Wittenberg, offered his students the sacraments in both bread and wine.

In terms of a public ecclesial controversy, the Reformation began with Gabriel Zwilling's (1487–1558) sermon against the Mass on October 6, 1521.[36] The Augustinians under Zwilling then stopped celebrating Mass in October of 1521. In the same month, Karlstadt and Melanchthon also publicly questioned the mass. Karlstadt was calling for a moderate reform at this time. In November the Augustinians started to break their vows and leave the cloister. At this time Elector Frederick was cautious about the changes and very concerned about what they would mean for his university town and for his status in the empire. In the tense situation of transition and controversy, "Karlstadt insisted that all the Wittenbergers must first be persuaded by preaching. Melanchthon, on the other hand, objected that there had been enough preaching. It was time to act!"[37] Against this radical approach, "Karlstadt urged that no action be taken without the consent of the Wittenberg magistracy."[38] Although Karlstadt originally wanted moderate reforms, the passions of reform could not be controlled. On December 3, 1521, students and townspeople "forcibly entered the parish church, threw away the missals and drove the priests from the altar. The next day they threw stones into the Franciscan cloister during Mass and pulled down the altar."[39] In response to this, Elector Frederick called for these people to be seized and demanded that an investigation follow the events.[40]

At this point the movement had largely developed without Luther.[41] At the beginning of December 1521 (probably arriving on the afternoon of the third), Luther visited Wittenberg. He wrote to Spalatin at this time. The editorial remarks in the Weimar Edition of Luther's works suggest that this letter to Spalatin was probably written on December 5, 1521, and certainly between the fourth and the ninth of December. The editorial remarks state, "What he [Luther] sees and hears in Wittenberg pleases him very much." Yet Luther was also "deeply moved by rumors that he had heard on the way there about the irresponsible actions of certain friends," to which he wanted to respond as soon as he returned to Wartburg Castle. In his letter Luther wrote to Spalatin, "Everything else that I hear and see pleases me very much. [*Omnia vehementer placent, quae video et audio.*] May the Lord strengthen the spirit of those who want to do right! Nevertheless I was disturbed on the way by various rumors concerning the improper conduct of some of our people, and I have decided to issue a public exhortation on that subject as soon as I have returned to my wilderness."[42]

Luther was clearly in agreement with the reform movement up to this point. While he supported the reform, he did not want a rebellion. Luther saw insurrection as the work of the devil.[43] This is why he wrote his "A Sincere Admonition by Martin Luther to All Christians against Insurrection and Rebellion." On December 14, 1521, he sent this to Spalatin for publication (as he promised in the letter cited above). Luther's "Sincere Admonition" was probably published in January of 1522.

In December of 1521, the reform movement was already taking hold in Wittenberg with the support of Karlstadt, Melanchthon, Nicholas von Amsdorf, Jerome Schurf, Zwilling, and many students and townspeople. The citizens of Wittenberg were calling for reforms, such as free preaching, reform of the Mass, Communion in bread and wine, and the abolishment of beer halls and houses of prostitution.[44] The conservative voices in the town resisted these reforms. Elector Frederick then sided decisively with the conservatives and demanded on December 19, 1521, that his representatives should "forbid the university and foundation [Collegiate Church] to introduce any innovations in the Mass."[45]

Up to this point, Karlstadt had been trying to cooperate with the authorities. In the midst of this controversy, he decided to resist the conservative agenda of the elector and some of the priests in Wittenberg who were resisting the reforms. A few days later, on Christmas Eve, a crowd of students took over the parish church. The protestors rejected the Mass, which they held to be blasphemous. On Christmas Day of 1521, Karlstadt then held the first Protestant church service of the Reformation. He did this without liturgical garments in a simple gown while addressing the people as "fellow laypeople" (*uns leyeen*). He encouraged the congregants to take Communion even if they had not confessed their sins to a priest. From this point on, faith was the issue that mattered, not confessions. They celebrated Communion in both bread and wine. Karlstadt simplified the liturgy and eliminated the language of sacrifice and the elevation of the host while speaking the words of institution in German for the first time ever.

During Communion, those taking Communion were permitted to take the bread and the cup in their own hands.[46] The people of Wittenberg had thus initiated the popular Reformation by pushing the Reformers to act upon and implement their own theology against the will of the elector. This Christmas Day church service was the high point of the Reformation from below in Wittenberg. The church services were full in the weeks to follow, and the congregants remarked on Karlstadt's good preaching.

Karlstadt's spirits had changed so much in the Wittenberg Movement that some congregants reported that "it was not the same Karlstadt."[47]

In the first week of January 1522, the Reform Congregation of Augustinians met in Wittenberg and introduced reforms, including provisions for the members to leave the order. Shortly after this, Zwilling and others destroyed various sacred objects, including altars and pictures in the cloister. Iconoclasm was a central aspect of the Protestant reforms in Germany, Switzerland, Scotland, and elsewhere. Those who were destroying the images were driven in part by an anger at "the deceit perpetrated on them by the pre-reformation church," as Hendrix remarks. The iconoclasts were also rejecting the theology behind the sacred objects. According to this theology, the objects were "sacred channels of divine power" through which one might come closer to God. The fragments of destroyed religious art, which can still be seen in museums and churches across Europe, are "reminders of the fierce emotions that also drove the Reformation."[48] Iconoclasm was one possible interpretation of the theology of divine grace, which rejected the claim that one could acquire grace through works, such as through the veneration of sacred images. The images became a major target of attack as the theologians and laity sought to overcome the works-based piety. They drew upon the Old Testament as a justification, for it teaches in the Ten Commandments, "You shall not make for yourself an idol, whether in the form of anything that is in heaven above, or that is on the earth beneath, or that is in the water under the earth" (Exod 20:4).[49]

The reforms continued on January 19, 1522, as Karlstadt married Anna von Monchau. He was the first leading figure of the Reformation to break his vows.[50] In the same month of January, the church reforms spread to other towns. When news of these events reached the imperial government, a condemnation of the reforms was issued on January 20.[51] From this point onward, Elector Frederick was under official imperial pressure to stop the reforms.

On January 24 the reforms were made a part of the Ordinance of the City of Wittenberg (*Löbliche Ordnung der Fürstlichen Stat Wittenberg*). The city council determined that there would be a reform of the Mass, a gradual removal of sacred images in the churches, an institution of a community chest for the poor and needy, and the prohibition of begging. As Appold specifies, this prohibition of begging was aimed at both the mendicant friars and the able-bodied laypeople who "should be put to work."[52] Here one can clearly see the Protestant work ethic in its early stages. At the same time, however, begging was also prohibited because the Reformers did not want people to think that they could acquire divine grace through works of charity. Some beer halls and houses of prostitution were also forbidden by the new ordinance.[53] As these examples show, the movement toward evangelical religion went hand in hand with social reforms. The social order was to be transformed and made to look more like the kingdom of God, not at some point in the eschatological future, but in the present.

Karlstadt then published a very popular tract that explained the reforms and encouraged their implementation ("On the Removal of Images and That There Should Be No Beggars among Christians," January 2, 1522). He wanted an orderly removal of the images, but this soon happened violently at the beginning of February in the parish church (St. Mary's) in Wittenberg, and then in other churches.[54] Both publicly and privately, Karlstadt rejected the iconoclastic activities of the townspeople and students. Zwilling, however, seems to have called for a direct removal of the images by "the common people" (*dye gemein*). Both of them were, however, associated with the iconoclastic activity of the riotous crowds because they were at the forefront of the reforms in Wittenberg.[55]

In January of 1522, the townspeople of Wittenberg; a group of theologians, priests, students; and even the city council had essentially taken over the church and reformed it with broad popular support and without the approval of the bishops, archbishops, or the pope. The mayor of the town, Christian Beyer, and the leadership of the university had, at this point, all endorsed the ordinances.[56] This was not a reformation from above but one from the middle of society. Neither the higher ranks of church leadership nor Elector Frederick were behind these reforms. In fact, both these realms of human power resisted the reforms. This power structure from the bottom and the middle of society would soon change, however, as Luther took up the cause of Elector Frederick.

Luther returned to Wittenberg on March 6, 1522, and then "energetically grabbed the rudder."[57] He preached his famous Invocavit Sermons from March 9 onward. He claimed that more teaching was necessary before the reforms could be implemented.[58] Some of the reforms were then turned back under Luther's watch. The laity was no longer granted access to the cup in Communion, the host was elevated again, and the words of institution were spoken in Latin.[59]

Although it is often claimed that Luther did this out of concern for the weak, this seems very unlikely. There are many examples of Luther not tolerating others who had not yet come to share his opinion. Furthermore, the townspeople in Wittenberg had actually strongly supported the reforms. It is more likely that Luther did this out of concern for Elector Frederick. Luther "satisfied the Elector's concern for law and order"[60]; indeed, "Luther could put his notion of not offending the weak at the service of Electoral demands."[61]

With some of the reforms turned back and the city ordinance suspended, Karlstadt's preaching was stopped, his writings were confiscated, and the authorities "lined up behind Luther."[62] Karlstadt then moved to Orlamünde, where he worked as a minister and became a farmer—Brother Andrew. In Orlamünde he introduced reforms to care for the poor. He also "gave concrete form to the priesthood of all believers by instituting democratic congregationalism."[63] In the Karlstadtian Reformation, the laity could elect their pastors, criticize them, and even preach themselves. In Orlamünde he stopped baptizing infants and interpreted the Lord's Supper as a memorial.[64] He became very influential among the Anabaptist theologians, and "second only to Luther in his use of the press, he produced some ninety works in over two hundred editions." Unlike the Anabaptists, however, "He advocated no separation from the established church. He was also no pacifist, though he rejected the use of force in religion. In this he differed from Thomas Müntzer."[65] They were also different from one another in that Karlstadt appealed to the Scriptures while Müntzer (ca. 1488–1525) appealed to religious experience and the Spirit. Luther was deeply irritated by Karlstadt's resistance to his authority, even after Karlstadt resigned his archdiaconate of the All Saints Collegiate Church in Wittenberg (on July 22, 1524).

In the summer of 1524, the princes encouraged Luther to suppress the reforming movements of the "fanatics." He was submissive to the political authorities and agreed with their agenda of suppressing the religious dissenters. While Luther clearly wanted to suppress the dissenters himself, he also became a tool in the hands of the political authorities. They must have been happy to have Luther on their side as they sought to insulate the authoritarian feudal order from any reforms from below. Luther's preaching tour around Thuringia was to be the beginning of the authoritarian "visitation" system in the Reformation from above. Dissenters, like Karlstadt, were to be excluded, silenced, and expelled.

On his tour, Luther went to Jena and preached against Karlstadt and Müntzer on the morning of August 22, 1524. Karlstadt was actually in the church service, but Luther did not see him. At Karlstadt's request,

Luther and Karlstadt then went to the Black Bear in Jena to have a meal and a conversation. Many other people witnessed this conversation, and a record of it was published. Karlstadt confronted Luther in the conversation because he had unfairly associated him with the revolutionary ideas of Müntzer (which both Karlstadt and the Orlamünde congregation rejected). Karlstadt said to Luther, "You treated me violently and improperly by putting me in the same pot with the murdering spirit. I protest publicly before all these brethren assembled together that I have nothing to do with the spirit in the rebellion!"[66] Luther answered, "That is not necessary. I have read the letter which you have written to Thomas from Orlamünde and have indeed noticed there that you are against and opposed to rebellion."[67] Although Karlstadt wanted to have a public debate with Luther, Luther later rejected this. As he had supreme authority in Wittenberg, why would he now wish to put his position up to debate with Karlstadt?

In the Black Bear, Karlstadt explicitly asked Luther not to censor his writings. Karlstadt said, "Mr. Doctor [Luther], I beg that you will not prevent me from printing nor otherwise wangle any persecution of me or impediment to my livelihood. For I intend to earn my living with the plow. You shall perceive what the plow will give." To this, Luther responded, "How could I want to prevent you if I want you to write against me?" Furthermore, the court preacher in Jena, who was also present at the meeting in the Black Bear, then said to Karlstadt, "The doctor will not harm your livelihood nor add injury."[68] As is clear from their conversation in Jena, Luther saw himself as the highest instance of authority in matters of censorship. In front of the public gathering at the Black Bear, Luther granted Karlstadt permission to write and publish his opinions against him. In private, however, Luther tried to silence him, like all his opponents.

A few days later, on August 24, 1524, Luther then went to Orlamünde to correct the congregation. He thought that it had been led astray by Karlstadt. Although Karlstadt wanted to participate in this meeting, Luther coldly rejected him. The congregation nevertheless defended Karlstadt against Luther. They supported the reforms that Karlstadt had introduced. The congregants actually used theological arguments to challenge Luther. This infuriated him. Orlamünde is proof of the fact that the reforms that Karlstadt had introduced were not too fast (as the political authorities and Luther had claimed). The simple people of the congregation were defending the reforms as legitimate. This exposed the logic of Luther's arguments about the reforms to be a contrived fabrication. "The Prophet of Patmos" (Luther) was therefore challenged by the Orlamünde congregation; "his role in Saxony of a quasi-bishop-like visitor was called into question." In Luther's mind there was "one person who was responsible for this: Andreas Karlstadt."[69]

Luther then resorted to political power to win a debate that he had lost with words. After Luther finished his tour, he "recommended to Duke John Frederick that the princes act against Karlstadt and remove him from Orlamünde. Ignoring Karlstadt's pleas for a public disputation to examine the truth of his doctrine, the princes decided not only to remove Karlstadt from the Saale valley as Luther had suggested, but also to banish him from all of Electoral Saxony."[70]

While the congregation of Orlamünde defended Karlstadt from Luther's criticisms and explicitly called upon the Wittenberg faculty and the authorities to allow Karlstadt to stay in the town and work as their pastor, the congregation could be overruled with the new Lutheran Reformation from above. Luther used his influence to silence Karlstadt, and he resisted the will of the congregation in Orlamünde.[71] He also encouraged the authorities to stop the publication of Karlstadt's work in Jena. In September of 1524, Karlstadt was then expelled from Electoral Saxony, even though his wife was pregnant and they had a small child.[72] In 1525 Karlstadt published his "Presentation of the Main Articles of Christian Teaching" ("Anzeyg etlicher Hauptartickeln Christlicher leere"), in which he defended himself and claimed that Luther was treating his opponents just like the pope had treated him. As Leppin remarks, this was not an "unjustified" conclusion.[73] Indeed, once Luther came into power, dissenters had to fear not a papal bull from Rome but a Lutheran bull from Wittenberg.

Initially, Luther supported an understanding of dispersed and localized authority in church government. In May of 1523, he published his "That a Christian Assembly or Congregation Has the Right and Power to Judge All Teaching and to Call, Appoint, and Dismiss Teachers, Established and Proven by Scripture."[74] Here he drew upon the teaching about the priesthood of all believers. In 1523 Luther also supported the right of local congregations to manage their finances and property, including the payment of their own pastors and care for the poor.[75] Later, in September of 1525, however, he changed his position on this matter in order to support a Reformation from above, one with the centralized authoritarian visitation system supported by politically backed "visitors."[76] As Appold summarizes, what happened in Wittenberg "would become the pattern throughout the German territories as the Reformation advanced: princes took charge of the reform process and used it to consolidate their authority over their subjects."[77] With Reformers like Luther, the Reformation from below and from the middle of society had become one from above.

4.4 DISCIPLINARY CONSOLIDATION

As the Wittenberg Reformation began to take shape in the 1520s, the secular authority effectively controlled the inner and the outer order of the church, including the pastorate, preaching, doctrine, counseling, and the administration of the sacraments. This control of the churches was carried out through the institution of visitation by the visitors who replaced the oversight of the bishops. These visitors were not coming to the churches to visit the congregation and the pastors (in the sense of this word "visitor" today) but to control them.[78]

Thomas A. Brady has summarized these reforms as they took shape in the 1520s and 1530s: "Protestant princes and magistrates suppressed Catholic worship, expelled pastors, dissolved the convents, and redirected ecclesiastical properties to other purposes—public or dynastic." They also "established evangelical (Lutheran) doctrine as the sole norm of preaching and practice" and "introduced reformed orders of worship and forbade all others." With this they "began to form an official regime for their churches" and replaced ecclesiastical institutions with territorial ones, such as marriage courts, poor relief, and schools. They also "encouraged the recruitment, training, ordination, and installation of a married evangelical clergy." In addition to this, they "crippled the Imperial Chamber Court, the only significant judicial instance from which the Catholics could seek redress and restoration."[79]

At the time, these reforms were illegal. For this reason the princes and magistrates "required divine authority for them, which the evangelical clergy happily supplied, as they placed themselves almost without reservation under princely and magisterial authority. In return, the rulers repressed all rivals—Catholics, Anabaptists, Zwinglians."[80] The anticlerical movement of the Reformation, which originally sought to transform the clergy, was thus reversed. As Oberman explains,

> Around the time of the reformation, anticlericalism's programmatic goal was to reform and discipline the clergy. In the post-reformation era we note the reversal of this tendency: now the clergy, as state-officials, turned their efforts more assertively than before to the problem of disciplining the laity; church and state cooperated to (re)form the laity into subjects. This gave rise to a new type of anticlericalism.[81]

Luther was one of the driving forces behind this reversal, and he was also quite proud of his achievement: "If I had never taught or done anything else than I had enhanced and illuminated secular rule and authority," he wrote in 1533, "this alone should deserve thanks." Indeed, "since the time of the apostles no doctor or writing, no theologian or lawyer has confirmed, instructed, and comforted secular authority more glorious and clearly than I was able to do through special divine grace."[82] He saw the secular authority as "God's fellow worker" (*cooperator dei*).[83]

While Luther was also critical of the princes and magistrates, he explicitly asked Elector John of Saxony to "supervise the reordering of parish life," as Hendrix remarks.[84] Luther encouraged a phasing in of the reforms and a systematic eradication of the older traditions with the help of political power. Rather than convincing people through theological argument and through debate on the basis of the Scriptures, rather than allowing the Holy Spirit to work on the hearts of the people, the ecclesial reforms were carried out on the basis of authoritarian power behind which stood the threat of violence.

As Heinz Schilling writes, in the Lutheran lands, "the powers of the local congregations were incorporated into the territorial bureaucracy, which allowed the state possibilities for influence and even control."[85] Luther encouraged this. On November 11, 1525, Luther wrote to Spalatin, "Our princes do not compel to faith and the gospel, but rather suppress external abominations." For example, they should suppress "manifest blasphemies of God's name."[86] This included the Catholic Mass. In Luther's sermon on November 27, 1524, he argued explicitly that the princes and magistrates should suppress the Mass. In all seriousness, he held this "abomination" to be worse than "manslaughter, theft, murder and adultery."[87] After these remarks he called upon the princes and magistrates to deal with this accordingly. In Luther's "On the Abomination of the Silent Mass" (1525) he also called for the celebration of the Mass to be punished by the secular authorities.[88]

Luther viewed errant church services as something to be controlled and corrected by the secular powers. As Armin Kohnle remarks, "Here one must ask themselves if the compulsion to the gospel, which Luther rejected, had not indeed been introduced in a different way."[89] Luther emphasized, with regard to Müntzer and the Peasants' Revolt, that the worldly authority had the responsibility "to take action against the public preaching of false teaching," as Christoph Strohm remarks.[90] The term "inquisition" is even used in some of the official instructions for the politically backed visitors in Saxony. These inquisitors (or visitors) effectively brought about the Reformation from above by quite literally forcing people to implement the new theology and practice.[91]

There are also other letters from Luther that show a more critical evaluation of the mixture of the two regiments—for example, a letter to Daniel Greiser from October 22, 1543.[92] By the 1540s, however, the disciplinary consolidation had been established. Many people did welcome the reforms and were happy to have the new order established by force. Andrew Pettegree argues that as the Protestant reforms became institutionalized, the idea of "utter passivity" was probably not the "normative experience."[93] For many, however, the reforms must have amounted to religious coercion. Scribner claims that "the majority of the population of Reformation Europe probably received the new ideas as 'involuntary Protestants,' for whom such radical changes were brought about by state action."[94] While some Reformers, like Karlstadt, offered an alternative conception of the Reformation, one that allowed for more congregational control, the politically backed Reformers, like Luther, rejected this option.

In theory Luther did reject a "compulsion to the gospel." This is expressed, for example, in his treatise "Temporal Authority: To What Extent It Should Be Obeyed" from 1523. In "Temporal Authority" Luther explained that the temporal authority of government "has laws which extend no further than to life and property and external affairs on earth, for God cannot and will not permit anyone but himself to rule over the soul."[95] He claims that it should "be content to attend to its own affairs and let men believe this or that as they are able and willing, and constrain no one by force. For faith is a free act, to which no one can be forced."[96] This was, of course, fundamentally contradicted by his own endorsement of the Reformation from above and its disciplinary consolidation.

As to the ecclesial authority of priests and bishops, "it is not a matter of authority or power, but a service and an office, for they are neither higher nor better than other Christians." Luther holds that ecclesial "ruling is rather nothing more than the inculcating of God's word, by which they guide Christians and overcome heresy." Thus "Christians can be ruled by nothing except God's word, for Christians must be ruled in faith, not with outward works. Faith, however, can come through no word of man, but only through the word of God."[97] Thus "God has ordained two governments [*Regimente*]: the spiritual [*geystliche*] by which the Holy Spirit produces Christian and righteous people under Christ; and the temporal [*welltliche*], which restrains the un-Christian and wicked so that [. . .] they are obliged to keep still and to maintain outward peace."[98]

Later Luther developed the "three-estate doctrine" of the *ordo economicus* (the household and communal order), the *ordo politicus* (the political order) and the *ordo ecclesiasticus* (the ecclesial order), as he referred to them in 1539. His conception of a division of oversight and a division of power is expressed in this system. The household is viewed as the instance of production, while the state is viewed as the instance of protection. The church transcends these but is only one of the orders in God's three regiments. All three have the purpose of resisting sin and promoting righteousness. In this sense, they were intended to be a symbol of the heavenly kingdom.[99] Both the two-governments doctrine and the three-estate doctrine have a positive potential for interpretation, as they emphasize the separation between the religious and political realms. Luther's theological articulations of an idealized relationship between the political and ecclesial orders were written in a context that did not reflect them. Luther's letter to Spalatin, his sermon as cited above, and his "On the Abomination of the Silent Mass" are far more representative of what actually happened in the 1520s and 1530s under Luther's watchful eye.

Social discipline in the confessional contexts was not unique to the Protestant tradition. Among both Catholics and Protestants there was an "intensification of church discipline after the Reformation."[100] While the Anabaptists also encouraged church discipline, they were not politically backed, and thus the nature of this was entirely different. The Anabaptists could only excommunicate someone from fellowship (the "ban"). The program of Karlstadt and the idea of a congregational control of the churches was ultimately, with Luther and the princes, turned into an authoritarian Reformation from above. Similar regimes were established in many of the politically backed reforms, such as the one in Geneva with Calvin.

The Reformation would not have been possible without the support of political authorities. At the same time, however, there was significant popular support for the reforms. It probably would not have been possible to execute the reforms without this support. In this sense, an overemphasis of the princes' role in the Reformation does not capture the full picture. As Manfred Schulze remarks, "That 'the' princes saved the Reformation is just as true as the fact that they destroyed it."[101] The Reformation was adopted in many of the imperial cities with significant support from the urban population. In some cases, as in Strasbourg, the elite embraced the reforms only after the townspeople had done so.[102] Nevertheless, the princes and magistrates greatly influenced the reforms. On this issue Erwin Iserloh correctly writes that as the authorities took the Reformation into their hands, they used it for their own interests: "Since then we may speak of the princes' Reformation. Instead of a congregational Christianity, with the free choice of the pastor, came the church of the land."[103]

4.5 RELIGIOUS DISSENT AND PERSECUTION

While Luther endorsed the freedom of conscience theoretically, in practice he rejected it. Those who did not agree with the new program were silenced and persecuted. As the Reformation continued, theologians returned to this issue. Calvin, for example, addressed the freedom of the conscience in his famous *Institutes*. Regarding "human laws," Calvin wrote that "our consciences have not to do with men but with God only." Furthermore, Paul's command to obey the authorities (Rom 13) "does not at all teach that the laws enacted by them reach to the internal government of the soul," for Paul "everywhere proclaims that the worship of God, and the spiritual rule of living righteously, are superior to all the decrees of men." In this sense, "human laws, whether enacted by magistrates or by the Church, are necessary to be observed (I speak of such as are just and good), but do not therefore in themselves bind the conscience, because the whole necessity of observing them respects the general end, and consists not in the things commanded."[104]

Later, in the same chapter, when addressing the "liberty of conscience" of a Christian, he holds that the human laws are "not fixed and perpetual obligations to which we are astricted, but external rudiments for human infirmity, which, though we do not all need, we, however, all use, because we are bound to cherish mutual charity towards each other." In addition to the laws of the land, Calvin has social and moral customs in mind here. He draws his reader to the example of women and their head coverings. He writes, "Should a woman require to make such haste in assisting a neighbour that she has not time to cover her head, she sins not in running out with her head uncovered." These kinds of things are different than the laws, for "the custom and institutions of the country, in short, humanity and the rules of modesty itself, declare what is to be done or avoided." This does not mean, however, that disregarding them intentionally will go unpunished. In Calvin's mind, these too must be followed: "Here, if any error is committed through imprudence or forgetfulness, no crime is perpetrated; but if this is done from contempt, such contumacy must be disapproved." Here in this paragraph it is clear that Calvin does not think that each individual can choose what is right in his or her own eyes. He writes, "For what a seed-bed of quarrels will confusion in such matters be, if every one is allowed at pleasure to alter what pertains to common order? All will not be satisfied with the same course if matters, placed as it were on debateable ground, are left to the determination of individuals."[105]

Calvin's theory of social order was essentially a Christian theocracy, like that of Luther's conception of the unified and harmonious political and ecclesial order, a "Christian body," a *corpus christianum*. This is an understanding of a unified social order based upon the Christian religion and controlled by its principles, teachings, and Christian customs. It is precisely what Luther argued for in his "Address to the Christian Nobility." The teaching was a conception of society that factually excluded the Jews from participation based upon their religious difference.[106] Already in the early 1536 edition of Calvin's *Institutes*, which was accompanied with a dedication to the French king Francis I, Calvin essentially sanctioned political control of the church, or rather, as he calls it, "the duty of rightly establishing religion":

> [Civil government] prevents idolatry, sacrilege against God's name, blasphemies against his truth, and other public offenses against religion from arising and spreading among the people [. . .]. Let no man be disturbed that I now commit to civil government the duty of rightly establishing religion, which I seem above to have put outside of human decision. For, when I approve of a civil administration that aims to prevent the true religion which is contained in God's law from being openly and with public sacrilege violated and defiled with impunity, I do not here, any more than before, allow men to make laws according to their own decision concerning religion and the worship of God.[107]

In line with this development in his thought, Calvin's later work, the *Defense of Orthodox Faith against the Prodigious Errors of the Spaniard Michael Servetus* (1554), was essentially a justification of intolerance.[108] It was published a few months after the execution of the non-Trinitarian "heretic" Michel Servetus (1511–1553). In it Calvin "justifies magisterial action against heresy."[109]

The execution of Servetus demonstrates how the original intentions of Calvin's social and political order were to take shape in Geneva in Calvin's own lifetime. On Calvin's order Servetus was incarcerated after being seen in a church service. Two and a half months later, following a legal trial in which Calvin's secretary Nicolas de La Fontaine was leading the accusation against Servetus, he was executed. Marian Hillar describes that day in Geneva:

> No cruelty was spared on Servetus as his stake was made of bundles of fresh wood of the live oak still green, mixed with its branches still bearing leaves. On his head a straw crown was placed sprayed with sulfur. He was seated on a log, with his body chained to a post with an iron chain, his neck was bound with four or five turns of a thick rope. This way Servetus was being fried at a slow fire for about a half hour before he died. To his side were attached copies of his book which he sent "confidentially" to Calvin for "his fraternal opinion." A legend has it that when a strong wind blew and separated the flames, Servetus exclaimed: "Poor me who cannot finish my life in this fire! The two hundred crowns and the golden necklace that they took from me should suffice to buy sufficient wood to burn me miserably."[110]

Here reference is made to books that Servetus sent to Calvin that Calvin released for the prosecution of Servetus. As Christoph Strohm remarks, in Calvin's conflict with Servetus and also Jérôme-Hermès Bolsec, "it must be noted in all clarity that Calvin could not imagine any religious tolerance."[111] As Strohm shows, the sentences arguing for a certain degree of toleration in the early 1536 edition of the *Institutes* were cut out of the later editions of the work by Calvin.[112] He eliminated these old arguments for tolerance from his *magnum opus* as the Reformation gained ground against the Catholics. As Turchetti has documented, Calvin did not support religious tolerance.[113] The idea of a "freedom of conscience," as addressed above in his works, was a purely theoretical construct that had no practical meaning in Geneva.

4.6 THE COUNTERMOVEMENT OF TOLERANCE

Very early in the Reformation, Protestant Reformers began to call for tolerance of dissent. The movement toward localized control of religion is an analogous phenomenon that begins at the same time. The idea that religion should be something that is controlled locally, by the congregation and the individual conscience before God, was one of the basic demands of Karlstadt and the German peasants in the 1520s. The first article of "The Twelve Articles of the Upper Swabian Peasants" states, "First, it is our humble desire and request, and the intention and conviction of us all, that henceforth we want to have the full power for a whole congregation to select and elect its own pastor; and also the power to remove him, if he acts improperly (1 Timothy 3, Titus 1, Acts 14, Deuteronomy 17, Exodus 31, Deuteronomy 10, John 6, and Galatians 2)."[114] The peasants wanted the congregation to control the religion, not a higher authority outside of the community. This demand was fundamentally rejected in the Reformation from above with Luther and the other magisterial Reformers.

Against the politically backed Reformers, Sebastian Franck (1499– 1542) provided a case for tolerance for all people and also strongly challenged the idea that political power and religion should unite in order to enforce one version of the faith, as was the case at this time.[115] Another impressive example of the countermovement of tolerance is found in a very early tract titled "Whether Secular Government Has the Right to Wield the Sword in Matters of Faith." It was published in 1530 anonymously. The author was probably someone from Nuremberg. The author addresses the problem at the outset:

> There is simply no end to executions and banishments for reasons of faith. Lutheran governments will not tolerate Anabaptists or Sacramentarians. Zwinglian governments also refuse to tolerate Anabaptists. Then come the papists, who burn, hang, or banish evangelicals, Lutherans, Zwinglians, Anabaptists and everyone who is not of their faith. [. . .] But from those governments that are evangelical, Lutheran, Zwinglian, and claim to hear God's word, to follow it, and in no way to act contrary to it, [. . .] I would very much like to hear where they get the right to control faith either by executing those who do not wish to be of their faith or else by tearing them from property and goods, wife and children, and banishing them from the territory.[116]

Later in the argument the author makes the case against such authority:

> Nowhere does one find [in the New Testament] that if someone did not adhere to their doctrine and preaching but rather believed or taught some other faith, that they [the Christians] appealed to the secular government either to force such a person to accept their faith or else not to tolerate him. Nor does one find anywhere in the New Testament that any government that did this of its own accord was praised for it.[117]

The author claims that "it is clear that Christ does not wish the sword of the secular government to be used to root anything out of his kingdom, but wishes rather to do combat there solely by his word until the end of the world."[118] Scripture is cited to support the case:

> And before Pilate he said: "My kingdom is not of this world." [John 18:36] He also taught his disciples, saying: "The secular kings exercise

lordship and the mighty are called gracious lords. But ye shall not be so!" etc. [Luke 22:25-26] From this one sees how God wishes to have the two kingdoms distinguished from one another. And since Christ remains in his kingdom and lets the secular kingdom go its own way, even though he is far mightier than all emperors and kings, it is all the more proper that the secular government should take care of its own kingdom and not attempt to govern that which belongs to Christ.[119]

Here in 1530, only around fifteen years after the short Reformation began, the basic program of religious tolerance was being established with theological arguments. The author points out that religious coercion is a contradiction to Christian teaching and emphasizes the difference between the "city of God" and the "earthly city" (to use Augustine's famous terms). Similar arguments can be found among many Anabaptists.

Another major voice to call for religious tolerance at this time was Sebastian Castellio (1515–1563). Shortly after the publication of Calvin's *Defense of Orthodox Faith*, Castellio responded anonymously with his *Whether Heretics Should Be Persecuted?* (*De haereticis an sint persequendi*, 1554). He essentially called for the tolerance of disagreement in matters of faith. He also emphasized the difference between matters of faith and outward acts of crime. Calvin thought that the arguments opened the door to all kinds of heresies. Castellio worked as a pastor in Geneva with Calvin. He later moved to Basel, where he tried to implement his principles of tolerance.[120]

In imperial politics a degree of tolerance was reached in 1555 with the Peace of Augsburg. There the principle was accepted: *cuius regio, eius religio* (whose region/territory, his religion). This popular Latin description of the Peace of Augsburg is from 1586, from Joachim Stephan, a Greifswald professor of law.[121] The allowance for multiple confessional identities (Catholic and Lutheran) within the Holy Roman Empire was the beginning of a process of pluralization and religious tolerance. It was not, however, an embrace of religious tolerance in the sense of the coexistence of different religions in one social and political order. As the Lutheran–Roman Catholic Commission on Unity states regarding the Peace of Augsburg of 1555, "The princes and magistrates had the right to determine the religion of their subjects. If the prince changed his religion, the people living in the territory would also have to change theirs, except in the areas where bishops were princes (*geistliche Fürstentümer*). The subjects had the right to emigrate if they did not agree with the religion of the prince."[122] Heinz Schilling argues that with the Peace of Augsburg of 1555 there was no individual freedom of conscience. This was the case even if paragraph 24 guaranteed that one could leave the territory.[123] Indeed, the Peace of Augsburg led to a new "decisive integration" within the various territories. In terms of the political relationship between territories, it also led to a "rigid and partly aggressive differentiation."[124]

By 1600 this turned into a "confessional fundamentalism," which radicalized the differences and brought with it new political consequences.[125] Internally this led to a disciplinary consolidation and integration of the religious identity of the specific territory. Externally it led to an aggressive posture toward the other political orders with a religiously legitimized hostility. This eventually culminated in the Thirty Years' War (1618–1648).[126] The imperial endorsement of Lutheranism in 1555 provided the Lutherans with a new agenda to defend the imperial constitution and the status quo. According to Philip Benedict, many Lutherans then "worked to cast Calvinism as seditious," which in turn made the Lutherans themselves "more reluctant than the Reformed to advocate resistance."[127]

As Protestantism spread into the Kingdom of France and both persecution and iconoclasm advanced the conflict about religion, only a small minority considered the option of religious tolerance of both Catholicism and Protestantism. One example of this call for toleration is an anonymously published worked titled *Exhortation to the Princes and Lords of the King's Privy Council* from 1561.[128] In the *Exhortation* the author calls for the allowance of two churches in one political order.[129] As the conflict about religion in the Kingdom of France advanced into a war, in October of 1562, Castellio anonymously published *Advice to a Desolate France*.[130] He also argued that both sides should grant tolerance. He used the Bible in his argument and claimed that there was no scriptural evidence for forcing conscience. Indeed, even if there had been such evidence, Castellio makes it clear that Christians should follow the example of Christ.[131] Of course, neither Calvin nor the authorities in Geneva were happy to see this work, and they did their best to destroy it.[132] Calvin and his followers were frightened by the idea of toleration and rejected it with the strongest terms. This also had to do with their hopes of seeing the Protestant Reformation expand in France. In 1570 Théodore de Bèze (Calvin's successor) wrote, "Will we say that freedom of conscience is to be granted? Not at all if it has to do with a freedom according to which everyone may worship God as he pleases: this is nothing but a diabolic dogma [*Est enim hoc mere diabolicum dogma*]."[133]

What was only a theoretical idea in France became a reality in the Dutch Republic. After the Protestant reform theologies started to infiltrate the Low Countries, which were the most urbanized part of Europe in the early modern period, the Catholic ruler Philip II, the king of Spain, introduced new heresy laws. This in turn provoked Calvinist opposition. After Philip II reinforced his commitment to the antiheresy laws in disregard of the nobility in 1565, a group of nobles formed the League of Compromise in November 1565. The compromise sought to relax the laws against heresy. In April of 1566, four hundred nobles, many of whom were Protestants, issue a moderate Petition of Compromise. This was then followed by a new resurgence of Protestant activity, preaching, and iconoclasm. The Spanish king then sent ten thousand troops to suppress the reforms. They executed two nobles and over one thousand people. New taxation laws were also introduced, which encouraged further popular resistance to the Spanish authority in the Low Countries. All this supported the cause of the Protestant opposition, which ultimately prevailed in the formation of the Dutch Republic.[134]

The Union of Utrecht from 1579, which essentially became the constitution of the Dutch Republic (founded in 1581 with the Act of Abjuration), states in article 13 "that everyone in particular will remain free in his religion, and that no one will be persecuted or questioned because of his religion."[135] The significance of this sentence cannot be overemphasized. Here in the sixteenth century in a Protestant-dominated political order—following the Hungarian Protestant Edict of Torda (1568)—religious tolerance had officially become law. Various forms of Protestantism and also Judaism were tolerated in the republic. While Catholic churches and religious services were officially banned in the republic, Catholics could continue to worship privately—and they did. In fact, Catholics thrived in the new Dutch Republic and sometimes even had their own "schools and poor reliefs."[136] Although Catholics were officially banned from holding public office, many continued to do so in the republic. Furthermore, private institutions in the republic welcomed Christians of all confessions. The oath of loyalty had to do with resisting Spain, not Catholicism. For this reason, most of the northern Catholics eventually came to accept the new political order, which was dominated by Protestants. In the provision of a compromise, Catholic funeral services were even permitted in the Protestant churches, although they were not allowed to use "papist" rituals. Of course, some Catholics also left the new republic and went into exile.[137] Many of these returned later, however, attracted by an economic boom in the republic.

Especially in Holland, the political leaders helped the Catholics "to participate in an inclusive *corpus christianum*." In Haarlem the elites went so far as to promote a "civic symbolism that transcended religious divisions. Emblems on public buildings avoided confessional sensitivities, expressing instead very general Christian values." Most of this tolerance followed from "practical necessity" and was, indeed, simply building upon "religious accommodations found elsewhere in post-Reformation Europe."[138] In fact, as the new Calvinist Church attempted to institute its reforms and radical Calvinist discipline in the republic, this was met with strong resistance from many other Protestant groups. Against the background of the tradition of local autonomy, with a booming economy, high levels of immigration, and an explosion of urban growth, the "urban authorities were often more concerned with preserving peace in these rapidly changing communities than with imposing religious uniformity."[139]

This tradition was advanced at the Peace of Westphalia (1648). The treaty set the foundation for the modern political order of Europe in that it effectively affirmed the confederation of independent political bodies in cooperative relationships.[140] Although there were some exceptions and conditions added to it, it essentially built upon the Peace of Augsburg and granted the Calvinist branch of Protestantism the status of a legitimate religion along with the Lutheran branch and Catholicism. According to the new treaty, officially recognized religion that was practiced privately or publicly (*exercitium privatum vel publicum*) before 1624 could continue to be practiced even if the princes converted or changed the official state church. The princes could therefore no longer demand that everyone in their respective territory practice the religion that they followed (according to the older principle of *cuius regio, eius religio*). Their power, or "right," to institute the reforms (*ius reformandi*) was therefore limited. The freedom to emigrate (*ius emigrandi*), as established in Augsburg in 1555, was both affirmed and advanced. Now people also had the freedom to remain in the territory and could continue to practice their religion privately rather than being forced to leave. In this, the private practice of religion was guaranteed as well as the freedom of conscience (*libertas conscientiae*).[141] Indeed, these people should be "patiently tolerated":

> It has moreover been found good, that those of the Confession of Augsburg, who are subjects of the Catholics, and the Catholic subjects of the states of the Confession of Augsburg, who had not the public or private exercise of their religion [*publicum vel etiam privatum religionis suae exercitium*] in any time of the year 1624 and who after the publication

of the Peace shall profess and embrace a religion different from that of the lord of the territory, shall in consequence of the said Peace be patiently tolerated without any hindrance or impediment to attend their devotions in their houses and in private, with all liberty of conscience, and without any inquisition or trouble [*patienter tolerentur et conscientia libera domi devotioni suae sine inquisitione aut turbatione privatim vacare*], and even to assist in their neighborhood as often as they have a mind at the public exercise of their religion, or send their children to foreign schools of their religion, or have them instructed in their families by private masters; provided the said vassals and subjects do their duty in all other things, and hold themselves in due obedience and subjection without giving occasion to any disturbance or commotion.[142]

This was a major step since it secured the rights of individuals to practice a religion different from the politically established religion of the territory. Of course, the practice of persecuting religious minorities, including the Jews and many other groups within Protestantism, continued. In the American context, however, a new level of religious tolerance was reached in the Rhode Island Royal Charter of 1663. The colony, which was founded by Baptists and Quakers, was to make a place where no one "shall be any wise molested, punished, disquieted, or called in question, for any differences in opinion in matters of religion" and where everyone may "freely and fully have and enjoy his and their own judgments and consciences, in matters of religious concernments," only that they behave themselves "peaceably and quietly" and that they not use "this liberty to licentiousness and profaneness."[143]

In the British context, John Locke's *Letter Concerning Toleration* (1689) advanced the theory of tolerance that had already been developed in the sixteenth century by Protestants. This work from the Latitudinarian churchman was an "olympian essay."[144] In his subsequent letters, which were published in the 1690s (and the posthumous fourth letter published in 1706), Locke promoted a "new type of churchmanship which sought to seize the pastoral initiative in the aftermath of the Act of Toleration [1689]."[145] With the Dutch Protestant invasion of England in 1688–1689, the Glorious Revolution brought about an overthrow of the Catholic monarchy and the establishment of a Protestant one. This revolution was essentially the creation of a new political order in England. The revolutionaries "*created* a new kind of modern state. It was that new state that has proved so influential in shaping the modern world."[146] With Locke's ideas regarding tolerance in mind, they ultimately "sought to promote a religiously tolerant society."[147] The Act of Toleration was precisely the result of this impulse.

It established the toleration of dissenting Protestant groups, such as the Presbyterians, Quakers, Baptists, and Congregationalists.

Locke's first letter had been written before this, however, and in Latin. It was published in Holland in 1685 and was written in the wake of the French king Louis XVI's annulment of the Edict of Nantes that same year. The edict had permitted the toleration of the Calvinist Protestants in the French kingdom. In this context, and with view to the situation in England as well, Locke argued for toleration in his first letter:

> If any person err from the right way, it is his own misfortune, no injury to you; nor therefore are you to punish him in the things of this life because you suppose he will be miserable in that which is to come. [...] Nobody, therefore, neither single persons nor churches, indeed, not even commonwealths, have any just title to invade the civil rights and worldly goods of each other upon pretence of religion. [...] No peace and security, and not even common friendship, can ever be established or preserved among people, so long as this opinion prevails "that dominion is founded in grace, and that religion is to be propagated by force of arms."[148]

Locke rejected with perfect clarity the claim that force in matters of religion could ever lead to peace among peoples. These movements toward tolerance in the religious history of the West after the Reformation were confirmed in the United States of America. The First Amendment of the Bill of Rights (ratified in 1791) states, "Congress shall make no law respecting an establishment of religion, or prohibiting the free exercise thereof; or abridging the freedom of speech, or of the press; or the right of the people peaceably to assemble, and to petition the Government for a redress of grievances." All the amendments were constructed to restrict the abuse of power. The anonymous Nuremberger of 1530 would have certainly been proud to see that his moral and spiritual intuitions were reflected in the government of these colonies thousands of miles away.

This was a continuation of the traditions in Europe, but it was also different in a fundamental way. In the European context, powerful authorities made small concessions for liberty. In the American context, free citizens, who had militarily overthrown despotism, instituted the control of power. As James Madison remarked, "In Europe, charters of liberty have been granted by power. America has set the example and France has followed it, of charters of power granted by liberty." As he continues, "We look back already with astonishment at the daring outrages committed by despotism on the reason and the rights of man;

We look forward with joy, to the period, when it shall be despoiled of all its usurpations and bound forever in the chains with which it had loaded its miserable victims."[149]

A new interpretation of this old theme was provided much later, in the twentieth century. With view to the horrors of modern European fascisms and totalitarianisms, Karl Popper emphasized the same theme in 1945. He was careful to qualify the idea, however, as he articulated what he called the "*paradox of tolerance.*" He writes, "Unlimited tolerance must lead to the disappearance of tolerance. If we extend unlimited tolerance even to those who are intolerant, if we are not prepared to defend a tolerant society against the onslaught of the intolerant, then the tolerant will be destroyed, and tolerance with them."[150] While Popper hoped that the radically intolerant could be met on the field of intellectual argument and that through this they could be held in check and would thus not need to be restrained by force, in certain cases he did claim that force was necessary. Regarding these extreme cases, he writes, "We should claim the *right* to suppress them if necessary even by force; for it may easily turn out that they are not prepared to meet us on the level of rational argument, but begin by denouncing all argument." Popper holds that "they may forbid their followers to listen to rational argument, because it is deceptive, and teach them to answer argument by the use of their fists or pistols. We should therefore claim, in the name of tolerance, the right not to tolerate the intolerant."[151] Of course, it is important to remember that the "intolerant" here are those who are essentially calling their followers to use violence against those who disagree with them.

The emergence of modern tolerance is one of the great achievements of Western civilization. The Reformation both encouraged this movement and resisted it. With the unification of political and religious authority in the Protestant territories, regimes of intolerance and persecution were established. Both Luther and Calvin emphasized the fact that faith cannot be coerced. Both of them, however, also contradicted this teaching with their actions. By the 1520s a countermovement of tolerance had already begun among many Protestants who drew upon the New Testament in their arguments. They claimed that intolerance conflicted with the Christian faith. Eventually their arguments were heard and accepted, and the countermovement prevailed in the West. This happened especially in places that were influenced by congregational and egalitarian impulses. It was the Reformation from below, not the one from above, that gave us religious tolerance.

«5»

MODERNITY, DEMOCRACY, CAPITALISM, AND SECULARISM

The Reformation's influence on the emergence of modernity, democracy, capitalism, and secularism is a major question that has been discussed in various fields of study since the nineteenth century. The interplay between religious beliefs and practices, on the one hand, and the cultural, social, and political realms of human life, on the other, has been analyzed from two extremes. On the one extreme, religion is the "unmoved mover" that is responsible for everything because it influences and determines everything. Culture, society, and politics then appear, in this paradigm, as passive instances of the more fundamental religious impulses. On the other extreme, religion is the purely passive instance, a mere product of cultural, social, political, or even biological phenomena. Standing behind these two extremes are, generally speaking, a philosophy of idealism, on the one hand, and, on the other, one of naturalistic materialism. While this rough outline is indeed a generalization of a very diverse landscape of theoretical inquiry, it nevertheless helps to describe one of the important philosophical conflicts in the academic discussion about the legacy of the Reformation. In order to strike a balanced analysis of the relationship between the Reformation and the phenomena addressed above, one must ponder the arguments on both sides and follow the evidence where it leads.

The need for a balanced analysis is especially evident when considering the controversial issues of modernity, democracy, capitalism, and secularism. Each of these terms represent broad subject areas that have long traditions of conflicting interpretation. In this chapter the relationship between the Reformation and these subject areas will be analyzed from different perspectives. An account of the Reformation's contribution will be presented that attempts to walk the fine line between the two extremes of interpretation. In this, the unique contribution of the Reformation can be appreciated in its true contours and not exaggerated. The Reformation was a significant part of a multidimensional process of dynamic cultural, social, and political transformation in the early modern period. In the history of the Reformation and the post-Reformation era, one can see that religion matters and that ideas have consequences. At the same time, in many cases the religious impulses were building upon older cultural, social, and political traditions.

5.1 THE REFORMATION AND MODERNITY

One of the major issues of historical research with regard to the Reformation and post-Reformation era of the sixteenth, seventeenth, and eighteenth centuries is the question about the influence of confessional regimes on the development of the cultural, social, and political mentalities of Western "modernity." The term "modernity" must be one of the most contested terms in modern intellectual history. It can be understood in at least two ways: as a historical epoch, and as a general agenda of liberalizing reform. The term "modernity" is sometimes used in the plural (modernities) in contemporary literature in order to emphasize the diversity of modernizing processes in different cultural and social contexts. In the singular sense, however, it usually refers to the general cultural, social, and political transition from the feudal Middle Ages to the period of history that came after it: the modern age. Modernity cannot be understood in a one-dimensional sense as an entirely positive era of human history. It brought about both positive and negative consequences. As a "general agenda of liberalizing reform," the concept of modernity is a collective term for the ideals of tolerance, democratic political order, egalitarianism, rule of law, freedom of movement, free trade, historical-critical research, individualism, and technological advances in medicine and science. While all these ideals were closely related to the Enlightenment of the eighteenth and nineteenth centuries, their roots are much older. By the end of the eighteenth century, the core principles of this agenda of modern reform, in different versions and interpretations (and still with many contradictions,[1] such as slavery and colonialism), had become established as an ideal in much of the Western world, and especially among many Protestants. In this chapter this general liberalizing agenda of modernity will be called "modern reforms" (what Ernst Troeltsch calls the "modern world").

The anti- or postmodern movements of the twentieth century are all a part of the historical epoch of modernity. Fascism, for example, is clearly a modern phenomenon. At the same time, however, many of these anti- or postmodern movements also tried to overturn the modern reforms. They were both in it and against it. For this reason they often adopted a critical posture toward the concept itself. In the radical political agenda of modern totalitarianism and fascism in the twentieth century, the critique of the modern reforms led to a rejection of the liberal political order, an overturning of the rule of law, a rejection of individualism, and the freedom of the press. Modern reforms, with all their diversity and tension, should not be conflated with the antimodern phenomena. These phenomena were a part of the historical epoch of modernity, but they opposed much of the general liberalizing agenda as it had advanced in the eighteenth and nineteenth centuries.[2]

Max Weber and Troeltsch both emphasized the uniqueness of the Protestant Reformation in this process of reform from the early modern period to the modern era. The idea that confessional systems (from the sixteenth century onward) influenced cultural, social, and political development is discussed in historical literature under the broad "theory of confessionalization." This theory was developed by Heinz Schilling and Wolfgang Reinhard in the 1970s and 1980s.[3] They drew upon the concepts of Ernst Walter Zeeden.[4] All these paradigms are, however, deeply related to Weber and Troeltsch's conception of the relationship of Protestantism and modernity. The process of confessionalization was closely related to the disciplinary consolidation of the Reformation in specific territorial regimes. This was enacted in a dynamic process of disciplinary control and reciprocal self-adjustment. The process was realized in the ecclesial realm through the visitation system, and in cultural, social, and political discipline.[5] Much of the literature on the subject continues to endorse some of the central claims of the theory of confessionalization. It is often held that the Protestant traditions drove forward these reforms even if they were not their sole progenitor. This is supported with evidence of book culture, literacy levels, and various statistical records of confessional differences in the realms of labor and society, as well as political sentiment, legal cultures of law and order, and egalitarian mentalities.

On the other hand, some surprising counterexamples have also been highlighted to show how some Protestant cultures—especially from the traditions of the Reformation from above—were very slow to introduce many of the modern reforms. A good example of this is Lutheran

Mecklenburg. It was a feudal order until the end of World War I in 1918, when both feudalism and the monarchy were brought to their final end in German history.[6] While the Reformation from above reinforced many sociopolitical hierarchies, the Reformation from below challenged them. These two contradictory aspects of the Reformation uniquely contributed to the modern reforms. A critical stage in the emergence of the modern reforms was the fundamental break with the authoritarianism of the papal order and the two-estate system of priesthood and laity. Another critical stage was the transformation of the feudal order itself. The Reformation from above clearly broke with the Roman hierarchy and rejected the two-estate system, while the Reformation from below contributed to the transformation of the feudal order.

The relationship between Protestantism and the modern world was one of the central questions that Troeltsch addressed. He emphasized a distinction between an older form of Protestantism that was authoritarian and a later form of Protestantism that was more focused on the individual. This later form contributed to the emergence of the modern individual in the Western world. At the same time, however, Troeltsch claimed that the modern world, in its political and social orders, emerged in many regards independently of Protestantism.[7] Protestantism, as Troeltsch argued, "often greatly and decisively encouraged the emergence of the modern world"; on the other hand, however, "in none of these areas is it simply their creator."[8]

The exclusivity of the claim that it was *only* Protestants who advanced the modern reforms has also been rightly overturned and rejected by many historians. Peter Canisius (1521–1597) claimed in 1576 that "the Catholics have so few universities, and such poor ones."[9] Through the work of the Jesuits, however, this quickly changed. Furthermore, Catholic educational reform, especially among Jansenists in France and in the Netherlands, is a clear example of Catholic modernization in post-Reformation Europe.[10] Other evidence, however, does support the theory that Protestantism uniquely advanced modernization. Christoph Strohm has analyzed the relationship between processes of confessionalization and the development of legal traditions in the Protestant territories. Strohm holds that jurisprudence was advanced and positively developed because of confessional competition. Whereas in many Protestant contexts jurisprudence was elevated in status, in many Catholic regions this development came later. The jurists of the Reformed and Lutheran Protestant traditions, who were often in constructive competition with one another because of their confessional differences, presumed that there was a consonance between the biblical religion and sound reason. They also emphasized the freedom of secular authority (often citing Rom 13).[11]

Philip Benedict does not see Calvinism as the causal force behind democracy or capitalism. Nevertheless, he holds that it "contributed powerfully to the spread of mass literacy and reinforcement of the individual conscience, those fundamental developments of the early modern centuries."[12] Among the Reformed churches of the sixteenth and seventeenth centuries, there was a clear emphasis on lay participation that worked to transform cultural norms, if only partially.[13] The new religious practice of piety in Reformed churches "created a new set of sensibilities over the long run." This led to a "distinctive religious culture."[14] Indeed, members must have felt like they were "living under a constant measure of surveillance by the church's elders." The core principle of church discipline was foundational in Reformed churches and "discipline truly was the sinews of the church."[15] This new religious culture certainly influenced the wider culture when it was dominated by the Protestants, even if it never transformed it entirely. In analysis of the period from 1517 to 1700, it is clear that Reformed churches often used the opportunities that they had to impose and to defend new ecclesial orders by force if necessary: "One cannot avoid concluding the Reformed embraced and acted upon such views more than any other confessional group."[16]

A recent presentation of the relationship of the Reformation to the modern Western world is found in Brad S. Gregory's *The Unintended Reformation*. The "unintended Reformation" is what he calls the secular "hyperpluralist" modern society of the contemporary Western world.[17] He sees this as having its primary roots in the Reformation-era developments that abandoned the relative unity of the Middle Ages and its unique ecclesial and political constitution.[18] He is also very skeptical about the future of the West, claiming that it is "failing."[19] By contrast, Troeltsch was more sensitive to the historical contingencies between the Reformation and the "modern world" (as he called it), and he focused on the discontinuity as well as the continuity. This is precisely the challenge that has been addressed in much of the literature on the relationship between the Reformation and the general liberalizing agenda of modernity. Gregory essentially adopts the old paradigm that says that the Reformation was, more or less, the sole progenitor of modernity. He then takes a completely different approach in his evaluation of modernity than that taken by the old paradigm. Rather than celebrating modernity as the child of the Reformation, he presents it as a failure. The problem with his theory is twofold: it has a monocausal account of the emergence of modernity, and a one-sided diagnosis of modernity. In both cases the issues are more complicated. For this reason it is important to emphasize the multidimensional and contingent nature of the historical emergence of modernity, and to provide a differentiated analysis of the contemporary Western world in its positive and problematic aspects.

The strongest argument that speaks for a substantial connection between Protestantism and the modern reforms is the simple fact that the modern reforms were fundamentally rooted in and advanced in the Protestant-dominated (and especially in the Reformation-from-below) countries. The various forms of Protestantism seem both to have inherited pre-1500 traditions of modern reform and also strongly encouraged these with new religious impulses and arguments. In this sense, the Reformation is rightly understood as one of the driving forces of modernization. This is not to assert that everything that emerged in modernity was good. It is also not to claim that Protestantism was the sole cause of all these developments. On the whole, however, it was Protestant-influenced countries that advanced the modern reforms in terms of political liberalism, capitalism, the separation of church and state, democracy, and individual freedoms.

This is not to claim that all Protestants supported the modern reforms. On the contrary, many Protestants radically rejected them. A good example of this is the Protestant ecclesial group in Nazi Germany called the German Christians. Many prominent Protestant theologians were also supportive of the general impulse of Nazi ideology and fascism.[20] German fascism was anti-Semitic and rejected the equality of all people, the freedom of the press, democracy, and the separation of powers in government. Another—and in this case, very different—exception to the rule is modern Protestant fundamentalism, which has a long prehistory in Protestantism. Protestant fundamentalism challenged, and continues to challenge, the modern reforms in a few specific areas: in the realms of science (Bible-as-science-book theory),[21] historical-critical research of the Bible, and the treatment of women (by excluding women from leading roles in ministry).[22] Of course, prominent evangelical theologians have also been working toward reform in all these areas.[23] The evangelical theologian Stanley J. Grenz, for example, started to call for women in ministry in the 1990s.[24]

In countries that were historically dominated by the Protestant traditions (like Germany, the Netherlands, the United Kingdom, and the

United States), or a very strong Enlightenment-oriented anticlericalism (like France), many Catholics and Catholic institutions (and even some individual Catholic congregations) embraced the modern reforms in the second half of the twentieth century. Historically, however, the Catholic Church largely supported fascism and resisted democracy. Pope Pius XI, for example, saw fascism as an ally in the struggle for "the establishment of an anti-liberal and anti-socialist, authoritarian and hierarchical State."[25] While the history of Catholic anti-Semitism in the twentieth century is well-known,[26] the local histories of this period are still being written, such as the history of the profascist British Catholics.[27]

Much has changed since the military defeat of fascism in Europe. In the second half of the twentieth century, the Catholic Church "was able to radically change its position and become a strong defender of the democratic form of government."[28] Many Western Catholics also turned away from the Catholic Church's conservative teachings on cultural and social issues in the twentieth century. In 1960, for the first time in American history, a Catholic, John F. Kennedy, was elected president of the United States of America. During the campaign, he explicitly affirmed the American tradition of the separation of church and state. In a speech he claimed, "I am not the Catholic candidate for President. I am the Democratic Party's candidate for President who happens also to be Catholic. I do not speak for my church on public matters—and the church does not speak for me."[29] While the Catholic Church continues to oppose the equality of women (by excluding women from leading roles in ministry), many Catholics in the Western world do not agree with the Catholic Church's teaching on this issue.[30]

It is important to remember that many Jews and Catholics also supported the modern reforms.[31] One of the classic examples of a Catholic contribution to modernization is the new "right of the peoples" (*ius gentium*) that was developed at the School of Salamanca in Spain with Francisco de Vitoria (1480–1546) and Francisco Suárez (1548–1617) under the "burdens of empire."[32] Both of these Catholic scholars contributed to the emergence of modern international law. The Protestant anti-Catholic polemic in the nineteenth and twentieth centuries actually contributed to the Catholic aversion toward modernity.[33] This polemic overlooked the fact that there have always been various streams of thought within Catholicism. In many cases, modern reforms have not been accepted in Rome. In other cases, however, they have been adopted—for example, at the Second Vatican Council.

The modern reforms did not emerge in a steady and upward-moving linear process. Over the course of modern history, there have been many setbacks and violent reversals. The rise of fascism in the twentieth century is the most obvious example of regressive development. The modern reforms also did not come from one source in the Western world. Many different religious, cultural, social, economic, and political forces drove them forward. In terms of the religious impetus, the Reformation's annulment of the two-estate system clearly promoted the movement toward modern society. The emphasis on the individual's immediate relationship to God (without ecclesial mediation) also raised the status of the individual and the individual's conscience. This emphasis on the freedom of the conscience was built upon by Protestants in later generations.

The traditions of the Reformation from below encouraged the modern reforms by promoting egalitarianism (the teaching about the priesthood of all believers) and by transforming the authority structure with a new focus on textual (biblical) authority (rather than personal authority). With a view to the American context, the emphasis on scriptural authority also contributed to the democratization of American Christianity. In many of the Protestant churches of the American context (such as the Baptists and the Methodists and many others), the laity acquired greater power and influence that the Scriptures could be read and proclaimed by anyone. This was, in many regards, the realization of the original program of reform with Karlstadt and the early Luther: a church of the laity for the laity.[34]

All these theological impulses of the Reformation worked to transform society and politics in the modern period. Even these, however, cannot be evaluated one dimensionally. As is well-known, modern Protestant fundamentalism is built upon, more than anything else, a modern biblicism. Modern biblicism is essentially a view of the Bible as a modern science book or a modern history book. While many factors contributed to the emergence of modern Protestant biblicism, it cannot be fully understood without the Reformers' emphasis on biblical authority. Many steps were necessary before modern biblicism could emerge, most importantly Protestant scholasticism (seventeenth century), the scientific revolution (seventeenth and eighteenth century), commonsense realism philosophy and theology at Princeton (eighteenth and nineteenth centuries, especially Charles Hodge, 1797–1878), and the debate about Darwinian evolution (nineteenth century). In this regard, there is no simple direct link between the sixteenth-century *sola scriptura* and modern biblicism. The Bible could only be read as a modern science book after the emergence of modern science in the seventeenth and eighteenth centuries. The Reformers did, however, contribute to this development by asserting the unique authority of Scripture. The movement in this direction begins before them in the fourteenth and fifteenth centuries, as Aristotelian scholasticism lost its prominence in theology.[35] Today, many Evangelical theologians have come around to affirming that the Bible is the final authority *in matters of Christian doctrine*. In this they reject the claim that the Bible is to be understood like a modern science book. The Protestant emphasis on biblical authority is also related to the anticlericalism of the Reformation. This phenomenon of biblical anticlericalism (the Bible is the authority, not the pope or other authorities in the church) is itself closely related to the emergence of modern democracy.

5.2 THE REFORMATION AND DEMOCRACY

The democracy (rule of the people) of the ancient Greek city-states, like Athens, became the model form of government in the modern period, in contrast to ochlocracy (rule of the mob) and systems of oligarchy (rule of the few), such as aristocracy (rule of the *aristos*, "best," the nobility) and monarchy (rule of one). In the ancient democratic system of Athens, only men had the right to vote, there was no formal division of power (in judicial, legislative, and executive branches), and slavery was practiced. In these regards modern democracy reformed the ancient Greek model. In the eighteenth and nineteenth centuries, the ideal of democracy as the self-government of the people became the defining feature of modern Western political theory. In the Middle Ages and before, principles of democratic self-government were already practiced among an exclusive group, such as the electors (for example, Elector Frederick) of the imperial diet of the Holy Roman Empire, who elected the emperor.[36]

The ancient tradition of democratic government slowly took hold in the Latin West in the city-states and imperial cities of the late Middle Ages as they introduced concepts of citizenship, representation, and the rule of law. In these cities, traditions of protodemocracy became early modern democracy. In 1457, for example, Geneva's general council was established, which exercised control over the city and ultimately enabled the Reformation to take the city by storm. Calvin came to Geneva in 1536, was exiled thereafter for his reform agenda, and then returned in 1541. As Calvin promoted his reforms, waves of Protestant refugees came to the city, and the new Protestants quickly overtook the old Genevans in number. This worked to support Calvin's reforming agenda since the new

Protestants were integrated into the political order and eventually swung the balance of power into Calvin's favor.[37]

While Calvin's conception of political order (which took concrete form in Geneva in the 1540s) has often been presented as a direct forerunner of modern democracy, he actually built upon older traditions of democracy within the city. There are certainly many parallels that can be drawn between the political order of Geneva and modern democracy. This is especially the case when considering the traditions of law and order in Calvin's Geneva, and in Reformed Protestantism in general.[38] On the other hand, there are also many points of discontinuity. After Calvin gained power, the city became a disciplinarian order that did not permit dissent. The city also supported an ecclesial system which went against the idea of a democratically organized religious community. Not only did Calvin reject the teaching that all men are created equal, he also promoted a very authoritarian vision of society and church. In this regard, Calvinism seems to have been a step on the way toward modern democracy rather than the full realization of it.

In Calvin's Geneva the general council of the city was made up of all the male inhabitants of Geneva over the age of twenty. One of the government's councils, which was established in the early 1540s, was called the "Consistory." The consistory answered to the executive "Small Council" in the city government and was responsible for handling "all problems involving marriage, and, in general, to see to it that everyone in town lived in a truly Christian manner."[39] This entailed, if necessary, sentences of excommunication, which, of course, humiliated the person being excommunicated. In some cases the punishment led to banishment. Those that challenged this practice of excommunication by the city government called themselves the "Children of Geneva," while Calvin called these critics the "Libertines."[40] In 1555 the conflict escalated into a riot. The Libertines were then removed from public office, expelled from the city, or executed.[41] From this point on, Calvin's authority was no longer challenged in Geneva.

The influential successor of Calvin, Théodore de Bèze (1519–1605), promoted the aristocratic system against the democratic system of church governance. On November 13, 1571, Bèze wrote a letter to Zwingli's successor in Zurich, Heinrich Bullinger (1504–1575), where he refers to "the most troublesome and mutinous democracy" (*perturbatissimam et seditiosissimam democratiam*). This had implications for an understanding of political order as well, since these kinds of arguments could easily be used to delegitimize democracy. Bèze claimed in the same letter that the French Reformed churches in Geneva had retained the "aristocratic principle of the Consistory" (*aristocratiam Consistorii*).[42] As Philip Benedict writes, "It is clearly anachronistic to consider Calvin's theory of church government democratic. He himself labeled it aristocratic."[43] While the political order itself in Geneva was democratic, the ecclesial order behind it was aristocratic.

Of course, this particular issue of ecclesial order was one of the great debates among the Protestant churches. While independent congregationalists emphasized a more democratic system of church government, the Presbyterians and Lutherans held to a more centralized authoritarian system. The case of Geneva suggests that once the external social and political order adopted a democratic or representational framework, the internal religious communities could continue to practice religion with aristocratic systems of authority. These two systems of social organization could run parallel to one another while, in some regards, contradicting one another.

Strong impulses toward the development of modern democracy can be found among the independent Reformers and the rebellious peasants, farmers, and commoners of the Reformation.[44] They promoted egalitarian thought in church and society and were critical of the aristocratic system. They called for the improvement of their social standing by providing compelling theological arguments. Fundamental legal arguments on the basis of natural law can also be identified in their questioning of the philosophical, theological, and legal legitimacy of the feudal system. The significance of this argumentation would be realized in the constitutional theory of law that emerged a century later across the English Channel.

It is one of the great ironies of history that the princes and magistrates unknowingly supported the democratic impulse in the early modern period. This was a consequence of their attempt to stop the peasants' rebellions. As the peasants began to protest, the princes and magistrates required the peasants to organize representative bodies by which their demands could be communicated. While the princes did this in order to suppress the reforms (by diffusing the insurrections through bureaucratic consultations), the process itself ultimately advanced the principle of popular representation among the common people. It encouraged the common people to believe that they had a right to be heard and represented. Of course, this was something that they also believed on theological grounds. These dynamics, which mutually reinforced one another, contributed to the emergence of representative government.[45]

The Reformation was very influential in the imperial cities, which already embraced many protodemocratic or early modern democratic institutions. The Peasants' Revolt, which drew upon Protestant theology, was also a central driving force in the advance of the democratic tradition. Furthermore, the basic teaching about the priesthood of all believers encouraged the principles of democracy and worked against the two-estate system of social order. In addition to this, the challenge to clerical authority in the "long" and "short Reformation," and especially in the traditions of the Reformation from below, supported the democratic impulse by shifting authority away from a centralized instance. The emphasis on the authority of Scripture, as found in Karlstadt and Luther, is a critical example of this movement of the center of authority from the few to the many. The emphasis on the congregational control of the church, as promoted by Karlstadt and the early Luther, clearly promoted the democratic impulse of bottom-up authority structures. In all these regards, and in others, the Reformation advanced the impulses of democracy.

As Alan Frederick Hattersley has argued, "The modern democratic movement may be traced to the political and religious conflicts of the era of the Reformation."[46] He writes,

> The Reformation paved the way for democratic government in both Church and state. German Protestantism found its justification in the principle of the direct relationship of the individual believer, through faith, with God. The substitution of free enquiry and private judgment for ecclesiastical authority could not but promote individualism in every sphere of thought and action. The overthrow of authority led logically to the recognition of the sovereignty of the community in matters of faith. Moreover, the Reformers were impelled by a strong desire to restore the primitive organisation and arrangements of the Christian Church, and this organization had been democratic in spirit.[47]

The emphasis on religious freedom in the Reformation from below provided a critical support for the theme of political freedom. A particular theology uniquely supported the emergence of modern democratic thought. It was grounded in at least two foundational principles: the priesthood of all believers (which went together with the rejection of the mediation of grace through the priesthood and the church[48]) and the sole authority of Scripture. Both of these principles worked to reverse the top-down authority structure of Christendom into a bottom-up authority structure. For this reason, both of these teachings were radically reinterpreted from their original senses in the politically backed Reformation from above, which developed after Luther took up the cause of Elector Frederick.

The teaching about the priesthood of all believers encouraged an egalitarian and participatory impulse in Christianity. Kaufmann calls this a "Copernican revolution" in the history of Western religion. He also emphasized that it had significant political implications.[49] Indeed, "the most important condition for the success of the Reformation" was the new conception of the laity and the idea of the one Christian estate, which was a unifying concept brought against the *ancien régime.*[50] The idea of the priesthood of all believers was understood in the sixteenth century by theologians, jurists, and political authorities to be both a theological and a political concept. In some cases it even functioned as the basis for the justification of resistance to unjust authority. In this regard, it contributed to the "relativization of the estate society."[51] A strong cultural impulse that went together with this new definition of the priesthood was the challenge to the clerical class, which was widespread at the time of the Reformation.[52] The turn toward a church of the laity is found first in the short Reformation with Karlstadt in the spring of 1519.[53]

Very quickly after the Reformation began to take shape (and especially after the Peasants' Revolt), the politically backed Reformers developed a highly specialized clerical class of Christians. The church and state also became closely intertwined in the Protestant territories. Many of the Reformed churches across Europe in the sixteenth and seventeenth centuries, for example, were "increasingly reclericalized."[54] In this sense, the teaching about the priesthood of all believers was essentially rejected, or radically reinterpreted. This was not the case with Brother Andrew (Karlstadt), however. He promoted a congregational church structure and encouraged the egalitarian impulse that went with the teaching about the priesthood of all believers.[55]

Nevertheless, the politically backed Reformation did take a big step toward the ideal of equality between laity and clergy in its explicit rejection of the formal priesthood. With the negation of the two-level Christianity, a transformative process was initiated that had long-term consequences for the Western world.[56] The ideal of a priesthood of all believers in the church would continue to be debated and practiced in different ways long after the sixteenth century. Today the idea is widespread in many churches that all members can participate in the ministry of the church in one way or another. To a large degree, this is a result of the teaching about the priesthood of all believers.

In the American context, these principles could flourish according to their original intention. Especially in the British colonies in North America, congregationalism became the dominant form of ecclesial government in the emerging democratic society. The township politics of the American context, as is also found in some Swiss cantons in the early modern period, reflected this movement from the Protestant ecclesiology to modern democracy. Just as the ministers of the church are merely servants of the congregation, so also are the political leaders merely elected servants. In the old patriarchal, aristocratic, clique-governed authoritarian system (in both ecclesiology and politics), the people are ruled; in the new democratic system (in both ecclesiology and politics), the people are corulers.[57]

Another mutually reinforcing cultural dynamic between Protestantism and democracy can be seen in the interplay between philosophical thought and political thought. The democratic tradition emerging from Protestantism tended to welcome a stream of philosophical thought that reflected and reinforced its own principles of egalitarianism. In the history of the emergence of modern democracy, one of the many important moments is the formation of the American system of government. As the ideal of democracy and the theoretical basis for egalitarianism (which were both older than the eighteenth century) took a new concrete form in the late eighteenth and early nineteenth centuries in the American Enlightenment, a specific school of philosophy became very popular. In the middle of the debates about the nature of human understanding and the human capacity to know the external world, Thomas Reid (1710–1796) asserted that every person has a common sense by which that person can understand the world and appropriately function within it. This school of philosophy challenged the radical skepticism of David Hume (1711–1776).

The commonsense realism of Reid and his followers had strong support among many of the proponents of the new political order in America. This is especially the case with John Witherspoon (1723–1794), the Presbyterian who became president of the College of New Jersey in 1768 (later Princeton University). He promoted the commonsense thought at the college. Many of his students would later play an important role in the new political order, such as President James Madison and Vice President Aaron Burr. Witherspoon also supported American independence and served in the Continental Congress from 1776 to 1782. He had a considerable intellectual influence over the course of twenty-five years of teaching. Among his students were "13 college presidents, 114 clergymen, 6 members of the Continental Congress, 23 United States senators, 24 members of the House of Representatives, 13 governors, and 3 Supreme Court justices."[58] Benjamin Franklin and Thomas Jefferson were also deeply influenced by commonsense realism. Indeed, "there is a consensus of opinion among scholars that the Scottish philosophy of Common Sense had a crucial function in the establishing of 'the American mind.' "[59] For the critical decades in the emergence of the new political order, it obtained the status of the "official metaphysics of America."[60] This was the case not only at Princeton but also at Harvard, Yale, and Andover.

The legal scholar James Wilson (1742–1798) also supported the commonsense approach against Hume's skepticism. He held Hume's philosophy to be subversive in issues of liberty and human responsibility. For Wilson the emphasis on common sense in Reid's thought affirmed that everyone had basic moral capacities. This had an important political dimension in its interpretation. Wilson argued that this teaching was a foundation for the establishment of an egalitarian legal and political order in the new republic.[61] In the political system of American democracy, which became the model for the Western world, every individual person, regardless of their background, social status or education, shall be deemed capable, by virtue of their common sense, to make moral decisions, to act responsibly, and to participate in the self-government of the democratically organized political order. It is not surprising that the Protestant minds of America's Enlightenment would find this egalitarian impulse in philosophical discourse to be more attractive than the alternatives. It was a philosophy that fundamentally affirmed the idea of equality and self-government. It worked for both the academic elite and the common people. More than any other philosophy, commonsense realism fit in the priesthood of all believers.

While Reidian thought took hold in the egalitarian culture of America's new republic, in the German lands it "clashed with the rationalistic tenor of German philosophy, seeming to offer little to thinkers writing in polities with weak middling classes and entrenched hierarchies and lacking republican institutions and a common public sphere of social and political interaction."[62] Although the commonsense approach had less appeal in the homeland of the Reformation from above, the egalitarian impulse in American theology, philosophy, and government was actually building on something that the independent Reformers, like Karlstadt, the early Luther, and the peasants (and many others) rediscovered: the principle of equality and the priesthood of all believers. In this sense, there is most certainly a jagged line to be drawn from "Wittenberg to Washington."[63]

It is older than Wittenberg, however, and its various roots also go back to Gansfort in Groningen, Hus in Prague, Tauler in Strasbourg, Wycliffe in Oxford, and Waldo in Lyon. In the long run, the ecclesial and theological movements from below, the desire for a self-governing church, and the textually based and decentralized authority system of *sola scriptura* all encouraged the movement in the Latin West toward self-government in politics.

While the Reformation and Protestantism did contribute to the emergence of modern democracy, many other cultural, social, political, and economic phenomena also played major roles. This is seen especially in the fact that the movement toward democracy was already underway in the early modern semiautonomous or autonomous cities of Europe in the pre-Reformation era. The Reformation built on these older trends and thrust them forward with strong theological arguments.

5.3 PROTESTANTISM AND CAPITALISM

The Reformation is often associated with the prehistory of modern capitalist societies. The relationship between Protestantism (especially Calvinism) and capitalism has been discussed since Max Weber's thesis. It is still a popular point of discussion when addressing the relationship between the Reformation and the modern Western world.[64] As will be argued here, there is some truth to the original thesis, but it must be modified. Protestantism is best understood as one factor among many and not the sole driving force behind modern capitalism.

Rejecting the materialism of Karl Marx's *Capital*, Weber wrote *The Protestant Ethic and the Spirit of Capitalism*. He wanted to show that there were many different issues that influenced the rise of capitalism, especially religion and culture, the "spirit" (*Geist*). After the publication of Weber's essay in 1905, Troeltsch gave a lecture in 1906 at a gathering of German historians in Stuttgart in which he endorsed many of Weber's claims. Both Weber and Troeltsch saw the genealogical prehistory of capitalism in ascetic Calvinism. In the Calvinist tradition, Troeltsch identified a rationalization of life driven forward by religious impulses. This was built on a general desire to give glory to God in Christian work. Once this understanding of human life was secularized, as the argument goes, it led to an ethical *habitus* that exemplifies the ideal of selfless and tireless work.[65] Troeltsch emphasized, stronger than Weber, that modern capitalism (in the early twentieth century) contrasted with classical Calvinism. This is because the ascetic striving for profit for the glory of man is fundamentally different than an inner-worldly asceticism for the honor of God.[66]

In the secondary literature on Weber's thesis, it is often presented in terms that are too exacting. Many scholars end up missing the sense of general affinity that he was attempting to establish between the habits and mentalities of ascetic Protestantism and modern capitalism.[67] Furthermore, it is important to remember that both Weber and Troeltsch tried to show that the industrious spirit of capitalism could be adopted by other cultures that did not have any background in Protestantism. In the first chapter of his book ("Religious Affiliation and Social Stratification"), Weber even mentioned the fact that it was those wealthier cities—the ones that were striving for economic and political power—that often introduced the Reformation in the early sixteenth century. With remarks like these, he tried to prevent a simple reading of his thesis as though theology was the sole driver of the trends toward modern capitalism. Clearly these kinds of examples show that there were movements toward capitalism before the Reformation. Furthermore, both Weber and Troeltsch were aware of the potential problems with capitalism.

Some endorse Weber's thesis with little reservation. Thomas Nipperdey, for example, draws upon Weber and claims that "the modern world [...] has been more strongly influenced by Protestantism than by Catholicism. In societies of mixed denomination Protestants produce from their ranks a greater number of entrepreneurs and professors, and a greater number of people with the vision and ability to get things done."[68] Nipperdey adds, "Protestants are not as happy as Catholics."[69] Heinz Steinert, by contrast, is more critical of the old theory. He points to contradictions in Weber's thought and a list of problems in his methodology, including the general vagueness of the arguments. Steinert also claims that Weber presented a deeply skewed interpretation of the Puritans.[70] Others have challenged Weber's thesis by claiming that capitalism can already be found before the Reformation and thus before the "Protestant work ethic." It is, of course, true that there was capitalism in pre-Reformation Renaissance Italy. At the same time, however, the capitalistic developments in the early modern period and in the seventeenth and eighteenth centuries (in connection with the scientific revolution) in predominately Protestant lands were quantitatively and qualitatively unique in comparison to the pre-Reformation developments in Italy.[71]

Weber argued that Calvinistic Protestantism encouraged the preconditions for modern capitalism in that it fostered an ascetic lifestyle of self-control. One of the principal causes of this was the Calvinist doctrine of double predestination. More precisely, it had to do with the desire to confirm one's election or predestination with good works. The theory goes back to the Protestant dogmatic controversy about the *syllogismus practicus* (practical syllogism). While this terminology emerged in the seventeenth century, the theology behind it is older. The practical syllogism says that a Christian may gain a degree of certainty regarding his salvation because of his good works. Teachings from the New Testament were drawn upon to support this theology. For example, regarding the false prophets, Jesus taught in the Sermon on the Mount, "You will know them by their fruits" and "every good tree bears good fruit, but the bad tree bears bad fruit. A good tree cannot bear bad fruit, nor can a bad tree bear good fruit" (Matt 7:16-18). In Calvinistic traditions and in many nonconformist churches, an anchor point for this teaching in the Reformation era is found in Calvin's *Institutes*. There Calvin writes,

> When believers therefore feel their faith strengthened by a consciousness of integrity, and entertain sentiments of exultation, it is just because the fruits of their calling convince them that the Lord has admitted them to a place among his children. Accordingly, when Solomon says, "In the fear of the Lord is strong confidence," (Prov 14:26), and when the saints sometimes beseech the Lord to hear them, because they walked before his face in simplicity and integrity (Gen 24:10; 2 Kings 20:3), these expressions apply not to laying the foundation of a firm conscience, but are of force only when taken *a posteriori*. For there is no where such a fear of God as can give full security, and the saints are always conscious that any integrity which they may possess is mingled with many remains of the flesh.[72]

In this citation Calvin clearly affirms that "fruits" of the "calling" may be rightly understood as convincing believers of their status as the elect. Yet, as he emphasizes, this is something that must be understood after the fact, "*a posteriori*." Interestingly, here the French version does not have the Latin term but rather "*comme enseigne de la vocation de Dieu*," that is, "as a sign of the calling of God."[73] The popular German translation of the Latin from Otto Weber translates "*a posteriori*" here with "*Rückschluß*" — that is, "inference."[74] Thomas Norton's English translation from 1561 has not "taken *a posteriori*" but rather "taken of the ensuing effect."[75] However one may choose to translate it, Calvin is saying that the good works may be rightly understood as an evidence of one's election. He does not say, of course, that they are the *reason* for the election. They are simply evidence of it after the fact.

This theology is not only found with Calvin. The very influential Calvinistic Reformed Heidelberg Catechism of 1563 also deals with this theme. Here Christians are given this question and answer to think about:

Q. Since we have been delivered from our misery by grace through Christ without any merit of our own, why then should we do good works?

A. Because Christ, having redeemed us by his blood, is also restoring us by his Spirit into his image, so that with our whole lives we may show that we are thankful to God for his benefits, so that he may be praised through us, *so that we may be assured of our faith by its fruits*, and so that by our godly living our neighbors may be won over to Christ.[76]

Later at the Canons of Dort (1619) the Reformed Protestants continued to affirm this teaching. In article 12 concerning "The Assurance of Election," it states,

Assurance of their eternal and unchangeable election to salvation is given to the chosen in due time, though by various stages and in differing measure. Such assurance comes not by inquisitive searching into the hidden and deep things of God, but by noticing within themselves, with spiritual joy and holy delight, the unmistakable fruits of election pointed out in God's Word—such as a true faith in Christ, a childlike fear of God, a godly sorrow for their sins, a hunger and thirst for righteousness, and so on.[77]

It is often claimed that this suggested a *syllogismus mysticus*, a mystical syllogism. That is, within the believer a mystical experience provides assurance of salvation by "noticing within themselves . . . the unmistakable fruits of election." So also the Calvinistic Westminster Confession of Faith of 1647 teaches concerning "Good Works":

These good works, done in obedience to God's commandments, are the fruits and evidences of a true and lively faith and by them believers manifest their thankfulness, strengthen their assurance, edify their brethren, adorn the profession of the gospel, stop the mouths of the adversaries, and glorify God, whose workmanship they are, created in Christ Jesus thereunto, that, having their fruit unto holiness, they may have the end, eternal life.[78]

Max Weber claimed that this theological tradition within the Calvinistic Reformed teachings ultimately provided an impetus for an inner-worldly asceticism. It provided an occasion to view the acquisition of wealth as the fruit of one's election. He remarks on the Calvinist theology,

> Good works are indispensable as *signs* of election. They are technical means, but not ones that can be used to purchase salvation. Rather good works serve to banish the anxiety surrounding the question of one's salvation. In this sense they are occasionally openly described as "indispensable for salvation" or directly linked to the *possessio salutis* [possession of salvation]. At a practical level, this doctrine basically means that God helps those who help themselves. Thus, as it is also noted on occasion, the Calvinist *himself creates* his salvation. More correctly: the Calvinist creates for himself the *certainty* of his salvation. *Unlike* in Catholicism, however, the creation of this certainty *cannot* be built from a gradual accumulation of single, service-oriented good works. It is comprised instead of the *systematic self-control* necessary, in *every moment*, when the believer stands before the alternatives: Am I among the saved or among the damned?[79]

This comes right down to financial issues in Weber's analysis, for "the acquisition of wealth, when it was the *fruit* of work in a vocational calling" was viewed as "God's blessing."[80]

There is something alluring about Weber's thesis. It draws upon a deep level of religious psychology to help explain a social and economic reality. He is right, of course, to point out that modern capitalism emerged in those parts of the Western world that were influenced not primarily by Lutheranism or Catholicism but by a version of Reformed or Calvinistic Christianity. Indeed, it seems plausible that the different versions of Calvinistic theology, which encouraged Christians to look for the "fruits of election," played a part in supporting a more productive society and thus encouraged the development of modern capitalism. There were, of course, other things that also contributed to the emergence of modern capitalism, such as the scientific revolution and cultures of trade and discovery that tended to flourish on Atlantic coastlines.

When encountering the bare bones presentation of Weber's thesis, one might get the impression that Lutheranism was the religion of grace and leisure, while Calvinism was the religion of fear and trembling and work. It is true that Lutheranism did not endorse the doctrine of double predestination. Yet, at the same time, one does find a similar emphasis on good works in the key texts of Lutheranism. Early in the Reformation,

Luther asserted that indulgences were, among other things, a way of *avoiding* good works: "For indulgences are and may continue to be nothing other than the neglect of good works [...]."[81] Furthermore, article 6 ("The New Obedience") of the Lutheran Augsburg Confession from 1530 teaches that the Christian faith "must bring forth good fruit and good works." The theme emerges more than once in the confession. Also in article 20 ("Faith and Good Works"), they teach that a Christian "should and must do good works."[82]

It is important to remember that Weber's thesis is dealing with a psychological reading of the consequences of theology in society. Taken at face value, the teachings addressed above never *explicitly* encourage Christians to create their own certainty of salvation in good works. From Augsburg to Boston, it is God who does the saving work. The point that Weber makes is that implicit content of the teaching became explicit in application. If understood in this way, the thesis becomes more convincing.

One can also take a wider view of the matter, rather than simply focusing on the doctrine of predestination and its consequences. For example, it is plausible that the teaching about the priesthood of all believers in Protestantism (depending on the degree that it was actually implemented) and the related emphasis on the necessity of every Christian to read the Scriptures also had a positive impact on societies in terms of education and productivity. It is also possible that the Reformers' emphasis on the reform of society increased the productivity of society. The emphasis on the reform of society is expressed in Luther's early work "To the Christian Nobility of the German Nation Concerning the Reform of the Christian Estate" (1520). Here the emphasis on social reform comes together with a criticism of gluttony and drinking on saints' days. Luther condemns the festivals because the "average man incurs two material disadvantages from this practice. First he neglects his work and spends more money than he would otherwise spend. Second, he weakens his body and makes it less fit."[83] In the early Luther's call to reform, he also claims that "they would be doing something far better if they honored the saint by turning the saint's day into a working day."[84] In this manifesto of the Reformation, the importance of work and the importance of thriftiness were both emphasized.

The Wittenberg Ordinances of the Reformation also called for the closure of some houses of prostitution and taverns while prohibiting begging (for spiritual reasons or otherwise). Furthermore, the Reformation led to the closure of many monasteries. In all these regards, the order, level of education, and productivity of society would have been improved by these changes. The educated men and women of the monasteries would now rejoin society and contribute to its improvement, rather than living separate from it, praying for it, and holding private masses. In the Reformation the most educated class of people in society, the priests, would now be married. They would then spread their knowledge to not only the congregants but also their children. In the Protestant territories, the pastor's home became the model family for society. The kingdom of God, once separate, celibate, and sacred, had become incorporated, fruitful, and worldly.[85] As mentioned above, the theme of good works is also found in the Augsburg Confession in multiple places and also in the condemnation of errors. The Protestants of 1530 called their followers to do good works diligently and to attend to one's vocation. Such emphases in these important documents of the Reformation show how the impulse of religious reform in the Reformation era was deeply connected with social reform. All this would have had an effect on the productivity, orderliness, and thus, finally, the influence and power of a given society.

While Weber saw pietism as a weaker force in the rationalization of human life in comparison to classical Calvinistic Protestantism, pietism did contribute to this reform of society in some regards.[86] Philipp Jacob Spener's *Pia desideria* (1675) encouraged a religious reform that was de facto a social reform. As the subtitle reads in the English translation, "Heartfelt Desire for a God-Pleasing Reform of the True Evangelical Church." One of the central concerns of his pious reforms was the idea that individual character should be more strongly emphasized than it was in Lutheran orthodoxy. For this reason he criticized the hierarchy of the university system in Germany. The outward form was not enough for Spener. The faith must transform the Christian in all dimensions of his or her life. This program of pious reform certainly encouraged the movement toward individualization and a heightened sense of spiritual reflection and moral duty in those cultures that were influenced by it, such as Swabia in Germany.

Although many have sought to overturn Weber's thesis, there is simply too much evidence that speaks for a positive collaborative relationship between Protestantism, thriftiness, productivity, and a strong work ethic. In this regard, ascetic Protestantism certainly contributed to the birth of the modern economy of free capitalism. At the same time, many other issues were probably just as important. Some of these factors are the nature of the political organization of a territory, the degree of authoritarianism in a society, the level of the freedom of movement, the level of the political control of the economy, the rules regarding taxation, the means of transportation, and the level of general education. On this scale, the further a society is from premodern structures of feudalism, the closer it would be to Weber's ideal concept of capitalism.

Did Protestantism contribute to a separation of morality from the market? While a capitalistic market has its own rules and governing principles (such as supply and demand), Protestants often sought to influence the markets and the economy by making them more Christian. Cotton Mather, for example, used his devout Reformed Protestantism to criticize the dangers of wealth.[87] At the same time, Protestants did emphasize the high standing of nonclerical occupations as vocations that could be done in honor of God.

While Weber's thesis and the related "Weber industry" of secondary literature on it will continue to be debated, other issues have emerged in recent history that raise new questions about the relationship between religion and capitalism. An economic study from 2014 claims that there is a direct correlation between secularity and productivity. The less religious the U.S. state, the more productive its economy. This may be because "religion imposes opportunity costs in terms of time and resources that may otherwise have been devoted toward productive entrepreneurship." An example of this is that "time spent in church reduces time available for engaging in business activity." On the subjective level, however, "religion may create psychic costs to pursuing worldly gains rather than salvation in the beyond." Thus, "One possibility is that productive entrepreneurial activities are largely substitutes for religious ones while unproductive entrepreneurial activities are complementary."[88]

Weber and Troeltsch would not have been surprised by this report or the speculative conclusions. It confirms the basic impulse of their theory about the relationship between inner-worldly asceticism (which they connected to Calvinism) and productivity. The difference here is the nature of the contemporary asceticism. As the authors of the study suggest, the asceticism that they analyze seems to be too ascetic for religion itself.

In summary, it seems that neither the Marxist view, which emphasizes the determinative power of the economy, nor the opposite view, in which religion determines everything, are adequate to explain the relationship between religion and the economy.[89] There is evidence that the influence goes in both directions; that is, religion influences the economy and the economy influences religion. Weber himself suggests this at the conclusion of his book when he remarks that there are many approaches to this issue:

> it is not, of course, my intention here to set a one-sided spiritualistic analysis of the causes of culture and history in place of an equally one-sided 'materialistic' analysis. *Both are equally possible.* Historical truth, however, is served equally little if either of these analyses claims to be the conclusion of an investigation rather than its preparatory stage.[90]

Weber apparently thought that a variety of things, and not only Calvinistic Protestantism, contributed to the emergence of modern capitalism.

5.4 NOMINALISM, EMPIRICISM, DISENCHANTMENT, AND SECULARISM

The Reformation is sometimes presented as popularizing nominalism, encouraging empiricism, and leading ultimately to the disenchantment and secularization of the world with univocal metaphysics.[91] Intellectual trends leading to the emergence of modern science have often been linked to the Reformation era, and especially to John Calvin and the Reformed traditions.[92] In Calvin's commentary to Genesis 1:16, for example, he states, "Astronomy is not only pleasant, but also very useful to be known: it cannot be denied that this art unfolds the admirable wisdom of God [*negari non potest quin admirabilem Dei sapientiam explicet ars illa*]." He goes on to argue that "as ingenious men are to be honored who have expended useful labor on this subject, so they who have leisure and capacity ought not to neglect this kind of exercise."[93] In the same commentary, Calvin also claims that Moses was "educated in all the science of the Egyptians" and "was not ignorant of geometry."[94] Calvin saw natural science as God's gift to mankind; he described the human understanding of the natural world as imbued by the activity of the Holy Spirit.

This theology helped him provide a very positive account of science. This, in turn, had a significant impact on the relationship between Protestantism and the natural sciences in the early modern and modern period: "Calvin's view of creation gave a significant impulse to the development of the natural sciences, which offers an explanation for the high percentage of Calvinists among the members of the *Académie Française* in the seventeenth century."[95] Of course, through the seventeenth century, Lutherans and Calvinists had also challenged the findings of science, such as Copernicanism, by citing Scripture. Furthermore, many Catholics supported heliocentricism both before and after Galileo was condemned by the Catholic Church in 1633.[96] In many regards, however, Protestants were at the forefront of the scientific revolution. This is especially evident in the English context of the seventeenth and eighteenth centuries. In order to explain this, some have drawn attention to the view of nature in Protestant theology and have come to focus on the influence of nominalism.

Duns Scotus (ca. 1270–1308) claimed that there is a univocal (as opposed to equivocal or analogical) concept of "being" that applies to both God and all beings. This, his critics argue, put God and creation on an even playing field as the existence of God could be understood in the same way as the existence of creation. As the argument goes, Scotus' philosophy eliminated the necessity of thinking about God in the philosophical analysis of the world. At this point, as his critics argue, God and the science of God (theology) were essentially being extracted from the academy. The next step in the argument moves to William of Ockham. He rejected the realist philosophy of Aquinas and Aristotle (and Plato), according to which terms, or concepts, have a real reference point in reality, in the sense of an absolute standard.

To simplify this, consider these two statements:

1. John Wycliffe and Jan Hus are both "humans" because they both possess the universal standard of "humanness"—that is, the eternal form of the "human."
2. When we say that John Wycliffe and Jan Hus are both "human;" this is our way of saying that they are similar to one another. "Human" is just a concept, or a mental name (*nomen mentale*), we use for thinking about this. Thus, there is no eternal form of the "human."[97]

The first statement accords with the realist view of the world; the second accords with the nominalist approach. Taken together, as the critics sometimes claim, Scotus and Ockham mark the watershed point for the decline of the Christian intellectual tradition in the West. For while Scotus taught us how to think of being without God, Ockham taught us that we can understand things without reference to the unseen world of eternal forms. As the argument goes, shortly after these medieval philosophers, and with the support of the Reformation theologians who were influenced by them, a disenchanting empiricism and finally an atomistic atheism would take hold of the Western mind. What had begun as innocent philosophy ended in the black hole of naturalistic atheism.

It is certainly true that Scotus (the "subtle doctor") had exposed errors in scholasticism with his logical arguments. It is also true that Ockham weakened the scholastic method as a whole by showing the inadequacies of many philosophical arguments for doctrinal positions— and thus the necessity of scriptural authority in these matters. Luther was working in this tradition when he criticized the scholastic theology in his "Disputation against Scholastic Theology" (1517). Luther's rejection of scholastic theology in these theses may have been extreme in some ways, but most would agree, even today, with thesis 43, which states, "It is an error to say that no man can become a theologian without Aristotle."[98] The rejection of Aristotelian scholasticism led to a new critical intellectual analysis of the nature of theological doctrine as based upon the Scriptures. In this regard, the intellectual shift was actually a reaffirmation of a classic position among the church fathers, who held the Scriptures to be the supreme authority in doctrinal issues.

The claim that this new philosophical and theological challenge to scholastic theology ultimately led to secularism simplifies the emergence of modern science as a one-track development toward modern atheism. Much of this question goes back to debates in the second half of the twentieth century about the birth of experimental science and the modern self-asserting individual. Hans Blumenberg and Amos Funkenstein were two key figures in the development of these theories. Some of these debates have been revived and modified in contemporary literature. In 2008 Michael Allen Gillespie committed chapter 1 of his book *The Theological Origins of Modernity* to the subject "The Nominalist Revolution and the Origin of Modernity."[99] One of the problems with many of these narratives of the birth of modernity is the overemphasis on theological and philosophical issues. These intellectual issues are sometimes isolated from the many other issues that were also very influential in the emergence of modernity. One is left with the impression that theology and philosophy are the chief, or indeed, the exclusive, reasons for the inauguration of the modern era.

This is not to suggest that Scotus' understanding of being and Ockham's nominalism were not an important part of the broad narrative from the late Middle Ages to modernity. Scotus was an important figure in the emergence of modern philosophy leading to Kant.[100] While Scotus' ontology and Ockham's theory of predication echoed into modern philosophy, these philosophical debates were not the fulcrum point, or the uniquely determinative factor, that brought about the birth of the modern world. They were simply one part of a much larger development that leads to modernity.

This debate actually goes back to Max Weber's thesis about the disenchantment (*Entzauberung*) of the natural world. Weber developed this theory in his address "Science as a Vocation" (1917). His thesis is essentially the observation that the process of rationalization, scientific method, and calculation, or the scientific progress of discovery, slowly replaced a magical view of the world. In Weber's analysis, this process of scientific advance begins in antiquity. Of course, the scientific revolution of the seventeenth and eighteenth centuries marked a new stage of discovery. An early form of empiricism can be found, for example, in Francis Bacon's *Novum Organum* (1620). Bacon's work is a good example of the scientific method that replaced Aristotelian scholasticism.

The process of intellectualization, rationalization, and scientific advance in the occidental tradition has realized itself in many different streams of thought. One of these is contemporary scientism. This is a belief that natural empirical science can provide insights not only about the workings of nature but also about the very meaning of the world and human existence. Scientism is, however, only one specific stream or branch within the broader process of scientific intellectualization. It is not the only expression of this process of critical scientific inquiry. Scientism is also not the necessary fulfilment of scientific intellectualization. On this subject Weber wrote,

> The fate of an epoch which has eaten of the tree of knowledge is that it must know that we cannot learn the meaning of the world from the results of its analysis, be it ever so perfect; it must rather be in a position to create this meaning itself. It must recognize that general views of life and the universe can never be the products of increasing empirical knowledge, and that the highest ideals, which move us most forcefully, are always formed only in the struggle with other ideals which are just as sacred to others as ours are to us.[101]

Weber knew that the intellectual mastery of the natural world in science does not have the capability of explaining the "meaning of the world." Weber believed, following Nietzsche, that meaning had to be transposed onto the world through a creative intellectual process of combination and evaluation.[102] Weber read Nietzsche in the 1890s, adopted many of his ideas, and cited some of his works in his own writings (such as *On the Genealogy of Morality* and *Thus Spoke Zarathustra*).[103] Among others, Peter Walkenhorst has shown how Max Weber addressed, in a discussion about the German and Polish relationships in 1894 and 1895, the physical and psychological "race-differences" and even addressed the different "race-qualities."[104] Walkenhorst also reports on Weber's "social-Darwinist" view of the world.[105] With Weber's call to create meaning, his thinking represents a second stream of thought from the general process of scientific intellectualization, one that integrated Nietzsche's ideas with a naturalism that was common to the later nineteenth century after Darwin.

While Weber knew the limitations of the "tree of knowledge," he was not critical enough of the popular moods of late romanticism. Gottfried Wilhelm Leibniz, by contrast, shows us that the scientific method and rational thinking can be used in understanding the divinely given meaning of the world.[106] This tradition is the third stream of thought, the rational one, that emerged before and went through the broader process that Weber described. The process of scientific intellectualization, which is much older than the Middle Ages, had many outcomes in the modern Western world. One of these, the most coherent and logical one, rejects both the simplistic conclusions of scientism and the Nietzschean conclusions of late romanticism. There is a living tradition of scientific intellectualization that is heir to that great process that Weber described.[107] It is therefore untenable to suggest that this process was essentially or necessarily a development that led to atheistic scientism or the Nietzschean *Übermensch*. Both of these phenomena are unique developments that cannot be explained exclusively in terms of the history of scientific intellectualization.

Another issue in this subject area is the related decline of the sacramental view of the world. The sacramental understanding of the world was challenged in the Reformation. Robert W. Scribner has analyzed this issue in terms of popular belief. The Reformation entailed an eventual rejection of purgatory, "the cult of the saints, relics, pilgrimages, and numerous other popular practices associated with belief in the salvific value of good works." The reforms led to a new orientation in religious life and an "attack on the notion of a sacramental world."[108] Scribner sees this rejection of a sacramental view of the world as "perhaps the most important mental shift" in this new orientation as it took away the salvific dimension of good works in the natural world and thus only allowed for the transmission of divine grace from above. What is left is an "inner-worldly realm of purely human action in which acts of piety had no transcendental efficacy."[109]

Scribner sees a dramatic shift taking place in the Reformation: "Sacred places and objects were destroyed (the entire Reformation process can be seen as a massive destruction of symbolic capital), sacred persons, especially the saints, denigrated and demythologized, significant religious communities uprooted or dissolved."[110] The reform of the ordinary faith of the people was eventually carried out through generational transfer as a new generation grew up without knowledge of the "old religion."[111] Scribner holds that this probably took around seventy years. At the same time, however, many of the reforms took much longer. In this sense, the old sacramental view of the world was actually not abolished but rather only replaced with a less sacramental religion.[112]

In evaluation of this general rejection of a sacramental view of the world, whereby one could acquire divine grace through good works, one must be careful not to romanticize the medieval traditions of piety as an ideal form of religious experience for all times. In some regards the religious traditions of the Middle Ages were certainly beautiful and worthy of preservation. This is especially the case when it comes to the issue of religious art, such as altar pieces, paintings, and sacred chalices and architecture. The desire to beautify religious spaces in these ways with symbolic and aesthetically attractive imagery was one of the things that was truly honorable about the pre-Reformation religious traditions. Many Reformed churches and free churches, however, even with their austere style, have their own aesthetic appeal that communicates a deeper meaning and provides occasion for religious reflection. In another sense, however, the practice of indulgences, which theologians like Luther denigrated and demythologized, was deeply connected to these same sacramental traditions of the "old religion," as Scribner calls it.[113] The idea that divine grace could be earned through good works based upon human efforts, or the idea that it could be purchased through worldly means, must be viewed from a theological perspective, even today, as an unacceptable corruption of the Christian teachings about God's gift of divine grace apart from works.

Connected to this discussion about the rise of natural sciences and the desacralization of the world is another discourse about Protestantism and secularism. The Reformation is sometimes presented as the most important historical source of modern secularism. Christian Smith of Notre Dame University (Indiana, U.S.), for example, claims that "it appears that something about Protestantism per se contains the seeds of and fertilizer for secularization."[114] Indeed, "Protestantism seems to itself embody elements that spawn and promote secularization, its own destruction, and then later to 'infect' Catholic countries and cultures."[115] This idea can already be found among many Catholic criticisms of Protestantism in the nineteenth century in the debates about Enlightenment philosophy and its Protestant roots.[116]

Since the trends of secularization advanced in the second half of the twentieth century, many cultural critics and historians have attempted to locate the roots of modern secularism in the early modern period and in the Reformation. Especially since the mid- and later 1980s in the American and British context, the study of the emergence of secularism became very popular among many authors, including some theologians. The theme has generated a great deal of secondary literature. In some of this literature, the Reformation is presented as the key event that led to modern secularism. This view is, however, problematic because it simplifies the historical development of secularism. Attempting to root the development of modern secularism in the sixteenth century in this way overlooks the importance of the many contingent developments that were necessary for bringing about contemporary secularism. As Troeltsch emphasized, there is not a straight line from sixteenth-century Protestantism to the modern secular state.[117]

Many developments after the Reformation contributed to what might be called the prehistory of modern secularism. These developments cannot be presented as determined consequences of previous influences. In each case, a mixture of unique conditions joined together at the inception of the unique cultural movements. Isolating the Reformation as the supreme source of secularism runs the risk of overlooking the critical importance of cultural-revolutionary developments in the 1960s across the Western world, for instance. Such an assertion is also in danger of overlooking the important developments around 1900 with the birth of classic modernism and its sense of reserve about traditional religion and moral norms. The effects of World Wars I and II would also be overlooked. These wars destabilized the legitimacy of old authorities and orders and contributed to the transformation processes in the twentieth century. An isolation of the Reformation as the sole originator of secularism would also fail to recognize the significance of the Industrial Revolution in the nineteenth century and its destabilizing effect on traditional society and religion. The importance of the French Revolution and European Enlightenment in the eighteenth century, both of which challenged the old order of things, would also be neglected. With such an emphasis on the Reformation of the sixteenth century, the significance of seventeenth-century Hobbesianism would also be ignored, particularly the swell of atheism in the English upper class that followed Hobbes.[118]

While the Reformation had a profound effect on Europe, the birth of the modern world should not be seen as a necessary consequence of the Reformation in the sense of a "paternal relationship." As Thomas Nipperdey argues, this is because "every age helps to determine the next."[119] He rightly claims that only in "a second phase of Protestantism" was the "potential for modernization [. . .] actually realized" as "pre-modern elements of the world and of early Protestantism became weaker."[120] Here he is thinking about developments in the seventeenth and eighteenth centuries that went together with the rise of the Enlightenment. The second phase (or the third, for that matter) was not, however, a necessary—or teleological—progression from the first phase in the sense of being its fulfilment. There are many Protestants today who continue to live, with minor qualifications, in the religious world of the first phase of Protestantism, just as there are Catholics who continue to live in the religious world of pre–Vatican II Catholicism. Both second-phase Protestantism and Vatican II Catholicism were unique developments that emerged in response to later cultural and social trends that were unique to their times.

When conceptualizing the emergence of secularism in the sense of the decline of the relevance of religion and the church, it is helpful to think of it in four phases, as described by Hugh McLeod: (1) toleration of alternative forms of Christianity, in the Reformation and post-Reformation eras; (2) publication of anti-Christian ideas, from around the eighteenth century onward; (3) the separation of church and state, from around the late eighteenth century onward; (4) and then the twentieth-century phenomenon, the "gradual loosening of the ties between church and society."[121]

The Enlightenment of the eighteenth century is a critical period for charting many of the trends toward the dechristianization of society. The laws of separation between church and state in the late eighteenth century in America, France, and the Netherlands are also critical signposts.[122] At the same time, there are many examples of the revitalization of religion in these periods of history (Pietism, the Great Awakenings, revivalism, Methodism, etc.).[123]

Theories of secularization today are very diverse. Some hold—such as Callum Brown (for Scotland), Peter van Rooden (for the Netherlands) and Thomas Großbölting (for Germany)—that religion was still an essential part of society through the 1950s. According to these theories, the major shift toward a secular society is found not in the eighteenth century (and not in the sixteenth century) but rather in developments in the middle of the twentieth century, which begin to take effect in the 1960s and 1970s.[124] It is too simplistic to single out the Reformation in the complex and regionally specific history of modern secularism.

Furthermore, there are forms of secularism that should be welcomed, and that were positive moments in the Reformation. The Reformation desacralized indulgences and rejected the claim that grace can be acquired through the veneration of sacred objects and works. The Reformation eliminated the two-estate system with the ecclesiastical courts for clergy. Of course, the Reformation also desacralized the pope and the councils. No longer would they be held to be absolute authorities (as they were at the execution of Hus). Finally, it desacralized the priesthood itself in allowing the clergy to marry. In all these cases, the secularization that the Reformation brought was actually a positive development.

« 6 »

THE WESTERN WORLD TODAY

At the outset of this book and in the preceding chapter, the historical relationship between the Reformation and the Western world was addressed. In this chapter some of the major issues today in the Western world will be analyzed with regard to the contemporary debates about these matters and especially with a view to the broader discourse about the legacy of the Reformation. As will be demonstrated, many of the historical issues that were addressed in the previous chapters, especially regarding religious difference and tolerance, remain challenges for societies in the Western world today. This will be addressed below with regard to multiculturalism and Islam. Before this, however, the general discourse about the Western world today will be evaluated. As will be seen, the Reformation still plays a role in these conversations about the contemporary Western world.

In this chapter the basic diagnostic framework is guided by a differentiated analysis. The problematic issues and the real challenges are acknowledged together with the positive and hopeful signs. In this, a realistic evaluation of our situation is provided that is informed by historical comparisons.

6.1 THE WESTERN DECLINE NARRATIVE

The Reformation is sometimes drawn into grand narratives of decline. These narratives often end in very negative presentations of the modern Western world. This assessment of the dominant cultural, social, and political order of the West can be found with differing emphases in many contemporary authors and cultural critics.[1] Some of these authors see the birth of nominalism in the thirteenth century as the beginning of the decline. Others see the Reformation as the primary point of decline. In these narratives the decline essentially ends in secularism and in a contemporary pluralistic culture, which is in turn described in negative terms. In many cases the accounts of the modern world are very critical of modernity. For example, Robert B. Pippin writes, "Modernity promised us a culture of unintimidated, curious, rational, self-reliant individuals, and it produced . . . a herd society, a race of anxious, timid, conformist 'sheep,' and a culture of utter banality."[2] Typical of these accounts of modernity is a deep skepticism about any positive account of the post-Enlightenment developments in Western cultures.

These analyses of the contemporary cultural situation were influenced by both older antimodernism from the early twentieth century and newer postmodern philosophy from the second half of the twentieth century. Most of them, however, emerged in the post-1960s environment of British and American culture. Following the new wave of de-churchization in Western society in the 1960s and 1970s, the cultural critics provided long prehistories of the rise of secularism. These analyses of the modern Western world are, however, largely one dimensional; most of these authors have chosen to focus on the problems. A fairer analysis of the situation would have to incorporate both the positive and the negative aspects of modernity.

Their skepticism is, nevertheless, well founded in some regards. The strongest argument against a one-dimensional positive analysis of modernity can be made by simply pointing to the violence of the twentieth century. In this century the Soviet Union killed around 62 million people, China around 45 million, Nazi Germany around 21 million, Japan around 6 million, Cambodia around 2 million, Turkey around 2 million, and another one hundred regimes killed over 10 million people between them.[3] Judged on this human destruction in the twentieth century, we are living in the wake of perhaps the most violent century recorded in human history, and most certainly since the early modern period.

While state-organized killing, both on the battleground and on the home front, is the usual example of the decline of modernity, the eugenics movement in the United States, Scandinavia, Great Britain, Germany, and elsewhere is another shocking illustration of modern man.[4] As much as his sympathizers have tried, Charles Darwin (1809–1882) himself cannot be neatly separated from social Darwinism. Citing Darwin's *The Descent of Man* (1871), Diane B. Paul writes, "Darwin would always see continuous gradations 'between the highest men of the highest races and the lowest savages.'"[5] This was, of course, in continuity with Darwin's famous letter to Charles Lyell from 1859. Addressing human "intellectual power," Darwin wrote, "I can see no difficulty in the most intellectual individuals of a species being continually selected; and the intellect of the new species thus improved, aided probably by effects of inherited mental exercise. I look at this process as now going on with the races of man, the less intellectual races being exterminated."[6] As Paul summarizes, "It is no coincidence that [Francis] Galton, the founder of modern eugenics, was his [Darwin's] cousin—or that Leonard Darwin, President of the Eugenics Society in Britain in the 1910s and 1920s, was his son."[7]

Modern conceptions of human progress in the early twentieth century were linked with Darwinist theories. The eugenics movement published slogans on their posters such as "Some people are born to be a burden on the rest." Eugenics was so popular in Western nations that the ideologues of Nazi Germany put the words "We do not stand alone" on their propaganda posters for the new eugenics program in Germany in the 1930s. On the same posters were British, American, Scandinavian, Swiss, and Japanese flags. All these countries had either introduced forced sterilization or were in the process of legally implementing it.

The eugenics movement was very much a part of modernity. It was also in part linked to the modern reforms addressed above. This is especially the case with view to the idea of human liberation. The eugenics movement sought to improve humanity through naturalistic means, to free it from those who were deemed to be a "burden on the rest." In this, however, it was also a fundamental rejection of the modern reforms that emphasized human equality, dignity, and sympathy.[8] The modern eugenics movement is best understood as a secular, naturalistic, scientific, ideological corruption of the modern agenda of reform. The eugenics movement was also a fundamental rejection of the Christian teaching about caring for the weak, poor, sick, and vulnerable.

Were the modern reforms, as addressed in the previous chapter, brought to their full manifestation in the brutality of the twentieth century? To reduce modernity to dictatorships, mass murder, nationalism, racism, and the eugenics movement is to overlook the fact that many of the dictators and ideologues of the twentieth century were themselves attempting to overturn the modern reforms of the seventeenth, eighteenth and nineteenth centuries (such as human equality, freedom of the press, the rule of law, and democracy). It would be reductionist to claim that the evils of the twentieth century represent the essence of modernity. To address the failures of the modern period alone is to say too little.

Another dimension of many contemporary Western decline narratives is the general analysis of modern philosophy and, ultimately, the rejection of it. For many critical intellectuals today, modern philosophy is a corruption of the true Christian tradition. Many of these critics suggest that it should be rejected in favor of premodern philosophies. Yet can some of modern philosophy also be understood as a unique unfolding of the truth in new modes of expression? Are there places where the "spermatic word" (*spermatikos logos*) can be identified, as Justin Martyr believed? With this term he refers to fragments of the truth spread around in the best intellectual traditions. In this sense, the truth can be articulated in different ways.

Pope John XXIII encouraged the church in this direction when he emphasized that "the deposit of the faith [*depositum fidei*] is one thing [. . .], the way it is expressed is another."[9] So also John Paul II in *Ut unum sint*, "the expression of truth can take different forms. The renewal of these forms of expression becomes necessary for the sake of transmitting to the people of today the Gospel message in its unchanging meaning."[10]

Both the total embrace of the thought of the modern period—as if it were, with all its tensions and diversity, a sealed package or "essence" to be accepted or rejected—and the total dismissal of modern philosophy appear to be insufficient responses. These approaches also overlook the hermeneutic assignment that the popes addressed. A middle path in this case is a differentiated analysis that seeks to identify the points of strength in modern thought and, at the same time, address its weaknesses.

While there is a time for criticism, there is also a time for praise. It is important that the diagnosis of modernity does not lose sight of the positive side. Pope John Paul II was critical of modernity in many ways, but his thoughts on "The Positive Fruits of the Enlightenment" in his *Memory and Identity: Conversations at the Dawn of a Millennium* capture the other side of the story well. He states,

> The European Enlightenment not only led to the carnage of the French Revolution, but also bore positive fruits, such as the ideals of liberty, equality and fraternity, values which are rooted in the Gospel. Even when proclaimed independently, these ideas point naturally to their proper origin. Hence, the French Enlightenment prepared the way for

a better understanding of human rights. Of course, the Revolution violated those rights in many ways. Yet this was also the time when human rights began to be properly acknowledged and put into effect more forcefully, leaving behind the traditions of feudalism.[11]

Diagnosing modernity in a well-balanced way, including both the positive and the negative sides, remains an important task. Although this is indeed a very challenging ideal to strive for, such a goal is better than the easier approaches of quietism, simple affirmation, or negation.

6.2 PLURALISM AND SOFT CONSENSUS

In some of the contemporary criticisms of the Reformation, the Reformation is presented as the main impulse of negative social and cultural fragmentation. This is actually a very old opinion. For example, Johann Tetzel remarked in his criticism of Luther in 1518:

> For because of them [Luther's articles] many people will hold the *magisterium* and jurisdiction of His Papal Holiness and the holy Roman See in contempt. The works of sacramental reparation will also cease. People will no longer believe preachers and theologians. Everyone will want to interpret Holy Scripture according to his own whim. Through this, all of holy Christendom must come into great spiritual danger, since each person will believe what best pleases him. In time, as the deceptive article announces, the modern revered theologians, in whom for many centuries Christianity has placed great confidence, shall no longer be considered credible.[12]

More recently, Brad Gregory has argued that the Reformation made the West "hyperpluralistic."[13] The first half of this argument has already been addressed above regarding the pluralization of the pre-Reformation period (see chap. 3, §3.2, "Pre-Reformation pluralization"). As was demonstrated in that section, there are many signs of pluralization before the Reformation. The second half of this issue will be addressed here. To put this in the form of a question: Is it true that the contemporary cultural context of the modern Western world is radically fragmented and "hyperpluralistic"? In the following section it is argued that although the contemporary Western world is indeed pluralistic, there is also evidence of a soft consensus in some basic values across the cultural, social, and political landscape. These can be seen especially in the foundational institutions of the Western world.

The term "hyperpluralism" is sometimes used in sociopolitical discourse to refer to the fragmentation of political interest groups and the resulting challenges associated with forming coalitions. Gregory, however, writes about "contemporary Western hyperpluralism" regarding the understanding of truth, the nature of meaning, the standards of morality, the values of society, the aims and priorities of Western culture, and its sense of purpose.[14] He thus uses the term in a more general sense, one which includes moral, philosophical, cultural, political, and theological aspects.

The discourse about pluralism in Gregory's book is related to the analysis found in Alasdair MacIntyre's *After Virtue*. There MacIntyre addresses the "self-avowed moral pluralism" of "liberal societies" that have "abandoned the moral unity of Aristotelianism, whether in its ancient or medieval forms."[15] Similar sentiment can be found in John Milbank's *Theology and Social Theory*. Milbank narrates, among other things, a long conflict between Christianity and the individualism of liberalism, as well as an older "incipient liberalism." Milbank finds the latter already with Augustine's opponents: "Augustine recognizes an individualizing degeneration in Rome's more recent history, and condemns the 'incipient liberalism.'"[16] More recently, in *A Secular Age*, Charles Taylor claims that "we are now living in a spiritual super-nova, a kind of galloping pluralism on the spiritual plane."[17] Taylor remarks that "the present scene, shorn of the earlier forms, is different and unrecognizable to any earlier epoch. It is marked by an unheard of pluralism of outlooks, religious and non- and anti-religious, in which the number of possible positions seems to be increasing without end."[18]

While these authors are certainly right to point out the great variety of worldviews, or, as others may prefer, expressions of the absolute, that currently coexist in the Western world, there is also significant agreement to be found. This agreement suggests the existence of a soft consensus, and not only regarding our selfish habits. To suggest that there is a soft consensus is not to posit a hard consensus, a "uniformity of belief and evaluation," as Nicholas Rescher has described it.[19] To claim that there is a soft consensus is also not to ignore the real plurality within the Western world. There are clearly some who entirely reject the soft consensus addressed below. These cases do not, however, discount the fact that there are broadly shared values that underlie and regulate the vast majority of social, political, educational, judiciary, cultural, and religious institutions in the Western world. What, then, are these points of soft consensus in the foundational institutions of the West?

The entire Western world has agreed (1) to live with a modern democratic political order, (2) to enforce concepts of unalienable human rights, (3) to uphold the rule of law, and (4) to secure the separation of powers. These four points suggest that there is a soft consensus in contemporary Western societies. These matters rest upon basic values that have correlations with views of the person and conceptions of the good.

The first two points especially draw upon a general view of the person, of the individual, that is more or less shared in Western society. In this regard, the high view of the individual, and thus the high view of that individual's opinion, is presumed in these points, but it could also be added as a fifth point in the soft consensus. This high view of the individual also has roots in religious traditions, which are reflected in the Scriptures. The Old Testament teaches that all people are made in the image of God: "Let us make humankind in our image, according to our likeness" (Gen 1:26). In the early church, furthermore, people like Onesimus could take advantage of the equality among the Christians. He himself went from being a "slave" to being "more than a slave" in that he was, according to the Christian teachings, "a beloved brother." His old master, Philemon, was now required by apostolic authority to see his old slave Onesimus as his own brother, "both in the flesh and in the Lord" (Phlm 1:16). Over the long run, these teachings had an impact in the Western intellectual tradition. While they were often ignored, they could never be forgotten because they were a part of the canon. There are many other values that follow from the high view of the individual and that also constitute elements of soft consensus in modern Western societies (such as the necessity of some kind of education and basic health care for every person, the legal equality of men and women, the legal indifference of race, background, or social class).

Another attribute could be added to the soft consensus in relation to the rule of law and the separation of powers. These points rest upon the idea of a limitation of government powers, oversight, and control. In this regard they presume the value of freedom. A high view of freedom could therefore be listed both as a presupposition of the third and fourth points and as an independent sixth point in the soft consensus. Freedom is articulated in a variety of ways in the modern Western world, such as the freedom of the press, of religion, of movement, the freedom to exchange ideas, thoughts, and writings—and, as one might add today, without a central government collecting the information—and the freedom to change religions without coercion, to associate with a group or a political party, to start a new business, to quit a job, to strike, to buy and to sell what one pleases, to own property, and to trade goods and services. All these expressions of freedom are presumed in all Western societies to differing degrees, and all of them rely upon basic views of the person as a responsible agent endowed with freedom. In the most coherent articulations of freedom, however, it is described as not only the absence of restriction but also the ability to flourish. In this sense, the idea of freedom presumes a conception of the good.

Another attribute of the soft consensus could be described in relation to the rule of law. The law is a concrete representation of the norms and principles that are held to be not only just and ethical but also reasonable. No individual authority or person is above the law: *lex rex* (law is king). In a related sense, all individuals are bound not by arbitrariness but by reason and by the reasonable justification of their actions. This principle presumes the human capacity, in normal cases, to make reasoned decisions and to be held accountable for them. The importance of reason and rational justification is therefore a part of the soft consensus as a presupposition of the rule of law, but also as an independent seventh point. In the most coherent articulations of reason, of course, it is situated within the relevant values, presuppositions, ideals, dialogical context, and religious faith, and thus in relation to a conception of the good: "Reason is beautiful and gentle."[20]

Another matter in the soft consensus relates to the idea of the separation of powers. This principle shows, of course, the importance of the limitation of power within government, but it also thereby postulates a presumed cooperation in the formal execution of power, administration, and management. A high regard for cooperation is therefore a part of the soft consensus as a presupposition of the separation of powers, but also as an independent eighth point. The most effective cooperation is, of course, dependent upon general agreements regarding shared goals and a basic goodwill between the cooperating parties.

In this brief sketch of some shared values, it has been presumed that the structuring principles of modern Western societies are not arbitrary assertions but rather mutually reinforcing concepts that are connected with one another, interwoven with historical developments, and representative of human life and ideals. The German historian Heinrich August Winkler is one author who has sought to show how the initial four points, as enumerated above, are positively connected with the history of the Western world.[21]

Other things could also be added to this list of common values in the soft consensus. One might mention the continual reaffirmation of basic moral virtues (and vices) in Hollywood films, which tend to exemplify the cultural expectations of modern moral norms and the implied soft consensus (such as the general honorableness of self-sacrifice, the good of compassion, the inescapable consequences of evil, the virtue of trusting in one's conscience against all odds, the victory of good over evil, etc.). The ecumenical movement, which reached its apex in the 1960s and 1970s, is another example of the trend in the second half of the twentieth century toward mutual understanding in Western societies. There is also a large corpus of literature, including the Bible and various classical works, that is generally recognized as a reference point for the ideals of human life in Western culture.

In addition to the soft consensus, the modern Western world seems to be much more unified today in its basic values than it was in the last century. We have come a long way since the bloody imperial wars a century ago, the great political, ideological, and military conflicts of the early and mid-twentieth century, the hardened positions of the cultural revolutions of the 1960s and 1970s, and the optimistic aspiration of a quick "end of history" with the spread of Western political ideals across the world.[22]

Even the plurality of religions in the West does not necessitate the postulation of a hyperpluralism. A variety of positions have been developed to conceptualize this issue in the history of theology and philosophy. As is already reported by Luke, the apostle Paul (drawing from Epimenides and Aratus) saw that God "is not far from each one of us. For 'In him we live and move and have our being'; as even some of your own poets have said, 'For we too are his offspring'" (Acts 17:27-28).

In the modern period, Rudolf Otto developed the conception of a shared basis in the "holy," and, before him, Hegel saw the world's religions as part of a unified process of the divine Spirit's self-realization.[23] Schleiermacher's conception of religion as the "feeling of absolute dependence" also allows for ways of seeing some commonality among different religions.[24] Of course, many of these religious-philosophical programs would require modifications in light of the warranted criticisms that have been brought against them.

Even viewed from the position of exclusivism, however, alterity is not usually understood in terms of hyperpluralism. In exclusivist systems the "other" is rather understood within the broader narrative of that particular religion's account of the world. This leads to vocabulary for designating those who are on the outside, which also presumes, in most cases, the associated guidelines for their respectful treatment. While the modern West is certainly a very diverse place culturally and socially, there is also evidence of a soft consensus in some shared values. Along with this, a general movement toward mutual understanding in the social, political, and religious spheres of Western societies is identifiable in the last century. Finally, contemporary figures in various religious traditions have been seeking to conceptualize pluralism, to understand it and to manage it, not necessarily from an abstract theoretical perspective (such as John Rawls' "original position"[25]) or through the negation of religious particularity (which has to do with personal identity), and not even in the negation of the idea of mission or evangelization, but by taking account of religion in all its facets and in many cases with the emphases that derive from the specific doctrinal traditions.[26]

This does not mean that the Western world is perfect. There is—especially in the age of "too-big-to-fail" banks—a need to make the economic markets free from the "oppressive genius of an exclusive company," to use Adam Smith's expression.[27] Granted, it is not only companies that have acted irresponsibly in recent history. The mountains of sovereign debt that many Western nations have created, and that continue to be loaded upon the coming generations, is also evidence of our imperfect political order. Protecting, supporting, educating, and training the poor, weak, and vulnerable, in order to ensure that everyone (and not only the privileged) can participate in and profit from the wealth of the nations, remains a challenging goal for all Western societies. The logic of the Levitical code provides a good example here in that it takes account of the specific situation of each individual: "if you cannot afford a sheep, you shall bring to the Lord [. . .] two turtledoves or two pigeons" (Lev 5:7).

With a view to contemporary society, Robert D. Putnam has analyzed the loss of "social capital" in modern American society.[28] Social capital is the collective value of various cultural and social interrelationships in a given society. It is measured by the levels of membership in clubs and other social organizations, including church membership and community support structures. If the level of social capital is high, there is a lot of support for people in a community. The decline of social capital can be identified in much of the Western world. David L. Tubbs has also addressed another issue that deserves more attention today. He argues that there is a danger for the well-being of children in a society that promotes moral indifference. Tubbs is no outsider to these issues. Before he became professor of politics at the King's College in New York City, he "worked in state government as a child-support investigator."[29] Regarding his work at that time, he states, "The most discouraging aspect of this work is parental indifference."[30] Later in his studies at graduate school, he "saw that contemporary liberal thinkers were minimizing or denying the importance of what were previously considered essential elements of children's welfare."[31]

Tubbs claims that "if we take account of the main currents of liberal thought over the last fifty to sixty years, we could say that it lacks the resources to criticize—in a truly cogent way—such parental indifference."[32] He draws upon many examples, such as child pornography, but his main diagnosis is concerned with the "moral reticence" (from the Latin, *reticere* [to keep silent]) of contemporary liberalism when it comes to affirming, supporting, and dutifully serving the interests of children. Rather than describing contemporary American liberalism as "radically subjectivist" (in the terms of MacIntyre and others), he calls it "morally reticent."[33] He analyzes a "permissive ethos" and a reluctance that helps "to obscure the difference between the responsible and the irresponsible exercise of freedom."[34] This was not always the case with liberalism. As he argues, nineteenth-century liberals were more concerned with emphasizing personal responsibility.

While there is a soft consensus in the modern Western world regarding many values, there is a need for a positive moral vision—one that is verified with moral examples in the family, in churches, and in the broader cultural, social, and political realm. We can build a better future for the coming generations by providing constructive responses to these issues rather than mere condemnation.

Today there is a growing anti-Muslim attitude in many parts of the Western world. If this attitude takes hold of us, we will forget the importance of communication, common humanity, and the many places of agreement and actual and potential collaboration between Muslims and Christians. With a view to the issue of immigration today, it is important to remember that the Western tradition and the Western world is not a static phenomenon. On the contrary, the West is best understood with the internal pluralism of the different cultures it contains, and especially with those cultures and those people—including their religions—who seek refuge in the Western world in order to receive protection and help.

The Western Judeo-Christian tradition is realized where the justice due to "the alien, the orphan, and the widow" is not perverted but is upheld (Deut 27:19), where a person in distress is brought "to an inn," where those who are "moved with pity" and show "mercy" say, "Take care of him; and when I come back, I will repay you whatever more you spend" (Luke 10:34-35). This is the spirit of Christian mercy, which Thomas Aquinas held to be the greatest of the virtues.[35]

6.3 THE WESTERN WORLD AND MULTICULTURALISM

When addressing the Western world, one is immediately confronted with the question regarding the oppressive nature of the concept itself and the violent history of colonialism. The discourse about multiculturalism is, in part, a response to this. There is little agreement about the definition of this term.[36] In general, the concept of multiculturalism represents an interpretive paradigm of cultural and social studies, and also politics, that emphasizes plurality and difference. Since the Western world is filled with many different cultures, traditions, languages, religious confessions, ethnic communities, and conflicting political parties, it is easy to view it in terms of plurality. There has also been a challenge to this interpretive paradigm of plurality and difference. Many hold that it neglects the commonality and universality of shared values in the Western world. For example, John M. Headley has recently sought to offer a criticism of this discourse. While some parts of Headley's analysis of the Western world are correct, his criticism of multiculturalism seems to go too far.

Headley, who calls himself a "political liberal, rather than a rock-solid Republican" and a "historian of the early modern period" and not the twentieth century,[37] is certainly correct to claim that he is "unwilling to argue that our civilization is *ipso facto* somehow the best and the greatest. Indeed, since the nineteenth century it has proved itself to be often ugly, extremely violent, and largely responsible for the exhaustion of the planet's resources."[38] Headley is obviously critical of the oppressive, colonial, and belligerent history of Western civilization. At the same time, he argues that "the West possesses a unique feature absent from all other civilizations or societies: a proclivity to create and expand programs, practices, and institutions that are suited not just to itself but also to all others—in appropriately modified form, to humankind in general." He sees this as the "universalizing process, which is ever bent upon connecting the disconnected."[39] Headley's articulation of this theory is sometimes insensitive to the real concerns and criticisms that have been brought against the destruction of local cultures and traditions in the processes of Westernization. It is important not to lose sight of the fact that the Western world has been a colonial force that has used its power to dominate other cultures.

On the other hand, Headley is correct to draw attention to the "West's uniqueness: the influence of its science and technology, the idea of a common humanity, the legitimacy of political dissent and diversity, the process of secularization and the universality of human rights."[40] It is possible to hold both of these views in harmony with one another. That is, one may affirm the view that the process of Westernization both inside and outside of the West has been filled with ambiguities, contradictions, coercion, and violence and therefore cannot be evaluated as a wholly positive development. At the same time, it is also possible to affirm the truly positive aspects of Western civilization that are deserving of praise.

When it comes to the issue of multiculturalism in the West, Headley seems to go too far in his criticism:

> Multiculturalism claims to be committed to the laudatory, if obvious, pursuit of engaging and understanding all the peoples of the earth. But its approach seeks instead to validate rather than to understand those societies and civilizations different from our own, to attribute to them a questionable or even undue priority in human advancement, and to denigrate or ignore the West's achievement and the uniqueness of American constitutionalism. The unhappy effect serves only to contribute to the degradation of American education.[41]

While it is a noble aim to defend American constitutionalism, this account of multiculturalism seems to be a mischaracterization. It is presented as essentially relativistic and anti-Western. Multiculturalism does not have to be understood in this way.

The contemporary Western world is influenced by immigration from the non-Western world.[42] A reactionary response to this immigration is the new right-wing political movements of various forms. They claim to represent the true Western tradition and view immigration as a threat to it. The new right wing has taken charge of the idea of the Western world and asserted itself as the protector of the West. Their possession of the term "Western world" has, in turn, caused many moderate voices to abandon it. In doing this, however, they abandon the field of argument and leave the interpretation of this great cultural legacy to the right wing. Beyond this basic polarity, there is a third position of moderation.

The hope for the future is to be found in the peaceful coexistence and cooperation of different cultures, peoples, and religious traditions. Such a hope does not require that religions stop proselytizing. Peaceful coexistence does require, of course, a rejection of all violent proselytizing and all forms of coercion. In this sense, the freedom of conscience is an important value to be rediscovered by every generation. Peaceful coexistence and cooperation does not require Western societies to stop the broad discussions about shared values that are foundational to the Western world. Many philosophers and theorists of religion, culture, and society in the second half of the twentieth century abandoned the language of commonality, common ground, and common values. This was done in order to promote the principle of plurality. In doing this, however, the practical realities of human life were sometimes overlooked, especially as they are lived out together in common education, common political systems, common law, and common social institutions. The academic fascination with plurality, difference, and diversity was certainly important in the wake of fascism. Many of the theorists of plurality and alterity were responding to fascism. While this response is praiseworthy, building healthy societies also requires communities to come together, to find agreement, and to make compromises in the interest of the common good. In this regard, there is a need to affirm cultural difference while also working toward social integration.

Along these lines, Daniel Weinstock argues that "the state should enact policies designed to achieve the requisite degree of social cohesion in as parsimonious a manner as possible." With this the state should seek to "draw as clear a line as possible between social integration on the one hand, and cultural integration, on the other." In this framework "social integration" is concerned with enabling everyone in society to participate in public institutions. "Cultural integration," on the other hand, has to do with "any policy designed to reduce the degree of cultural variety in a society in ways that are not justified by the requirements that justify social integration." In this conception of multiculturalism, "cultural integration" is to be rejected, but "social integration" is to be encouraged.[43] Measures toward "social integration" should be, however, as limited and reserved as possible.

Historically, the Western world has not always been a place where everyone has been encouraged to participate in public life as full members. As the history of the Reformation and the post-Reformation era shows, there is a long and bumpy path that brought us to our contemporary social, religious, and political framework. Today, much of the discussion about multiculturalism in the Western world is related to the discussion about Islam. Many Muslim people live in the West today, and thus the influence of Islam is growing. How should these new developments be interpreted?

6.4 ISLAM IN THE WESTERN WORLD

The contemporary relationship between Islam, in its many forms, and the Western world is strained by geopolitical conflicts, war, and terrorism. The positive sides to this "troubled history" (to use Rollin Armour's term) are often forgotten in light of the contemporary conflicts.[44] While it is true that "meaningful differences did and still do exist between the two worlds,"[45] our contemporary situation provides us with an opportunity to work toward a different future of peace and cooperation.

New research on the history of the emergence of Islam has shown that it should be understood within the broader framework of late antiquity, which links its genesis closely to the cultural dynamics of the Mediterranean world. Rather than seeing Islam in radical alterity to the occidental traditions, it can be understood as a critical and reflective movement that was modifying and reconceptualizing the language and narratives of the Bible in postbiblical theology and exegesis: "Paleo-Islam and its deity need to be regarded more as points of arrival, and less as generic beginnings. They did not arise from or act upon a tabula rasa, but brought to conclusion a constellation of long-term developments, Hellenistic and late antique, religious, social and political, but also ones that are specifically Arab."[46] This is significant because it shows that religious traditions from Judaism and early Christianity were adopted and developed in both the Western and the Islamic world.

The formation of a new cultural, linguistic, and religious community on the Arabian Peninsula became an imperial threat to the Western world. It conquered a significant part of the territory previously controlled by Christian rulers. At the same time, it was also connected to the very political, social, and religious frameworks that it defeated, colonized, and converted. The religious motivation of the Arab conquest is undeniable, but it was only one part of the larger social, economic, and cultural dynamic that enabled the expansion of the Islamic empire.[47] The response of Latin Christendom in the Crusades, in which untold thousands of Muslims and Jews were killed, and in the Reconquista (reconquest) of the Iberian Peninsula remain defining features of the image of the West in the Islamic world.[48] Beyond this, colonialism and modern war (such as the Iraq War) have been extremely damaging to the relationship between Islam and the West.

In the Western world today, there are still many challenges with regard to integration and mutual acceptance on both sides: "Muslim integration into Christian heritage societies of the West is by and large a failure."[49] What is needed in this case is "positive action from both the host society and Muslim immigrants."[50] While many are attempting to overcome this tension by building relationships of trust and cooperation, the integration of Muslim communities in the Western world remains a major challenge.

There is a debate going on about traditional Islamic conceptions of family and society within Muslim communities and among Islamic scholars in the Western world. Those who are not members of this religion cannot significantly influence this debate. At the same time, understanding some of the challenges and some of the issues is important. With a better understanding of these matters we can develop a well-balanced outlook regarding our shared future together.

One of the major points of debate, in some Muslim communities, is the status of women.[51] Radical interpretations of this issue in Islam have occupied much of the public's attention. Two examples of this interpretation are radical Islam and the anti-Islam discourse that emerged after September 11, 2001. Radical Islam has drawn upon the religion to create a "vast system of rape."[52] The anti-Islam discourse, on the other hand, claims that Islam is fundamentally antiwoman and that it is impossible to reform it. The latter view fails to see the significance of theological interpretation and the living dynamic of traditions in processes of reform.

Moderate voices within Islam are developing innovative interpretations of the Qur'an in order to improve the status of women. For example, this text from the Qur'an teaches something very positive: "Their Lord has answered them: 'I will not allow the deeds of any one of you to be lost, whether you are male or female, each is like the other" (Qur'an 3:195). According to this text, all people are equal, "like the other."

Traditional Islamic conceptions of social and political order are also undergoing reinterpretation. This is the case with the qur'anic and post-qur'anic concept of jihad. This concept has been interpreted in very different ways. As Bernard Lewis has explained, "There were some who argued that *jihād* should be understood in a moral and spiritual, rather than a military sense." While these arguments have been made by "Shi'ite theologians in classical times, and more frequently by modernizers and reformists in the nineteenth and twentieth centuries," Lewis holds that the "overwhelming majority of classical theologians," including the legal interpreters of the religion, "understood the obligation of *jihād* in a military sense, and have examined and expounded it accordingly."[53] Even if this is the case in the premodern era, modern theologians are reinterpreting this theme today.[54] Jihad has also been addressed by Francesca Forte. She situates it in the context with other issues related to Islamic law and calls for new interpretations of these themes in Islam:

> *Shari'a*, or rather its traditional interpretations, presents elements which are explicitly in contrast with human rights (male guardianship of women—*qiwama*; sovereignty of Muslims over non-Muslims—*dhimma*; and violently aggressive *jihad*). It is thus necessary to reassess the interpretation of religious law in order to make it an instrument of promotion and protection of rights.[55]

The diversity of interpretations in the history of Islam is evidence of the fact that these contemporary challenges in reinterpretation are not insurmountable. Through this process of reinterpretation, Islam can be reformed, just like other religions have been. It can become a defender and supporter of the traditions of freedom and equality in the Western world.

In the German context, the recent establishment of various university centers for the study of Islamic theology is a very good example of a positive contribution to this process of reform and reinterpretation in Islam. As millions of Muslims now live in Germany, these centers were arranged to be theological institutions rather than only religious-studies institutions. A theological debate within Islam is necessary for this process of reform and reinterpretation. After the first center for the study of Islamic theology was established in Tübingen in January of 2012, the German federal minister for education, Annette Schavan, praised the new center in Tübingen, calling it a "milestone for integration."[56]

Islam is not the only religion that has had to come to terms with traditions of inequality, oppression, and violence. In the history of Christianity, the classic example of this is the Crusades, which were explicitly supported by the popes. Another example is the persecution of "heretics" and "witches."[57] Many religious traditions have found ways of reforming religious ethics in order to respect the equality of all people.

Another major issue with regard to Islam in the Western world is Islamic terrorism. In the wake of terrorist attacks, like those in New York in 2001 or those in Paris in 2015, Christians are challenged to respond in a way that supports the long-term goal of peace. In these critical times, it is important to avoid two dangerous pitfalls. The first pitfall is simply forgetting the message of the Bible about seeking both justice (that is, true judgments) and reconciliation. Zechariah 7:9, for example, teaches, "Thus says the Lord of hosts: Render true judgments, show kindness and mercy to one another.'" Jesus' teachings also challenge us in difficult times like these: "You have heard that it was said, 'You shall love your neighbor and hate your enemy.' But I say to you, Love your enemies and pray for those who persecute you" (Matt 5:43-44). Paul also taught this: "Beloved, never avenge yourselves, but leave room for the wrath of God [. . .] Do not be overcome by evil, but overcome evil with good" (Rom 12:19-21). There is a dual impulse in the Judeo-Christian tradition in this regard. One impulse is to seek justice; the other impulse is to seek reconciliation. The difficult challenge is to do both.

With a view to our contemporary context in the Western world, there are many divisions between Muslims and Christians. Radical Islamic terrorists want to exploit this division and turn the world into an "us" versus "them" conflict. The biblical teaching about reconciliation, by contrast, encourages us to establish positive relationships. A hand of peace should be extended to Muslims everywhere, which reflects a hope for a positive and harmonious future together, one marked by freedom, peace, and cooperation. If we forget the principles of justice and reconciliation, we can easily get led down the wrong path—the path of division and resentment. This path is easy, but it is actually very dangerous and ultimately counterproductive.

The second pitfall is a dangerous simplification of our understanding of Islam. This simplification claims that terrorist attacks are representative of the essence of Islam. This goes together with a view of all of Islam as inherently violent and incapable of reform. This view leads to a general rejection of the religion as a whole. It supports a view of Muslims that says that these people are incapable of fitting into the Western world. It suggests that they are inherently foreign because of their religion. All this ultimately encourages an exclusion of these people from participating in our societies. This, in turn, reinforces divisions and prejudices among us. This simplification of Islam overlooks four important issues:

First of all, the people who are carrying out these attacks are, numerically, actually a very small minority of Muslims; they are not representative of the majority. Furthermore, terrorism has been done in the name of many religions and ideologies. Second, the people that are carrying out these terrorist attacks have diverse motivations. While radical Islam certainly plays a very important role in their motivations, it is not the only issue. Other factors also play a role in the process of radicalization, such as personal biographies of disillusionment, identity crisis, and radical conversion. In other cases, young people are radicalized in the context of a youthful adventure or because of political fantasies.

Third, while terrorists claim to represent Islam and follow the teaching of the Qur'an, they are actually only following a radical interpretation of this religious document. In truth, their interpretation is not the only one, and it is not a necessary interpretation. Other interpretations are also possible. It is important to remember the ambiguity of religious texts in this regard. Religious texts that are full of various ideas, like the Qur'an, require interpretation. In this process of interpretation, one is required to balance out one claim with another claim. This is done in order to provide a systematization of the basic principles of the religion. In this process, the Qur'an can be read in very different ways. For example, the Qur'an actually calls for the rejection of hatred. It teaches, "You who believe, be steadfast in your devotion to God and bear witness impartially: do not let hatred of others lead you away from justice, but adhere to justice, for that is closer to awareness of God" (5:8). It also teaches that there is a dignity of human beings and that human beings should therefore not be unjustly murdered (5:32). Furthermore, it teaches that God has made human life "sacred" (6:151). A positive interpretation of the Qur'an can be—and is being—reached through a balanced theology. The religion has been reformed in the past and it can continue to be reformed.

Fourth, the attacks are being rejected by leaders of Islam today. This rejection is coming not only from liberal Muslim scholars in the Western world but also from traditional voices in the religion. For example, the leading Muslim cleric in Egypt, Sheikh Ahmed El-Tayyeb, strongly distanced the Islamic religion from the Paris attacks by calling them "hideous" and "hateful" and by arguing that they lacked "religion and humanity." Indeed, he claims that this radicalism is actually a "frantic monster."[58]

Today one of the great challenges in the Western world is the task of establishing and building upon constructive relationships with the vast majority of Muslims even when a small minority of radical Islamic terrorists are seeking to destroy Western civilization. Here we must ask ourselves if our behavior toward these people and our opinions about Islam support a positive and long-term vision of cooperation. We must ask ourselves if we are encouraging Muslims to participate in the modern social and political system as equal citizens or if we are seeking to exclude them. Are we working toward the goal of a social order in which everyone can participate—regardless of their religion—or are we abandoning this great vision? If we consider our ways and our thoughts, we will avoid the dangerous pitfalls that are around us. If we hold to the spirit of justice and reconciliation, and the hope for a cooperative relationship, we will not be swept away in division and resentment. The narrow path is difficult, but it leads to life.

The social dynamics of multiculturalism and the specific issue regarding growing populations of Muslim people in the West are contemporary developments that will bring about some degree of social and cultural transformation. The interpretation of these events should not be radicalized, however, since these issues simply do not warrant an apocalyptic evaluation. Christians can do their part to make these contemporary processes of transformation peaceful and help to steer them in a positive direction. In doing this we can support human flourishing and the common good in the hopes that the gesture of goodwill will be returned by the other side. Furthermore, we can apply those lessons that we have learned from the Reformation era about the necessity of tolerance.

≪7≫

THE REFORMATION AND ECUMENISM

Is the Reformation still a living issue at all, or is it over? How should we think about the Reformation today? When looking back at this historical event and the division of Western Christendom, it is important to consider the fact that many generations before us have worked toward Christian unity and have attempted to heal the divisions. There are also some positive things that have come from the Reformation. Perhaps we can look back together, as both Protestants and Catholics, and see the positive sides of the history and the problematic ones too. In this chapter these issues will be addressed and an ecumenical view of the Reformation will be proposed. With this, the contemporary history of ecumenism will be introduced along with some of its greatest achievements, such as the joint statement on the doctrine of justification. Finally, the theological foundations of ecumenism will be addressed.

7.1 CONTEMPORARY HISTORY OF ECUMENISM

The contemporary situation in ecumenism is closely related to historical developments after World War II.[1] After the war there was a general cultural and sociopolitical swing toward unity in the West. This created a background mood that encouraged consensus. The classic example of this is the formation of the North Atlantic Treaty Organization (NATO) in 1948. Many authoritarian regimes transformed into democracies in the 1970s and 1980s. The Communist Eastern Bloc also disintegrated in the later 1980s and early 1990s while the European Union emerged with the Maastricht Treaty in 1992.

These developments accompanied the liberalization of economic policies and societies around the Western world in the later twentieth century. In the second half of the twentieth century, there was also a general consolidation of Western values in many of these Western nations, all of which have Christian backgrounds. Seen from this perspective, the swing toward theological consensus in the ecumenism of churches in the second half of the twentieth century reflected the broader swing toward a cultural, social, and political unity in the modern Western nations.

The striving for universal consensus regarding the catalogue of Western values (freedom of the press, separation of powers in government, democracy, the rule of law, social equality, human rights, justice, freedom, etc.) was also legitimized by the religious program of ecumenism. This is because ecumenism generally encouraged many of these themes in the spirit of peace and cooperation. This interrelated cultural framework, and specifically the hope for overcoming divisions after the "age of extremes," provided a common language and a shared impulse for the progress of Christian relations in the second half of the twentieth century in the shadow of the Cold War.

After the establishment of the Protestant "fellowship of churches"—the World Council of Churches (WCC), in 1948—ambitious, institutionally supported, consensus-oriented modern ecumenism emerged in the 1960s. The sense of momentum was confirmed in November of 1964 at the Second Vatican Council when the Catholic Church issued this statement in the Decree on Ecumenism: "Everywhere large numbers have felt the impulse of this grace, and among our separated brethren also there increases from day to day the movement, fostered by the grace of the Holy Spirit, for the restoration of unity among all Christians." [2] The ecumenical spirit is strongly expressed in the reference to non-Catholics as "brethren" and the emphasis on the "restoration of unity."

The document also remarks that those who are participating in the ecumenical movement "invoke the Triune God and confess Jesus as Lord and Savior." This remark seeks to show that there is a general doctrinal consensus with these "brethren" in the most important parts of Christian teaching, the doctrine of God and in the understanding of Christ. It holds that everyone involved "longs that there may be one visible Church of God." [3] It also called for participation: "The Sacred Council exhorts all the Catholic faithful to recognize the signs of the times and to take an active and intelligent part in the work of ecumenism." [4]

In the second half of the twentieth century, there were many great ecumenical achievements. One example of this is the work done between the Roman Catholic Church and the Orthodox churches. On December 7, 1965, the ancient Church Schism of 1054 was cast in a new light by Pope Paul VI and Patriarch Athenagoras I of Constantinople. The pope and the patriarch jointly declared that they regretted "the offensive words, the reproaches without foundation, and the reprehensible gestures which, on both sides, have marked or accompanied the sad events of this period." They also declared that they "regret and remove both from memory and from the midst of the Church the sentences of excommunication which followed these events, the memory of which has influenced actions up to our day and has hindered closer relations in charity; and they commit these excommunications to oblivion."[5] While differences remain between these churches, the spirit of communion and the desire for reconciliation were strengthened by this gesture of humility. As the "Joint Declaration" between them states,

> They hope that the whole Christian world, especially the entire Roman Catholic Church and the Orthodox Church will appreciate this gesture as an expression of a sincere desire shared in common for reconciliation, and as an invitation to follow out in a spirit of trust, esteem and mutual charity the dialogue which, with God's help, will lead to living together again, for the greater good of souls and the coming of the kingdom of God, in that full communion of faith, fraternal accord and sacramental life which existed among them during the first thousand years of the life of the Church.[6]

Inner-Protestant movement toward fellowship and mutual understanding was also pushed forward at this time. In 1973 the theological statement of common understanding called the "Agreement of the Churches of the Reformation in Europe," usually referred to as the Leuenberg Agreement, was completed.[7] Today, over ninety churches belong to this fellowship, which affirms the gospel as the basis of the church and a common understanding of many central doctrinal teachings among Protestants. It followed the principles of reconciled difference between various theological traditions. It permits different Protestant churches to maintain their doctrinal distinctions on the common basis of the shared foundation of Christian teachings. After laying out a consensus statement on the Lord's Supper, the document states, "Where there is such consensus between churches, the condemnations pronounced by the Reformation confessions of faith are inapplicable to the doctrinal position of these churches."[8]

This document from the 1970s is a good example of the strong impulse toward fellowship and mutual acceptance in the wake of the cultural transitions of the 1960s. In many ways it provided the theological groundwork for ecumenism today. Paragraph 28 states, "There remain considerable differences between our churches in forms of worship, types of spirituality, and church order." Yet, "in fidelity to the New Testament and Reformation criteria for church fellowship, we cannot discern in these differences any factors which should divide the church."[9]

One of the other major modern works of ecumenism at this time was the WCC's convergence paper, "Baptism, Eucharist, and Ministry" (1982).[10] Based upon the agreements reached, it states, "Mutual recognition of baptism is acknowledged as an important sign and means of expressing the baptismal unity given in Christ."[11] Regarding the Lord's Supper, it declared that "the increased mutual understanding expressed in the present statement may allow some churches to attain a greater measure of eucharistic communion among themselves and so bring closer the day when Christ's divided people will be visibly reunited around the Lord's Table."[12]

There has been significant work toward mutual recognition in these areas. In 2007, in Magdeburg, Germany, many churches—Protestant, Catholic, and Orthodox—signed a declaration entitled "Mutual Recognition of Baptism." It affirms that "baptism signifies our new birth in Jesus Christ. [. . .] Despite differences in our understanding of the Church, there exists between us a common understanding on baptism."[13] The spirit of ecumenism was also supported by Pope Benedict XVI's visit to Luther's Augustinian monastery in Erfurt in 2011. Pope Francis has also sent a strong message in support of unity.

In the 1950s and 1960s there was a general push toward "convergence ecumenism."[14] The hope was for an ecumenical and universal church that would be, according to George Lindbeck, "richer and more variegated than anything we could imagine, and yet it would be genuinely one." Yves Congar's *Chrétiens désunis* (1937)[15] is an example of this ambitious ecumenism. This was "the first and, in some respects, still the greatest catholic ecumenical manifesto" that was, at the same time, "officially silenced in 1954."[16] Nevertheless, his theology influenced Vatican II and Pope Paul VI (indeed, later in 1994 he was made a cardinal). This was the new approach, "convergence ecumenism," that would come to "dominate the ecumenical establishment." This approach, according to Lindbeck, was represented in the WCC's statement "The Unity We Seek" (1961, New Delhi, India), in *Unitatis redintegratio*, and in "Baptism, Eucharist, and Ministry" (1982, WCC).[17] Since then, however, "ecumenism has been in decline." While the Lutheran–Roman Catholic *Joint Declaration on the Doctrine of Justification* (1999) was a major step, it followed more from "institutional inertia" than from "continuing enthusiasm."[18] Already at the WCC assembly in 1968 in Uppsala, Sweden, "the unity of the world, not that of the church in service to the world's unity," became "more and more the direct goal." Those who were not pleased with this transition often claim that the "world sets the agenda" in the new ecumenism.[19]

Statements from the executive director of the Institute for Ecumenical and Cultural Research, Patrick Henry, confirm this analysis. Henry refers to a meeting of ecumenical leaders from around the world in July of 2003 in Bossey, Switzerland. He claimed that there was "nearly unanimous and almost immediate resistance" among these leaders of ecumenism to the idea

> that the ecumenical movement has a single nature and a single goal.
> [. . .] Negotiating doctrines is giving way to [. . .] ecumenical
> spirituality. [. . .] Most people don't believe unity is the goal anymore;
> now it's dialogue, the sharing of stories. At Bossey it became clear [. . .]
> that the nature of the ecumenical movement is to have many goals, and
> the goal of the ecumenical movement is to let its many natures flourish
> and interact. [. . .] Nearly everyone in the seminar, including those
> who have devoted careers of many decades to the movement, responded
> positively to this new focus.[20]

This may be understood as "wider ecumenism" because it is more focused on "interreligious rather than intra-Christian relations." Lindbeck challenges this approach with a convincing argument: "What is problematic about this focus is not interfaith dialogue but the failure to realize that this dialogue differs categorically from the search for Christian unity: the first is a matter of learning how to communicate with strangers, and the second, of overcoming estrangement within the family."[21] Lindbeck sees the emphasis in this as moving from concerns about "Christian disunity" to concerns about "religious pluralism."[22] He argues that the older hopes of a convergence ecumenism have been lost in this trend.

Lindbeck finds hope in the work of Michael Kinnamon and the *Princeton Proposal*.[23] While there are differences between them, Kinnamon and the *Princeton Proposal* both challenge the eroding theological foundation of ecumenism. They also strongly hold to the view, as Lindbeck remarks, that ecclesial unity is "an end in itself."[24] In the dedicatory letter for the *Princeton Proposal*, Carl E. Braaten and Robert W. Jenson write, "The institutions of conciliar ecumenism are largely captive to a 'new ecumenical paradigm' which subordinates the concern of the 'faith and order' movement, for the visible unity of Christians, to social and political agendas which are themselves divisive."[25] Even though convergence ecumenism lost significant momentum in the later twentieth century, it was still possible to address one of the major issues of the Reformation, the doctrine of justification, in the 1990s.

7.2 CONSENSUS IN THE BASIC DOCTRINE OF JUSTIFICATION

As addressed in the preceding chapters of this book, one of the major issues in the Reformation was the teaching about salvation by grace. In the 1990s this subject became a major issue in ecumenism. Catholic and Evangelical theologians from the Evangelicals and Catholics Together working group issued an ecumenical document in 1997 titled "The Gift of Salvation." One of the most important statements in this document reads:

> We agree that justification is not earned by any good works or merits of our own; it is entirely God's gift, conferred through the Father's sheer graciousness, out of the love that he bears us in his Son, who suffered on our behalf and rose from the dead for our justification. [. . .] The New Testament makes it clear that the gift of justification is received through faith. [. . .] Faith is not merely intellectual assent but an act of the whole person, involving the mind, the will, and the affections, issuing in a changed life. We understand that what we here affirm is in agreement with what the Reformation traditions have meant by justification by faith alone (*sola fide*).[26]

In 1999 the *Joint Declaration on the Doctrine of Justification* between the Lutheran World Federation and the Roman Catholic Church was signed. It holds, "Together we confess: By grace alone, in faith in Christ's saving work and not because of any merit on our part, we are accepted by God and receive the Holy Spirit, who renews our hearts while equipping and calling us to good works."[27] The *Joint Declaration* "shows that a consensus in basic truths of the doctrine of justification exists between Lutherans and Catholics." Thus, "the remaining differences of language, theological elaboration, and emphasis in the understanding of justification [. . .] are acceptable."[28] From this standpoint, "the doctrinal condemnations of the 16th century, in so far as they relate to the doctrine of justification, appear in a new light" for the "teaching of the Lutheran churches presented in this Declaration does not fall under the condemnations from the Council of Trent. The condemnations in the Lutheran Confessions do not apply to the teaching of the Roman Catholic Church presented in this Declaration."[29]

The *Joint Declaration* was signed on Reformation Day, October 31, 1999, in Augsburg, the city of the Augsburg Confession, where Cardinal Cajetan also summoned Luther in 1518 and unsuccessfully demanded his revocation. Before the official signing of the *Joint Declaration* in the fall of 1999, the final version of the document was released and discussed publicly in 1998 and 1999. While there were some critics, many more welcomed the document as evidence of progress in ecumenism. The vast majority of the Lutheran churches in the world affirm the document, as does the World Methodist Council.[30]

The Protestant criticisms of the *Joint Declaration* exemplified the transition in ecumenism. The resistance to it came from various angles, both from older traditionalist theology and from the newer postmodern theology of difference. This can be understood in part because of the broad reception of new philosophy from the 1960s and 1970s in theological faculties. The philosophical discourse of postmodernism, dialogical rationality, pragmatism, and the hermeneutical approach were all being adopted by theologians in the 1980s and 1990s. With this came a new emphasis on the good of difference and diversity. The pragmatic-idealist philosopher Nicholas Rescher, for example, wrote a book with this title in the early 1990s: *Pluralism: Against the Demand for Consensus.*[31]

All this ran parallel to the rise of the agenda of multiculturalism in politics in Western societies in the late twentieth century. The new philosophy and the cultural mood provided many theologians with a conceptual basis to challenge the agenda of unity, and, in some cases, a rationale to abandon the notion of consensus itself. The forces behind the *Joint Declaration* were, however, still driven by the older ecumenism of unity and consensus.

Whether the shift in ecumenism should be viewed negatively or positively depends upon, among other things, theological and philosophical presuppositions. On the one hand, this shift could be understood as the rebirth of ecumenism with more sober aims and with more pragmatic methods. Some might also view it positively as a movement away from an unrealistic idealism, or a false conception of unity. On the other hand, it could also be seen as evidence of the general decline of interest in ecumenism. Jürgen Moltmann writes, "The conservative programme of 'reconciled difference' promoted by the Lutheran World Federation became the sleeping pill of the ecumenical movement. We all stay as we are and are nice to each other."[32]

In another regard, the shift can be understood as an adaptation to a new view of religion as, in the first order, a cultural construct. This philosophy sees Christianity primarily at the cultural level. According to this viewpoint, it is not necessary to come to consensus in terms of faith, or in the concrete doctrinal expressions of faith, since these are understood as cultural symbols that are unique to a specific culture or society. The hope of the older consensus ecumenism has been lost in this thinking, and, with it, something of the universality of Christianity itself.

In this sense, Lindbeck correctly emphasizes the need for a sense of "a common peoplehood, transcending cultures and boundaries."[33] He calls the church to reconsider its identity in relationship to Judaism: "What we need to do is to find out that we are indeed one people, the people of Israel, as an interlocking part of the Jews as Israel. It is a very difficult thing to do." According to this theology, "we have to be nonsupersessionists; we don't replace Israel. We're in the very strange position of being part of the chosen people of God, even while there is another branch of the chosen people of God, most of whom do not accept Jesus Christ as Savior."[34] Lindbeck is correct to remind us of the origin of our faith in God's promise to Abraham. It is, indeed, the foundation upon which Paul's account of the gospel was built (see Gal 3:6-14; Gen 15:16). The core message of this theology is precisely the teaching that was affirmed in the *Joint Declaration*. While there are differences in the interpretation, there is also a fundamental agreement among many Christians today about this biblical teaching of justification.

7.3 ECUMENISM TODAY

There are many indicators today that seem to foretell challenging days ahead for ecumenism. Many have pointed out that there is a lack of interest today. This seems to be confirmed by anecdotal evidence. In 2013 in Tübingen, for example, there was a very sparsely attended lecture series jointly organized by the Catholic and Protestant faculties for the University of Tübingen's university-wide lecture series (Studium Generale) titled "Multifaceted Christianity" ("Vielfältiges Christentum"). On January 17, 2013, Theodor Dieter, from the Institute for Ecumenical Research in Strasbourg, gave a lecture in the series titled, "What Is and to Which End Does One Do Consensus Ecumenism?"[35] In the question-and-answer time following his lecture, I asked him about the status of ecumenism in Christianity today.

Making use of the story of the children of Israel wandering in the desert for forty years (Num 14) or of Jesus fasting in the desert for forty days (Matt 4), he responded by claiming that ecumenism is now in a "desert time" (*Wüstenzeit*). Dieter is certainly not alone in this observation.

Michael Kinnamon sees a decline in the interest in ecumenism as well. He also holds that the commitment to ecumenism is waning and that there are new divisions in the movement. He sees a decline in the overall relevance of ecumenical working groups and councils.[36] Many of the older mainline liberal denominations were at the forefront of the ecumenical movement. Their decline has certainly taken a toll on ecumenical vitality. In 1966 Bryan R. Wilson had already argued that the shift toward the ecumenical movement followed the beginnings of decline in mainline denominations.[37] Others have argued that the rise of Pentecostalism has done little to bolster the ecumenical institutions, although some participation is identifiable. David M. Thompson wrote in 2006 that charismatic or Pentecostal Christianity, which has been spreading across Europe since the 1960s, seems to be "generally unsympathetic to ecumenism."[38]

Analyzing the American context, Adelle M. Banks wrote in 2012, "The National Council of Churches, the flagship agency of ecumenism, has shrunk from some 400 staffers in its heyday in the 1960s to fewer than 20."[39] In a publication from 2012, Wesley Ariarajah holds that "the financial support" for the WCC is "decreasing, with serious impact on its programmatic life." He writes about a "decline of the influence of the voice of the WCC in international affairs." As he continues, "Some have begun to speak of an 'ecumenical winter.'"[40] In addition to this, a criticism of the politicization of the ecumenical movement has become a standard point of reference in many discourses about the movement. The same sentiment is found in the *Princeton Proposal*.[41]

While there are many examples that point to challenges ahead for institutional ecumenism, the various academic inquiries about ecumenism sometimes overlook the grassroots of ecclesial relations that emerged in the second half of the twentieth century. There are many examples of church fusions and ecumenical agreements, such as pulpit fellowships. The Lutheran and Reformed Churches of France recently joined together to form the United Protestant Church of France. There are also countless smaller ecumenical working groups that have emerged in the last forty years at the congregational level. Furthermore, with the continual rise of interconfessional marriages, many modern families have become miniature ecumenical associations. Perhaps some of these trends reflect Steven R. Harmon's call for "ordinary Christians" to take the lead in working toward the goal of ecclesial unity.[42]

Ecumenism is undergoing a process of transformation today. Jenson encourages us to "cling to baptism, and after that not be too precise about further conditions of fellowship."[43] His remark echoes the formulation found in *Unitatis redintegratio*: "All who have been justified by faith in Baptism are members of Christ's body, and have a right to be called Christian, and so are correctly accepted as brothers by the children of the Catholic Church."[44]

Following the Leuenberg Agreement and ecumenical work of the Lutheran World Federation in the 1970s, an understanding of fellowship was developed that made room for the idea of reconciled difference without identical confessional formulations. The continuing relevance of this approach was recently analyzed by theologians at a conference in 2013, at the celebration of the fortieth anniversary of the Leuenberg Agreement from 1973. The conference emphasized, as Michael Welker summarizes, the strength of this approach in its ability to conceptualize diversity in a polyphonic unity: "Ecclesial unity cannot have at its goal uniformity, homogeneity and integration through only a clerical hierarchy. The church as the body of Christ realizes itself in a differentiated unity of the different members under the one head, Jesus Christ, in a differentiated unity of the different gifts of the one Holy Spirit."[45]

Progress in ecumenism is also seen in the Catholic Church and the Orthodox churches. The fiftieth anniversary of the meeting in Jerusalem between Pope Paul VI and Patriarch Athenagoras was celebrated and confirmed by Pope Francis and Ecumenical Patriarch Bartholomew I of Constantinople in the same city. They also signed a "Common Declaration of Pope Francis and the Ecumenical Patriarch Bartholomew I" on May 25, 2014.[46] In this declaration they state that they "look forward in eager anticipation to the day in which we will finally partake together in the Eucharistic banquet."[47] They also affirm the work of the Joint International Commission, which is searching for the way to "full communion among Catholics and Orthodox."[48]

A new impulse of ecumenical theology is found in this document. They affirm that dialogue is "about deepening one's grasp of the whole truth that Christ has given to his Church, a truth that we never cease to understand better as we follow the Holy Spirit's promptings."[49] This is indeed a challenging call for ecumenism today. Such a deepening of our understanding of the "whole truth" seems to suggest that the different parts of "his Church" have something to learn from one another. Today the Orthodox churches are continuing to move toward more ecumenical collaboration and conversation.[50]

One of the major contemporary discussions in ecumenism is concerned with church unity. This is seen in the recent convergence document of the WCC, "The Church: Towards a Common Vision." It was accepted by the central committee of the WCC in Crete, Greece, in 2012. It describes the contemporary situation in ecumenism as entailing deep contradictions in the very understanding of church unity. It states,

> Currently, some identify the Church of Christ exclusively with their own community, while others would acknowledge in communities other than their own a real but incomplete presence of the elements which make up the Church. Others have joined into various types of covenant relationships, which sometimes include the sharing of worship. Some believe that the Church of Christ is located in all communities that present a convincing claim to be Christian, while others maintain that Christ's church is invisible and cannot be adequately identified during this earthly pilgrimage.[51]

The document nevertheless lays out some basic theological principles regarding the nature of the church as a missional fellowship. This subject of ecclesial unity was addressed further in a document that was accepted at the assembly of the WCC in Busan, Korea, in 2013. It is called "God's Gift and Call to Unity—and Our Commitment." There it states regarding the unity of the church, "The unity of the Church is not uniformity; diversity is also a gift, creative and life-giving. But diversity cannot be so great that those in Christ become strangers and enemies to one another, thus damaging the uniting reality of life in Christ."[52] It goes on to remark, "We are hardly a credible sign as long as our ecclesial divisions, which spring from fundamental disagreements in faith, remain."[53]

As the Christians working toward unity in the WCC know, the contemporary situation of Christianity in the world has brought new challenges. The major liberal mainline and established churches across the Western world have all gone into decline, while new Evangelical and Pentecostal churches are growing all over the world. Kurt Cardinal Koch, the president of the Pontifical Council for Promoting Christian Unity, has argued on many occasions that ecumenism today must work to include these traditions in the ecumenical discussion. The future of ecumenism will be strongly influenced by these churches. The groundbreaking achievements of past generations in ecumenism, such as the development of the idea of reconciled difference,[54] serve as examples for the contemporary context. We can build upon these accomplishments and address those issues that have not yet been addressed. Today, one of these major issues is the Reformation itself.

7.4 IS THE REFORMATION OVER?

This question was the title of a book from Geoffrey Wainwright that was published in 2000. It was also the title of another book from Mark A. Noll and Carolyn Nystrom in 2005. They write that "among evangelicals and Catholics who are open to cooperation there now exists a broad and deep foundation of agreement on the central teachings of Christianity."[55] They also see "the openness at many levels of the Catholic Church to a Bible-centered and Christ-focused religion that looks strangely like evangelical Christianity."[56] Noll and Nystrom do, however, point out that the nature of the church is the major issue that shows a fault line. They write,

> In sum, the central difference that continues to separate evangelicals and Catholics is not Scripture, justification by faith, the pope, Mary, the sacraments or clerical celibacy—though the central difference is reflected in differences on these matters—but the nature of the church. For Catholics, the visible, properly constituted, and hierarchically governed church is the principal God-ordained agent for the work of apostolic ministry. For evangelicals, the church is the body of Christ made up of all those who have responded to the apostolic proclamation of the God-given offer of the forgiveness of sins in Jesus Christ.[57]

In these remarks Noll and Nystrom echo the insight of Wainwright. He holds, "Are doctrinal matters between Catholics and Protestant now settled? The appropriate answer is: More than they were."[58]

While there are indeed many points of agreement that can be identified, the Reformation is not over in the theological sense. This is especially the case if the Reformation is understood as a re-formation of the church to an authority structure that is closer to the egalitarian impulses of the New Testament church and especially the idea of a priesthood of all believers. Pope Francis is encouraging this impulse today in the Catholic Church. Officially, however, the Catholic Church continues to assert absolute authority. As an institution that asserts "jurisdictional and magisterial primacy within the universal church," the papacy "dates only from the

Middle Ages in the Latin west."⁵⁹ The Roman bishops' attempts to assert primacy were "always rejected by the majority of the church and especially by the Eastern churches."⁶⁰

Until the Roman Catholic Church finds a way of officially reinterpreting this assertion of authority over the universal church, there will be no unity in Christianity. It is also necessary for the Catholic Church to address officially its excommunication of Luther (even if the church cannot revoke it officially as he is dead). The excommunication signifies a fundamental rejection of his entirely legitimate calls for reform. While it is certainly possible for the Catholic Church officially to reject the spirit of this excommunication (and apologize for it) and to develop officially a new understanding of the papacy, at the moment it continues to teach officially that the pope has "supreme" power over the whole church.

If one did not hold the Catholic Church to be a part of the one church of Christ, it would not be necessary to address this issue. As it is a part of the one church of Christ, however, it is necessary to address this absolute claim to authority as an issue between brothers and sisters in the one faith. In *Lumen gentium* (*Dogmatic Constitution on the Church*, Vatican Council II) and in the Catechism of the Catholic Church, the Catholic Church teaches officially that the pope is "Vicar of Christ, and as pastor of the entire Church has full, supreme, and universal power [*plenam, supremam et universalem potestatem*] over the whole Church, a power which he can always exercise unhindered."⁶¹

Many Christians in the world today reject this idea of the pope as the "Vicar of Christ" and this claim to "full, supreme, and universal power." This is because both the papacy and this assertion of authority have no foundation in the Scriptures. The passage that is always cited to support these claims (Matt 16:18-19) does not justify them.⁶² While Roman bishops were important and influential in the early church, they never had supreme authority. The modern papacy is a creation of the Middle Ages and the nineteenth century (when Rome asserted papal infallibility at the First Vatican Council). Both the idea that all the succeeding bishops of Rome since Peter had supreme authority over the church, and the idea that they were, or are, in any way infallible, cannot be established from the New Testament. David L. Turner writes,

> This dogma is anachronistic for Matthew, who knows nothing about Peter being the first pope or of the primacy of Rome over other Christian churches. Matthew would not have endorsed the idea of Peter's infallibility or sole authority in the church, since Peter speaks as

a representative of the other apostles and often makes mistakes ([Matt] 15:15; 16:16; 17:4, 25; 18:21; 19:27; 26:33-35; cf. Acts 11:1-18; Gal. 2:11-14). In 18:18, binding and loosing is a function of the church, not Peter. Peter is later sent by the church and is accountable to the church (Acts 8:14; 11:1-18). James presides over Peter, and Paul rebukes Peter (Acts 15; Gal. 2:11-14). Peter himself speaks of Jesus as the chief shepherd, senior pastor, or *pontifex maximus* of the church (1 Pet. 5:4).[63]

As Donald A. Hagner remarks, "to allow this passage its natural meaning, that Peter is the rock upon which the church is built, is by no means either to affirm the papacy or to deny that the church, like the apostles, rests upon Jesus as the bedrock of its existence. Jesus is after all the builder, and all that the apostles do they do through him."[64] It is, furthermore, impossible to separate the declaration of Jesus in verse 18 from the confession of Peter in verse 16. Peter is the rock upon which Jesus will build his church insofar as it has been revealed to him (through what was heard and seen, Matt 11:4) that Jesus was the Christ.[65] To claim that Jesus was establishing the papacy with these remarks is, simply put, bad exegesis. Even the current prefect of the Congregation for the Doctrine of the Faith (of the Roman Catholic Church), Gerhard Cardinal Müller, openly admits that the New Testament sources do not speak of a Petrine succession. Nevertheless, he endorses the idea because of tradition.[66] In his explanation of the First Vatican Council, he writes that the pope can "at any time exercise his full power directly over all of the faithful and the bishops."[67] Where is the Scripture to support this claim?

In the context of his confession about Jesus, Peter is singled out by Jesus for a special ministry in the early church. The fact that Peter was influential in the early church was already well known—indeed, common knowledge—among Christians at the time of the writing of the Gospel of Matthew. Matthew's first readers would have understood this passage in this way: *Jesus was the one who determined that Peter, the individual apostle, would play an important role in the first generation of the church (as we all know to be the case). Furthermore, this great man of God, Peter (who is now dead), understood what the story is all about: Jesus is the Christ.* Clearly, the passage does not endorse the idea of apostolic succession, infallibility, or the Roman bishop's "full, supreme, and universal power" over all the church.

The Roman assertion of "full, supreme, and universal power" keeps the Protestant protest against this authoritarianism alive. It necessarily evokes a protest from all Christians who do not agree with this claim since there is no foundation for it in the Scriptures. The Catholic Church's assertion of "full, supreme, and universal power" shows that the basic issue of authority, as addressed in the Reformation five hundred years ago, has not yet been resolved. In this sense, the Reformation is not over.

A contemporary assignment for Catholic theologians, one started in the Farfa Sabina dialog, is to reinterpret these claims in *Lumen gentium* to fit with the Bible. Only Jesus Christ has supreme authority in the church (Matt 28:18: "And Jesus came and said to them, 'All authority in heaven and on earth has been given to me'"; Col 1:18: "he [Jesus Christ] is the head of the body, the church"; see also Eph 1:22). Furthermore, all Christians are able to instruct one another in the faith without the magisterium. As Paul teaches, "I myself feel confident about you, my brothers and sisters, that you yourselves are full of goodness, filled with all knowledge, and able to instruct one another" (Rom 15:14).[68] By providing a new interpretation of these passages in *Lumen gentium*, Catholic theologians can affirm the teaching in *Dei verbum*: "This Magisterium [teaching office] is not superior to the Word of God [*non supra verbum Dei*], but is its servant."[69]

Historically, however, the Reformation is over. With the Peace of Augsburg in 1555, a political order was established allowing for the two confessions. This event marked the end of an epoch and the beginning of a new one. What followed was the confessional era. This too, however, has passed. As Brady argues, the "age of reformations is over and so is the confessional era."[70] Secularization has transformed the old landscape of confessional identities. In this historical, cultural, and social sense, the Reformation is clearly over.

On the other hand, the term "Reformation" stands for more than the historical events, although it is closely related to them. The term is associated with a living debate within Christianity about articles of the Christian faith (such as the understanding of justification), about the church (the Lord's Supper, priesthood, papacy, celibacy, etc.), and about the sources and methods of theology (the understanding of Scripture, tradition, and ecclesial authority). While these doctrinal disputes are connected to the sixteenth century, they also transcend it. The precise meaning of these historical-theological matters and the correct interpretations of the positions also remain contested issues. While the Reformation is over in the historical sense, it lives on as a debate within Christianity about the Christian faith. The creedal formulas of the fourth and fifth centuries or the Enlightenment of the eighteenth and nineteenth centuries are similar examples of completed events that are simultaneously living debates.

In this sense, the Reformation can be understood as a living debate and an unfinished project. The transformational processes that took shape in the Reformation were viewed as a historical break by many in the first half of the sixteenth century. Kaufmann holds that the church that took shape after this process of reform was no longer the church of the pope, and, in this regard, the "Reformation failed."[71] According to the Lutheran theologian Wolfhart Pannenberg, "the existence of specific Protestant churches manifests the failure of the Reformation."[72] The quest for ecclesial unity today, insofar as it is a promotion of the gospel message as the foundation of the unity of the church, is an attempt at the "completion of the failed, or at least discontinued, Reformation of Christianity in the sixteenth century."[73] As long as there is still a need for a new focus on the gospel, the grace of God, the teaching about the priesthood of all believers, and the authority of the Scripture, the Reformation remains an unfinished project in Christianity today.

In the aftermath of the Reformation, many Protestants adopted the expression *ecclesia semper reformanda est* (the church is always to be reformed).[74] Since John Henry Newman (1801–1890), the idea of doctrinal "development" also became very popular among many Catholics. All Christians hear the call of Christ: "Be perfect, as your heavenly Father is perfect" (Matt 5:48). Beyond the historical and doctrinal sense of the Reformation, there is a deeper principle of Christian renewal—reform— that is shared by all Christians.

7.5 COMMEMORATING THE REFORMATION TOGETHER

How then should the historical Reformation of the sixteenth century be remembered by a Christian? Can Orthodox, Catholic, and Protestant Christians commemorate positive aspects of the Reformation together? If so, which aspects? A foundational achievement of the ecumenical movement was the reappraisal of the mutual condemnations of the Reformation era. The Protestant condemnations applied to teachings that were common in the Reformation era. Since the Second Vatican Council, however, the Catholic Church has changed in many ways. For this reason, the old condemnations do not apply to the Catholic Church today. A new relationship has been established between these churches, even if there continue to be differences.[75]

Following on the ecumenical work of Catholic and Lutheran theologians from the last thirty years, in 2013 the Lutheran–Roman Catholic Commission on Unity issued a common statement on the celebration of the Reformation in 2017.[76] The Ecumenical Working Group of Protestant and Catholic Theologians has also issued a statement on the Reformation with a view to the five hundredth anniversary of the Reformation, titled "Reformation 1517–2017: Ecumenical Perspectives." It is a positive signal for ecumenism today because it shows how both traditions have learned from one another. Catholics have learned from the Protestant emphasis on Scripture and on the priesthood of believers.[77] The statement also affirms the "acceptance of Roman Catholic insights in the Protestant churches."[78] The Protestant churches have learned to make themselves "jointly perceptible in the global context."[79] This seems to be a reference to the inner-Protestant work in ecumenism, such as the Leuenberg Agreement, which led to the formation of the Community of Protestant Churches in Europe. The document also holds that Protestants have learned from Catholics about the importance of the ancient and the medieval church as a source of wisdom to be rediscovered.[80]

Some open questions are also addressed. The statement claims that Catholics and Protestants have dealt with the Enlightenment in different ways. It raises the question about "how churches should respond in their self-organization to the trends and values of modernity." Here it refers to matters such as "the consistent division of powers, issues of participation and gender equality or of human rights." These subjects are "compelling both denominational traditions to further reflections."[81]

The statement suggests that the commemoration of the Reformation is an opportunity to focus on reading the Scriptures in groups and as individuals.[82] It also affirms, for both Catholics and Protestants, that "all religions and cultures in the history of mankind should be treated with respect, even if Christians are committed to witness to Jesus Christ as the light of the world and thus also to formulate the Christian faith as a religious alternative for the adherents of other religions."[83] This goes together with an emphasis on ecumenical dialogue as cooperation and collaboration.[84] Regarding the history of division in the Reformation, "it is appropriate to commemorate the Reformation in a double-edged way: both with joyous celebration of the Reformation as well as with self-critical reflection."[85] The ecumenical statement also asserts that "no church can fulfil the catholicity of the church without the other churches."[86] It goes on to encourage church leaders to promote ecumenism at the local level.

The Reformation is a unique event in the history of Christianity. If one compares the split of Latin Christendom in the sixteenth century to the split of Anglicanism in the eighteenth century, for example, one will find that the Reformation was far more violent. After John Wesley attended a Moravian service in May of 1738 and claimed to feel his "heart strangely warmed,"[87] he committed himself to a new movement in Christianity that focused on the lived experience of salvation. As the Methodist Society grew, the relationship with the Church of England fell apart. Once the bishop of London rejected the Methodists within the Church of England for ordination, and as the need for new ministers grew in the American context, John Wesley ultimately appointed a general superintendent, which was then followed with the Methodist "Deed of Declaration" (1784). This provided the formal establishment of the Society of Methodists and ultimately led to the split with the Anglican Church. No one lost their life for this, and no wars followed this fundamental break between the Methodists and the Anglicans.

The Reformation was very different in this regard. As Bob Scribner writes, the Reformation "was driven forward not by coolheaded discussion and debate, but by passionate polemic and fevered propaganda."[88] This applies to both the Protestants and the Catholics. It is difficult to celebrate something that is described in these terms. Indeed, the Reformation as a historical event is inseparable from the Papal Bull of Pope Leo X, issued on June 15, 1520, *Exsurge domine*, "Condemning the Errors of Martin Luther." It is also inseparable from his excommunication of Luther on January 3, 1521 (*Decet romanum pontificem*), and the consequent divisions of Western Christianity.

The division of Latin Christendom in the sixteenth century brought another division in the body of Christ. This division, and the others before it and after it, cannot be celebrated by a Christian because it contradicts the biblical message of unity. Furthermore, many of the things that happened in the Reformation, on both sides, are not worthy of celebration. In fact, one of the most important historical events of the Reformation—the shift of power in church matters from an imperfect but semiautonomous ecclesial structure to the German princes as virtually miniature popes in their territories, which was later reaffirmed at the Peace of Augsburg in 1555—led to a problematic new fusion of the religious and the political realms and a significant reduction of the autonomy of the church.

This fusion is certainly understandable from a historical perspective; furthermore, it was not entirely new. Herzog Georg von Sachsen is a good example of a pre-Reformation political figure who exercised significant influence over the church in his territory. The fusion is, nevertheless, a central aspect of what we today call "the Reformation."

This aspect would be difficult to celebrate as it weakened the autonomy of the church. The relationship between the ecclesial order and the regional political authorities went far beyond a relationship of cooperation in freedom. What emerged was a direct correlation between the ecclesial and the political realms. It led to a new system of religious coercion and disciplinary consolidation.

Although the Reformation cannot be celebrated in its totality, in terms of general history it must be remembered as a whole as a very significant event in Western history. Furthermore, good things also came from the impulses of reform. A few things that were emphasized in the Reformation also have been acknowledged and affirmed in the Catholic Church. The positive aspects of the Reformation can be commemorated by both Catholics and Protestants together, indeed, by all Christians.

Liberal Protestants sometimes celebrate the "Luther to the modern individual" account of the Reformation. Luther's challenge to authority is presented as the beginning of the turn from the authoritarianism of the Middle Ages to the Enlightenment, leading ultimately to the autonomous individual of the modern world. Ulrich Barth, for example, sees the "birth of religious autonomy" in Luther's Ninety-Five Theses.[89] The theses offer a "compendium of social critique, moral critique, critique of religion, critique of ideology and critique of institutions."[90] In the theses he sees the methodological and the material sense of "Enlightened Protestantism."[91] At the same time, however, it is important to remember that Luther was popularizing medieval mysticism and biblical theology, as well as Augustinian theology and Pauline theology. In all these regards, one could say that Luther was regressive. Indeed, his rejection of Erasmus is perhaps the best example of this.

Nevertheless, it is certainly true that the Reformation encouraged the recognition of the freedom of conscience. At the Diet of Worms in 1521, Luther said, "It is neither safe nor right to go against conscience."[92] This emphasis on personal conscience was a positive moment in the Reformation. He claimed that his conscience was ultimately only answerable to the evidence of Scripture and reason. This was a foundational challenge to otherwise absolute human authority at this time.

The emphasis on the individual conscience went together with an emphasis on the individual and the local congregation. As Karlstadt wrote in 1524 regarding the implementation of the ecclesial reforms, "God issued a general law by which the entire believing community, every congregation and each person, is to be guided and directed." God works not only on the level of the "entire believing community" and "every congregation" but also concretely in "each person."[93] For this reason he called for more congregational autonomy in the implementation of the reforms (rather than centralized control). This was the true spirit of the original Wittenberg Reformation. This was also closely related to the mystical theology of yieldedness (*Gelassenheit*). The individual conscience, "each person," answers to Scripture and reason and should yield only to God in the final instance. This is not to disregard the importance and necessity of pastors, teachers, and parents. Rather it situates them all *sub verbo Dei* (under the word of God). The forerunner of the Reformation, Jan Hus, and so many others who were executed for their faith, embody the true meaning of this teaching. The importance of the individual conscience has also been emphasized by Catholics, for example, in Pope John Paul II's *Ut unum sint*.[94]

The emphasis on the authority of the Scriptures was also a positive development that has been acknowledged by Protestants and Catholics. *Dei verbum* of Vatican II explicitly states that the magisterium is *non supra verbum Dei* (not above the word of God). The emphasis on scriptural authority in the Reformation, which is also found with Hus, was one of the things that was used to challenge the coercion of otherwise absolute human authority.

The interest in reforming the social order and helping the poor is another area that both Catholics and Protestants can positively commemorate. Thesis 43 of Luther's Ninety-Five Theses states, "Christians are to be taught that he who gives to the poor or lends to the needy does a better deed than he who buys indulgences."[95] Karlstadt was also a strong voice for the poor. He wrote, "As Christians we are not to let anyone descend to such poverty and need that they are driven and forced to cry and search for bread." Indeed, "we must eagerly look to our neighbors and fellow Christians and together help them in their need before they cry to us for help. If we fail to do this, we are simply not being Christian."[96] Karlstadt also argued for the liberation of slaves:

> This should also be done by all slave traders in Rome and elsewhere in the world. They should set the slaves free, without later enslaving them by force. [. . .] Accordingly, abbots, vicars, provincials, clergy, and monks should set their sold brothers free—and not only when they express a desire to be free. In addition, they are to give them money and other aid and help them toward the trade they might enjoy doing. Thus they will be able to feed and maintain themselves in a Christian manner.[97]

The cultural heritage of the Reformation is another positive moment in the history, such as the emphasis on vernacular translations of the Bible. The Reformation also brought a reform of education. As the church service was reformed, Protestants also emphasized the sermon. This focus on intellectual communication in the context of religious ritual is a central part of the educational legacy of the Reformation.[98]

The artistic and musical impulses of the Reformation, like the educational impulse, were connected to both the religious renewal and the general cultural movements of humanism and the Renaissance.[99] These developments in education and culture are positive moments in the history of the Reformation. The same applies to the basic idea of reform or renewal, and the many figures who worked for reform before 1517.

The teaching about the priesthood of all believers is one of the great inheritances of the Reformation. Before this, the Hussite Articles also encouraged this theological impulse. This is a biblical theme from 1 Peter 2:5: "Like living stones, let yourselves be built into a spiritual house, to be a holy priesthood, to offer spiritual sacrifices acceptable to God through Jesus Christ." In *Lumen gentium*, the "Dogmatic Constitution on the Church" from the Second Vatican Council, this theme of the "common priesthood of the faithful" (*sacerdotium commune fidelium*) is specifically highlighted and emphasized.[100] While the Catholic view is articulated differently than Protestant views on this matter, there is nevertheless a consensus in the basic teaching that all Christians belong to the "holy priesthood." The gospel message and the teaching about divine grace were central concepts in the tracts and literature of the Reformation. All Christians celebrate this gospel message. As addressed above, this was affirmed in the *Joint Declaration on the Doctrine of Justification*.

Commemorating the Reformation is a very challenging assignment, but it brings with it an opportunity to reaffirm the principle of Christian unity in love. The Reformation is not only an issue among Protestants and Catholics, however; it is also an issue for all those traditions that "protested" against the papacy. For the Mennonites and other members of the sidelined traditions of Anabaptism, the Reformation is remembered as an era of persecution and human brutality. The Lutherans and the Calvinists, and the other politically powerful streams of the Reformation, must continually seek reconciliation with their brothers and sisters in Christ. It is therefore critical that the commemoration of the Reformation include these stories about the persecution of the Anabaptists as an important dark chapter of the Reformation. It is a positive sign of this reconciliation that after nearly five hundred years, in 2010 in Stuttgart, the Lutheran World Federation asked the Mennonites for forgiveness for the sins of their spiritual ancestors. The same can be said of Pope Francis' recent trip to Turin, where he asked the Waldensians for forgiveness. Much work has been done toward reconciliation, but there is still a lot of work to do.

The commemoration of the Reformation is an opportunity to work toward reconciliation, to contribute to ecumenical work, to proclaim the gospel, to make the Scriptures accessible to everyone, to take on responsibility for our neighbors, to strengthen the church, and to praise "the triune God as origin and goal of all life."[101] Indeed, commemorating the Reformation ecumenically means celebrating Christ together, not divisions.[102] Thomas Söding is correct when he writes about the commemoration of the Reformation "from a Catholic perspective." The commemoration provides us with an opportunity "in the globalized and secular world to call the Reformation to memory in such a way that it does not, like in past jubilees, deepen the division of the church but rather heals it."[103]

7.6 THEOLOGICAL FOUNDATIONS OF ECUMENISM

While the push to consensus has lost its momentum and its background cultural energy from the 1950s and 1960s, the abiding call of Christ in John 17:22-23 remains a guiding light for the church today: "The glory that you have given me I have given to them, so that they may be one, as we are one, I in them and you in me, that they may become completely one, so that the world may know that you have sent me and have loved them even as you have loved me." From a historical-critical perspective, this verse is itself evidence of the early church's struggles with disunity and fragmentation. The problem of disunity and fragmentation has been with Christianity from its birth. In theological analysis of this passage, we learn that the impulse toward Christian unity is one that has its ultimate foundation in divine unity. The unity of the Father, Son, and Holy Spirit offers an example of unity in difference, a oneness that is differentiated and based upon love. This concept of differentiated unity is the key to ecclesial unity today. As the passage teaches, the unity of the church also strengthens the witness of the church in the world. Furthermore, "the unity of which Jesus speaks must be in some way visible, because it is meant to be *seen* by the world."[104]

Another important passage that provides guidance is Ephesians 4:1–13. This passage teaches us to make "every effort to maintain the unity of the Spirit in the bond of peace," for "there is one body and one Spirit" and "one Lord, one faith, one baptism, one God and Father of all." It also teaches that "each of us was given grace" so that some are apostles, others prophets, others evangelists and still others pastors and teachers. All these are given "to equip the saints for the work of ministry, for building up the body of Christ, until all of us come to the unity of the faith and of the knowledge of the Son of God." It follows that we should be eager to maintain the unity because there is, in fact, only "one faith" and "one baptism." This passage speaks to a fundamental unity of the Christian faith that exists even when there are divisions between Christians.

Many of these impulses toward a concept of ecclesial unity have been affirmed in modern Catholic theology. *Lumen fidei* affirms that "by professing the same faith, we stand firm on the same rock."[105] The unity of the church is based not on personalities but on a common faith. As Luther remarked, "All churches are equal, and their unity does not depend on the sovereignty of this one man [the pope]; but as St. Paul says in Eph. 4[:5], their unity depends on one faith, one baptism, one Lord Jesus Christ, and these are all the common and equal possession of all the parishes in the world."[106]

Striving toward more unity means expanding our horizons in order to see not only the differences but also the points of agreement. First Corinthians 12:12 teaches in this sense that "For just as the body is one and has many members, and all the members of the body, though many, are one body, so it is with Christ." A body with many members is not the only image that illustrates the church's unity in diversity. The fourth-century theologian Pacian of Barcelona provides these other analogies:

> The church is "the queen in clothing embroidered with gold adorned with diverse colors" [Ps 45:12]; "a fruitful vine on the walls of the house of the Lord" [Ps 128:3]; the mother of "young maidens without number" [Song 6:8]; "the one beautiful and perfect dove, the chosen of her mother" [Song 6:9]; the very mother of all, "built on the foundations of the apostles and prophets, Christ Jesus himself being the cornerstone" [Eph 2:20]; and "a great house" made sumptuous with a diversity of every kind of vessel [2 Tim 2:20].[107]

In the "diverse colors," there is, however, "one faith" that is shared by all Christians, a faith laid forth in the Scriptures and summarized in the ancient creeds. This was acknowledged in Luther's rejection of the partisan term "Lutheran." While he would accept it later, early on in 1522 (after the 1521 excommunication), he argued that Christians should call themselves "Christians" and not "Lutherans." We should "abolish all party names and call ourselves Christians after him whose teaching we hold."[108] Luther knew that the unity of the church has its foundation in the gospel, which unites all congregations.[109] Katharina Zell (1497/98–1562), perhaps the most important woman Reformer of the sixteenth century, remarked in 1557, in a published "Letter to the Whole City of Strasbourg," that she wanted to be called neither after the name of the Reformers (whether it were Luther, Zwingli, Schwenckfeld, Bucer, etc.) nor after the name of all the preachers, prophets, and apostles, for "these did not become a sacrifice for me on the cross, but only Christ the Son of God; why then would I want to be named after them?" She adds, "I don't want to be named after them, but rather want to be called a 'Christian,' after my only lord and master Christ, about whom all of these [Reformers] taught and whom they confessed."[110]

By acknowledging the common faith laid forth in the Scriptures and summarized in the ancient creeds, the positive contributions of all the traditions can be understood as enriching the whole. *Lumen gentium* brings this to expression: "In virtue of this catholicity [*catholicitatis*] each individual part contributes through its special gifts [*propria dona*] to the good of the other parts and of the whole Church." In turn, through "the common sharing of gifts and through the common effort to attain fullness in unity, the whole and each of the parts receive increase."[111] This teaching emphasizes the unique gifts, the *propria dona*, of specific parts of the whole. In this way, plurality and diversity are evaluated positively. This positive evaluation of diversity is also central to the document "Reformation 1517–2017: Ecumenical Perspectives":

> The paths of Western Christendom, which diverged in the 16th century, have converged, touched and connected to one another over the past century in a hopeful manner. The denominational polyphony of Christian witness and service in the present day world may be seen as an expression of the diverse gifts in the one body of Christ, as long as they do not contain mutual condemnation or fundamental criticism. One may hope and seek to ensure that the brotherhood of the different churches and congregation in the *one* Church of Jesus Christ that has already been reached may lead more and more to visible unity.[112]

This is a very hopeful development in ecumenism. It challenges us to think about a "polyphony of Christian witness." This is a fundamentally biblical theology because the church's birth in the Pentecost event was precisely that—a polyphony of Christian witness.

After the Jerusalem church was "filled with the Spirit" (Acts 2:4), people from all over the world heard them in their own languages "speaking about God's deeds of power" (2:11). Many were "amazed and perplexed, saying to one another, 'What does this mean?'" (2:12). According to Luke's account of the event, Peter then recited Joel 2:28-32 at length in order to explain the Spirit's work at Pentecost (Acts 2:14-21). Peter referred to Joel who prophesied that God would pour out the Spirit "on *all* flesh" (Acts 2:17; Joel 2:28) for "*everyone* who calls upon the name of the Lord shall be saved" (Acts 2:21; Joel 2:32). The same verse from Joel is cited verbatim by Paul at Romans 10:13. Paul saw this fulfilled in the work of Jesus Christ, for now "there is no distinction between Jew and Greek; the same Lord is Lord of *all* and is generous to *all* who call on him." (Rom 10:12).

The emphasis on the universality of the Christian message and the universality of the Spirit's work in the church was adopted by the church fathers.[113] To Joel 2:28 ("I will pour out my Spirit on *all flesh*"), Cyril of Jerusalem taught that "the Holy Spirit is no respecter of persons, for he seeks no dignities but piety of soul. Let neither the rich be puffed up nor the poor be dejected, but only let each prepare himself for reception of the heavenly gift."[114] It was in this tradition that the Anabaptists (such as Melchior Hoffman) referred to Joel 2:28-29 ("your sons *and your daughters* shall prophesy") in their arguments for raising the status of women in the church. The true "polyphony of Christian witness" requires the voices of women as equal voices in every respect.

Some of the most beautiful descriptions of the "polyphony of Christian witness" are found with Cyprian of Carthage. In his *On the Unity of the Church*, he outlines the principle of subsidiarity. This theology holds together both the universality of the church and its local particularity. Cyprian writes, "The Church forms a unity, however far she spreads [. . .]; just as the sun's rays are many, yet the light is one [. . .]; it is one and the same light that is spread everywhere." He also writes, "A tree's branches are many, yet the strength deriving from its sturdy root is one. [. . .] Though many streams flow from a single spring [. . .] yet their oneness abides by reason of their starting point."[115] The image of catholicity here is so impressive because it is articulated in terms of plurality.

These illustrations of the church in its unity and diversity have been summarized by the Jesuit theologian Maurice Bévenot. Cyprian's understanding of the church "may in part be illustrated by the propagation of the strawberry plant, whose runners give birth to fresh strawberry plants, each as complete as itself. Cyprian maintains the persistence of the 'oneness' [of the church] *in spite of* this, as also *in spite of* the fact that the Apostles were all shepherds equally."[116] For this reason, the unity of the church is best understood in participatory language rather than institutional or hierarchical categories. By virtue of the Spirit of God, various parts jointly *participate* in the shared fellowship of Jesus Christ.

The concept of *koinonia* (communion, fellowship, or participation) is used in the description of the early church at Acts 2:42: "They devoted themselves to the apostles' teaching and fellowship [κοινωνία], to the breaking of bread and the prayers." Michael Kinnamon has drawn attention to the importance of this idea of "fellowship." He writes, *"Koinonia is expressed in the relationship of the local and universal church*; or, to say it more directly, the universal church is a communion of local churches, in each of which the fullness of the church resides."[117] This understanding of the universal church as a fellowship of local churches was already addressed at the beginning of the Reformation.

At the Leipzig Debate in 1519, Luther said, "As long as the excellent doctor [Eck] insists on throwing the Hussites, who have only been around a century, in my face I will respond with the Eastern Church—the better part of the Universal Church—and its fourteen centuries. If their refusal to accept the Pope makes them heretics then I call my opponent [Eck] an heretic for saying that all these saints, famous throughout the universal church, are damned."[118] The universality and catholicity of the church can never be secured by demanding submission to a higher instance of ecclesial authority in an institutional hierarchy.[119] There must be a way of understanding Christian unity that acknowledges the history of various traditions within Christianity and their respective institutional frameworks. The visible unity, catholicity, and universality of the church does not require institutional conformity. Each strawberry plant is going to grow differently. The unity of the church exists in this plurality of its local expressions. While the different strawberry plants may grow together naturally, they cannot and should not be forced to do this.

At Pope Francis' visit to the Waldensian temple, he spoke about the unity of the church. He emphasized the fruit of the ecumenical movement as "the rediscovery of the fraternity which unites all those who believe in Jesus Christ and have been baptized in his name." Rediscovering this fraternity "allows us to perceive the profound bond which already unites us, despite our differences." This is a very important point in his address. In this sentence he affirms that there is already a unity *in difference*. He goes on to explain that the "unity produced by the Holy Spirit does not mean uniformity. Indeed, brothers are united by one and the same origin but they are not identical to each other." Pope Francis emphasizes that there is a basis in the New Testament for this theology. He points to the teaching about the different gifts of the Spirit in the one Christian community (see 1 Cor 12–14). He also points to the "differences and sometimes contention" in the proclamation of the gospel in the New Testament (see Acts 15:36-40). Pope Francis regrets that Christians often fail to "accept their differences" and rather turn to "acts of violence committed in the name of our faith." The significance of these statements can hardly be overemphasized. He calls upon Christians to accept one another's differences and thus to see difference itself in a positive light.[120]

Understanding how the different parts make up the whole and how they enrich the whole requires a widening of our horizons and a deepening of our faith. Christian unity is, however, more than mutual understanding, prayer, and dialogue—as important as this is. The importance of working together for the common good was addressed in *Ut unum sint*: "Relations between Christians [...] call for every possible form of practical cooperation at all levels: pastoral, cultural and social, as well as that of witnessing to the Gospel message."[121] While Christian unity becomes visible in cooperation, cooperation itself requires a goodwill on the part of the participants.[122] Goodwill imbues the other with trust and strengthens those who are working for the common good. With goodwill, a common understanding of our unity in difference, and practical cooperation, Christians can "offer a radiant and attractive witness of fraternal communion."[123]

Along these lines, Pope Francis has called for a new understanding of the church today as a missional church, one that imbues the joy of the gospel. The Roman bishop declares that the church should fulfill this assignment not with a centralized, top-down authority structure but in a decentralized network of local congregations. The local congregation is the place where the whole church is concretely present, and it is the place where the gospel is proclaimed. Pope Francis asks us to consider if the message of the church today is a message of division and exclusion, or a message of the good news (the gospel), which brings joy, liberation, and renewal.

When reflecting on the Reformation, now five hundred years later, we have an opportunity to remember what was truly at stake in the old debates about the indulgences: the joy of the gospel as a freely given gift, "grace given for grace out of mercy and compassion."[124] In this joy of the gospel, we can continue the work of reconciliation and affirm the one Christian faith as a faith that unites us in a differentiated unity. The church's service and witness is, of course, made more effective in this unity. Christian unity is, however, more than just a means to an end. Maintaining "the unity of the Spirit in the bond of peace" (Eph 4:3) is also an end in itself, just as a fellowship of sisterly and brotherly kindness is an end in itself. With a deeper faith and goodwill, with dialogue and cooperation, the pragmatic, positive consensus can be strengthened and developed. This is, after all, the true sense of *reformatio* (reformation): the Spirit of God improving the church and leading it toward a more visible unity as the body of Christ.

CONCLUSION
The Future of Reformation

The Scriptures teach at 1 Peter 4:8, "Above all, maintain constant love for one another, for love [Gr. *agape*; Lat. *caritas*] covers a multitude of sins." This teaching presumes that which is true; namely, that the virtue of love (or charity) is indispensable for successful coexistence in close communities that share a sense of mutual belonging and that seek to create a future together.[1] Sins that have been committed against God and between brothers and sisters in Christ, both in the history of the church and today, are an injury to communion. The tragic story of the Dutch Anabaptist Dirk Willems is a painful reminder of this.[2] He is a virtually mythological figure in many Mennonite circles because of his compassion. He was imprisoned for his Anabaptist faith by the Catholic authorities. After escaping, a guard pursued him across the ice and fell through. Rather than continuing his escape, Willems turned back to rescue him. After being saved by Willems, the guard was then forced to take him into custody, where Willems was later burned at the stake. Similar stories of injustice can be told in which the Protestants were the aggressors. So much of the Reformation era is stained by injustice and brutality.

While much work has been done to subdue the pain of these memories, they have a habit of resurfacing. If there has been an attempt to reestablish a just relationship through the righting of wrongs, love can make forgiveness possible. Of course, the righting of wrongs, as necessary as this is, cannot force forgiveness (a contradiction in terms). At best, the righting of wrongs or the seeking after reconciliation through action can increase the chances that forgiveness and reconciliation might actually happen.[3]

Only God can forgive sins in the absolute sense. Christians are, however, called to love one another and to forgive one another. The relationship of love and reconciliation is beautifully illustrated with the story of Jacob and Esau. Jacob cheated his brother Esau and forced him to sell his birthright. Jacob even deceived his own father, Isaac, to get the paternal blessing that was intended for Esau (Gen 25–27). Esau was justified in his anger toward Jacob as this was a grave injustice. Later, however, when Esau and four hundred of his men could have destroyed Jacob and his family, he showed mercy on Jacob and forgave him his sins. As Jacob and his family approached Esau with gifts of recompense and in a spirit of contrition, "Esau ran to meet him, and embraced him, and fell on his neck and kissed him, and they wept" (Gen 33:4).

If this story is taken in the allegorical sense, we can see that many Christians today and many of our spiritual ancestors in the faith have acted like Jacob in doing violence and injustice. The hope of the story is seen in both Jacob and Esau. Jacob gives us hope in that he sought reconciliation through action. We too are called to this active posture that seeks reconciliation through deeds and words. We are also encouraged in the example of Esau in his spirit of mercy and forgiveness. The Spirit of God alone can draw us to this posture as we are reminded that we too have been reconciled to God through the work of Jesus Christ on the cross.

Understanding the Reformation and its complicated legacy and influence on the Western world today is very important for many reasons. It provides a foundation for reflecting on our contemporary situation and our future together. It cannot stop with academic work or historical reflection, however. As Christians who are members of various churches, we are also called to be "kind to one another, tenderhearted, forgiving one another, as God in Christ has forgiven you" (Eph 4:32). The commemoration of the Reformation is an opportunity to do just that—to look together at our divisive and painful past in light of our hopes for reconciliation and unity.

NOTES

Introduction

1 See Mark A. Noll, *Protestantism: A Very Short Introduction* (Oxford: Oxford University Press, 2011), 9.

2 Especially Leopold von Ranke (1795–1886), Max Weber (1864–1920), and Ernst Troeltsch (1865–1923).

3 Carlos M. N. Eire, "The Reformation," in *The Blackwell Companion to Catholicism*, ed. James J. Buckley et al. (Chichester: Wiley-Blackwell, 2011), 63–80, here 72.

4 Martin Luther translated a version of the plan into German and offered therein his own "sardonic glosses." Hubert Jedin, *Geschichte des Konzils von Trient, 1: Der Kampf um das Konzil* (Freiburg: Herder, 1949), 346, see also 341ff.; Alfred Kohler, *Von der Reformation zum Westfälischen Frieden* (München: Oldenbourg, 2011), 51; John C. Olin, *The Catholic Reformation: Savonarola to Ignatius Loyola* (New York: Fordham University Press, 1992).

5 Eire, "Reformation," 72.

Chapter 1

1 To this theme, see my *"Civitas terrena:* On Heinrich August Winkler's *Geschichte des Westens," Theologie.Geschichte: Zeitschrift für Theologie und Kulturgeschichte* 6 (2011), http://universaar.uni-saarland.de/journals/index.php/tg/article/view/656/701.

2 Cf. Wolfgang Pfeifer, ed., *Etymologisches Wörterbuch des Deutschen* (München: DTV, 2005), 1560–61.

3 Robert Gordis, *The Judeo-Christian Tradition: Illusion or Reality* (New York: Judaica, 1965), 19.

4 Daniel R. Langton, *The Apostle Paul in the Jewish Imagination: A Study in Modern Jewish-Christian Relations* (Cambridge: Cambridge University Press, 2010), 176. See also Bernard Heller, "About the Judeo-Christian Tradition," *Judaism* 1 (1951): 260–61; Arthur Allen Cohen, *The Myth of the Judeo-Christian Tradition, and Other*

Dissenting Essays (New York: Schocken, 1971); Isaac Rottenberg, "The Idea of a Judeo-Christian Worldview: Religiopolitical Reflections," *Journal of Ecumenical Studies* 37 (2000): 401–20; Adam H. Becker and Annette Yoshiko Reed, eds., *The Ways That Never Parted: Jews and Christians in Late Antiquity and the Early Middle Ages* (Minneapolis: Fortress, 2007); S. C. Mimouni, *Early Judaeo-Christianity: Historical Essays* (Leuven: Peeters, 2012); Peter Schäfer, *Anziehung und Abstoßung: Juden und Christen in den ersten Jahrhunderten ihrer Begegnung* [Attraction and Repulsion: Jews and Christians in the First Centuries of their Encounter], ed. Jürgen Kampmann, trans. P. S. Peterson (Tübingen: Mohr Siebeck, 2015). Emmanuel Nathan and Anya Topolski have provided a helpful analysis of this term in its intellectual-historical development. As they show, the term "has had and continues to have many different meanings and usages." See Nathan and Topolski, "The Myth of a Judeo-Christian Tradition: Introducing a European Perspective," in *Is There a Judeo-Christian Tradition? A European Perspective*, ed. idem (Berlin: de Gruyter, 2016), 1–15, here 14. Richard H. Popkin and Gordon M. Weiner, eds., *Jewish Christians and Christian Jews: From the Renaissance to the Enlightenment* (Dordrecht: Kluwer, 1994).

5   See Roberto Tottoli, ed., *Routledge Handbook of Islam in the West* (London: Routledge, 2015); Karl Vocelka, *Geschichte der Neuzeit, 1500–1918* (Vienna: Böhlau, 2010), 165ff., 233ff.; David L. Lewis, *God's Crucible: Islam and the Making of Europe, 570 to 1215* (New York: Norton, 2008); Michael Bonner, ed., *Arab-Byzantine Relations in Early Islamic Times* (Aldershot: Ashgate, 2004); Rollin Armour, *Islam, Christianity and the West: A Troubled History* (Maryknoll, N.Y.: Orbis, 2003); Toby E. Huff, *The Rise of Early Modern Science: Islam, China, and the West* (Cambridge: Cambridge University Press, 2003); Maria Rosa Menocal, *The Ornament of the World: How Muslims, Jews, and Christians Created a Culture of Tolerance in Medieval Spain* (Boston: Little, Brown, 2002); David B. Burrell, "Aquinas and Islamic and Jewish Thinkers," in *The Cambridge Companion to Aquinas*, ed. Norman Kretzmann and Eleonore Stump (Cambridge: Cambridge University Press, 1993), 60–84; Titus Burckhardt, *Moorish Culture in Spain*, trans. Alisa Jaffa (New York: McGraw-Hill, 1972); Norman Daniel, *Islam and the West: The Making of an Image* (Edinburgh: Edinburgh University Press, 1960). See also the section below dealing with Islam in the Western world.

6   Cf. Ronald Inglehart and Christian Welzel, "Changing Mass Priorities: The Link between Modernization and Democracy," *Perspectives on Politics* 8 (2010): 551–67.

7   Cf. Heinrich August Winkler, *Geschichte des Westens*, 4 vols. (München: Beck, 2009–2015).

8   See Jürgen Leonhardt, *Latin: Story of a World Language*, trans. Kenneth Kronenberg (Cambridge, Mass.: Belknap Press of Harvard University Press, 2013).

9   Winkler, *Geschichte des Westens*, 4 vols.; John M. Headley, *The Problem with Multiculturalism: The Uniqueness and Universality of Western Civilization* (New Brunswick, N.J.: Transaction, 2012); idem, *The Europeanization of the World: On the Origins of Human Rights and Democracy* (Princeton, N.J.: Princeton University Press, 2008); Niall Ferguson, *Civilization: The West and the Rest* (London: Allen Lane, 2011); Jean-Paul Rosaye and Charles Coutel, *Les Sens de l'Occident* (Arras: Artois Presses Université, 2006); Philippe Nemo, *Qu'est-ce que l'Occident?* (Paris: Presses universitaires de France, 2005); Michael Hochgeschwender, "Was ist der

Westen? Zur Ideengeschichte eines politischen Konstrukts," *Historisch-politische Mitteilungen. Archiv für Christlich-Demokratische Politik* 11 (2004): 1–30; Alastair Bonnet, *The Idea of the West: Culture, Politics and History* (New York: Palgrave Macmillan, 2004); David Gress, *From Plato to NATO: The Idea of the West and Its Opponents* (New York: Free Press, 1998); Thomas C. Patterson, *Inventing Western Civilization* (New York: Monthly Review, 1997); Douglass C. North, "The Paradox of the West," in *The Origins of Modern Freedom*, ed. Richard W. Davis (Stanford, Calif.: Stanford University Press, 1995), 7–34; Rémi Brague, *Europe: La voie romaine* (Paris: Criterion, 1992); Oskar Köhler, "Abendland (Occident, Europa)," in *Theologische Realenzyklopädie*, vol. 1 (Berlin: de Gruyter, 1977), 17–42; William H. McNeill, *The Rise of the West: A History of the Human Community* (Chicago: University of Chicago Press, 1963); Peter Rassow, *Die geschichtliche Einheit des Abendlandes: Reden und Aufsätze* (Köln: Böhlau, 1960); Jürgen Fischer, *Oriens–Occidens–Europa: Begriff und Gedanke 'Europa' in der späten Antike und im frühen Mittelalter* (Wiesbaden: Steiner, 1957); Oskar Halecki, *The Limits and Divisions of European History* (London: Sheed & Ward, 1950); Heinrich Dannenbauer, *Die Entstehung Europas*, 2 vols. (Stuttgart: Kohlhammer, 1959, 1962); Christopher Dawson, *Religion and the Rise of Western Culture* (London: Sheed & Ward, 1950; The Gifford Lectures); Gonzague de Reynold, *La formation de l'Europe*, 7 vols. (Fribourg: Egloff, 1944–1957); Arnold Toynbee, *Civilisation on Trial* (New York: Oxford University Press, 1948); Will Durant and Ariel Durant, *The Story of Civilization*, 11 vols. (New York: Simon & Schuster, 1935–1975); Christopher Dawson, *The Making of Europe: An Introduction to the History of European Unity* (London: Sheed & Ward, 1932); Oswald Spengler, *Der Untergang des Abendlandes* (München: Beck, 1918–1922); Max Weber, "Vorbemerkung" (foreword), in *Gesammelte Aufsätze zur Religionssoziologie* (Tübingen: Mohr, 1920).

10 Thomas A. Brady Jr., *German Histories in the Age of Reformations, 1400–1650* (Cambridge: Cambridge University Press, 2009), 4.

11 Euan Cameron, *The European Reformation*, 2nd ed. (Oxford: Oxford University Press, 2012), 1.

12 Thomas Kaufmann, *Geschichte der Reformation* (Frankfurt: Verlag der Weltreligionen, 2009), 21.

13 Jacques Le Goff, *Must We Divide History into Periods?*, trans. Malcolm DeBevoise (New York: Columbia University Press, 2015), 2.

14 Leopold von Ranke (1795–1886) transformed Reformation historiography with his six-volume work *Deutsche Geschichte im Zeitalter der Reformation* (Leipzig: Duncker & Humblot, 1838–1847). Troeltsch was also very familiar with Ranke, and many of his theories can be seen in Ranke's work. For more on Ranke as a historian of the Reformation, see Arthur G. Dickens, *Reformation Studies* (London: Hambledon, 1982), 565–82. While Ranke is usually praised for his new achievements in historical research and the idea of world history, there was also a strong nationalistic-liberal reception of his Reformation history in the nineteenth century. See, for example, Wolfgang Menzel's review of the first two volumes from 1838 in Menzel's *Literaturblatt* for the *Morgenblatt für gebildete Leser* 33, no. 99 (1839): 393–96.

15 Andrew Pettegree, *Reformation and the Culture of Persuasion* (Cambridge: Cambridge University Press, 2005), 1.

16 See Peter Blickle, *From the Communal Reformation to the Revolution of the Common Man*, trans. Beat Kümin (Leiden: Brill, 1998).

17 Robert W. Scribner, "Elements of Popular Belief," in *Handbook of European History 1400–1600: Late Middle Ages, Renaissance and Reformation*, ed. Thomas A. Brady Jr. et al., vol. 1: *Structures and Assertions* (Leiden: Brill, 1994), 231–62, here 253.

18 For a recent account of the history of reception of the Reformation, see C. Scott Dixon, *Contesting the Reformation* (Malden, Mass.: Wiley-Blackwell, 2012); see also these studies on the history of the reception of Luther: Christian Danz and Rochus Leonhardt, eds., *Erinnerte Reformation: Studien zur Luther-Rezeption von der Aufklärung bis zum 20. Jahrhundert* (Berlin: de Gruyter, 2008). For more on the Reformation, see Volker Leppin, *Transformationen: Studien zu den Wandlungsprozessen in Theologie und Frömmigkeit zwischen Spätmittelalter und Reformation* (Tübingen: Mohr Siebeck, 2015), 1–15.

19 See Volker Reinhardt, *Luther, der Ketzer: Rom und die Reformation* (München: Beck, 2016).

20 For more on the complicated history, involving multiple layers of ecclesial and political corruption and power interests, see Luther, "[The Ninety-Five Theses, or] Disputation for Clarifying the Power of Indulgences," in *The Annotated Luther*, vol. 1: *The Roots of Reform*, ed. Timothy J. Wengert (Minneapolis: Fortress, 2015), 13–46, here 18.

21 Luther, "Wider Hans Worst," in *WA* 51:538: "Johannes Detzel [. . .] verkaufft gnade umbs Gelt [. . .]." The following abbreviations will be used to refer to Luther's works: *LW*: *Luther's Works*, ed. Jaroslav Pelikan and Helmut T. Lehmann, 55 vols. (St. Louis, Mo.: Concordia, 1955–1986). *WA*: *Luthers Werke: Kritische Gesamtausgabe [Schriften]*, 73 vols. (Weimar: Böhlau, 1883–2009). *WA Br*: *Luthers Werke: Kritische Gesamtausgabe: Briefwechsel*, 18 vols. (Weimar: Böhlau, 1930–1985). *WA TR*: *Luthers Werke: Kritische Gesamtausgabe: Tischreden*, 6 vols. (Weimar: Böhlau, 1912–1921).

22 See *WA* 1:138–41, here 141. See also *WA* 1:63–65, 94–99. To the dating of the "Sermo de Indulgentiis," see Berndt Hamm, *Der frühe Luther: Etappen reformatorischer Neuorientierung* (Tübingen: Mohr Siebeck, 2010), 109. See also Martin Brecht, *Martin Luther*, vol. 1: *Sein Weg zur Reformation, 1483–1521* (Stuttgart: Calwer Verlag, 1981), 183, 215–16. Luther's initial criticism of the indulgences was deeply influenced by medieval mysticism. See also Luther, "Ninety-Five Theses," in Wengert, *Roots of Reform*, 13–46, esp. 17ff. On the pre-1517 criticism of the indulgences, see Wilhelm Ernst Winterhager, "Ablaßkritik als Indikator historischen Wandels vor 1517: Ein Beitrag zu Voraussetzungen und Einordnung der Reformation," *Archiv für Reformationsgeschichte* 90 (1999): 6–71.

23 Joachim Rogge, *Anfänge der Reformation*, 2nd ed. (Berlin: Evangelische Verlagsanst., 1985), 142–44. Wilhelm Borth suggests that Elector Frederick criticized Luther's preaching that was opposed to the sale of indulgences, to which Luther reacted by ceasing his criticism. Wilhelm Borth, *Die Luthersache (causa Lutheri), 1517–1524: Die Anfänge der Reformation als Frage von Politik und Recht* (Lübeck: Matthiesen, 1970), 20.

24 There is reliable historical evidence for this claim. Much of the information here on Karlstadt and Luther is drawn from Ulrich Bubenheimer, "Karlstadt, Andreas Rudolff Bodenstein von (1486–1541)," in *Theologische Realenzyklopädie*, vol. 17

(Berlin: de Gruyter, 1988), 649–57; and Martin Brecht, Karl-Heinz zur Mühlen, and Walter Mostert, "Luther, Martin (1483–1546)," in *Theologische Realenzyklopädie*, vol. 21 (Berlin: de Gruyter, 1991), 513–94.

25 See Thomas Kaufmann, *Der Anfang der Reformation: Studien zur Kontextualität der Theologie, Publizistik und Inszenierung Luthers und der reformatorischen Bewegung* (Tübingen: Mohr Siebeck, 2012), 178–80. On the theological conflicts at the beginning of the Reformation in Wittenberg, see Volker Leppin, *Reformatorische Gestaltungen: Theologie und Kirchenpolitik in Spätmittelalter und Früher Neuzeit* (Leipzig: Evangelische Verlagsanstalt, 2016), 153–76.

26 Ronald J. Sider, *Andreas Bodenstein von Karlstadt: The Development of His Thought 1517–1525* (Leiden: Brill, 1974), 9.

27 He had the "second highest income among the sixty-four clerics at All Saints." Sider, *Andreas Bodenstein von Karlstadt*, 10–15.

28 On the transition in his thought, see Hermann Barge, *Andreas Bodenstein von Karlstadt*, vol. 1: *Karlstadt und die Anfänge der Reformation* (Leipzig: Brandstetter, 1905), 69–81; vol. 2: *Karlstadt als Vorkämpfer des laienchristlichen Puritanismus* (Leipzig: Brandstetter, 1905).

29 See Staupitz, *Libellus de Executione Aeternae Praedestinationis—Ein Büchlein von der entlichen Volziehung ewiger Fürsehung* (1517), in *Johann von Staupitz, Sämtliche Schriften*, ed. Lothar Graf zu Dohna and Albrecht Endriss, vol. 2 (Berlin: de Gruyter, 1979); Heiko Oberman, *Forerunners of the Reformation: The Shape of Late Medieval Thought; Illustrated by Key Documents*, trans. Paul L. Nyhus (New York: Holt, Rinehart, & Winston, 1966), 175–203. It was published on February 2, 1517. See Sider, *Andreas Bodenstein von Karlstadt*, 18.

30 Theologically, Karlstadt was probably more influenced by Staupitz than Luther. See Ernst Kähler, *Karlstadt und Augustin: der Kommentar des Andreas Bodenstein von Karlstadt zu Augustins Schrift De spiritu et litera; Einführung und Text* (Halle: Niemeyer, 1952), 7; Sider, *Andreas Bodenstein von Karlstadt*, 20.

31 Bernhard Lohse, *Luthers Theologie in ihrer historischen Entwicklung und in ihrem systematischen Zusammenhang* (Göttingen: Vandenhoeck & Ruprecht, 1995), 88–89. The term is already found in Luther's lectures on Romans in 1515–1516. *WA* 56:272: "Nunquid ergo perfecte Iustus? Non, Sed simul peccator et Iustus; peccator re vera, Sed Iustus ex reputatione et promissione Dei certa, quod liberet ab illo, donec perfecte sanet." ("Now, is he perfectly righteous? No, for he is at the same time both a sinner and a righteous man; a sinner in fact, but a righteous man by the sure imputation and promise of God that He will continue to deliver him from sin until he has completely cured him.") *LW* 25:260 is commentary on Rom 4:7, with verse 8: "Blessed are those whose iniquities are forgiven, and whose sins are covered; blessed is the one against whom the Lord will not reckon sin."

32 These first theses are cited below in the section dealing with Scripture and the magisterium.

33 Andreas Bodenstein von Karlstadt, *Centum quinquagintaunum conclusiones de natura, lege et gratia, contra scolasticos et usum comunem*, 26 April 1517, in *Kritische Gesamtausgabe der Schriften und Briefe Andreas Bodensteins von Karlstadt, Teil I (1507–1518)*, ed. Thomas Kaufmann (Wolfenbüttel: Herzog-August-Bibliothek, 2012). The theses were edited by Martin Keßler. The German translation provided by Alejandro Zorzin and Martin Keßler at the Herzog-August-Bibliothek

Wolfenbüttel was consulted for the translation above. The theses: "[24.] Nulla bona merita precedunt gratiam. Contra communem." "[38.] Gratia facit ut invocetur deus. Contra communem." "[81.] Peccator sine omni dispositione sufficienti de congruo ex parte eius iustificatur." "[83.] Iustificatio factores legis precedit. non sequitur. Contra quasi omnes." "[85.] Gratia facit nos legis dilectores et factores." "[88.] Non iustificatur homo preceptis bon[a]e vit[a]e. [89.] Non lege operum, nec litera nec factorum meritis. [90.] Sed per fidem Hiesu Christi spiritu, lege fidei et gratia." "[133.] Vita eterna est gratia data pro gratia ex misericordia et miseratione." "[138.] Iustus ergo simul est bonus et malus: filius dei et filius seculi." "[151.] Fecunda veritatis authoritas sepius discussa melius cognoscitur: et veram convenientiam parit: quam manifestis sermonibus abscondit." Karlstadt, like Luther, sees this teaching about grace hidden in the Old Testament; see thesis 107; see also thesis 79. An edition of the 151 Theses is also found in Theodor Kolde, "Wittenberger Disputationsthesen aus den Jahren 1516–1522," in *Zeitschrift für Kirchengeschichte* 11 (1890): 448–71, here 450–56. In Kolde's edition, however, there are a few minor variances in comparison to the new Wolfenbüttel edition. Kaufmann provides an explanation of the dating of the theses and a reference to all the relevant secondary literature. Kaufmann, *Der Anfang der Reformation*, 178. Kolde remarks regarding thesis 151 that Karlstadt wanted to emphasize that debate about the Scriptures leads to more clarity and agreement than determined statements about it, which, in fact, often hide this true harmony and agreement. Kolde, "Wittenberger Disputationsthesen aus den Jahren 1516–1522," 456.

34 See Sider, *Andreas Bodenstein von Karlstadt*, 57ff.

35 See Volker Leppin, *Die fremde Reformation: Luthers mystische Wurzeln* (München: Beck, 2015); idem, "Tauler, Johannes (ca. 1300–1361)," in *Theologische Realenzyklopädie*, vol. 32 (Berlin: de Gruyter, 2001), 745–48.

36 "Auszlegung und lewterung etzlicher heyligenn geschrifften," postscript dated March 18, 1519.

37 See Kaufmann, *Geschichte der Reformation*, 523f.; and Alejandro Zorzin, *Karlstadt als Flugschriftenautor* (Göttingen: Vandenhoeck & Ruprecht, 1990), 37–40. His work was also influenced by Tauler and the idea of a mystical-pious yieldedness (*abnegatio sui, Gelassenheit*, placidness, serenity).

38 Barge, *Andreas Bodenstein von Karlstadt*, 1:234: "Schon seit Frühjahr 1519 hat Karlstadt mit stets wachsendem Eifer die Befriedung laienchristlicher Bedürfnisse von der kirchlich-priesterlichen Gnadenvermittlung loszulösen und auf inneren Voraussetzungen aufzubauen gesucht."

39 See Christopher Spehr, *Luther und das Konzil: Zur Entwicklung eines zentralen Themas in der Reformationszeit* (Tübingen: Mohr Siebeck, 2010), 210. In a letter on December 18, 1519, *WA Br* 1:595; no. 231 (Luther to Spalatin, Wittenberg). In the fall of 1519, Luther began to call for Communion to be served in both bread and wine (like the Hussites). See Kaufmann, *Der Anfang der Reformation*, 514.

40 See Bernd Moeller, "Klerus und Antiklerikalismus in Luthers Schrift An den christlichen Adel deutscher Nation von 1520," in *Anticlericalism in Late Medieval and Early Modern Europe*, ed. Peter A. Dykema and Heiko A. Oberman (Leiden: Brill, 1993), 353–65, here 353. See the classic remarks in his "Address to the Christian Nobility," in *WA* 6:407–13.

41 *LW* 31:320–21. See *WA Br* 1:420–24. Luther's letter to Spalatin from July 20, 1519.

42 *LW* 31:323.

43 See Karlstadt, "CCCLXX et Apologeticae Conclusiones," in Kaufmann, *Kritische Gesamtausgabe der Schriften und Briefe Andreas Bodensteins von Karlstadt.* Translation cited in Sider, *Andreas Bodenstein von Karlstadt,* 48. They were published before June 11, 1518.

44 To Karlstadt's account of the authority of Scripture at Leipzig, see his *protestatio* for June 27: "Sacris autem scripturis hunc honorem impendimus, quod nihil sine his aut asserere aut praecipere volumus. In caeteris autem, quae non liquide hinc doceri possunt, solis ecclesiasticis primas damus." *WA* 59:433. See Leppin's remarks about Luther and Karlstadt at the Leipzig Debate in Leppin, *Transformationen,* 378ff. See also idem, ed., *Reformatorische Theologie und Autoritäten: Studien zur Genese des Schriftprinzips beim jungen Luther* (Tübingen: Mohr Siebeck, 2015).

45 This is addressed in chap. 4. While Luther was at the Wartburg, there was no correspondence between Luther and Karlstadt. Luther corresponded with Melanchthon. See Bubenheimer, "Karlstadt." For more on Karlstadt's time in Denmark, see James L. Larson, *Reforming the North: The Kingdoms and Churches of Scandinavia, 1520–1545* (Cambridge: Cambridge University Press, 2010), 89–92; Barge, *Andreas Bodenstein von Karlstadt* 1:249ff.; 467ff.

46 See Volker Leppin, *Martin Luther* (Darmstadt: Primus, 2006), and also Hamm, *Der frühe Luther,* 25–64. According to Hamm, the first reorientation (*Umorientierung*) in Luther's theology can be seen in his first lectures on the Psalms from 1513 to 1515 (49). This process begins earlier, however.

47 Borth, *Die Luthersache,* 21. See also Lohse, *Luthers Theologie in ihrer historischen Entwicklung,* 116.

48 The official papal teaching about indulgences was first issued in 1518. Borth, *Die Luthersache,* 24.

49 Borth, *Die Luthersache,* 23.

50 See Leppin, *Die fremde Reformation.*

51 The story about him posting his theses on the door of the church is offered by Philip Melanchthon (1497–1560), as recorded decades later in 1546 in his preface to Luther's Latin works; see *Corpus reformatorum* 6:161–62. Volker Leppin, "Die Monumentalisierung Luthers. Warum vom Thesenanschlag erzählt wurde—und was davon zu erzählen ist," in *Luthers Thesenanschlag—Faktum oder Fiktion?,* ed. Joachim Ott and Martin Treu (Leipzig: Evangelische Verlagsanstalt, 2008), 69–92; Kaufmann, *Der Anfang der Reformation,* 176–80; Luther, "Ninety-Five Theses," in Wengert, *Roots of Reform,* 23; Volker Leppin and Timothy J. Wengert, "Sources for and against the Posting of the Ninety-Five Theses," *Lutheran Quarterly* 29 (2015): 373–98, esp. 388–89. The counterarguments are less convincing. Regarding the historicity of the posting of the Ninety-Five Theses, see Leppin, *Martin Luther,* 125f.

52 See Luther, "A Sermon on Indulgences and Grace, 1518," in Wengert, *Roots of Reform,* 57–66, here 61f.; reference to the "new teachers" is made on p. 60. See "Ein Sermon von Ablaß und Gnade," in *WA* 1:244.

53 Luther, "Disputation of Martin Luther on the Power and Efficacy of Indulgences" (October 31, 1517), in *LW* 31:31. See *WA* 1.233–38. See also no. 55: "the gospel, which is the very greatest thing . . . ," *LW* 31:30.

54 Luther, "Power and Efficacy," in *LW* 31:29. See *WA* 1.233–38.

55 Luther, "Power and Efficacy," in *LW* 31:33. See *WA* 1.233–38.

56 Luther, "Explanation of the Ninety-Five Theses," in *LW* 31:249. These were written in late 1517 and early 1518 and then revised and published in August of 1518.

57 Luther, "Power and Efficacy," in *LW* 31:33.

58 Luther, "Power and Efficacy," in *LW* 31:26.

59 Luther, "Power and Efficacy," in *LW* 31:26.

60 Luther, "Power and Efficacy," in *LW* 31:33.

61 Luther, "Power and Efficacy," in *LW* 31:30.

62 Kaufmann, *Der Anfang der Reformation*, 184.

63 Borth, *Die Luthersache*, 29f.

64 Dewey Weiss Kramer, ed. and trans., *Johann Tetzel's Rebuttal against Luther's Sermon on Indulgences and Grace* (Atlanta: Pitts Theology Library, 2012), 21.

65 Kramer, *Johann Tetzel's Rebuttal*, 26.

66 Kramer, *Johann Tetzel's Rebuttal*, 28.

67 Kramer, *Johann Tetzel's Rebuttal*, 29.

68 Borth, *Die Luthersache*, 33f.

69 Borth, *Die Luthersache*, 37.

70 See *LW* 31:31–69.

71 Berndt Hamm, "Staupitz, Johann[es] von (ca. 1468–1524)," in *Theologische Realenzyklopädie*, vol. 32 (Berlin: de Gruyter, 2001), 119–27, here 124: "Mit seiner außergewöhnlichen Neuinterpretation Augustins hat Staupitz nicht nur junge Theologen seines Ordens wie Luther, Linck, Johannes Lang und Kaspar Güttel (1471–1542) beeindruckt, sondern auch entscheidenden Einfluß auf die Wende seines Wittenberger Kollegen A. Karlstadt von der scholastischen Theologie zu einem gnadentheologischen Augustinismus mit spiritualistischen Zügen genommen." See also Hamm, "Johann von Staupitz (ca. 1468–1524)—spätmittelalterlicher Reformer und 'Vater' der Reformation," *Archiv für Reformationsgeschichte* 92 (2001): 6–42; Markus Wriedt, *Gnade und Erwählung: Eine Untersuchung zu Johann von Staupitz und Martin Luther* (Mainz: Zabern, 1991). The critical edition of his work (currently 3 vols.): Lothar zu Dohna and Richard Wetzel, eds., *Sämtliche Schriften* (Berlin: de Gruyter, 1979–2001). On Luther and Staupitz, see also Hamm, *Der frühe Luther*, 15ff. Further Henrik Otto, *Vor- und frühreformatorische Tauler-Rezeption: Annotationen in Drucken des späten 15. und frühen 16. Jahrhunderts* (Gütersloh: Gütersloher Verlagshaus, 2003).

72 Franz Posset, *The Front-Runner of the Catholic Reformation: The Life and Works of Johann von Staupitz* (Aldershot: Ashgate, 2003), 228.

73 Leppin, *Martin Luther*, 116–17. See also Leppin's "Eine neue Luther-Debatte: Anmerkungen nicht nur in eigener Sache," *Archiv für Reformationsgeschichte* 99 (2008): 297–307, and his *Die fremde Reformation*.

74 Kaufmann, *Geschichte der Reformation*, 146. By 1520, and especially after 1521 (following the excommunication), Luther eventually embraced his role (which the ecclesial authorities had given to him) as a rebellious Reformer in confrontation with the church.

75 Hamm, "Staupitz, Johann[es] von (ca. 1468–1524)," 120.

76 Hamm, "Johann von Staupitz," 13.

77 Hamm, "Johann von Staupitz," 26.

78 Hamm, "Johann von Staupitz," 26f.

79 In his *Table Talk*, Luther, *WA TR* 1:80 (no. 173): "Ex Erasmo nihil habeo. Ich hab all mein ding von Doctor Staupiz; der hatt mir occasionem geben." Cf. Hamm, "Johann von Staupitz," 31.

80 Leppin, *Transformationen*, 254: "Dieser Satz stimmt biographisch und er stimmt theologisch."

81 Leppin, *Transformationen*, 241–59, here 245; *WA TR* 5:99 (no. 5374).

82 See also David C. Steinmetz, *Luther and Staupitz: An Essay in the Intellectual Origins of the Protestant Reformation* (Durham, N.C.: Duke University Press, 1980); Wriedt, *Gnade und Erwählung*.

83 Hamm, "Staupitz, Johann[es] von (ca. 1468–1524)," 120: "Staupitz zog sich nach Salzburg zurück. Er suchte, dem geistlichen Ideal der 'Gelassenheit' entsprechend, äußere und innere Ruhe in der Distanz zum Kampf um Luther, ohne sich von ihm und seiner Theologie zu distanzieren."

84 Hamm, "Staupitz, Johann[es] von (ca. 1468–1524)," 125: "Diese klare Haltung des Augustinervikars schirmte Luther gegen die römische Ordensleitung ab und veranlaßte wohl auch, daß Kurfürst Friedrich der Weise an Luther festhielt."

85 *WA Br* 3:263f.; as cited in Hamm, "Staupitz, Johann[es] von (ca. 1468–1524)," 125.

86 Borth, *Die Luthersache*, 25.

87 On Luther's criticism of the scholastic and Aristotelian theory of justification, see Theodor Dieter, *Der junge Luther und Aristoteles: Eine historisch-systematische Untersuchung zum Verhältnis von Theologie und Philosophie* (Berlin: de Gruyter, 2001), 149–256, esp. 193–201.

88 Borth, *Die Luthersache*, 27.

89 Scott Hendrix, "Martin Luther, Reformer," in *Cambridge History of Christianity*, vol. 6: *Reform and Expansion, 1500–1660*, ed. R. Po-Chia Hsia (Cambridge: Cambridge University Press, 2007), 3–19, here 7.

90 Luther, "Vorrede zu der vollständigen Ausgabe der deutschen Theologie" (1518), *WA* 1:378; *LW* 31:75. 1 Cor 4:10: "We are fools for the sake of Christ, but you are wise in Christ. We are weak, but you are strong. You are held in honor, but we in disrepute."

91 Luther's "Disputation against Scholastic Theology," in *LW* 31:15. In the last thesis he sought to assert the continuity of his theology with the tradition: "In all we wanted to say, we believe we have said nothing that is not in agreement with the Catholic church and the teachers of the church," *LW* 31:16.

92 Luther, "Vorrede zur Promotionsdisputation von Palladius und Tilemann" (1537): "Articulus iustificationis est magister et princeps, dominus, rector et iudex super omnia genera doctrinarum, qui conservat et gubernat omnem doctrinam ecclesiasticam et erigit conscientiam nostram coram Deo," *WA* 39/1:205; as cited in Lohse, *Luthers Theologie in ihrer historischen Entwicklung*, 275. For more on the genesis of the emphasis on *sola fide* and the amalgamation of Pauline theology and mystical theology from medieval Christianity, see Leppin, *Transformationen*, 333–54.

93 Hendrix, "Martin Luther, Reformer," in Hsia, *Reform and Expansion*, 3.

94 See Heiko Oberman, *The Reformation: Roots and Ramifications*, trans. Andrew C. Gow (London: T&T Clark, 1994), 118ff.

95 Karlstadt, "Tract on the Supreme Virtue of *Gelassenheit* [yieldedness] (1520)," in *The Essential Carlstadt: Fifteen Tracts*, ed. and trans. Edward J. Furcha, Classics of

the Radical Reformation 8 (Waterloo: Herald, 1995), 30f., 34, 37. Job 13:15: "Though he slay me, I will hope in him" (ESV).

96 See Brecht, Mühlen, and Mostert, "Luther, Martin (1483–1546)," 518.

97 Hendrix, "Martin Luther, Reformer," in Hsia, *Reform and Expansion*, 9. For the rest of his life, Luther "was confined to Electoral Saxony" under the protection of Frederick, his brother John, and John's son, John Friederick I.

98 See Leppin, *Die fremde Reformation*, 194; Sider, *Andreas Bodenstein von Karlstadt*, 174ff. This transition in the Reformation is addressed further below in chap. 4, §4.3.

99 Sider, *Andreas Bodenstein von Karlstadt*, 177.

100 "Resolution of the Majority, 7 April 1529," in *Documents Illustrative of the Continental Reformation*, ed. B. J. Kidd (Oxford: Clarendon, 1911), 242; as cited in William Roscoe Estep, *Renaissance and Reformation* (Grand Rapids: Eerdmans, 1986), 149. See George Huntston Williams, *The Radical Reformation*, 3rd ed. (Kirksville, Mo.: Truman State University Press, 1992), xxviii.

101 Cf. Hsia, *Reform and Expansion*, xvii–xxi.

102 William R. Estep, *The Anabaptist Story: An Introduction to Sixteenth-Century Anabaptism* (Grand Rapids: Eerdmans, 1996), 103.

103 Hans Joachim Hillerbrand, *The Division of Christendom: Christianity in the Sixteenth Century* (Louisville, Ky.: Westminster John Knox, 2007), 163.

104 These are the final remarks from his statement, which is edited in Herbert Immenkötter, *Die Confutatio der Confessio Augustana vom 3. August 1530* (Münster: Aschendorff, 1978), German version on p. 206 (Latin on p. 207); as cited in Hillerbrand, *Division of Christendom*, 165.

105 Hillerbrand, *Division of Christendom*, 169.

106 Hillerbrand, *Division of Christendom*, 169.

107 See Hendrix, "Martin Luther, Reformer," in Hsia, *Reform and Expansion*, 9.

108 Diarmaid MacCulloch, *Reformation: A History* (New York: Viking, 2004), xix.

Chapter 2

1 Volker Leppin, *Martin Luther: vom Mönch zum Feind des Papstes* (Darmstadt: Lambert Schneider, 2013), 107ff. Cf. idem, *Die Reformation* (Darmstadt: Wissenschaftliche Buchgesellschaft, 2013).

2 On the publicity of the Reformation, see Thomas Kaufmann, *Der Anfang der Reformation: Studien zur Kontextualität der Theologie, Publizistik und Inszenierung Luthers und der reformatorischen Bewegung* (Tübingen: Mohr Siebeck, 2012), 231ff., 266ff.

3 George Huntston Williams, *The Radical Reformation*, 3rd ed. (Kirksville, Mo.: Truman State University Press, 1992), xxx. Williams' study is the standard work on this issue. He sees the "radical Reformation" in three groups: Anabaptism, spiritualism, and evangelical rationalism. For a helpful collection of the sources, see Michael G. Baylor, ed., *The Radical Reformation* (Cambridge: Cambridge University Press, 1991). On the Peasants' Revolt, see Williams, *Radical Reformation*, 137–74; to the Münster Rebellion, see Williams, *Radical Reformation*, 553–88.

4 See Baylor, Introduction to *Radical Reformation*, xi–xxvi, here xii.

5 Baylor, Introduction to *Radical Reformation*, xii.

6 Baylor, Introduction to *Radical Reformation*, xvi.

7 Baylor, "Introduction to *Radical Reformation*, xvi.

8   C. Scott Dixon, *The Reformation in Germany* (Oxford: Blackwell, 2002), 111.

9   Jacob Rabus, *Christliche bescheidne und wolgegründts ablähnung der vermeindten Bischoffs Predigt* (Cologne, 1570), fol. 30r; as cited in Thomas A. Brady Jr., "'In Search of the Godly City': The Domestication of Religion in the German Urban Reformation," in *The German People and the Reformation*, ed. R. Po-Chia Hsia (London: Cornell University Press, 1988), 14–31, here 28–29.

10 Heiko A. Oberman, *Luther: Mensch zwischen Gott und Teufel* (Berlin: Severin & Siedler, 1981), 242; trans. Eileen Walliser-Schwarzbart, *Luther: Man between God and the Devil* (New Haven, Conn.: Yale University Press, 2006), 227–28. Here Oberman uses an analogy to describe the "fanatics" (*Schwärmer*) that gets lost in translation. In German he writes that Luther thought of these people as if they "schwärmen wie aufgescheuchte Bienen um den Korb." In the translation above, this phrase is translated with "restless, roaming spirits." The sense is certainly there in this translation; literally, however, it would be something more like "swarming like agitated bees around a basket." The best translation of *Schwärmer* is probably "fanatics," but literally it means "swarmers," like swarming bees or insects. For Luther, these Reformers were driven by Satan, heretical, destructive, and seditious.

11 See Meinulf Barbers, *Toleranz bei Sebastian Franck* (Bonn: Röhrscheid, 1964).

12 Carter Lindberg, *The European Reformations* (Chichester: Wiley-Blackwell, 2010), 12.

13 Williams, *Radical Reformation*, xxx.

14 Williams, *Radical Reformation*, xxx.

15 Williams, *Radical Reformation*, xxviii–xxix.

16 William Roscoe Estep, *Renaissance and Reformation* (Grand Rapids: Eerdmans, 1986), 149.

17 Williams, *Radical Reformation*, xxix.

18 Here I agree with much of what Brad Gregory has said about the significance of political power in the formation of these confessional identities and historiographical categories. Brad Gregory, Randall Zachman, and I discussed this matter at length in Heidelberg in September 2016. I am grateful for this conversation. Gregory has also addressed this in his *The Unintended Reformation: How a Religious Revolution Secularized Society* (Cambridge, Mass.: Belknap Press of Harvard University Press, 2012).

19 See also Müntzer's "Prague Protest" (1521) in Baylor, *Radical Reformation*, 1–10.

20 Peter Blickle, "Communal Reformation: Zwingli, Luther, and the South of the Holy Roman Empire," in *Cambridge History of Christianity*, vol. 6: *Reform and Expansion, 1500-1660*, ed. R. Po-Chia Hsia (Cambridge: Cambridge University Press, 2007), 75–89, here 76.

21 On Memmingen as a "center of the Reformation," see Peter Blickle, *From the Communal Reformation to the Revolution of the Common Man*, trans. Beat Kümin (Leiden: Brill, 1998), 16–80.

22 "The Twelve Articles of the Upper Swabian Peasants," in Baylor, *Radical Reformation*, 234. In this edition it is dated from February 27 to March 1, 1525. The editorial remarks explain that the articles were written by Sebastian Lotzer, "a tanner and lay reformer," and Christoph Schappele, the "evangelical pastor in St. Martin's church in Memmingen." They summarized the grievances and provided scriptural support. The articles were "the most widely circulated program produced by the rebellious

peasants in 1525" (231). According to Estep (*Renaissance and Reformation*, 144), Balthasar Hubmaier, a priest in Waldshut, confessed while being tortured that he wrote the articles. Estep dates the publication March 1. Blickle, "Communal Reformation," in Hsia, *Reform and Expansion*, 81, also dates to March. Even after the suppression of the peasants in 1525, they nevertheless remained a political force. Blickle, *Communal Reformation*, 178–88. Regarding the Peasants' Revolt, see 94–116.

23 See Luther, *WA TR* 4:247 (no. 4346).

24 Hans-Jürgen Goertz, *Thomas Müntzer: Revolutionär am Ende der Zeiten* (München: Beck, 2015), 27.

25 Tom Scott, *Thomas Müntzer: Theology and Revolution in the German Reformation* (Basingstoke: Macmillan, 1989), 1–16, here 13.

26 R. Emmet McLaughlin, "The Radical Reformation," in Hsia, *Reform and Expansion*, 37–55, here 41.

27 *WA TR* 1:195 (no. 446).

28 Luther called them new prophets, so they became known as the "Zwickau Prophets." Some of this information about the "prophets" is drawn from Heinz Schilling, *Martin Luther Luther: Rebell in einer Zeit des Umbruchs* (München: Beck, 2012), 289–92.

29 Ronald J. Sider, *Andreas Bodenstein von Karlstadt: The Development of His Thought 1517–1525* (Leiden: Brill, 1974), 162.

30 Kaufmann, *Der Anfang der Reformation*, 467.

31 Such as in his "Address to the Christian Nobility"; see Kaufmann, *Der Anfang der Reformation*, 469.

32 Nikolaus Müller, *Die Wittenberger Bewegung 1521 und 1522* (Leipzig: Heinsius, 1911), 143; as cited in Sider, *Andreas Bodenstein von Karlstadt*, 162. For more on their theology, see Thomas Kaufmann, *Thomas Müntzer, "Zwickauer Propheten" und sächsische Radikale: eine quellen- und traditionskritische Untersuchung zu einer komplexen Konstellation* (Mühlhausen: Thomas-Müntzer-Ges., 2010). See also Kaufmann's *Der Anfang der Reformation*, 466ff.

33 Baylor, Introduction to *Radical Reformation*, xii.

34 Sider, *Andreas Bodenstein von Karlstadt*, 162.

35 *LW* 48:371f.; *WA Br* 2:427; as cited in Oberman, *Luther: Man between God and the Devil*, 229f.

36 Luther, "Ein Brief an die Fürsten zu Sachsen von dem aufrührerischen Geist" (1524), *WA* 15:216; *LW* 40:54–55; before this (see *WA* 15:215) Luther asserts his authority because he risked his life (*leyb und leben*). Cf. Scott Hendrix, "Martin Luther, Reformer," in Hsia, *Reform and Expansion*, 14.

37 Luther to Landgraf Philipp, November 20, 1538; Hessisches Staatsarchiv Marburg, Best. 3 (Landgrafschaft Hessen, Politisches Archiv Landgraf Philipps des Großmütigen), Nr. 2687; see the transcription provided by Clemens Joos, "Luther rät Landgraf Philipp zur Vertreibung der Täufer aus Hessen" in der Digitales Archiv der Reformation: "[. . .] ist nicht allein mein bedencken, sondern auch demutiges bitten, E[uer] f[urstlich] g[naden] wolten sie ernstlich des lands verweisen. Denn es ist gleichwol des teuffels samen [. . .] E[uer] f[urstlich] g[naden] haben sich auch des nicht zu beschweren, das sie vertrieben anderswo schaden thün mugen. Denn anderswo haben sie nicht viel mehr raüm, und ob sie es hetten, sollen die zusehen,

so des orts das regiment und kirchen haben. Denn ob ich sorgen mocht, der wolff, so ynn meinem stal wurget, mocht ynn andern stellen mehr wurgen, kan ich yhn darumb unverjagt nicht lassen. Ein iglicher hute seins stalles."

38 Luther, "Dass diese Worte, 'Das ist mein Leib' noch fest stehen wider die Schwarmgeister," *WA* 23:71; *LW* 37:18: "It is precisely the same devil [*der selbige teufel*] who now assails us through the fanatics [*die schwermer*] by blaspheming the holy and venerable sacrament [*mit lesterunge des heiligen hochwirdigen sacraments*] of our Lord Jesus Christ, out of which they would like to make mere bread and wine as a symbol or memorial sign of Christians, in whatever their dream or fancy dictates." Cf. Hendrix, "Martin Luther, Reformer," in Hsia, *Reform and Expansion*, 14.

39 Jörg Trelenberg, "Luther und die Bestrafung der Täufer," in *Zeitschrift für Theologie und Kirche* 110 (2013): 22–49, here 49: "zweifellos eine generelle, aber auch sehr konkrete Mitschuld an der gewalttätigen Unterdrückung des devianten Täufertums im 16. Jahrhundert." The grievances of the peasants were, of course, not unique to the sixteenth century. There were various revolts by peasants going back at least two centuries from this point. See Juliet R. V. Barker, *1381: The Year of the Peasants' Revolt* (Cambridge, Mass.: Belknap Press of Harvard University Press, 2014). See also David M. Whitford's analysis in "Luther's Political Encounters," in *The Cambridge Companion to Martin Luther*, ed. Donald McKim (Cambridge: Cambridge University Press, 2003), 178–92, here 190.

40 Michael G. Baylor, *The German Reformation and the Peasants' War: A Brief History with Documents* (Boston, Mass.: Bedford St. Martin's, 2012), 128–29. Also in *Luther's Works*, vol. 46, ed. Robert C. Schultz (Philadelphia: Fortress, 1967). For the full story about Luther's attempt to deal with the Peasants' War, and how Luther's theology was deeply involved in his view of it, see Volker Leppin, "Das Gewaltmonopol der Obrigkeit: Luthers sogenannte Zwei-Reiche-Lehre und der Kampf zwischen Gott und Teufel," in *Krieg und Christentum: religiöse Gewalttheorien in der Kriegserfahrung des Westens*, ed. Andreas Holzem (Paderborn: Schöningh, 2009), 403–14. See also Bernhard Lohse, *Luthers Theologie in ihrer historischen Entwicklung und in ihrem systematischen Zusammenhang* (Göttingen: Vandenhoeck & Ruprecht, 1995), 175ff.

41 Andrea Strübind, *Eifriger als Zwingli: die frühe Täuferbewegung in der Schweiz* (Berlin: Duncker & Humblot, 2003); Mira Baumgartner, ed., *Die Täufer und Zwingli: eine Dokumentation* (Zurich: Theologischer Verlag, 1993); Mirjam G. K. van Veen, "'Cruel, cold and false': Calvin and the Calvinists through the Eyes of Their Dutch Opponents (1566–1619)," in *John Calvin, Myth and Reality: Images and Impact of Geneva's Reformer*, ed. Amy Nelson Burnett (Eugene, Ore.: Cascade, 2011), 126–38.

42 Born in Donauwörth; studied in Ingolstadt and in Heidelberg; priest in Benzenzimmern (Diocese Augsburg); adoption of Protestantism in 1524 or 1525; call to pastoral ministry in Büchenbach (Roth) from the Protestant councilmen in Nuremberg; publication of *Von dem greulichen Laster der Trunckheit* (Augsburg 1528), in which he defends the idea that true faith leads to sanctification; 1528 or 1529 abandoned his pastorate; 1530 or 1531 moved to Strasbourg, where he published his *Chronica* (1531), where the criteria of ecclesial judgements on heretics is presented as arbitrary and institutionally motivated rather than being based

on inherent spiritual arguments. In his *Paradoxa* (1534; see Sebastian Franck, *Paradoxa*, ed. Siegfried Wollgast [Berlin: Akademie-Verlag, 1966]), he emphasized the freedom of the human person to choose between good and evil; the importance of an ethical life; a view of God in idealistic and mystical terms; a mystical piety of inner experience; a direct connection of the individual person with the absolute; the Bible as a historical witness to revelation, not itself revelation; and that tolerance is necessary because every individual has in their own subjectivity direct relationship to the absolute. See André Séguenny, "Franck, Sebastian (ca. 1500–1542)," in *Theologische Realenzyklopädie*, vol. 11 (Berlin: de Gruyter, 1983), 307–12; Siegfried Wollgast, ed., *Beiträge zum 500. Geburtstag von Sebastian Franck: (1499–1542)* (Berlin: Weidler, 1999); Patrick Hayden-Roy, *The Inner Word and the Outer World: A Biography of Sebastian Franck* (New York: Lang, 1994); see also Williams, *Radical Reformation*, 394–98, 694ff. Franck thought of God like an inexpressible "sigh" (*Seüfftz*) of the soul (Williams, *Radical Reformation*, 397); this theme is found in some contemporary Pentecostal theology in the description of the work of the Holy Spirit. Franck was critical of the Anabaptists because of their strict biblicism and separatism.

43   Carter Lindberg argues that they have always been floating around in Lutheranism: *The Third Reformation? Charismatic Movements and the Lutheran Tradition* (Macon, Ga.: Mercer University Press, 1983).

44   Harry Loewen, *Luther and the Radicals: Another Look at Some Aspects of the Struggle between Luther and the Radical Reformers* (Waterloo: Wilfred Laurier University, 1974), 151.

45   For the background of the rhetoric of liberation of the German nation around 1500, see Jost Hermand, *Verlorene Illusionen: eine Geschichte des deutschen Nationalismus* (Köln: Böhlau, 2012), 18–37 ("Vom Mittelalter bis zum Beginn des 18. Jahrhunderts.")

46   Dixon, *Reformation in Germany*, 14. Dixon points to many examples of this.

47   Luther also believed that the Roman papacy (which he came to see as the antichrist) reinstated the fallen Roman Empire, and thus brought the empire from the Greeks "to the Germans." He held that this *translatio imperii* was allegorically prefigured in the book of Revelation. Luther's preface to the book of Revelation from 1530, *WA Deutsche Bibel*, 7:415: "Denn der Bapst hat das gefallen Roemisch Reich, widder auffgericht, vnd von den Griechen zu den Deudschen bracht." Luther attacks the same theory elsewhere (*WA* 6:462); see Bernhard Lohse, *Martin Luther: eine Einführung in sein Leben und sein Werk* (Munich: Beck, 1997), 105.

48   Volker Reinhardt, *Luther, der Ketzer: Rom und die Reformation* (München: Beck, 2016).

49   See Caspar Hirschi, *The Origins of Nationalism: An Alternative History from Ancient Rome to Early Modern Germany* (Cambridge: Cambridge University Press, 2012), 199.

50   Hirschi, *Origins of Nationalism*.

51   Hirschi, *Origins of Nationalism*, 204.

52   Hirschi, *Origins of Nationalism*, 204f.

53   Hirschi, *Origins of Nationalism*, 205.

54   Hirschi, *Origins of Nationalism*, 206.

55 Luther, *An die Ratherren aller Städte deutsches Lands*, in *WA* 15:53; as cited in Hirschi, *Origins of Nationalism*, 199.

56 Luther, "Warnung an seine lieben Deutschen," *WA* 30:291; *LW* 47:29; as cited in Hendrix, "Martin Luther, Reformer," in Hsia, *Reform and Expansion*, 9.

57 Luther, "Vorrede zu der vollständigen Ausgabe der deutschen Theologie" (1518), *WA* 1:378; *LW* 31:76.

58 Luther, "To the Christian Nobility of the German Nation concerning the Reform of the Christian Estate," in *LW* 44:141.

59 Luther, "To the Christian Nobility," 142.

60 Luther, "To the Christian Nobility," 143.

61 Letter to Blumenthal (May 28, 1819), as cited in Heinrich Bornkamm, *Luther im Spiegel der deutschen Geistesgeschichte* (Göttingen: Vandenhoeck & Ruprecht, 1970), 217. *Volk* is the German term for "people" in the singular sense.

62 Houston Stewart Chamberlain, *Auswahl aus seinen Werken: Die Rassenfrage—Die germanische Rasse—Martin Luther—Die deutsche Sprache—Heimat—Bismarck der Deutsche—Bayreuth—Adolf Hitler* (Breslau: Hirt, 1934), 27: "Für meine Deutschen bin ich geboren; ihnen will ich dienen!" Luther wrote this in a letter to Nikolaus Gerbel in 1521 ("Germanis meis natus sum, quibus et serviam"). This sense of utter devotedness was famous in German romanticism, for example, in Friedrich Hölderlin's "The Death for the Fatherland" (*Der Tod fürs Vaterland*). Hölderlin also propagated the idea of a mythical (non-Jewish) "Greek Jesus." Éva Kocziszky writes, "The image of the *Greek* Jesus nourishes itself from the anti-Semitism of both friends [Hegel and Schelling], from their rejection of everything positive, of all legalism in favor of the faith of love and freedom of the Greeks." Kocziszky, *Mythenfiguren in Hölderlins Spätwerk* (Würzburg: Königshausen & Neumann, 1997), 129.

63 Chamberlain, *Auswahl aus seinen Werken*, 39: "'Wenn Deutschland nur *einen* Herrn hätte, so wäre es nicht zu gewinnen' (das heißt nicht zu besiegen): so ruft er [Luther] 350 Jahre vor Bismarck!" See Luther, *WA TR* 3:470 (no. 3636): "sicut Germania si sub uno domino esset, esset invicibilis."

64 Heinrich Bornkamm, *Luthers geistige Welt* (Gütersloh: Bertelsmann, 1953), chap. 11. After World War II the essay was slightly modified and republished again in 1947, and then again in 1953, 1959, and for the last time in 1960. See Harry Oelke et al., eds., *Martin Luthers "Judenschriften": die Rezeption im 19. und 20. Jahrhundert* (Göttingen: Vandenhoeck & Ruprecht, 2016).

65 Georg Wilhelm Friedrich Hegel, *Lectures on the History of Philosophy* [*Vorlesungen über die Geschichte der Philosophie*], trans. E. S. Haldane and Frances H. Simson, vol. 3 (London: Routledge, 1955), 146–47. These were held multiple times from 1819 to 1831.

66 Georg Wilhelm Friedrich Hegel, *Lectures on the Philosophy of History* [*Vorlesungen über die Philosophie der Geschichte*], trans. J. Sibree (London: Henry G. Bohn, 1861), 434. The lectures were held several times from 1822 to 1831.

67 Hegel, *Lectures on the Philosophy of History*, 437.

68 Hegel, *Lectures on the Philosophy of History*, 437f.; emphasis in original.

69 Hegel, *Lectures on the Philosophy of History*, 440.

70 Hegel, *Lectures on the Philosophy of History*, 445f; emphasis in original.

71   On this theme, see Heiko A. Oberman, *The Roots of Antisemitism in the Age of Renaissance and Reformation*, trans. James I. Porter (Philadelphia: Fortress, 1984).

72   Martin Greschat, *Martin Bucer: A Reformer and His Times*, trans. Stephen E. Buckwalter (London: Westminster John Knox, 2004), 158.

73   John Calvin, *Commentaries on the Book of the Prophet Daniel*, trans. Thomas Myers, 2 vols. (Edinburgh: Calvin Translation Society, 1852–1853), 1:185; on Dan 2:44 see *Calvini Opera* 40:605; as cited in J. Marius J. Lange van Ravenswaay, "Calvin and the Jews," in *The Calvin Handbook*, ed. Herman J. Selderhuis (Grand Rapids: Eerdmans, 2009), 143–46, here 146.

74   *WA* 53:417–552. See Thomas Kaufmann, *Luthers "Judenschriften": ein Beitrag zu ihrer historischen Kontextualisierung* (Tübingen: Mohr Siebeck, 2013).

75   Karl Jaspers, *Philosophie und Welt: Reden und Aufsätze* (München: Piper, 1958), 162: "Was Hitler getan, hat Luther geraten, mit Ausnahme der direkten Tötung durch Gaskammern."

76   See Debra Kaplan, "Sharing Conversations: A Jewish Polemic against Martin Luther," in *Archiv für Reformationsgeschichte* 103 (2012): 41–63, esp. 49. This is especially concerned with Luther's work "Against the Sabbatarians."

77   Kaufmann, *Luthers "Judenschriften*," 154: "Was Luther allerdings von den anderen, im wesentlichen gleich gesinnten Zeitgenossen unterschied, war die Maßlosigkeit seiner Polemik, die Offensivität seines Kampfgeistes, wohl auch die Tiefe seines Sendungsbewußtseins und die Intensität einer obsessiven Gewissensnot, als einstmals geirrt habender Prophet nun dazu berufen und dafür verantwortlich zu sein, definitive und 'letzte Worte' über die Juden als verstockte Feinde Christi sprechen zu müssen." Regarding this, see Volker Weymann, "Luthers Schriften über die Juden Theologische und politische Herausforderungen," *Texte aus der VELKD* 168 (2013): 3–33; Dorothea Wendebourg, "Martin Luther und die Juden," *Evangelische Verantwortung: Magazin des EAK* 13 (2013): 5–10. The historical context of his different writings on the Jews are also addressed by Kaufmann in his recent book *Luthers Juden* (Stuttgart: Reclam, 2014).

78   Thomas Kaufmann, "Antisemitische Lutherflorilegien. Hinweise und Materialien zu einer fatalen Rezeptionsgeschichte," *Zeitschrift für Theologie und Kirche* 112 (2015): 192–228, here 228.

79   Martin Sasse, *Martin Luther über die Juden: Weg mit ihnen!* (Freiburg im Breisgau: Sturmhut-Verlag, 1938); to "the prehistory of the Holocaust," see Götz Aly, *Why the Germans? Why the Jews?: Envy, Race Hatred, and the Prehistory of the Holocaust*, trans. Jefferson S. Chase (New York: Metropolitan, 2014).

80   Nicola Willenberg, "'Mit Luther und Hitler für Glauben und Volkstum': der Luthertag 1933 in Dresden," in *Spurenlese—Reformationsvergegenwärtigung als Standortbestimmung (1717–1983)*, ed. Klaus Tanner and Jörg Ulrich (Leipzig: Evangelische Verlagsanstalt, 2012), 195–237; Julie M. Winter, *Luther Bible Research in the Context of Volkish Nationalism in the Twentieth Century* (New York: Lang, 1998); Hartmut Lehmann, "Luther als Kronzeuge für Hitler: Anmerkungen zu Otto Scheels Lutherverständnis in den 1930er Jahren," in idem, *Protestantische Weltsichten* (Göttingen: Vandenhoeck & Ruprecht, 1998), 153–73. Heinz Kremers, ed., *Die Juden und Martin Luther, Martin Luther und die Juden: Geschichte, Wirkungsweise, Herausforderung* (Neukirchen-Vluyn: Neukirchener Verlag, 1985).

81 Thomas Kaufmann, "Evangelische Reformationsgeschichtsforschung nach 1945," *Zeitschrift für Theologie und Kirche* 104 (2007): 404–54, here 434; see also Christian Wiese, "'Unheilsspuren': Zur Rezeption von Martin Luthers 'Judenschriften' im Kontext antisemitischen Denkens in den Jahrzehnten vor der Shoah," in *Das mißbrauchte Evangelium: Studien zu Theologie und Praxis der Thüringer Deutschen Christen*, ed. Peter von der Osten-Sacken (Berlin: Institut Kirche & Judentum, 2002), 91–135.

82 William M. MacGovern, *From Luther to Hitler: The History of Fascist-Nazi Political Philosophy* (London: Harrap, 1941); see also Wolfram von Hanstein, *Von Luther bis Hitler: ein wichtiger Abriss deutscher Geschichte* (Dresden: Voco-Verl, 1947).

83 Christoph Strohm, *Die Kirchen im Dritten Reich* (München: Beck, 2011), 16. The traditional Catholic party was the "Center Party."

84 See James M. Stayer, *Martin Luther, German Saviour: German Evangelical Theological Factions and the Interpretation of Luther, 1917–1933* (Montreal: McGill-Queen's University Press, 2000).

85 Hendrix, "Martin Luther, Reformer," in Hsia, *Reform and Expansion*, 18.

86 See, for example, Robert W. Jenson and Eugene Korn, eds., *Covenant and Hope: Christian and Jewish Reflections: Essays in Constructive Theology from the Institute for Theological Inquiry* (Grand Rapids: Eerdmans, 2012).

87 See Dorothee Kommer, *Reformatorische Flugschriften von Frauen: Flugschriftenautorinnen der frühen Reformationszeit und ihre Sicht von Geistlichkeit* (Leipzig: Evangelische Verlagsanstalt, 2013); Kirsi Irmeli Stjerna, *Women and the Reformation* (Malden, Mass.: Blackwell, 2009).

88 Merry Wiesner-Hanks, "Women and Religious Change," in Hsia, *Reform and Expansion*, 465–82, here 468.

89 Wiesner-Hanks, "Women and Religious Change," in Hsia, *Reform and Expansion*, 470.

90 Wiesner-Hanks, "Women and Religious Change," in Hsia, *Reform and Expansion*, 470.

91 Wiesner-Hanks, "Women and Religious Change," in Hsia, *Reform and Expansion*, 471.

92 Wiesner-Hanks, "Women and Religious Change," in Hsia, *Reform and Expansion 1500–1660*, 473. The Luther household—between thirty and forty people—consumed between sixty to eighty liters of beer daily. For this reason Katharina had her own brewery. See Volker Leppin et al., eds., *Das Luther-Lexikon* (Regensburg: Bückle & Böhm, 2014), 113.

93 Charlotte Methuen, "'And Your Daughters Shall Prophesy!' Luther, Reforming Women and the Construction of Authority," *Archiv für Reformationsgeschichte* 104 (2013): 82–109, here 107.

94 Robert W. Scribner, "Elements of Popular Belief," in *Handbook of European History 1400–1600: Late Middle Ages, Renaissance and Reformation*, vol. 1: *Structures and Assertions*, ed. Thomas A. Brady Jr. et al. (Leiden: Brill, 1994), 254.

95 Luther, WA 49:303; as cited in John Witte, *Law and Protestantism: The Legal Teachings of the Lutheran Reformation* (Cambridge: Cambridge University Press, 2002), 119.

96 Cf. Susan C. Karant-Nunn and Merry E. Wiesner-Hanks, eds., *Luther on Women: A Sourcebook* (Cambridge: Cambridge University Press, 2003).

97   Luther, *WA TR* 1:19, no. 55 (cited in Karant-Nunn and Wiesner-Hanks, *Luther on Women*, 28).

98   Luther, "The Estate of Marriage" (1522), in *LW* 45:33.

99   Luther, "Sermon on Exodus" (1526), *WA* 16:551 (cited in Karant-Nunn and Wiesner-Hanks, *Luther on Women*, 231; emphasis in original. See also 12f., 228f.).

100   Luther, *Commentary on 1 Peter* (1522), in *LW* 30:91 (cited in Karant-Nunn and Wiesner-Hanks, *Luther on Women*, 232–33).

101   Luther's *Table Talk, Tischreden*, no. 5207 (*WA TR* 5:8f.), no. 2528–29 (*WA TR* 2:503ff.), no. 3676 (*WA TR* 3:515ff.), no. 4513 (*WA TR* 4:357f.); see Paul Althaus, *Die Ethik Martin Luthers* (Gütersloh: Mohn, 1965), 101; Eberhard Jüngel, *Indikative der Gnade—Imperative der Freiheit* (Tübingen: Mohr Siebeck, 2000), 79.

102   Hubertus Mynarek, *Luther ohne Mythos: das Böse im Reformator* (Freiburg: Ahriman-Verlag, 2012); Bernd Rebe, *Die geschönte Reformation: warum Martin Luther uns kein Vorbild mehr sein kann; ein Beitrag zur Lutherdekade* (Marburg: Tectum Verlag, 2012).

103   See Luther, *WA* 18:164.

104   Peter Harrison, "Philosophy and the Crisis of Religion," in *The Cambridge Companion to Renaissance Philosophy*, ed. James Hankins (Cambridge: Cambridge University Press, 2007), 234–49, here 245.

105   Matthew Becker, "Werner Elert (1885–1954)," in *Twentieth-Century Lutheran Theologians*, ed. Mark Mattes (Göttingen: Vandenhoeck & Ruprecht, 2013), 93–135, here 128. Becker writes, "scores of students flocked to" Erlangen to study with Elert, Paul Althaus, and Otto Procksch (94). Elert and Althaus were two very influential German Lutheran theologians in Nazi Germany. Both of them supported the "Aryan-Paragraph" for the church. (111f.) See Robert P. Ericksen, *Theologians Under Hitler* (New Haven, Conn.: Yale University Press, 1985).

106   Oswald Bayer, *Martin Luther's Theology: A Contemporary Interpretation*, trans. Thomas Trapp (Grand Rapids: Eerdmans, 2008), 202.

107   Ockham: "quia creatio et conservatio per nihil positivum differunt"; *Commentary on the Sentences*, II, qu. 3f.; in *Opera Theologica*, vol. 5: *Quaestiones in secundum librum sententiarum, Reportatio* (St. Bonaventure, N.Y.: The Franciscan Institute, 1981), 65. This and the following citation are drawn from Johannes Schwanke, *Creatio ex nihilo: Luthers Lehre von der Schöpfung aus dem Nichts in der großen Genesisvorlesung (1535–1545)* (Berlin: de Gruyter, 2004), 141f.

108   Luther in his lectures on Genesis (here to Gen 22:13): "Nos Christiani scimus, quod apud Deum idem est creare et conservare." *WA* 43:233.

109   Luther, *WA* 18:615.

110   Calvin, *Institutes of the Christian Religion*, vols. 1 and 2, trans. Henry Beveridge (Edinburgh: T&T Clark, 1863), 1:177 (bk. 1, ch. 16, par. 5).

111   Kathleen D. Vohs and Jonathan W. Schooler, "The Value of Believing in Free Will: Encouraging a Belief in Determinism Increases Cheating," *Psychological Science* 19 (2008): 49–54, here 54.

112   Max Weber, *The Protestant Ethic and the Spirit of Capitalism*, trans. Talcott Parsons (New York: Scribner, 1958), 104; emphasis in German original: *Die protestantische Ethik und der Geist des Kapitalismus: Vollständige Ausgabe*, ed. Dirk Kaesler (Tübingen: Mohr, 1904/1905, 1920; München: Beck, 2004), 145. Here is the first part of the citation in German: "In ihrer pathetischen Unmenschlichkeit mußte

diese Lehre nun für die Stimmung einer Generation, die sich ihrer grandiosen Konsequenz ergab, vor allem eine Folge haben: ein Gefühl einer unerhörten inneren *Vereinsamung des einzelnen Individuums*."

113   Calvin, *Institutes*, bk. 3, chap. 21.

114   Calvin writes, "By predestination we mean the eternal decree of God, by which he determined with himself whatever he wished to happen with regard to every man. All are not created on equal terms, but some are preordained to eternal life, others to eternal damnation; and, accordingly, as each has been created for one or other of these ends, we say that he has been predestinated to life or to death." Calvin, *Institutes*, 2:206 (bk. 3, ch. 21, par. 5).

Chapter 3

1   Heiko Oberman, *Forerunners of the Reformation: The Shape of Late Medieval Thought; Illustrated by Key Documents*, trans. Paul L. Nyhus (New York: Holt, Rinehart & Winston, 1966), ix. Alternatively, the Reformation has also been presented as a story about Luther's biography and his theology. These developments are then transcribed onto the history of the Reformation. This is another form of history that overlooks the significance of the prehistory. In the Reformation there was a process of the monumentalization of Luther. This process of monumentalization was pushed forward by theologians and church historians. In this process they presented the story about Luther's nailing of the Ninety-Five Theses on the Wittenberg Collegiate Church door as the monumental starting point of the Reformation. In this way Luther and his theology were cemented together with the historical movement of the Reformation. This view of Luther as a monocausal source of the Reformation fails to acknowledge the prehistory of the conflicts that enabled the reforming process, and it overlooks the contingencies from the 1517 event to the decisive years in the 1520s when the process of reform took political shape. Luther himself contributed to this process especially by writing his biography in the preface to his Latin works. Volker Leppin, *Transformationen: Studien zu den Wandlungsprozessen in Theologie und Frömmigkeit zwischen Spätmittelalter und Reformation* (Tübingen: Mohr Siebeck, 2015), 528. Regarding the transformation of the Reformation from a charismatically led movement to an institution, see 519–29.

2   See Oberman, *Forerunners of the Reformation*. In his introductory essay (1–49), he addresses all the important academic debates about the forerunners of the Reformation. In his volume he then offers a selection of readings from these forerunners, including, among others, John Brevicoxa (on Scripture and tradition), Staupitz (on justification), Jan Hus (on the church), Cornelisz Hoen (on the Eucharist), and Erasmus (on exegesis). On the prehistory of the Reformation, see Heiko Oberman, *The Reformation: Roots and Ramifications*, trans. Andrew C. Gow (London: T&T Clark, 1994), 8. He emphasizes various issues, including the princes within the empire, the social crisis of the time, the cities, and the Reformers.

3   Euan Cameron, *The European Reformation*, 2nd ed. (Oxford: Oxford University Press, 2012), 26; emphasis in original; for a summary of some of "The Background," see 11–100.

4   See Anne Hudson, *The Premature Reformation: Wycliffite Texts and Lollard History* (Oxford: Clarendon, 1988).

5   See Euan Cameron, *The Waldenses: Rejections of Holy Church in Medieval Europe* (Oxford: Blackwell, 2000).

6   Charles Taylor, *A Secular Age* (Cambridge, Mass.: Belknap Press of Harvard University Press, 2007), 68.

7   Taylor, *Secular Age*, 69.

8   Taylor, *Secular Age*, 70

9   Marsilius of Padua, *The Defender of the Peace*, ed. Annabel Brett (Cambridge: Cambridge University Press, 2005).

10 William of Ockham, *A Short Discourse on Tyrannical Government*, ed. Arthur Stephen McGrade (Cambridge: Cambridge University Press, 1992), bk. 1, ch. 8, p. 13.

11 See Erika Rummel, ed., *Biblical Humanism and Scholasticism in the Age of Erasmus* (Leiden: Brill, 2008), esp. 39–56. The humanists often fought out the confessional battles of the Reformation in satire, rather than in strict theological argument. For some examples of this, see idem, ed., *Scheming Papists and Lutheran Fools: Five Reformation Satires* (New York: Fordham University Press, 1993).

12 David Daniell, *William Tyndale: A Biography* (New Haven, Conn.: Yale University Press, 1994), 122.

13 Nancy Bisaha, *Creating East and West: Renaissance Humanists and the Ottoman Turks* (Philadelphia: University of Pennsylvania Press, 2004), 133–34.

14 Emidio Campi, "Was the Reformation a German Event?" in *The Myth of the Reformation*, ed. Peter Opitz (Göttingen: Vandenhoeck & Ruprecht, 2013), 9–31, here 10–11. He also points to Joachim of Fiore (1130/35–1202) as an example of the hopes for spiritual renewal in the church.

15 Wolf-Friedrich Schäufele, *"Defecit ecclesia": Studien zur Verfallsidee in der Kirchengeschichtsanschauung des Mittelalters* (Mainz: Veröffentlichungen des Instituts für Europäische Geschichte, 2006).

16 Campi, "Was the Reformation a German Event?" 11.

17 See *Patrologiae cursus completus, Series Latina* (PL) 200:743.

18 See PL 216:824.

19 Luther, *WA* 1:627 (*Resolutiones*, 1518, *Conclusio* 89); as cited in translation in Campi, "Was the Reformation a German Event?" 25.

20 As an example of this, Campi points to James D. Tracy, *Europe's Reformations, 1450–1650* (Lanham: Rowman & Littlefield, 1999); Andrew Pettegree, *The Early Reformation in Europe* (Cambridge: Cambridge University Press, 1992); idem, *The Reformation World* (London: Routledge, 2000); Diarmaid MacCulloch, *Reformation: Europe's House Divided, 1490–1700* (London: Allen Lane, 2003); Peter G. Wallace, *The Long European Reformation: Religion, Political Conflict, and the Search for Conformity, 1350–1750* (Basingstoke: Palgrave Macmillan, 2004); Ronnie Po-Chia Hsia, *A Companion to the Reformation World* (Malden, Mass.: Blackwell, 2004); Ulinka Rublack, *Reformation Europe* (Cambridge: Cambridge University Press, 2005); see Campi, "Was the Reformation a German Event?" 18.

21 Campi, "Was the Reformation a German Event?" 19.

22 See Volker Reinhardt, *Luther, der Ketzer: Rom und die Reformation* (München: Beck, 2016).

23 Thomas A Brady Jr., *German Histories in the Age of Reformations, 1400–1650* (Cambridge: Cambridge University Press, 2009), 149.

24 See especially Franz Machilek, "Einführung: Beweggründe, Inhalte und Probleme kirchlicher Reformen des 14./15. Jahrhunderts (mit besonderer Berücksichtigung der Verhältnisse im östlichen Mitteleuropa)," in *Kirchliche Reformimpulse des 14./15. Jahrhunderts in Ostmitteleuropa*, ed. Winfried Eberhard and Franz Machilek (Köln: Böhlau, 2006), 1–121. The other essays in this volume also address this matter.

25 See Leppin, *Transformationen*, 56, 121, 228, 416. Tauler himself developed this from the theology of Meister Eckhart.

26 See František Šmahel, "Die Vier Prager Artikel: Das Programm der Hussitischen Reformation," in Eberhard and Machilek, *Kirchliche Reformimpulse des 14./15.*, 329–39.

27 In 1620 the Bohemian Hussites were finally overcome by the Habsburg Counter-Reformation. See the essays in Franz Machilek, ed., *Die hussitische Revolution: religiöse, politische und regionale Aspekte* (Köln: Böhlau, 2012); e.g., Georg Denzler, "Reform der Kirche um 1400," 9–24; Peter Hilsch, "Jan Hus: ein Reformator als Bedrohung von Reich und Kirche?," 25–37; Blanka Zilynská, "Hussitische Synoden: die Vorläufer der reformatorischen Synodalität," 57–75; Franz Machilek, "Jan Hus und die Hussiten in der Oberpfalz," 181–222; Michael Van Dussen, *From England to Bohemia: Heresy and Communication in the Later Middle Ages* (Cambridge: Cambridge University Press, 2012); Thomas A. Fudge, *The Magnificent Ride: The First Reformation in Hussite Bohemia* (Aldershot: Ashgate, 1998); Frederick Heymann, *John Žižka and the Hussite Revolution* (Princeton, N.J.: Princeton University Press, 1955).

28 Here I am drawing upon Kaufmann, "Jan Hus und die frühe Reformation," in *Biblische Theologie und historisches Denken*, ed. Martin Kessler and Martin Wallraff (Basel: Schwabe, 2008), 62–109; see also Bernhard Lohse, "Luther und Huß," in *Luther: Zeitschrift der Luthergesellschaft* 36 (1965): 108–22.

29 See Helmar Junghans, ed., *Die Reformation in Augenzeugenberichten* (Munich: DTV, 1973), 84.

30 See Junghans, *Die Reformation in Augenzeugenberichten*, 86.

31 Luther, "To the Christian Nobility of the German Nation concerning the Reform of the Christian Estate," in *LW* 44:196.

32 See Michael G. Baylor, ed., *The Radical Reformation* (Cambridge: Cambridge University Press, 1991), 1.

33 The break with Rome was a contingent process. As Luther was declared a new heretical Hus, and as the Reformation became a public spectacle, Luther adopted this Hus role and made it his own. In this context, and in his self-understanding as a heretic in the eyes of Rome, the connection with Hus became a framework for reflection on his own resistance to papal authority in 1519 and 1520. Once Luther was excommunicated in 1521, the split of Latin Christendom began to take shape. Thomas Kaufmann, *Der Anfang der Reformation: Studien zur Kontextualität der Theologie, Publizistik und Inszenierung Luthers und der reformatorischen Bewegung* (Tübingen: Mohr Siebeck, 2012), 54–67.

34 German: "Von der Abtuung der Bilder und dass keine Bettler unter den Christen sein sollen" (1522); Karlstadt, "On the Removal of Images and That There Should Be No Beggars among Christians (1522)," in *The Essential Carlstadt: Fifteen Tracts*, ed. and trans. Edward J. Furcha, Classics of the Radical Reformation 8 (Waterloo: Herald, 1995).

35 "Article XXVII, of Monastic Vows," in *The Book of Concord: The Confessions of the Evangelical Lutheran Church*, ed. Theodore Gerhardt Tappert (Philadelphia: Fortress, 1959), 79; this is the English translation of the Latin version of the confession (it was issued in both German and Latin); see the Latin in *Confessio Augustana*, in *Corpus reformatorum*, 26:263–336.

36 Campi, "Was the Reformation a German Event?," 13.

37 On this issue, see also the many essays in Ole Peter Grell and Andrew Cunningham, eds., *Health Care and Poor Relief in Protestant Europe, 1500–1700* (New York: Routledge, 1997); Irene Dingel and Armin Kohnle, eds., *Gute Ordnung: Ordnungsmodelle und Ordnungsvorstellungen in der Reformationszeit* [Good Order: Models and Ideas of Order in the Reformation Period] (Leipzig: Evangelische Verlagsanstalt, 2014).

38 *Deutsche Reichstagsakten, Jüngere Reihe*, vol. 3: *Deutsche Reichstagsakten unter Kaiser Karl V.*, ed. Adolf Wrede (Göttingen: Vandenhoeck & Ruprecht, 1901), 397. This seems to be an acknowledgment of errors. In 1999 the International Theological Commission of the Catholic Church declared, "In the entire history of the Church there are no precedents for requests for forgiveness by the Magisterium for past wrongs. Councils and papal decrees applied sanctions, to be sure, to abuses of which clerics and laymen were found guilty, and many pastors sincerely strove to correct them. However, the occasions when ecclesiastical authorities—Pope, Bishops, or Councils—have openly acknowledged the faults or abuses which they themselves were guilty of, have been quite rare." International Theological Commission (of the Roman Catholic Church), *Memory and Reconciliation: The Church and the Faults of the Past*, December 1999 (London: Catholic Truth Society, 2000), no. 1.1. The document goes on to discuss John Paul II's work of reconciliation.

39 Karl Fink, *Papsttum und Kirche im abendländischen Mittelalter* (München: Beck, 1981), 59; as cited in Machilek, "Einführung," in Eberhard and Machilek, *Kirchliche Reformimpulse des 14./15.*, 82. There Machilek addresses a variety of opinions.

40 Scott Hendrix, "Martin Luther, Reformer," in *Cambridge History of Christianity*, vol. 6: *Reform and Expansion, 1500–1660*, ed. R. Po-Chia Hsia (Cambridge: Cambridge University Press, 2007), 14.

41 Johannes Eck, *Enchiridion locorum communium adversus Lutherum et alios hostes ecclesiae (1525–1543)* in *Corpus Catholicorum*, vol. 34, ed. P. Fraenkel (Münster: Aschendorff, 1979), 38: "Tollatur conciliorum authoritas, et omnia in ecclesia erunt ambigua, dubia, pendentia, incerta."

42 A lot of this goes back to Étienne Gilson's narrative of the Middle Ages and the deterioration of Western thought after Aquinas leading to the Reformation and then to modernity. See, for example, E. Gilson, *History of Christian Philosophy in the Middle Ages* (London: Sheed & Ward, 1955); Philip Daileader, "Étienne Gilson (1884–1978)," in *French Historians, 1900–2000*, eds. Philip Daileader and Philip Whalen (Oxford: Blackwell, 2010), 285–305; C. Scott Dixon, *Contesting the Reformation* (Malden, Mass.: Wiley-Blackwell, 2012), 57. In a related form, it is also found with Alasdair MacIntyre, *After Virtue: A Study in Moral Theory* (Notre Dame, Ind.: University of Notre Dame Press, 1981; London: Bloomsbury, 2013), John Milbank, Brad Gregory, and many others. See my "Diagnosing Western Modernity: A Review Article," *Neue Zeitschrift für Systematische Theologie und Religionsphilosophie* 57 (2015): 267–84.

43 Johannes Grabmayer, *Europa im späten Mittelalter 1250–1500: eine Kultur- und Mentalitätsgeschichte* (Darmstadt: Primus Verlag, 2004), 10.

44 Michael Mitterauer, *Why Europe?: The Medieval Origins of Its Special Path*, trans. Gerald Chapple (Chicago: University of Chicago Press, 2010), 146.

45 See Monika Asztalos, "The Faculty of Theology," in *A History of the University in Europe*, vol. 1: *Universities in the Middle Ages*, ed. Hilde de Ridder-Symoens (Cambridge: Cambridge University Press, 1992), 409–41, here 434.

46 Cf. Sonja Dünnebeil and Christine Ottner, eds., *Außenpolitisches Handeln im ausgehenden Mittelalter: Akteure und Ziele* (Vienna: Böhlau, 2007); Lars Börner, *Making Medieval Markets: A Formal Institutional Analysis* (Ph.D. diss., Humboldt University of Berlin, 2007).

47 Michael North, "Charakter der Epoche," in idem, *Europa expandiert, 1250–1500* (Stuttgart: Ulmer, 2007), 13–24, here esp. 22–23.

48 Deno John Geanakoplos, "Church and State in the Byzantine Empire: A Reconsideration of the Problem of Caesaropapism," *Church History* 34 (1965): 381–403.

49 North, "Charakter der Epoche," 23f.

50 Peter Bernholz et al., eds., *Political Competition, Innovation and Growth: A Historical Analysis* (Berlin: Springer, 1998); Johannes Fried, *Das Mittelalter: Geschichte und Kultur* (München: Beck, 2008), 192ff.; Douglass North, *Structure and Change in Economic History* (New York: Norton, 1981); idem, "The Paradox of the West," in *The Origins of Modern Freedom*, ed. Richard W. Davis (Stanford, Calif.: Stanford University Press, 1995), 7–34; Eric L. Jones, *The European Miracle: Environments, Economies, and Geopolitics in the History of Europe and Asia* (Cambridge: Cambridge University Press, 1981). Kant already identified this theory, which was popularized later by Weber in his *General Economic History: Wirtschaftsgeschichte: Abriss der universalen Sozial- und Wirtschaftsgeschichte* (München: Duncker & Humblot, 1923); trans., General Economic History (New York: Collier Books, 1961). The following subtitle was added to this translation: "A Penetrating Analysis of the Origins of Our Economic System and Its Relation to Ethics and Religion." This was put together from various lecture notes from students from his final lecture in Munich (1919/1920). In these lectures, he also addresses the relationship of Protestantism to capitalism.

51 Michael A. R. Graves, *The Parliaments of Early Modern Europe: 1400–1700* (London: Routledge, 2001), 14; on the point regarding the transfer of this idea from the ecclesial realm, Graves refers to Helmut G. Koenigsberger, *A History of Europe*, vol. 1: *Medieval Europe: 400–1500* (London: Longman, 1987), 300f.

52 Fried, *Das Mittelalter*, 109ff., 233ff. (regarding the role that universities played).

53 This information about the life of commoners and peasants in the sixteenth century is drawn from Kenneth G. Appold, *The Reformation: A Brief History* (Malden, Mass.: Wiley-Blackwell, 2011), 3. For more on life in the early sixteenth century, see Cameron, *European Reformation*, 4–5.

54 Brady, *German Histories in the Age of Reformations*, 62.

55 Brady, *German Histories in the Age of Reformations*, 62.

56 Brady, *German Histories in the Age of Reformations*, 62.

57 Brady, *German Histories in the Age of Reformations*, 63.

58 Appold, *Reformation*, 5.

59 Klaus Schatz, *Papal Primacy: From Its Origins to the Present* (Collegeville, Minn.: Liturgical, 1996), 86.

60 See Hans Küng, "Preface for the English Edition," in idem, *Can We Save the Catholic Church?—We Can Save the Catholic Church!* (London: William Collins, 2013), 3–4. Regarding the tensions between papal power in the polycentric Europe of the High Middle Ages, see Volker Leppin, *Geschichte des mittelalterlichen Christentums* (Tübingen: Mohr Siebeck, 2012), 273ff.

61 Appold, *Reformation*, 5.

62 Leppin, *Transformationen*, 51: "durchaus heterogenes Gesicht." On the processes of religious transformation in Europe at the time of the Reformation, see pp. 17–68.

63 For more on the tensions and polarities of the late Middle Ages leading up to the Reformation, see Leppin, "Polaritäten im späten Mittelalter (ca. 1300–1500)," chap. 5 in *Geschichte des mittelalterlichen Christentums*, 375ff.

64 Dorothea Sattler and Volker Leppin, eds., *Reformation 1517–2017: Ökumenische Perspektiven; für den ökumenischen Arbeitskreis evangelischer und katholischer Theologen* (Freiburg im Breisgau: Herder, 2014), 111.

65 See Walter Bauer, *Orthodoxy and Heresy in Earliest Christianity*, trans. Paul J. Achtemeier et al., ed. Robert R. Kraft and Gerhard Krodel (Philadelphia: Fortress, 1971); originally published in German as *Rechtgläubigkeit und Ketzerei im ältesten Christentum* (Tübingen: Mohr, 1934); Hans Dieter Betz, "Orthodoxy and Heresy in Primitive Christianity," *Interpretation* 19 (1965): 299–311; James D. G. Dunn, *Unity and Diversity in the New Testament: An Inquiry into the Character of Earliest Christianity* (London: SCM Press, 1977).

66 Gotthold Ephraim Lessing, "The Religion of Christ, 1780," in *Lessing's Theological Writings*, ed. Henry Chadwick (London: Black, 1956), 106.

67 Roger Haight, *Christian Community in History*, vol. 1: *Historical Ecclesiology* (New York: Continuum, 2004), 133.

68 John Henry Newman's criticism is a good example of this; see See John Henry Newman, "Lectures on the Scripture Proof of the Doctrines of the Church (pt. 1)" (1838), tract no. 85 in idem, *Tracts for the Times*, vol. 5 (London: Gilbert & Rivington, 1840); Frank M. Turner, *John Henry Newman: The Challenge to Evangelical Religion* (New Haven, Conn.: Yale University Press, 2002), 275–83.

69 See Irenaeus, *Against Heresies*, 1.10, in *Ante-Nicene Fathers* (*ANF*) 1:330f.; on the "rule of truth," see *Against Heresies*, 1.9, 2.27, 4.35.

70 Irenaeus, *Against Heresies* 3.2, *ANF* 1:415.

71 Tertullian, *Prescription against Heretics*, chap. 13, *ANF* 3:249.

72 Augustine, "On Baptism, Against the Donatists," bk. 2, chap. 3 in *Nicene and Post-Nicene Fathers, Series I*, 4:427; PL 43:128; *Corpus Scriptorum Ecclesiasticorum Latinorum* 51.

73 Vincent of Lérins, *Commonitory*, chap. 2 in *Nicene and Post-Nicene Fathers*, Series II, 11:132. Cf. *Corpus Christianorum, Series Latina* 64:125–231. See also Thomas G. Guarino, *Vincent of Lérins and the Development of Christian Doctrine* (Grand Rapids: Baker Academic, 2013); Michael Fiedrowicz, ed., *Vinzenz von Lérins—Commonitorium: Mit einer Studie zu Werk und Rezeption*, trans. Claudia Barthold (Mühlheim: Carthusianus Verlag, 2011); Martien Parmentier, "Vinzenz von Lérins," *Theologische Realenzyklopädie* 35 (2003): 109–11.

74 As cited in Margaret Deanesly, "The Prohibitions of Vernacular Bible Reading in France, Italy and Spain," chap. 2 in idem, *The Lollard Bible: And Other Medieval Biblical Versions* (Cambridge: Cambridge University Press, 1920), 36f.

75 As cited in Deanesly, "Prohibitions of Vernacular," 36–37.

76 As cited in Deanesly, "Prohibitions of Vernacular," 37.

77 As cited in Deanesly, "Prohibitions of Vernacular," 38.

78 Frans van Liere, *An Introduction to the Medieval Bible* (New York: Cambridge University Press, 2014), 177–207, esp. 190ff.

79 Thomas A. Fudge, *The Trial of Jan Hus: Medieval Heresy and Criminal Procedure* (Oxford: Oxford University Press, 2013), 324.

80 Thomas A. Fudge, "Hussite Theology and the Law of God," in *The Cambridge Companion to Reformation Theology,* ed. David Bagchi and David C. Steinmetz (Cambridge: Cambridge University Press, 2004), 22–27, here 25. For Hus' works in the critical edition, see *Magistri Iohannis Hus Opera omnia (Prag: Academia Scientiarum Bohemoslavaca, 1959–1988),* now with *Corpus Christianorum, Continuatio mediaevalis* (Turnhout: Brepols, 2004–).

81 As reported by the chronicler Peter of Mladoňovice in his account of the execution of Hus in "Relatio de Magistro Johanne Hus." See the translation in Matthew Spinka, *John Hus at the Council of Constance* (New York: Columbia University Press, 1965), 233. The Latin edition: Václav Novotný, ed., *Fontes rerum bohemicarum,* vol. 8 (Prague: Palacky, 1932), 119: "In ea vero ewangelii [*sic*] veritate, quam scripsi, docui et predicavi ex dictis et exposicionibus sanctorum doctorum, hodie letanter volo mori." I am very thankful to Prof. Dr. Thomas A. Fudge for guiding me to this source. See also David S. Schaff, *John Huss: His Life, Teachings and Death, after Five Hundred Years* (London: Allen & Unwin, 1915), 257.

82 Gillian R. Evans, *Problems of Authority in the Reformation Debates* (Cambridge: Cambridge University Press, 1992), ix; regarding the council, see esp. 241–47.

83 Regarding the scholastic rift that emerged in the late Middle Ages, see Heiko Oberman, *Masters of the Reformation: The Emergence of a New Intellectual Climate in Europe,* trans. Dennis Martin (Cambridge: Cambridge University Press, 1981), 23–44, here 40.

84 The biblical theology went together with the emergence of critical nominalism. The latter questioned the plausibility of the scholastic philosophical realism and reasserted the unique authority of the Scriptures above the scholastic philosophy. See Heiko A. Oberman, *Spätscholastik und Reformation,* vol. 1: *Der Herbst der mittelalterlichen Theologie* (Zurich: EVZ-Verlag, 1965), 335ff., 343.

85 Wessel Gansfort, "From the Letter in Reply to Jacob Hoeck," chap. 8, as cited in Oberman, *Forerunners of the Reformation,* 109. See also Fokke Akkerman et al., eds., *Wessel Gansfort (1419–1489) and Northern Humanism* (Leiden: Brill, 1993). Already in the fourteenth century many theologians were discussing the differences between traditions of the church and the authentic doctrines of Scripture in contrast to these.

86 See especially the Antiochian interpretations, which emphasize the literal and historical meaning (in the premodern sense): Manlio Simonetti, *Biblical Interpretation in the Early Church: An Historical Introduction to Patristic Exegesis,* trans. John A. Hughes (Edinburgh: T&T Clark, 1994), 59ff.

87 See Kaufmann, *Der Anfang der Reformation*, 88ff. *WA TR* 5:99, no. 5374. Luther held that Staupitz' biblical theology was similar to another Tübingen theologian, Konrad Summenhart.

88 Andreas Bodenstein von Karlstadt, *Centum quinquagintaunum conclusiones de natura, lege et gratia, contra scolasticos et usum comunem*, April 26, 1517; the German translation provided by Alejandro Zorzin and Martin Keßler (Wolfenbüttel: Herzog-August-Bibliothek) was consulted for this translation: "[1.] Dicta sanctorum patrum non sunt neganda. [2.] Nisi essent correcta vel retractata. [3.] Si fuerint diversa non secundum nudum placitum sunt eligenda. [4.] Sed ea que divinis testimoniis magis vel ratione iuvantur."

89 Karlstadt, "151 Theses," "[151] Fecunda veritatis authoritas sepius discussa melius cognoscitur: et veram convenientiam parit: quam manifestis sermonibus abscondit."

90 Translation cited in Ronald J. Sider, *Andreas Bodenstein von Karlstadt: The Development of His Thought, 1517–1525* (Leiden: Brill, 1974), 49. See also his remarks about the Bible in his 370 Conclusions from 1518, as cited above in chap. 1.

91 Sylvester Prierias, "Dialogue de potestate papae," in *Dokumente zur Causa Lutheri (1517–1521)*, ed. P. Fabisch and E. Iserloh, vol. 1 (Münster: Aschendorff, 1988), 55; as cited in Lutheran–Roman Catholic Commission on Unity, *From Conflict to Communion: Lutheran-Catholic Common Commemoration of the Reformation in 2017* (Leipzig: Bonifatius, 2013), 72.

92 Eck, *Enchiridion locorum communium adversus Lutherum et alios hostes ecclesiae*, 30, 27. See also the Lutheran–Roman Catholic Commission on Unity, *From Conflict to Communion*, 72. As Evans explains, Eck thought of the bishops as though they were "carrying their subjects [sc. members of the church] with them as a king carries his people in committing his country to war or peace." Evans, *Problems of Authority in the Reformation Debates*, 250ff. Later, Luther would explicitly reject this view of the representative power of the bishops. See also Christopher Spehr, *Luther und das Konzil: Zur Entwicklung eines zentralen Themas in der Reformationszeit* (Tübingen: Mohr Siebeck, 2010), 39–68.

93 *WA* 2:11: "cum Papa non super, sed sub verbo dei sit." A summary of this issue is provided by Scott Hendrix, "Luther," in Bagchi and Steinmetz, *Cambridge Companion to Reformation Theology*, 39–56, here 45–46. Gal 1:8: "But even if we or an angel from heaven should proclaim to you a gospel contrary to what we proclaimed to you, let that one be accursed!"

94 Hendrix, "Luther," in Bagchi and Steinmetz, *Cambridge Companion to Reformation Theology*, 46. In August of 1518, Luther had claimed that the pope and councils could err. See his exchange with Silvester Prierias, *WA* 1:656: "quia tam Papa quam concilium potest errare." Regarding the date, see *WA* 1:645–46. See Spehr, *Luther und das Konzil*, 61; Leppin, *Transformationen*, 385.

95 To Karlstadt's account of the authority of Scripture at the Leipzig Debate, see his *protestatio* for June 27: "Sacris autem scripturis hunc honorem impendimus, quod nihil sine his aut asserere aut praecipere volumus. In caeteris autem, quae non liquide hinc doceri possunt, solis ecclesiasticis primas damus," *WA* 59:433. See Leppin's remarks about Karlstadt's theology at the Leipzig Debate in Leppin, *Transformationen*, 378. This is also addressed by Hermann Barge, *Andreas Bodenstein von Karlstadt*, vol. 1: *Karlstadt und die Anfänge der Reformation* (Leipzig: Brandstetter, 1905), 155.

96 Leppin, *Transformationen*, 378.
97 *LW* 31:318. Luther claims that Eck tried to exclude the stenographers from the debate in order that there would be no official record of it. Karlstadt forced Eck to hold to the agreement, however, according to which the debate would be recorded with stenographers (*LW* 31:319). Before this, in a letter from the spring of 1518, Luther had already remarked on the fact that his scholastic teachers taught him that only the canonical books are deserving of "faith" (*fides*), while all others are only deserving of an "opinion/belief/judgment" (*iudicium*). See *WA Br* 1:171, no. 74, letter to Jodocus Trutfetter, May 9, 1518: "solis canonicis libris deberi fidem." See Bernhard Lohse, *Luthers Theologie in ihrer historischen Entwicklung und in ihrem systematischen Zusammenhang* (Göttingen: Vandenhoeck & Ruprecht, 1995), 40, 204–5. See Kaufmann, *Der Anfang der Reformation*, 88ff.
98 Leppin, *Transformationen*, 396: "Zwingend konnten nur solche Argumente sein, die der Schrift selbst entstammten. Kirchenväter und erst recht Konzilien traten demgegenüber in eine dienende und verweisende Funktion ein, nicht aber in eine generell erschließende, wie sie ihnen noch in den *Asterisci* bei Luther selbst und während der Leipziger Disputation nach Ecks Argumentation zugekommen war." On the genesis of the emphasis on *sola scriptura*, see 335–97.
99 Leppin, *Transformationen*, 473.
100 *LW* 31:385. See *WA* 7:161–82. See also the editorial introduction in *LW* 31:381ff.
101 *LW* 31:387.
102 *LW* 31:389.
103 *LW* 31:391.
104 *LW* 31:392.
105 *LW* 31:392.
106 Luther, "Defense and Explanation of All the Articles," in *LW* 32:81. Here Luther also defends Hus. Here he remarks that "all the articles of John Huss, condemned at Constance, are altogether Christian" (*LW* 32:82).
107 *LW* 32:81.
108 *LW* 32:81–82.
109 *LW* 32:112–13.
110 See Oberman, *Reformation*, 15–18. See also John Brevicoxa's treatise on this matter in idem, *Reformation*, 67ff.
111 Alfred Kohler, *Karl V: 1500–1558: Eine Biographie* (München: Beck, 2013), 154–56.
112 See David M. Whitford, "Luther's Political Encounters," in *The Cambridge Companion to Martin Luther*, ed. Donald McKim (Cambridge: Cambridge University Press, 2003), 182.
113 Spehr, *Luther und das Konzil*, 271.
114 *Dogmatic Constitution on Divine Revelation; Dei verbum* (Washington, D.C.: United States Catholic Conference, 1994), §10. Cf. *Acta Apostolicae Sedis* 58 (1966): 817–36.
115 *Dogmatic Constitution on Divine Revelation; Dei verbum*, §9.
116 *Dogmatic Constitution on Divine Revelation; Dei verbum*, §9.
117 *Dogmatic Constitution on Divine Revelation; Dei verbum*, §10.
118 United States Catholic Conference, *Catechism of the Catholic Church* (New York: Doubleday, 1994), pt. 1, sec. 1, chap. 2, art. 2, III. "The Interpretation of the Heritage of Faith," §86, p. 32.

119 Paul VI, *Apostolic Exhortation Evangelii nuntiandi* (London: Catholic Truth Society, 1976), 78; *Acta Apostolicae Sedis* 68 (1976): 71.

120 John Paul II, *Ut unum sint: On Commitment to Ecumenism* (Washington, D.C.: United States Catholic Conference, 1995), §4. See *Acta Apostolicae Sedis* 87 (1995): 921–82.

121 John Paul II, *Ut unum sint*, §39.

122 Pope Francis, *The Light of Faith; Lumen fidei* (Washington, D.C.: United States Conference of Catholic Bishops, 2013), §49.

123 Avery Dulles, "Revelation, Scripture, and Tradition," in *Your Word Is Truth: A Project of Evangelicals and Catholics Together*, ed. Charles Colson and Richard John Neuhaus (Grand Rapids: Eerdmans, 2002), 35–58, here 57–58.

124 See Colson and Neuhaus, *Your Word Is Truth*, 3–4.

125 Colson and Neuhaus, *Your Word Is Truth*, 5.

126 Daniel J. Treier, "Scripture and Hermeneutics," in *The Cambridge Companion to Evangelical Theology*, ed. idem and Timothy Larsen (Cambridge: Cambridge University Press, 2007), 35–49, here 35. The modern Catholic recognition of the importance of Scripture in "Your Word Is Truth" is also stated with careful qualifications regarding its interpretation.

127 Wolfhart Pannenberg, *Systematic Theology*, vol. 3, trans. G. W. Bromiley (London: T&T Clark, 1998), 420–21. As the Lutheran–Roman Catholic Commission on Unity recalls, "In the Augsburg Confession (1530), the reformers declared that they were prepared to obey the bishops if the bishops themselves would allow the preaching of the gospel according to Reformation beliefs." Lutheran–Roman Catholic Commission on Unity, *From Conflict to Communion*, 32.

128 Pannenberg, *Systematic Theology*, 421.

129 Pannenberg, *Systematic Theology*, 430.

130 Robert W. Jenson, "The Church as *Communio*," in *The Catholicity of the Reformation*, ed. idem and Carl E. Braaten (Grand Rapids: Eerdmans, 1996), 1–12, here 10; emphasis in original.

131 Pope Francis, *The Joy of the Gospel; Evangelii gaudium* (Washington, D.C.: United States Conference of Catholic Bishops, 2013), §32.

132 The Ecumenical Working Group of Protestant and Catholic Theologians recently issued a statement in 2014. They hold that the emphasis on scriptural authority from the Reformation has been taken up in the Catholic tradition. As the document affirms, "The Constitution on Divine Revelation adheres to the priority of Scripture over the ecclesiastical tradition: the 'Sacred Scripture is the word of God,' while sacred tradition (simply) hands it on (see *Dei verbum* 9)." Sattler and Leppin, *Reformation 1517–2017*, 104.

133 See the books in the Five Solas Series: What the Reformers Taught . . . And Why It Still Matters, edited by Matthew Barrett (Grand Rapids: Zondervan, 2015–2017): Thomas Schreiner, *Faith Alone: The Doctrine of Justification* (2015); David VanDrunen, *God's Glory Alone: The Majestic Heart of Christian Faith and Life* (2015); Matthew Barrett, *God's Word Alone: The Authority of Scripture* (2016); Carl Trueman, *Grace Alone: Salvation as a Gift of God* (2017); and Stephen Wellum, *Christ Alone: The Uniqueness of Jesus as Savior* (2017). *Soli Deo gloria* was added later to this classic list of four. These also go back to Staupitz' sermons in German ("*genad . . . alain*," grace alone), see Volker Leppin, *Die fremde Reformation: Luthers*

mystische Wurzeln (München: Beck, 2015), 14–15. To the genesis of the emphasis on *solus Christus* from medieval Christianity, see Leppin, *Transformationen*, 279–302.

134 Gansfort, "From the Letter in Reply to Jacob Hoeck," chap. 8, as cited in Oberman, *Forerunners of the Reformation*, 109.

Chapter 4

1 See Günther Gaßmann et al., *Historical Dictionary of Lutheranism*, 2nd ed. (Lanham, Md.: Scarecrow, 2011), 395.

2 According to Brady, the Protestant reforms required the idea of political protection. For while the church was "no longer the vessel of God's saving grace," it was still the "speaker of His saving Word. Without the ruler's aid, they believed, their mission could not be fulfilled." Thomas A. Brady Jr., *German Histories in the Age of Reformations, 1400–1650* (Cambridge: Cambridge University Press, 2009), 263–64.

3 *Sophocles*, trans. by Hugh Lloyd-Jones (Cambridge, Mass.: Harvard University Press, 1984), *Antigone*, 450f.

4 See Alexander Weiß, *Soziale Elite und Christentum: Studien zu ordo-Angehörigen unter den frühen Christen* [Social Elite and Christianity: Studies on the Ordo-Members among the Early Christians] (Berlin: de Gruyter, 2015); my review was published in *Reviews in Religion and Theology* 22, no. 4 (2015): 386–88.

5 Augustine, *City of God*, vol. 4: *Books 12–15*, Loeb Classical Library 414, trans. Philip Levine (Cambridge, Mass.: Harvard University Press, 1966), 14:28, p. 405.

6 Christine Caldwell Ames, *Medieval Heresies: Christianity, Judaism, and Islam* (Cambridge: Cambridge University Press, 2015), 51–53, here 52–53; see also Jennifer Ebbeler, *Disciplining Christians: Correction and Community in Augustine's Letters* (Oxford: Oxford University Press, 2012), 151ff.

7 Augustine, "Against the Letters of Petilian," 1.18.20; as cited in Ames, *Medieval Heresies*, 53.

8 Anders Winroth, *The Age of the Vikings* (Princeton, N.J.: Princeton University Press, 2014), 42.

9 As cited in Oliver O'Donovan and Joan Lockwood O'Donovan, eds., *From Irenaeus to Grotius: A Sourcebook in Christian Political Thought, 100–1625* (Grand Rapids: Eerdmans, 1999), 179.

10 Christian Igelbrink, *Kanonische Ideale und politische Pragmatik: das Wormser Konkordat im Spannungsfeld hochmittelalterlicher Herrschaftspraxis* (München: AVM, 2014); Uta-Renate Blumenthal, *The Investiture Controversy: Church and Monarchy from the Ninth to the Twelfth Century* (Philadelphia: University of Philadelphia Press, 1988).

11 James Atkinson Introduction to *LW* 44:117–21, here 117.

12 Luther, "To the Christian Nobility of the German Nation concerning the Reform of the Christian Estate," in *LW* 44:126. In this work, Luther initiated a reforming process that was no longer working within the confines of the Roman ecclesial structure or the older tradition of ecclesial reform that sought to improve this system. Martin Luther, *An den christlichen Adel deutscher Nation von des christlichen Standes Besserung*, ed. Thomas Kaufmann (Tübingen: Mohr Siebeck, 2014), 15.

13 Luther, "To the Christian Nobility," 161.

14 Luther, "To the Christian Nobility," 129.

15 Luther, "To the Christian Nobility."

16 Luther, "To the Christian Nobility."

17 Luther, "To the Christian Nobility," 130.

18 Hartmut Boockmann, *Einführung in die Geschichte des Mittelalters* (München: Beck, 2007), 50.

19 John. W. Baldwin, *The Government of Philip Augustus: Foundations of French Royal Power in the Middle Ages* (Berkeley: University of California Press, 1991), 185.

20 In modern Western nations there are, nevertheless, still some vestiges of the old protected status for political leaders in criminal matters. In the United States, for example, there is the controversial state secrets privilege: "The state secrets privilege is a judicially created evidentiary privilege that allows the federal government to resist court-ordered disclosure of information during litigation if there is a reasonable danger that such disclosure would harm the national security of the United States." Todd Garvey and Edward C. Liu, *The State Secrets Privilege: Preventing the Disclosure of Sensitive National Security Information During Civil Litigation* (Washington, D.C.: Congressional Research Service, Library of Congress, 2011), ii.

21 See Bernd Moeller, "Klerus und Antiklerikalismus in Luthers Schrift An den christlichen Adel deutscher Nation von 1520," in *Anticlericalism in Late Medieval and Early Modern Europe*, ed. Peter A. Dykema and Heiko A. Oberman (Leiden: Brill, 1993).

22 Luther, "To the Christian Nobility," 135.

23 "The Twelve Articles of the Upper Swabian Peasants," in *The Radical Reformation*, ed. Michael G. Baylor (Cambridge: Cambridge University Press, 1991), 234.

24 Luther, "To the Christian Nobility," 135.

25 Luther, "To the Christian Nobility," 136.

26 See Henning Graf Reventlow, *History of Biblical Interpretation*, vol. 3: *Renaissance, Reformation, Humanism*, trans. James O. Duke (Leiden: Brill, 2010), 65–198. This also entailed Sebastian Franck, who focused on the "inner word," not the letter (see 165–75), and Müntzer, who sought to advance the kingdom of God with the sword (see 137–54).

27 Luther, "To the Christian Nobility," 137.

28 Luther, "To the Christian Nobility," 182.

29 Luther, "To the Christian Nobility."

30 Luther, "To the Christian Nobility," 183.

31 Luther, "To the Christian Nobility," 158.

32 See Armin Kohnle, "Luther und das Landeskirchentum," *Luther: Zeitschrift der Luthergesellschaft* 85 (2014): 9–22. Kohnle claims that for "most of the sovereign princes" around 1500, this was "self-evident" (*selbstverständlich*), see 11. Christoph Volkmar, *Reform statt Reformation: die Kirchenpolitik Herzog Georgs von Sachsen, 1488–1525* (Tübingen: Mohr Siebeck, 2008). George saw himself as a Reformer but did not support the Reformation.

33 See Kenneth G. Appold, *The Reformation: A Brief History* (Malden, Mass.: Wiley-Blackwell, 2011), 9.

34 See Mark U. Edwards, *Luther and the False Brethren* (Stanford, Calif.: Stanford University Press, 1975), 7–20; Appold, *Reformation*, 83ff.; Scott H. Hendrix, *Martin Luther: Visionary Reformer* (New Haven, Conn.: Yale University Press,

2015), 119–34; Heinz Schilling, *Martin Luther: Rebell in einer Zeit des Umbruchs* (München: Beck, 2012), 289–92; Euan Cameron, *The European Reformation*, 2nd ed. (Oxford: Oxford University Press, 2012), 215–19; Stefan Oehmig, "Die Wittenberger Bewegung 1521/22 und ihre Folgen im Lichte alter und neuer Fragestellungen. Ein Beitrag zum Thema (Territorial-) Stadt und Reformation," in *700 Jahre Wittenberg. Stadt, Universität, Reformation*, ed. idem (Weimar: Böhlaus, 1995), 97–130; Martin Brecht, *Martin Luther*, vol. 2: *Ordnung und Abgrenzung der Reformation 1521–1532* (Stuttgart: Calwer Verlag, 1986), 11–65; trans. James L. Schaff as *Martin Luther*, vol. 2, *Shaping and Defining the Reformation, 1521–1532* (Minneapolis: Fortress, 1990); Volker Leppin, *Transformationen: Studien zu den Wandlungsprozessen in Theologie und Frömmigkeit zwischen Spätmittelalter und Reformation* (Tübingen: Mohr Siebeck, 2015), 31–68; Thomas Kaufmann, *Der Anfang der Reformation: Studien zur Kontextualität der Theologie, Publizistik und Inszenierung Luthers und der reformatorischen Bewegung* (Tübingen: Mohr Siebeck, 2012), 201–20, 464–505; James S. Preus, *Carlstadt's Ordinaciones and Luther's Liberty: A Study of the Wittenberg Movement 1521–1522* (Cambridge, Mass.: Harvard University Press, 1974).

35 See Kaufmann, *Der Anfang der Reformation*, 185–265.

36 Hermann Barge, *Andreas Bodenstein von Karlstadt*, vol. 1: *Karlstadt und die Anfänge der Reformation* (Leipzig: Brandstetter, 1905), 313ff.; Ronald J. Sider, *Andreas Bodenstein von Karlstadt: The Development of His Thought 1517–1525* (Leiden: Brill, 1974), 153ff.

37 Sider, *Andreas Bodenstein von Karlstadt*, 155.

38 Sider, *Andreas Bodenstein von Karlstadt*. See Nikolaus Müller, *Die Wittenberger Bewegung 1521 und 1522* (Leipzig: Heinsius, 1911), 34.

39 Sider, *Andreas Bodenstein von Karlstadt*, 157.

40 Edwards, *Luther and the False Brethren*, 8.

41 See Ernst Troeltsch, *Protestantisches Christentum und Kirche in der Neuzeit (1906/1909/1922)*, Kritische Gesamtausgabe 7, ed. Volker Drehsen (Berlin: de Gruyter, 2004), 179.

42 Luther to Spalatin, *LW* 48:351–52; *WA Br* 2:409–11, here 410. See also Hendrix, *Martin Luther*, 123. The editorial remarks suggest that Luther probably arrived in Wittenberg on the afternoon of December 3.

43 Hendrix, *Martin Luther*, 123; Sider, *Andreas Bodenstein von Karlstadt*, 154ff.

44 Edwards, *Luther and the False Brethren*, 8.

45 Sider, *Andreas Bodenstein von Karlstadt*, 157.

46 Sider, *Andreas Bodenstein von Karlstadt*, 160; to the history of these events, see also Barge, *Andreas Bodenstein von Karlstadt*, 1:358; Müller, *Die Wittenberger Bewegung*, 170.

47 Sider, *Andreas Bodenstein von Karlstadt*, 160; Müller, *Die Wittenberger Bewegung*, 153f.

48 Hendrix, *Martin Luther*, 127.

49 Peter Jezler, "Von den Guten Werken zum reformatorischen Bildersturm—Eine Einführung," in *Bildersturm: Wahnsinn oder Gottes Wille?* ed. Cécile Dupeux, Peter Jezler, and Jean Wirth (Munich: Wilhelm Fink, 2000), 20–27, here 23.

50 Hendrix, *Martin Luther*, 125. Regarding Karlstadt and die events in Wittenberg in 1521 and 1522, see Markus Matthias, "Die Anfänge der reformatorischen Theologie

des Andreas Bodenstein von Karlstadt," in *Querdenker der Reformation Andreas Bodenstein von Karlstadt und seine frühe Wirkung*, ed. Stefan Oehmig (Würzburg: Religion-und-Kultur-Verlag, 2001), 87–109. Volker Leppin, "Die Wittenbergische Bulle. Andreas Karlstadts Kritik an Luther," in *Die Kirchenkritik der Mystiker. Prophetie aus Gotteserfahrung*, ed. Mariano Delgado, vol. 2 (Stuttgart: Academic, 2005), 117–29; Barge, *Andreas Bodenstein von Karlstadt*, 2 vols.

51   Volkmar, *Reform statt Reformation*, 488. Herzog Georgs von Sachsen had part in this. He used every opportunity to move the princes and magistrates to resist the reforms. See also Christopher Spehr, *Luther und das Konzil: Zur Entwicklung eines zentralen Themas in der Reformationszeit* (Tübingen: Mohr Siebeck, 2010), 267.

52   Appold, *Reformation*, 84. See also Leppin, "Die Wittenbergische Bulle," 120.

53   See Hans-Jürgen Goertz, *Religiöse Bewegungen in der Frühen Neuzeit* (München: Oldenbourg, 1993), 9.

54   Ulrich Bubenheimer, "Karlstadt, Andreas Rudolff Bodenstein von (1486–1541)," in *Theologische Realenzyklopädie*, vol. 17 (Berlin: de Gruyter, 1988), 649–57.

55   Sider, *Andreas Bodenstein von Karlstadt*, 169.

56   Edwards, *Luther and the False Brethren*, 10.

57   Schilling, *Martin Luther*, 289.

58   Cameron, *European Reformation*, 216.

59   Sider, *Andreas Bodenstein von Karlstadt*, 171–73, here 172–73: "Luther restored the old custom. He again spoke the words of institution softly in Latin while facing the altar. The cup was again denied to the laity in public services, although special services were made available for those who wanted both. [...] The practice of placing the sacrament in the hands of the communicant received Luther's particularly vigorous condemnation"; John S. Oyer, *Lutheran Reformers against Anabaptists: Luther, Melanchthon and Menius and the Anabaptists of Central Germany* (The Hague: Nijhoff, 1964), 23.

60   Sider, *Andreas Bodenstein von Karlstadt*, 172.

61   Sider, *Andreas Bodenstein von Karlstadt*, 200. In a letter on March 19, 1521, Luther explained that he returned to Wittenberg from the Wartburg Castle in order to "destroy this theatre of Satan." *WA Br* 2:478. Luther to Wenzeslaus Linck. As cited in Sider, *Andreas Bodenstein von Karlstadt*, 173. In his second Invocavit Sermon, Luther wrote, "Had I desired to foment trouble, I could have brought great bloodshed upon Germany; indeed, I could have started such a game that even the emperor would not have been safe." *LW* 51:78; *WA* 10/3:19; translation cited in Eric Lund, ed., *Documents from the History of Lutheranism, 1517–1750* (Minneapolis: Fortress, 2002), 38.

62   The power play that Luther worked in 1522 was "not Luther fighting against the vastly superior powers of pope and emperor; this was Luther fighting for control." Appold, *Reformation*, 85.

63   R. Emmet McLaughlin, "The Radical Reformation," in *Cambridge History of Christianity*, vol. 6: *Reform and Expansion 1500–1660*, ed. R. Po-Chia Hsia (Cambridge: Cambridge University Press, 2007), 39.

64   See Sider, *Andreas Bodenstein von Karlstadt*, 187ff.

65   McLaughlin, "The Radical Reformation," in Hsia, *Reform and Expansion*, 40.

66 Ronald J. Sider, ed., *Karlstadt's Battle with Luther: Documents in a Liberal-Radical Debate* (Philadelphia: Fortress, 1978), 41.

67 Sider, *Karlstadt's Battle with Luther*, 41.

68 Sider, *Karlstadt's Battle with Luther*, 48.

69 Volker Leppin, *Martin Luther* (Darmstadt: Primus, 2006), 219. Regarding the preaching tour, and Luther's later relationship with Karlstadt (after he was humiliated and expelled from Electoral Saxony), see 215–20.

70 Sider, *Andreas Bodenstein von Karlstadt*, 196f.

71 See Sider, *Andreas Bodenstein von Karlstadt*, 196. See also Appold, *Reformation*, 85.

72 See Sider, *Andreas Bodenstein von Karlstadt*, 194ff. Karlstadt rejected Luther's teaching about the baptism of children. He specifically rejected the idea of a vicarious *fides aliena* of the godparents. He never called for rebaptisms, however. That was the classic Anabaptist position. He held against Luther that the bread and wine are symbols of the spiritual presence of Christ. From 1522 or 1533 he had contact with Müntzer. In 1523, however, he distanced himself from his understanding of revelation (*Ursachen, daß Andreas Karlstadt ein Zeit still geschwiegen*). In July of 1524, during the Peasants' Revolt, he rejected Müntzer's revolutionary approach. He was, nevertheless, branded by Luther to be an insurrectionist, even if he encouraged the Franconian groups not to resort to violence. After a long and complicated journey through Protestant Europe—also for a time returning to Wittenberg, where he stayed with Luther (and had to remain silent)—he eventually found a place in Zurich with the Swiss Reformers. Although he did not support them entirely, there he could continue to publish and promote his cause. Karlstadt's works (especially the mystical theology, such as *Was gesagt ist: Sich gelassen*, 1523) were read well into the seventeenth century, although sometimes without his name attached to them. He was rehabilitated in pietism. See Bubenheimer, "Karlstadt, Andreas Rudolff Bodenstein von (1486–1541)," 649–57.

73 Leppin, "Die Wittenbergische Bulle," 117. Both Luther and Karlstadt were influenced by medieval mysticism and especially Staupitz (122–23).

74 *WA* 11:408–16; *LW* 39:305–14.

75 See Leisnigers' common-chest ordinance and Luther's preface to it in *WA* 12:11–30; *LW* 45:163–94.

76 To this see James Martin Estes, *Peace, Order and the Glory of God: Secular Authority and the Church in the Thought of Luther and Melanchthon; 1518–1559* (Leiden: Brill, 2005), 1–52; Susan C. Karant-Nunn, *Luther's Pastors: The Reformation in the Ernestine Countryside* (Philadelphia: American Philosophical Society, 1979); Karl Trüdinger, *Luthers Briefe und Gutachten an weltliche Obrigkeiten zur Durchführung der Reformation* (Münster: Aschendorff, 1975), 68–71.

77 Appold, *Reformation*, 85.

78 Regarding the visitation institution, see Herman Speelman, *Melanchthon and Calvin on Confession and Communion: Early Modern Protestant Penitential and Eucharistic Piety* (Göttingen: Vandenhoeck & Ruprecht, 2016), 97–128.

79 Thomas A. Brady, "Emergence and Consolidation of Protestantism in the Holy Roman Empire to 1600," in Hsia, *Reform and Expansion*, 20–36, here 21.

80 Brady, "Emergence and Consolidation," in Hsia, *Reform and Expansion*, 22.

81 Heiko A. Oberman, "Anticlericalism as an Agent of Change," in Dykema and Oberman, *Anticlericalism*, ix–xi, here x. This is a part of a new definition of anticlericalism that various scholars contributed to at a conference from September 20 to 22, 1990, at the University of Arizona.

82 *WA* 38:102–3; as cited in translation in Brady, "Emergence and Consolidation," in Hsia, *Reform and Expansion*, 22. See also *WA* 19:625.

83 Kohnle, "Luther und das Landeskirchentum," 17.

84 See Luther and Melanchthon, "Unterricht der Visitatoren an die Pfarrherrn im Kurfürstentum Sachsen" (1528); *WA* 26; *LW* 40. Scott Hendrix, "Martin Luther, Reformer," in Hsia, *Reform and Expansion*, 11.

85 Heinz Schilling, "Confessional Europe," in *Handbook of European History 1400–1600: Late Middle Ages, Renaissance and Reformation*, ed. Thomas A. Brady Jr. et al., vol. 2: *Visions, Programs and Outcomes* (Leiden: Brill, 1995), 641–81, here 649.

86 *WA Br* 3:616: "Deinde principes nostri non cogunt ad fidem et Euangelion, sed cohibent externas abominationes."

87 *WA* 15:774: "todtschleg, diebstal, mord uund eebruch nitt also schedlich seyn als dieser grewel der Papisten Mess."

88 *WA* 18:36. "Vom Greuel der Stillmesse" (1525).

89 Kohnle, "Luther und das Landeskirchentum," 15; see Luther, *WA Br* 3:615–17 (no. 946).

90 Christoph Strohm, "Calvin und die religiöse Toleranz," in *1509—Johannes Calvin—2009. Sein Wirken in Kirche und Gesellschaft. Essays zum 500. Geburtstag*, ed. Martin E. Hirzel and Martin Sallmann (Zurich: Theologischer Verlag, 2008), 219–36, here 225.

91 Kohnle, "Luther und das Landeskirchentum," 16; see Emil Sehling, ed., *Die evangelischen Kirchenordnungen des XVI. Jahrhunderts*, vol. 1: *Sachsen und Thüringen nebst angrenzenden Gebieten; Hälfte 1: Die Ordnungen Luthers, die Ernestinischen und Albertinischen Gebiete* (Leipzig: Reisland, 1902), 144.

92 Kohnle, "Luther und das Landeskirchentum," 18; see Luther, *WA Br* 10:436–7 (no. 3930).

93 Andrew Pettegree, *Reformation and the Culture of Persuasion* (Cambridge: Cambridge University Press, 2005), 3.

94 Robert W. Scribner, "Elements of Popular Belief," in *Handbook of European History 1400–1600: Late Middle Ages, Renaissance and Reformation*, ed. Thomas A. Brady Jr. et al., vol. 1: *Structures and Assertions* (Leiden: Brill, 1994), 254.

95 Martin Luther, "Temporal Authority: To What Extent It Should Be Obeyed," in *LW* 45:105.

96 Luther, "Temporal Authority," 108.

97 Luther, "Temporal Authority," 117.

98 Luther, "Temporal Authority," 91.

99 For an analysis of this theme, see John Witte, *Law and Protestantism: The Legal Teachings of the Lutheran Reformation* (Cambridge: Cambridge University Press, 2002), 93–94. Volker Leppin et al., eds., *Das Luther-Lexikon* (Regensburg: Bückle & Böhm, 2014), 174–76.

100 Ute Lotz-Heumann, "Imposing Church and Social Discipline," in Hsia, *Reform and Expansion*, 244–60, here 247. See also Philip S. Gorski, *The Disciplinary Revolution: Calvinism and the Rise of the State in Early Modern Europe* (Chicago: University of

Chicago Press, 2003); Ronnie Po-Chia Hsia, *Social Discipline in the Reformation: Central Europe 1550–1750* (London: Routledge, 1989); Heinz Schilling, ed., *Institutionen, Instrumente und Akteure sozialer Kontrolle und Disziplinierung im frühneuzeitlichen Europa* (Frankfurt: Klostermann, 1999); idem, ed., *Kirchenzucht und Sozialdisziplinierung im frühneuzeitlichen Europa* (Berlin: Duncker & Humblot, 1994).

101 Manfred Schulze, *Fürsten und Reformation: Geistliche Reformpolitik weltlicher Fürsten vor der Reformation* (Tübingen: Mohr, 1991), 1.

102 See Peter Blickle, "Communal Reformation: Zwingli, Luther, and the South of the Holy Roman Empire," in Hsia, *Reform and Expansion,* 75–89. Bernd Moeller, *Reichsstadt und Reformation* (Gütersloh: Gütersloher Verlagshaus, 1962; Tübingen: Mohr Siebeck, 2011); Steven E. Ozment, *The Reformation in the Cities: The Appeal of Protestantism to Sixteenth-Century Germany and Switzerland* (New Haven, Conn.: Yale University Press, 1975); Thomas A. Brady, *Communities, Politics, and Reformation in Early Modern Europe* (Leiden: Brill, 1998); idem, *Ruling Class, Regime and Reformation at Strasbourg: 1520–1555* (Leiden: Brill, 1978).

103 Erwin Iserloh, "Die protestantische Reformation," in *Handbuch der Kirchengeschichte*, vol. 4: *Reformation, katholische Reform und Gegenreformation,* ed. Hubert Jedin (Freiburg: Herder, 1967), 3–446, here 145.

104 Calvin, *Institutes of the Christian Religion*, vols. 1 and 2, trans. Henry Beveridge (Edinburgh: T&T Clark, 1863), bk. 4, chap. 10, par. 5, 2:416–17.

105 Calvin, *Institutes*, bk. 4, chap. 10, par. 31, 2:436–37.

106 Thomas Kaufmann, *Luthers "Judenschriften": ein Beitrag zu ihrer historischen Kontextualisierung* (Tübingen: Mohr Siebeck, 2013), 148; Kaufman, "Das Bekenntnis im Luthertum des konfessionellen Zeitalters," *Zeitschrift für Theologie und Kirche* 105 (2008): 281–314. He points to Dean Phillip Bell, *Sacred Communities: Jewish and Christian Identities in Fifteenth Century Germany* (Boston: Brill, 2001). Arnold Hirsch, "Luther et le Corpus Christianum," in *Revue d'histoire moderne et contemporaine* 4 (1957): 81–111.

107 Calvin, *Institutes of the Christian Religion, 1536 Edition,* trans. Ford Lewis Battles (Grand Rapids: Eerdmans, 1995), 208–9; emphasis added. Cf. Strohm, "Calvin und die religiöse Toleranz," in Hirzel and Sallmann, in *1509—Johannes Calvin—2009,* 227. See also Herman A. Speelman, *Calvin and the Independence of the Church* (Göttingen: Vandenhoeck & Ruprecht, 2014).

108 Calvin, *Defensio orthodoxae fidei de sacra Trinitate contra prodigiosos errores Michaelis Serveti Hispani;* see Joseph Lecler, *Geschichte der Religionsfreiheit im Zeitalter der Reformation,* vol. 1 (Stuttgart: Schwabenverl., 1965), 459. Cf. Strohm, "Calvin und die religiöse Toleranz," in Hirzel and Sallmann, *1509—Johannes Calvin—2009,* 228.

109 Wulfert Greef, *The Writings of John Calvin: An Introductory Guide,* trans. Lyle D. Bierma (Louisville, Ky.: Westminster John Knox, 2008), 164.

110 Marian Hillar, *Michael Servetus: Intellectual Giant, Humanist and Martyr* (Lanham, Md.: University Press of America, 2002), 185. On the execution, Cotton Mather's brother, Samuel Mather, wrote, "It is none of my Business to defend the *Execution*. I own, I am not for any Persecution, much less, *ad sanguinem.*" *A Discourse concerning the Necessity of Believing the Doctrine of the Holy Trinity* (London: Pater-Noster-Row, 1719), 71.

111 Strohm, "Calvin und die religiöse Toleranz," in Hirzel and Sallmann, *1509—Johannes Calvin—2009*, 222: "Es muss aber in aller Klarheit festgehalten werden, dass sich Calvin in den Auseinandersetzungen mit Bolsec wie auch mit Servet zu keinerlei religiöser Toleranz im Stande gesehen hat."

112 Cf. Strohm, "Calvin und die religiöse Toleranz," in Hirzel and Sallmann, *1509—Johannes Calvin—2009*, 226-27.

113 Mario Turchetti, "Der Beitrag Calvins und des Calvinismus zur Entstehung der modernen Demokratie," in Hirzel and Sallmann, *1509—Johannes Calvin—2009*, 237-66, here 252ff.

114 "Twelve Articles of the Upper Swabian Peasants," in Baylor, *Radical Reformation*, 232. See also the first Anabaptist confession of faith (the Schleitheim Confession, 1527), drafted primarily by Michael Sattler. Article five states that the pastors shall be appointed by the congregation that supports them. Article six states that they will not use force in matters of faith. *The Schleitheim Confession*, trans. John H. Yoder (Scottdale, P.: Herald Press, 1977), 13-14. Critical edition: *Das Schleitheimer Bekenntnis 1527: Einleitung, Faksimile, Übersetzung und Kommentar*, eds. Urs B. Leu and Christian Scheidegger (Zug: Achius, 2004), 69.

115 See Meinulf Barbers, *Toleranz bei Sebastian Franck* (Bonn: Röhrscheid, 1964). See also Harry Loewen, *Luther and the Radicals: Another Look at Some Aspects of the Struggle between Luther and the Radical Reformers* (Waterloo: Wilfred Laurier University, 1974), 146-47. Regarding Franck, see above, chap. 2, §2.1.

116 Anonymous, *Whether Secular Government Has the Right to Wield the Sword in Matters of Faith: A Controversy in Nürnberg, 1530*, trans. James M. Estes (Toronto: Center for Reformation and Renaissance Studies, 1994), 41; Anonymous, "Ob ein weltlich oberkait recht habe, in des glaubens sachen mit dem schwert zu handeln," ed. Martin Brecht, *Archiv für Reformationsgeschichte* 60 (1969): 65-75.

117 Anonymous, *Whether Secular Government*, 43.

118 Anonymous, *Whether Secular Government*, 43.

119 Anonymous, *Whether Secular Government*, 44.

120 See Stefan Zweig, *The Right to Heresy: Castellio against Calvin*, trans. Eden Paul and Cedar Paul (New York: Viking, 1936). This work is now in its fifteenth edition in the German original: *Castellio gegen Calvin oder ein Gewissen gegen die Gewalt* (Frankfurt am Main: Fischer, 2009). See also Ferdinand Buisson, *Sébastien Castellion, sa vie et son oeuvre, 1515-1563* (Genève: Librairie Droz, 2010).

121 See Brady, "Emergence and Consolidation," in Hsia, *Reform and Expansion*, 25.

122 Lutheran–Roman Catholic Commission on Unity, *From Conflict to Communion: Lutheran-Catholic Common Commemoration of the Reformation in 2017* (Leipzig: Bonifatius, 2013), 35.

123 Heinz Schilling, "Der Augsburger Religionsfriede als deutsches und europäisches Ereignis. Festvortrag am 25. September 2005 in Augsburg," *Archiv für Reformationsgeschichte* 98 (2007): 244-50, here 246.

124 Schilling, "Der Augsburger Religionsfriede," 248.

125 Schilling, "Der Augsburger Religionsfriede," 249: "*Konfessionsfundamentalismus*."

126 Schilling, "Der Augsburger Religionsfriede."

127 Philip Benedict, *Christ's Churches Purely Reformed: A Social History of Calvinism* (New Haven, Conn.: Yale University Press, 2002), 535.

128 *Exhortation aux princes et seigneurs du Conseil privé du roy.* The authorship of this text is disputed by scholars; it has been attributed to the Catholic Étienne Pasquier (1529–1615); see idem, *Ecrits politiques*, ed. D. Thickett (Geneva: Droz, 1966), 33–90. Cf. Malcolm Smith, *Montaigne and Religious Freedom: The Dawn of Pluralism* (Geneva: Droz, 1991), 196–97.

129 As John M. Headley remarks, "for the first time" it entertained "the arresting thought of the necessity for two churches within a single realm." In light of the political and religious crisis in France, the author of the text saw that "if the unity of the realm was to be preserved," then "the links between the secular and the spiritual" had to be "loosened." Headley, "The Continental Reformation," in *The Meaning of the Renaissance and Reformation*, ed. Richard L. DeMolen (Boston: Houghton Mifflin, 1974), 131–211, here 199.

130 In 1561 the followers of Calvin began "systematically to seize churches and to destroy statues of the Virgin and saints, crucifixes and altarpieces." Robert J. Knecht, *The French Civil Wars, 1562–1598* (Harlow: Longman, 2000), 73.

131 Sebastian Castellio, *Advice to a Desolate France*, trans. Wouter Valkhoff (Shepherdstown, W.Va.: Patmos, 1975), 19.

132 Knecht, *French Civil Wars*, 79f.

133 Théodore de Bèze to Andreas Dudith, Geneva, June 18, 1570, *Correspondance de Theodor de Bèze*, vol. 11, no. 780, p. 179; as drawn from Turchetti, "Der Beitrag Calvins und des Calvinismus zur Entstehung der modernen Demokratie," in Hirzel and Sallmann, *1509—Johannes Calvin—2009*, 254.

134 See Graham Darby, *The Origins and Development of the Dutch Revolt* (London: Routledge, 2001), 17.

135 As cited in Martin van Gelderen, *The Political Thought of the Dutch Revolt, 1555–1590* (Cambridge: Cambridge University Press, 1992), 52.

136 Nicolette Mout, "Peace without Concord: Religious Toleration in Theory and Practice," in Hsia, *Reform and Expansion*, 227–43, here 237.

137 Geert H. Janssen, *The Dutch Revolt and Catholic Exile in Reformation Europe* (Cambridge: Cambridge University Press, 2014), 170–71.

138 Janssen, *Dutch Revolt and Catholic Exile in Reformation Europe*, 159. See also Benjamin J. Kaplan, *Divided by Faith: Religious Conflict and the Practice of Toleration in Early Modern Europe* (Cambridge, Mass.: Belknap Press of Harvard University Press, 2007).

139 Janssen, *Dutch Revolt and Catholic Exile in Reformation Europe*, 161.

140 John Huxtable Elliott, *Spain, Europe and the Wider World, 1500–1800* (New Haven, Conn.: Yale University Press, 2009), 92.

141 Antje von Ungern-Sternberg, *Religionsfreiheit in Europa: die Freiheit individueller Religionsausübung in Großbritannien, Frankreich und Deutschland—ein Vergleich* (Tübingen: Mohr Siebeck, 2008), 8.

142 Antje Oschmann, ed., *Acta Pacis Westphalicae, Serie III Abteilung B: Verhand-lungsakten*, vol. 1: *Die Friedensverträge mit Frankreich und Schweden. 1: Urkunden* (Münster: Aschendorff, 1998), art. 5, §34 (110–28); trans.: *A General Collection Of Treatys*, vol. 2 (London, 1713), 404–5, modified. Another paragraph (§36) determined that when the authorities practiced expulsion, then the person being expelled from the territory should have three to five years. On the conflicting interpretations of the paragraph, see Martin Heckel, "Zu den Anfängen der

Religionsfreiheit im Konfessionellen Zeitalter," in *"Ins Wasser geworfen und Ozeane durchquert": Festschrift für Knut Wolfgang Nörr*, ed. Mario Ascheri et al. (Köln: Böhlau, 2003), 349–402, esp. 365ff.

143 See Conrad H. Moehlman, ed., *The American Constitutions and Religion: Religious References in the Charters of the Thirteen Colonies and the Constitutions of the Forty-Eight States: A Source-Book on Church and State in the United States* (Berne, Ind.: C. H. Moehlman, 1938; Clark, N.J.: Lawbook Exchange, 2007), 27.

144 Mark Goldie, "John Locke, Jonas Proast and Religious Toleration 1688–1692," in *The Church of England, c. 1689–c. 1833: From Toleration to Tractarianism*, ed. John Walsh, Colin Haydon, and Stephen Taylor (Cambridge: Cambridge University Press, 1993), 143–71.

145 Goldie, "John Locke, Jonas Proast and Religious Toleration 1688–1692," 145.

146 Steven Pincus, *1688: The First Modern Revolution* (New Haven, Conn.: Yale University Press, 2009), 3; emphasis in original.

147 Pincus, *1688*, 8.

148 John Locke, *Letter Concerning Toleration* (1689), in idem, *The Works of John Locke, in Nine Volumes*, 12th ed. (London, 1824), 5:18, 20–21; the language has been modernized. With this, in the same volume, the second, third, and fourth letters are provided. These other letters were more focused on the Anglican clergyman Jonas Proast and thereby the opinions of the Anglican church regarding the establishment of religion. For more on this theme, see John Marshall, *John Locke, Toleration and Early Enlightenment Culture: Religious Intolerance and Arguments for Religious Toleration in Early Modern and "Early Enlightenment" Europe* (Cambridge: Cambridge University Press, 2010).

149 James Madison, *Selected Writings of James Madison*, ed. Ralph Ketcham (Indianapolis, Ind.: Hackett, 2006), 213; published originally in his "Charters" (1792).

150 Karl Popper, *The Open Society and Its Enemies* (orig. 2 vols., 1945; repr., London: Routledge, 2002), 668; emphasis in original.

151 Popper, *Open Society and Its Enemies*; emphasis in original.

Chapter 5

1 Steffen Martus has drawn attention to some of the peculiarities and seeming contradictions of the eighteenth-century German Enlightenment, such as the interest in esoteric traditions: *Aufklärung: Das deutsche 18. Jahrhundert—ein Epochenbild* (Berlin: Rowohlt, 2015), 370–75. He also draws attention to occultism. Martus demonstrates that the Enlightenment contained many different impulses.

2 On this term in contemporary debate, see my "Diagnosing Western Modernity: A Review Article," *Neue Zeitschrift für Systematische Theologie und Religionsphilosophie* 57 (2015): 267–84. See also Shmuel N. Eisenstadt, who has coined the term "multiple modernities": *Multiple Modernities and Comparative Civilisations*, 2 vols. (Leiden: Brill, 2003).

3 A brief history of the theory is provided by Ute Lotz-Heumann, *Die doppelte Konfessionalisierung in Irland: Konflikt und Koexistenz im 16. und in der ersten Hälfte des 17. Jahrhunderts* (Tübingen: Mohr Siebeck, 2000), 4ff.

4 Ernst Walter Zeeden, *Konfessionsbildung: Studien zur Reformation, Gegenreformation und katholischen Reform* (Stuttgart: Klett-Cotta, 1985).

5   Andrew Pettegree, "Confessionalization in North Western Europe," in *Konfessionalisierung in Ostmitteleuropa: Wirkungen des religiösen Wandels im 16. und 17. Jahrhundert in Staat, Gesellschaft und Kultur*, ed. Joachim Bahlcke and Arno Strohmeyer (Stuttgart: Steiner, 1999), 105-20, here 112.

6   Hans-Ulrich Wehler, *Deutsche Gesellschaftsgeschichte*, vol. 1: *Vom Feudalismus des Alten Reiches bis zur Defensiven Modernisierung der Reformära 1700-1815*, 3rd ed. (München: Beck, 1996), 229. See also the collection of essays titled "Forschungen zur Geschichte Mecklenburgs: Volle Entfaltung des Feudalismus in Mecklenburg," in *Wissenschaftliche Zeitschrift der Universität Rostock* 36 (1987): 3-89; on the history of the Reformation in Mecklenburg, see Michael North, *Geschichte Mecklenburg-Vorpommerns* (Munich: Beck, 2008), 38-50.

7   Ernst Troeltsch, "Die Bedeutung des Protestantismus für die Entstehung der modernen Welt," in idem, *Kritische Gesamtausgabe, 8: Schriften zur Bedeutung des Protestantismus für die moderne Welt (1906-1913)*, ed. Trutz Rendtorff and Stefan Pautler (Berlin: de Gruyter, 2001), 201-316, here 314; cf. Georg Pfleiderer and Alexander Heit, eds., *Protestantisches Ethos und moderne Kultur: zur Aktualität von Ernst Troeltschs Protestantismusschrift* (Zurich: Theologischer Verlag, 2008).

8   Troeltsch, "Die Bedeutung des Protestantismus für die Entstehung der modernen Welt," 297.

9   As cited in Heinz Schilling, "Confessional Europe," in *Handbook of European History 1400-1600: Late Middle Ages, Renaissance and Reformation*, ed. Thomas A. Brady Jr. et al., vol. 2: *Visions, Programs and Outcomes* (Leiden: Brill, 1995), 641-81, here 649.

10   Regarding the role of confessional identities and the influence of the Reformation on educational reforms, see the essays in *Archiv für Reformationsgeschichte* 95 (2004): 240-300. See also Wolfgang Mager, "Jansenistische Erziehung und die Entstehung des modernen Individuums," in *Im Spannungsfeld von Staat und Kirche: "Minderheiten" und "Erziehung" im deutsch-französischen Gesellschaftsvergleich 16.-18. Jahrhundert*, ed. Heinz Schilling and Marie-Antoinette Gross (Berlin: Duncker & Humblot, 2003), 313-55. See also Willem Frijhoff, "Calvinism, Literacy, and Reading Culture in the Early Modern Northern Netherlands: Towards a Reassessment," *Archiv für Reformationsgeschichte* 95 (2004): 252-65.

11   Christoph Strohm, "Konfessionelle Einflüsse auf das Werk reformierter Juristen," in *Konfessionalität und Jurisprudenz in der frühen Neuzeit*, ed. Christoph Strohm and Heinrich de Wall (Berlin: Duncker & Humblot, 2009), 1-32, esp. 14ff. See also Christoph Strohm, *Calvinismus und Recht: Weltanschaulich-konfessionelle Aspekte im Werk reformierter Juristen in der Frühen Neuzeit* (Tübingen: Mohr, 2008).

12   Philip Benedict, *Christ's Churches Purely Reformed: A Social History of Calvinism* (New Haven, Conn.: Yale University Press, 2002), 543; see also idem, 460-89 (on the exercise of discipline in Calvinism), 509ff. (on piety and bible reading), and 526ff. and 533ff. (on the overall impact of these traditions).

13   Benedict writes, "Nonetheless, a measure of lay participation in the administration of the church and considerable lay involvement in the exercise of discipline did continue to characterize many Reformed churches throughout the sixteenth and seventeenth centuries. In this way, they differed from Lutheran churches and may have been well suited institutionally to attempt a reformation of manners and the inculcation of new habits of worship and belief among their members. Of course,

altering long-established patterns of behavior and belief was no easy matter." *Christ's Churches Purely Reformed*, 459.

14 Benedict, *Christ's Churches Purely Reformed*, 532.

15 Benedict, *Christ's Churches Purely Reformed*, 489.

16 Benedict, *Christ's Churches Purely Reformed*, 535.

17 Brad S. Gregory, *The Unintended Reformation: How a Religious Revolution Secularized Society* (Cambridge, Mass.: Belknap Press of Harvard University Press, 2012). Regarding this book, see my "On Brad S. Gregory's *The Unintended Reformation*," *Theologie.Geschichte: Zeitschrift für Theologie und Kulturgeschichte* 9 (2014), universaar.uni-saarland.de/journals/index.php/tg/article/view/656/701.

18 Gregory remarks about his book in response to a review: "I sought to explain [. . .] the formation of the West's hyperpluralism [. . .]." Brad S. Gregory, "Responses to the Reviewers," in *Pro Ecclesia* 22 (2013): 429–36, here 434.

19 Gregory, *Unintended Reformation*, 365; see also Brad S. Gregory, "The Unintended Reformation: Historical Arguments and Omissions," *The Immanent Frame* (blog), February 7, 2014, http://blogs.ssrc.org/tif/2014/02/07/historical-arguments-and-omissions/.

20 See Robert P. Ericksen, *Theologians under Hitler* (New Haven, Conn.: Yale University Press, 1985).

21 See Barry Hankins, ed., *Evangelicalism and Fundamentalism: A Documentary Reader* (New York: New York University Press, 2008), 97–116; Christopher M. Rios, *After the Monkey Trial: Evangelical Scientists and a New Creationism* (New York: Fordham University Press, 2014).

22 Pentecostalism is different on the last point as many Pentecostal churches embraced and continue to embrace women ministers. See Chas H. Barfoot, *Aimee Semple McPherson and the Making of Modern Pentecostalism, 1890–1926* (London: Routledge, 2015). McPherson was the founder of the Foursquare Church. See also the important studies on this issue from George M. Marsden, *Fundamentalism and American Culture*, 2nd ed. (New York: Oxford University Press, 2006); idem, *Understanding Fundamentalism and Evangelicalism* (Grand Rapids: Eerdmans, 1991).

23 See, for example, Christopher M. Hays and Christopher B. Ansberry, eds., *Evangelical Faith and the Challenge of Historical Criticism* (Grand Rapids: Baker Academic, 2013). Jan Stievermann has shown how the "first American Evangelical" (Cotton Mather) integrated the historical-critical perspective of his time: *Prophecy, Piety and the Problem of Historicity: Interpreting the Hebrew Scriptures in Cotton Mather's "Biblia Americana"* (Tübingen: Mohr Siebeck, 2016).

24 See Stanley J. Grenz and Denise Muir Kjesbo, *Women in the Church: A Biblical Theology of Women in Ministry* (Downers Grove, Ill.: InterVarsity, 1995).

25 See Jan Nelis, Anne Morelli, and Danny Praet, "The Study of the Relationship between Catholicism and Fascism, beyond a Manichean Approach?" in *Catholicism and Fascism in Europe, 1918–1945*, ed. idem (Hildesheim: Olms, 2015), 9–14, here 9; capitalization in original.

26 See Robert Michael, *A History of Catholic Antisemitism: The Dark Side of the Church* (Basingstoke: Palgrave Macmillan, 2011).

27 Tom Villis, *British Catholics and Fascism: Religious Identity and Political Extremism between the Wars* (Basingstoke: Palgrave Macmillan, 2013).

28 Carsten Anckar, *Religion and Democracy: A Worldwide Comparison* (London: Routledge, 2011), 43.

29 As cited in Shaun A. Casey, *The Making of a Catholic President: Kennedy vs. Nixon, 1960* (Oxford: Oxford University Press, 2009), 168. He gave the speech on September 12, 1960, in Houston, Texas. He was a student of Princeton and Harvard.

30 See Kelley A. Raab, *When Women Become Priests: The Catholic Women's Ordination Debate* (New York: Columbia University Press, 2000). Ida Raming, *A History of Women and Ordination*, ed. and trans. Bernard Cooke and Gary Macy, vol. 2: *The Priestly Office of Women: God's Gift to a Renewed Church*, 2nd ed. (Lanham, Md.: Scarecrow, 2004); Deborah Halter, *The Papal "No": A Comprehensive Guide to the Vatican's Rejection of Women's Ordination* (New York: Crossroad, 2004).

31 See the great collection of modern Jewish thought in Daniel H. Frank, Oliver Leaman, and Charles H. Manekin, eds., *The Jewish Philosophy Reader* (London: Routledge, 2000), 303ff. See also Jonathan I. Israel, *Radical Enlightenment: Philosophy and the Making of Modernity, 1650–1750* (Oxford: Oxford University Press, 2001). Jay P. Corrin has offered an analysis of Catholicism in modernity that points to some of the progressive voices of social reform before this era of transformation. These older voices of reform are, unfortunately, sometimes forgotten: *Catholic Intellectuals and the Challenge of Democracy* (Notre Dame, Ind.: University of Notre Dame Press, 2002).

32 See André Azevedo Alves and José Manuel Moreira, *The Salamanca School* (New York: Continuum, 2010), 39–64; Anthony Pagden, *The Burdens of Empire: 1539 to the Present* (New York: Cambridge University Press, 2015), 45–74.

33 Elizabeth Fenton has drawn attention to the deep anti-Catholic attitude in much of American culture in the nineteenth century. This worked to exclude Catholics from the national identity: *Religious Liberties: Anti-Catholicism and Liberal Democracy in Nineteenth Century U.S. Literature and Culture* (Oxford: Oxford University Press, 2011). Jenny Franchot showed how anti-Catholic attitudes were used in American culture of the antebellum period as a negative foil for the Protestant culture: *Roads to Rome: The Antebellum Protestant Encounter with Catholicism* (Berkeley: University of California Press, 1994). To the contemporary debate about modernism in Catholicism as a whole, especially since the later nineteenth century leading up to the contemporary context, see Claus Arnold, *Kleine Geschichte des Modernismus* (Freiburg: Herder, 2007).

34 Nathan O. Hatch, *The Democratization of American Christianity* (New Haven, Conn.: Yale University Press, 1989).

35 On the theological origins of modern Protestant fundamentalism, which go back to the Reformed tradition at Princeton, see Gary J. Dorrien, *The Remaking of Evangelical Theology* (Louisville, Ky.: Westminster John Knox, 1998), 13–48. A contemporary discussion about fundamentalism can be found in Kevin T. Bauder, R. Albert Mohler Jr., John G. Stackhouse Jr., and Roger E. Olson, *Four Views on the Spectrum of Evangelicalism* (Grand Rapids: Zondervan, 2011), 19–67. In the first of the four parts, Bauder defends "Fundamentalism" and the other three respond to this. In the final section, Roger E. Olson defends "Postconservative Evangelicalism." See also Vincent Bacote et al., eds., *Evangelicals and Scripture: Tradition, Authority and Hermeneutics* (Downers Grove, Ill.: InterVarsity, 2004).

On the prehistory of the Reformers' emphasis on scriptural authority, see Heiko Oberman, *Forerunners of the Reformation: The Shape of Late Medieval Thought; Illustrated by Key Documents*, trans. Paul L. Nyhus (New York: Holt, Rinehart & Winston, 1966), 51–120.

36   See Günter Figal, "Demokratie," in *Religion in Geschichte und Gegenwart*, 4th ed., vol. 2 (Tübingen: Mohr Siebeck, 1999), 649–53. Regarding the history of political representation in the Middle Ages, see Michael A. R. Graves, *The Parliaments of Early Modern Europe: 1400–1700* (London: Routledge, 2001), 14f.; Helmut G. Koenigsberger, *A History of Europe*, vol. 1: *Medieval Europe: 400–1500* (London: Longman, 1987), 300–301.

37   Nicholas Terpstra, *Religious Refugees in the Early Modern World: An Alternative History of the Reformation* (New York: Cambridge University Press, 2015), 171.

38   See John Witte, *The Reformation of Rights: Law, Religion and Human Rights in Early Modern Calvinism* (Cambridge: Cambridge University Press, 2007).

39   Robert M. Kingdon, "The Calvinist Reformation in Geneva," in *Cambridge History of Christianity*, vol. 6: *Reform and Expansion, 1500–1660*, ed. R. Po-Chia Hsia (Cambridge: Cambridge University Press, 2007), 90–103, here 94.

40   Kingdon, "Calvinist Reformation in Geneva," in Hsia, *Reform and Expansion*, 98.

41   Kingdon, "Calvinist Reformation in Geneva," in Hsia, *Reform and Expansion*, 98.

42   Théodore de Bèze, *Correspondance de Théodore de Bèze*, vol. 12: *1571*, ed. Hippolyte Aubert et al. (Geneva: Droz, 1986), no. 871, p. 220; as cited in Mario Turchetti, "Der Beitrag Calvins und des Calvinismus zur Entstehung der modernen Demokratie," in *1509—Johannes Calvin—2009. Sein Wirken in Kirche und Gesellschaft. Essays zum 500. Geburtstag*, ed. Martin E. Hirzel and Martin Sallmann (Zurich: Theologischer Verlag, 2008), 237–66, here 244.

43   Benedict, *Christ's Churches Purely Reformed*, 536. See also Robert M. Kingdon, *Church and Society in Reformation Europe* (London: Variorum, 1985).

44   See Peter Blickle, *From the Communal Reformation to the Revolution of the Common Man*, trans. Beat Kümin (Leiden: Brill, 1998), 162–77.

45   Blickle, *From the Communal Reformation*, 117–28.

46   Alan Frederick Hattersley, *A Short History of Democracy* (Cambridge: Cambridge University Press, 1930), 106. As was addressed above in the discussion about the Reformation from above, the history was not, however, a direct movement without setbacks and contradictions (108). Calvin limited democratic principles in the government of the church and thus "the significance of the co-operation of the congregation in the election of a minister was minimized by the rule that the pastor must preside" (109).

47   Hattersley, *Short History of Democracy*, 109. See also James Hastings Nichols, *Democracy and the Churches* (Philadelphia: Westminster, 1951).

48   The shift toward this is already in Eckhart and Tauler, who emphasized inner devotion and repentance as the ultimate priority. Staupitz, Luther, and Karlstadt all drew upon this theme, which necessarily relativized the role of the priesthood and the practice of confession. See Volker Leppin, *Die fremde Reformation: Luthers mystische Wurzeln* (München: Beck, 2015).

49   Thomas Kaufmann, "Luthers kopernikanische Wende," *Frankfurter Allgemeine Zeitung*, October 28, 2013, p. 7.

50 Thomas Kaufmann, *Der Anfang der Reformation: Studien zur Kontextualität der Theologie, Publizistik und Inszenierung Luthers und der reformatorischen Bewegung* (Tübingen: Mohr Siebeck, 2012), 549.

51 Chang Soo Park, "Das Prinzip des allgemeinen Priestertums, ein politisches Konzept?" *Archiv für Reformationsgeschichte* 105 (2014): 129–58, esp. 149 and 156, here 156: "Relativierung der ständischen Gesellschaft." Cf. Thomas Kaufmann, *Das Ende der Reformation: Magdeburgs "Herrgotts Kanzlei" (1548–1551/2)* (Tübingen: Mohr Siebeck, 2003), 145ff., 176ff., 189.

52 Hans-Jürgen Goertz, *Antiklerikalismus und Reformation: sozialgeschichtliche Untersuchungen* (Göttingen: Vandenhoeck & Ruprecht, 1995); idem, *Pfaffenhaß und groß Geschrei: die reformatorischen Bewegungen in Deutschland, 1517–1529* (München: Beck, 1987).

53 See above, chap. 1, on Karlstadt's 151 Theses.

54 Benedict, *Christ's Churches Purely Reformed*, 458.

55 Regarding Karlstadt's ecclesiology and his conception of the full power of the laity, see Kaufmann, *Der Anfang der Reformation*, 522–27.

56 See Thomas Kaufmann, *Geschichte der Reformation* (Frankfurt: Verlag der Weltreligionen, 2009), 715.

57 See Max Weber, *Economy and Society: An Outline of Interpretive Sociology*, ed. Guenther Roth and Claus Wittich, 2 vols. (Berkeley: University of California Press, 2013); Regina F. Titunik, "Democracy, Domination and Legitimacy in Max Weber's Political Thought," in *Max Weber's Economy and Society: A Critical Companion*, ed. Charles Camic et al. (Stanford, Calif.: Stanford University Press, 2005), 143–63.

58 James Oscar Farmer, *The Metaphysical Confederacy: James Henley Thornwell and the Synthesis of Southern Values* (Macon, Ga.: Mercer University Press, 1986), 96. See also Scott Philip Segrest, *America and the Political Philosophy of Common Sense* (Columbia: University of Missouri Press, 2010).

59 Terence Martin, *The Instructed Vision: Scottish Common Sense Philosophy and the Origins of American Fiction* (Bloomington: Indiana University Press, 1961), vii; as cited in Farmer, *Metaphysical Confederacy*, 96.

60 Perry Miller, Introduction to *American Thought from the Civil War to World War I*, ed. idem (New York: Holt, Rinehart & Winston, 1954), ix–lxii, here ix; as cited in Farmer, *Metaphysical Confederacy*, 96.

61 Benjamin W. Redekop, "Reid's Influence in Britain, Germany, France, and America," in *The Cambridge Companion to Thomas Reid*, ed. Terence Cuneo and René van Woudenberg (Cambridge: Cambridge University Press, 2004), 313–39, here 327.

62 Redekop, "Reid's Influence in Britain, Germany, France, and America," 335

63 Heinrich August Winkler, *Geschichte des Westens*, 4 vols. (München: Beck, 2009–2015), 1:111.

64 See Gordon Marshall, *Presbyteries and Profits: Calvinism and the Development of Capitalism in Scotland, 1560–1707* (Oxford: Clarendon, 1980). See Max Weber, *Die protestantische Ethik und der Geist des Kapitalismus: Vollständige Ausgabe*, ed. Dirk Kaesler (Tübingen: Mohr, 1904/1905, 1920; München: Beck, 2004).

65 Hans-Georg Drescher, *Ernst Troeltsch: Leben und Werk* (Göttingen: Vandenhoeck & Ruprecht, 1991), 397. Weber was initially asked to give the lecture, but he suggested that his friend Troeltsch should take his place.

66 See Volkhard Krech, "Moderner Kapitalismus und Protestantismus: Wahlverwandt-schaft oder Heterogenese?: die 'Weber-Troeltsch-These' und ihre Aktualität," in Pfleiderer and Heit, *Protestantisches Ethos und moderne Kultur*, 107–17, esp. 113–14.

67 Krech, "Moderner Kapitalismus und Protestantismus," in Pfleiderer and Heit, *Protestantisches Ethos und moderne Kultur.*

68 Thomas Nipperdey, "The Reformation and the Modern World," in *Politics and Society in Reformation Europe*, ed. E. I. Kouri und Tom Scott (Hampshire: Macmillan, 1987), 535–52, here 540.

69 Nipperdey, "Reformation and the Modern World," 548.

70 See Heinz Steinert, *Max Webers unwiderlegbare Fehlkonstruktionen: Die protestantische Ethik und der Geist des Kapitalismus* (Frankfurt am Main: Campus Verlag, 2010).

71 See Jere Cohen, "Rational Capitalism in Renaissance Italy," *American Journal of Sociology* 85 (1980): 1340–55; for a critique of Cohen's reading of Weber, see Malcolm H. MacKinnon, "The Longevity of the Thesis: A Critique of the Critics," in *Weber's Protestant Ethic: Origins, Evidence, Contexts*, ed. Hartmut Lehmann and Guenther Roth (Cambridge: Cambridge University Press, 1993), 211–43.

72 Calvin, *Institutes of the Christian Religion*, vols. 1 and 2, trans. Henry Beveridge (Edinburgh: T&T Clark, 1863), bk. 3, chap. 14, par. 19, 2:87. See the Latin version, which reads, "sed tum demum valent si a posteriori sumuntur." In *Joannis Calvini Opera selecta*, ed. Peter Barth and Wilhelm Niesel, vol. 4: *Institutionis Christianae religionis 1559 librum III continens* (Munich: Kaiser, 1959), 237.

73 See *Corpus reformatorum* 32:291.

74 Calvin, *Unterricht in der christlichen Religion*, trans. O. Weber (1955; repr., Neukirchen-Vluyn: Neukirchener Verlag, 1997), 515.

75 John Calvin, *The Institution of Christian Religion*, trans. Thomas Norton (London: Wolfe & Harison, 1561), 192.

76 *The Heidelberg Catechism: 450th Anniversary Edition* (Grand Rapids: Faith Alive, 2013), pt. 3, Q & A 86, p. 51, emphasis added. Regarding the passage about being "assured of our faith by its fruits," the following verses are cited: Matt 7:17-18 (as cited above); Gal 5:22-24; 2 Pet 1:10-11.

77 *Canons of Dort: A New Translation for the Reformed Church in America* (New York: Reformed Church, 1991), pt. 1, art. 12.

78 Westminster Confession of Faith, chap. 16, par. 2; in *Creeds of the Churches: A Reader in Christian Doctrine from the Bible to the Present*, ed. John H. Leith (Louisville: John Knox, 1982), 210.

79 Max Weber, *The Protestant Ethic and the Spirit of Capitalism*, trans. Stephen Kalberg (London: Fitzroy Dearborn, 2001), 68–69; emphasis in original. Cf. Weber, *Die protestantische Ethik und der Geist des Kapitalismus*, 153.

80 Weber, *Protestant Ethic and the Spirit of Capitalism*, 116, cf. 109; emphasis in original.

81 See Luther, "A Sermon on Indulgences and Grace, 1518," in *The Annotated Luther*, vol. 1: *The Roots of Reform*, ed. Timothy J. Wengert (Minneapolis: Fortress, 2015), 62; see "Ein Sermon von Ablaß und Gnade," in *WA* 1:244.

82 See the Augsburg Confession in *Die Bekenntnisschriften der Evangelisch-Lutherischen Kirche*, vol. 1: *Von den altkirchlichen Symbolen bis zu den Katechismen*

Martin Luthers, ed. Irene Dingel (Göttingen: Vandenhoeck & Ruprecht, 2014), 100, 120.

83 Luther, "To the Christian Nobility of the German Nation concerning the Reform of the Christian Estate," in *LW* 44:183.

84 Luther, "To the Christian Nobility," 183.

85 Bodo-Michael Baumunk, Stiftung Deutsches Historisches Museum et al., eds., *Leben nach Luther: eine Kulturgeschichte des evangelischen Pfarrhauses* (Bönen: Kettler, 2013).

86 Weber, *Protestant Ethic and the Spirit of Capitalism*, 89.

87 See Jan Stievermann, "Writing 'To Conquer All Things': Cotton Mather's *Magnalia Christi Americana* and the Quandary of *Copia*," *Early American Literature* 39 (2004): 263–97.

88 Travis Wiseman and Andrew Young, "Religion: Productive or Unproductive?" *Journal of Institutional Economics* 10 (2014): 21–45, here 42.

89 Gisela Kubon-Gilke, "Verwischte Spuren in wechselnder Richtung?: Anmerkungen zur Interdependenz von Ökonomie und Protestantismus," in *Spurenlese: kulturelle Wirkungen der Reformation*, ed. Reformationsgeschichtliche Sozietät der Martin-Luther-Universität Halle-Wittenberg (Leipzig: Evangelische Verlagsanstalt, 2013), 155–80.

90 Weber, *Protestant Ethic and the Spirit of Capitalism*, 125; emphasis in original.

91 This is what Michael Allen Gillespie argues; see his *The Theological Origins of Modernity* (Chicago: University of Chicago Press, 2008). The same theory is found among many other authors. See my "Diagnosing Western Modernity" for an analysis of these claims and a prehistory of the theories. See also Daniel P. Horan's critical analysis of these theories: *Postmodernity and Univocity: A Critical Account of Radical Orthodoxy and John Duns Scotus* (Minneapolis: Fortress, 2014), 59–96.

92 Cf. Reijer Hooykaas, *Religion and the Rise of Modern Science* (Edinburgh: Scottish Academic, 1972), 98ff.

93 John Calvin, *Commentaries on the First Book of Moses Called Genesis*, trans. J. King, vol. 1 (Edinburgh: Calvin Translation Society, 1847), 86; cf. *Corpus reformatorum*, vol. 51 (= *Calvini Opera* 23:22).

94 At Gen 6:14; cf. Calvin, *Commentaries on the First Book of Moses Called Genesis*, 256; *Corpus reformatorum*, 51:123.

95 Cf. Herman Selderhuis, "Calvin 1509–2009," in *Calvin and His Influence, 1509–2009*, ed. Irena Backus and Philip Benedict (Oxford: Oxford University Press, 2011), 144–58, here 155. Michael D. Bush, "Calvinrezeption im 18. Jahrhundert," in *Calvin Handbuch*, ed. Herman J. Selderhuis (Tübingen: Mohr Siebeck, 2008), 474–80. On this theme, see Peter Harrison, *The Bible, Protestantism, and the Rise of Natural Science* (Cambridge: Cambridge University Press, 1998). In a lecture ("The Protestant Reformation and the Rise of Modern Science," Heidelberg, September 23, 2016), Harrison showed how early modern Protestants attached a religious significance to scientific research.

96 Ann Blair, "Science and Religion," in Hsia, *Reform and Expansion*, 425–43, here 434–35.

97 For a similar account of these two statements, see Rik Van Nieuwenhove, *An Introduction to Medieval Theology* (Cambridge: Cambridge University Press, 2012), 254–55.

98   Luther, "Disputation against Scholastic Theology," in *LW* 31:12.

99   Regarding Luther, he writes, "This was the God that so terrified the young Luther, the omnipotent and transrational God of nominalism." Gillespie, *Theological Origins of Modernity*, 114.

100 See Ludger Honnefelder, *Scientia transcendens: die formale Bestimmung der Seiendheit und Realität in der Metaphysik des Mittelalters und der Neuzeit (Duns Scotus–Suárez–Wolff–Kant–Peirce)* (Hamburg: Meiner, 1990); Maarten J. F. M. Hoenen, "Scotus and the Scotist School: The Tradition of Scotist Thought in the Medieval and Early Modern Period," in *John Duns Scotus (1265–1308): Renewal of Philosophy*, ed. E. P. Bos (Amsterdam: Rodopi, 1998), 196–210; on Ockham and the scientific revolution: André Goddu, "Medieval Natural Philosophy and Modern Science: Continuity and Revolution," in *Philosophy and Theology in the Long Middle Ages: A Tribute to Stephen F. Brown*, ed. Kent Emery et al. (Leiden: Brill, 2011), 213–33; see also Ludger Honnefelder, "Metaphysics as a Discipline: From the 'Transcendental Philosophy of the Ancients' to Kant's Notion of Transcendental Philosophy," in *The Medieval Heritage in Early Modern Metaphysics and Modal Theory, 1400–1700*, ed. R. L. Friedman and L. O. Nielsen (Dordrecht: Kluwer Academic, 2003), 53–74; Thomas Williams, ed., *The Cambridge Companion to Duns Scotus* (Cambridge: Cambridge University Press, 2003).

101 Max Weber, *The Methodology of the Social Sciences* (New York: Free Press, 1949), 57.

102 Gilbert G. Germain, *A Discourse on Disenchantment: Reflections on Politics and Technology* (Albany: State University of New York Press, 1993), 41.

103 Michael Sukale, *Max Weber—Leidenschaft und Disziplin: Leben, Werk, Zeitgenossen* (Tübingen: Mohr Siebeck, 2002), 487f.

104 Peter Walkenhorst, *Nation—Volk—Rasse: Radikaler Nationalismus im Deutschen Kaiserreich, 1890–1914* (Göttingen: Vandenhoeck & Ruprecht, 2007), 105.

105 Walkenhorst, *Nation—Volk—Rasse*, 122. Not only Thomas Mann but also Ernst Troeltsch (58) praised Paul de Lagarde (1827–1891), the anti-Semitic German nationalist and promoter of a "genuine German religion." Regarding Lagarde, see Richard S. Levy, ed., *Antisemitism: A Historical Encyclopedia of Prejudice and Persecution*, vol. 1 (Santa Barbara, Calif.: ABC-CLIO, 2005), 409–10.

106 For a contemporary example of this tradition, see my article "Friedrich Hermanni's Metaphysics," *Neue Zeitschrift für Systematische Theologie und Religionsphilosophie* 55 (2013): 526–38. Friedrich Hermanni, *Metaphysik: Versuche über letzte Fragen* (Tübingen: Mohr Siebeck, 2011). See also Thomas Buchheim et al., eds., *Gottesbeweise als Herausforderung für die moderne Vernunft* (Tübingen: Mohr Siebeck, 2013).

107 Cf. Simon Conway Morris, *Life's Solution: Inevitable Humans in a Lonely Universe* (Cambridge: Cambridge University Press, 2003); idem et al., eds., *Fitness of the Cosmos for Life: Biochemistry and Fine-Tuning* (Cambridge: Cambridge University Press, 2008); Thomas Nagel, *Mind and Cosmos: Why the Materialist Neo-Darwinian Conception of Nature Is Almost Certainly False* (Oxford: Oxford University Press, 2012); J. P. Moreland, Chad Meister, and Khaldoun A. Sweis, eds., *Debating Christian Theism* (New York: Oxford University Press, 2013). Holm Tetens, *Gott denken: Ein Versuch über rationale Theologie* (Stuttgart: Reclam, 2015).

108 Robert W. Scribner, "Elements of Popular Belief," in *Handbook of European History, 1400–1600: Late Middle Ages, Renaissance and Reformation*, ed. Thomas A. Brady Jr. et al., vol. 1: *Structures and Assertions* (Leiden: Brill, 1994), 253.

109 Scribner, "Elements of Popular Belief," in Brady et al., *Structures and Assertions*.

110 Scribner, "Elements of Popular Belief," in Brady et al., *Structures and Assertions*.

111 Scribner, "Elements of Popular Belief," in Brady et al., *Structures and Assertions*.

112 Scribner, "Elements of Popular Belief," in Brady et al., *Structures and Assertions*, 254.

113 On this theme, see Euan Cameron, *Enchanted Europe: Superstition, Reason, and Religion, 1250–1750* (Oxford: Oxford University Press, 2011).

114 Christian Smith, *How to Go from Being a Good Evangelical to a Committed Catholic in Ninety-Five Difficult Steps* (Eugene, Ore.: Cascade, 2011), 68. See also Christian Smith, ed., *The Secular Revolution: Power, Interests, and Conflict in the Secularization of American Public Life* (Berkeley: University of California Press, 2003).

115 Smith, *Good Evangelical to a Committed Catholic*, 69.

116 See Josephus Kleutgen, SJ, *Die Philosophie der Vorzeit vertheidigt*, vol. 1 (Münster: Theissing, 1860), §1, 4. He links Protestantism with all the ails of modern philosophy.

117 See Reiner Anselm, "Den modernen Staat . . . hat der Protestantismus nicht geschaffen," in Pfleiderer and Heit, *Protestantisches Ethos und moderne Kultur*, 93–106.

118 David Berman, *A History of Atheism in Britain: From Hobbes to Russell* (London: Croom Helm, 1988), 48.

119 Nipperdey, "Reformation and the Modern World," 539.

120 Nipperdey, "Reformation and the Modern World," 540.

121 Hugh McLeod, Introduction to *The Decline of Christendom in Western Europe, 1750–2000*, ed. Hugh McLeod and Werner Ustorf (Cambridge: Cambridge University Press, 2003), 1–26, here 5.

122 McLeod, Introduction to McLeod and Ustorf, *Decline of Christendom*, 7–8. McLeod draws upon Ralph Gibson, Michel Vovelle, and Michael MacDonald.

123 See Hartmut Lehmann, *Säkularisierung: der europäische Sonderweg in Sachen Religion* (Göttingen: Wallstein, 2004), 66–69.

124 Regarding this theme, see Nancy Christie, *The Sixties and Beyond: Dechristianization in North America and Western Europe, 1945–2000* (Toronto: University of Toronto Press, 2013); Hugh McLeod, "The Sixties: Writing the Religious History of A Crucial Decade," *Kirchliche Zeitgeschichte* 14 (2001): 36–48; Brown and Rooden's essays are in McLeod and Ustorf, *Decline of Christendom;* Thomas Großbölting, *Der verlorene Himmel. Glaube in Deutschland seit 1945* (Göttingen: Vandenhoeck & Ruprecht, 2013).

Chapter 6

1 See, for example, the works of Alasdair MacIntyre, Michael J. Buckley, Charles Taylor, Colin E. Gunton, Stanley Hauerwas, John Milbank, Michael Allen Gillespie, and, more recently, David B. Hart, Adrian Pabst, Brad S. Gregory, and Thomas Pfau, among others. On this issue, see my "Diagnosing Western Modernity: A Review Article," *Neue Zeitschrift für Systematische Theologie und Religionsphilosophie* 57 (2015): 267–84; and my "Gesellschaftliche Folgen der Entkirchlichung

Deutschlands? Überlegungen zu einer umstrittenen Frage," *Deutsches Pfarrerblatt* 115 (2015): 312–18.

2   Robert B. Pippin, *Modernism as a Philosophical Problem: On the Dissatisfactions of European High Culture* (Cambridge, Mass.: Blackwell, 1991), 22.

3   See Rudolph J. Rummel, *Statistics of Democide: Genocide and Mass Murder since 1900* (Münster: Lit, 1998). Other scholars put these estimates much lower.

4   See Stefan Kühl, *For the Betterment of the Race: The Rise and Fall of the International Movement for Eugenics and Racial Hygiene*, trans. Lawrence Schofer (New York: Palgrave Macmillan, 2013).

5   Diane B. Paul, "Darwin, Social Darwinism and Eugenics," in *The Cambridge Companion to Darwin*, ed. Jonathan Hodge and Gregory Radick (Cambridge: Cambridge University Press, 2003), 219–45, here 223.

6   Charles Darwin to Charles Lyell (October 11, 1859), in Darwin, *The Correspondence of Charles Darwin*, vol. 7: *1858–1859*, ed. Frederick Burkhardt and Sydney Smith (Cambridge: Cambridge University Press, 1991), 345.

7   Paul, "Darwin, Social Darwinism and Eugenics," 241.

8   See Michael L. Frazer, *The Enlightenment of Sympathy: Justice and the Moral Sentiments in the Eighteenth Century and Today* (Oxford: Oxford University Press, 2010); Oliver Sensen, *Kant on Human Dignity* (Berlin: de Gruyter, 2011).

9   Pope John XXIII, "Address for the Opening of the Second Vatican Council" (October 11, 1962), in *Acta Apostolicae Sedis* 54 (1962): 792: "Est enim aliud ipsum depositum fidei, seu veritates, quae veneranda doctrina nostra continentur, aliud modus, quo eaedem enuntiantur"; as cited in Pope Francis, *The Joy of the Gospel: Evangelii gaudium* (Washington, D.C.: United States Conference of Catholic Bishops, 2013), §41.

10 Pope John Paul II, Encyclical Letter *Ut unum sint: On Commitment to Ecumenism* (Washington, D.C.: United States Catholic Conference, 1995), 19; *Acta Apostolicae Sedis* 87 (1995): 933; as cited in Pope Francis, *The Joy of the Gospel*, §41.

11 Pope John Paul II, *Memory and Identity: Conversations at the Dawn of a Millennium* (London: Weidenfeld & Nicolson, 2005), 107.

12 Dewey Weiss Kramer, ed. and trans., *Johann Tetzel's Rebuttal against Luther's Sermon on Indulgences and Grace* (Atlanta: Pitts Theology Library, 2012), 30; emphasis in original.

13 Did the emphasis on scriptural authority cause or contribute to the pluralization of Christendom (as Brad S. Gregory suggests in chap. 2 of his *Unintended Reformation: How a Religious Revolution Secularized Society* [Cambridge, Mass.: Belknap Press of Harvard University Press, 2012])? The methodological principle of theological discourse, which scientifically focused theological disputes on their biblical exegetical foundations, may have contributed to pluralization in a secondary or tertiary sense. As addressed above, however, the pluralization of the Latin West was long underway before 1500. Modern pluralism has many causes, not one. A shortened and simplified version of this section was first published online as "The Unintended Reformation: Conceptualizing Pluralism and Consensus in the Modern Western World," *The Immanent Frame* (blog), October 16, 2013, http://blogs.ssrc.org/tif/2013/10/16/conceptualizing-pluralism -and-consensus-in-the-modern-western-world/.

14   See Gregory, *Unintended Reformation*, 369. For more on this work, see my "On Brad S. Gregory's *The Unintended Reformation*," *Theologie.Geschichte: Zeitschrift für Theologie und Kulturgeschichte* 9 (2014).

15   Alasdair MacIntyre, *After Virtue: A Study in Moral Theory* (Notre Dame, Ind.: University of Notre Dame Press, 1981; London: Bloomsbury, 2013), 183.

16   John Milbank, *Theology and Social Theory: Beyond Secular Reason* (Cambridge, Mass.: Blackwell, 1993), 9.

17   Charles Taylor, *A Secular Age* (Cambridge, Mass.: Belknap Press of Harvard University Press, 2007), 300.

18   Taylor, *Secular Age*, 437.

19   Nicholas Rescher, *Pluralism: Against the Demand for Consensus* (Oxford: Clarendon, 1993), 1.

20   Plato, *Laws*, 645, in *Dialogues of Plato*, vol. 4, trans. Benjamin Jowett (Cambridge: Cambridge University Press, 2010), 166.

21   Heinrich August Winkler, *Geschichte des Westens*, 4 vols. (München: Beck, 2009–2015).

22   Francis Fukuyama, "The End of History?" *The National Interest* 16 (1989): 3–18; idem, *The End of History and the Last Man* (New York: Free Press, 1992).

23   Rudolf Otto, *The Idea of the Holy: An Inquiry into the Non-rational Factor in the Idea of the Divine and Its Relation to the Rational*, trans. John W. Harvey (Oxford: Oxford University Press, 1978); Georg Wilhelm Friedrich Hegel, *Lectures on the Philosophy of Religion: The Lectures of 1827*, ed. Peter C. Hodgson, trans. R. F. Brown (Oxford: Clarendon, 2006).

24   Regarding the bedrock of liberal Protestantism's understanding of religion, the theological category of the "feeling of absolute dependence," see Friedrich Schleiermacher, *The Christian Faith*, trans. H. R. Mackintosh and J. S. Stewart (Edinburgh: T&T Clark, 1999), §4, pp. 12–19, esp. 16.

25   See Samuel Freeman, "Introduction: John Rawls, an Overview," in *The Cambridge Companion to Rawls*, ed. idem (Cambridge: Cambridge University Press, 2003), 1–61, esp. 10–28, here 14: "The idea of the original position is to devise a choice situation where *rational decision is subject to reasonable (moral) constraints* imposed by the conditions on choice in the original position"; emphasis in original.

26   See David Cheetham et al., eds., *Understanding Interreligious Relations* (Oxford: Oxford University Press, 2013); Christoph Schwöbel, *Christlicher Glaube im Pluralismus: Studien zu einer Theologie der Kultur* (Tübingen: Mohr Siebeck, 2003).

27   Adam Smith, *An Inquiry into the Nature and Causes of the Wealth of Nations*, 2 vols., 1st ed. (Dublin: Whitestone et al., 1776), 2:516.

28   Robert D. Putnam, *Bowling Alone: The Collapse and Revival of American Community* (New York: Simon & Schuster, 2000); idem et al., *Better Together: Restoring the American Community* (New York: Simon & Schuster, 2004).

29   David L. Tubbs, *Freedom's Orphans: Contemporary Liberalism and the Fate of American Children* (Princeton: Princeton University Press, 2007), 7.

30   Tubbs, *Freedom's Orphans*.

31   Tubbs, *Freedom's Orphans*, 8.

32   Tubbs, *Freedom's Orphans*.

33   Tubbs, *Freedom's Orphans*, 19.

34 Tubbs, *Freedom's Orphans*, 20.

35 Thomas Aquinas, *Misericordia est maxima virtutum*, S.th., IIa IIae, q. 30, art. 4. Aquinas explains that love, or charity, is the greatest virtue with regard to our relationship to God, but mercy is the greatest with regard to human relationships.

36 For more on this subject and the very disputed term, see these recent studies: George Crowder, *Theories of Multiculturalism: An Introduction* (Cambridge: Polity, 2013); Michael Kearney, *From Conflict to Recognition: Moving Multiculturalism Forward* (Amsterdam: Rodopi, 2012); Michael Murphy, *Multiculturalism: A Critical Introduction* (London: Routledge, 2012); Imke Leicht, *Multikulturalismus auf dem Prüfstand: Kultur, Identität und Differenz in modernen Einwanderungsgesellschaften* (Berlin: Metropol-Verlag, 2009).

37 John M. Headley, *Problem with Multiculturalism*, xii; idem, *The Europeanization of the World*. Demographic shifts have provoked strong challenges to multiculturalism and immigration, as seen, for example, in the conservative cultural commentator Christopher Caldwell, *Reflections on the Revolution in Europe* (London: Allen Lane, 2009).

38 Headley, *Problem with Multiculturalism*, xiv.

39 Headley, *Problem with Multiculturalism*, xv.

40 Headley, *Problem with Multiculturalism*, ix.

41 Headley, *Problem with Multiculturalism*, xii.

42 On theological engagement with the issue of immigration, see Alexander Y. Hwang et al., eds., *Strangers in This World: Multi-religious Reflections on Immigration* (Minneapolis: Fortress, 2015).

43 Daniel Weinstock, "Liberalism and Multiculturalism," in *The Cambridge Companion to Liberalism*, ed. Steven Wall (Cambridge: Cambridge University Press, 2015), 305–28, here 308.

44 Many historians have, however, drawn attention to these forgotten aspects of the history. See the literature cited above in the section dealing with the definitions of the Western world and the influence of Islam on the Western world (§1.1). The term "Troubled History" comes from Rollin Armour, *Islam, Christianity and the West: A Troubled History* (Maryknoll, N.Y.: Orbis Books, 2003).

45 Michael Curtis, *Orientalism and Islam: European Thinkers on Oriental Despotism in the Middle East and India* (Cambridge: Cambridge University Press, 2009), 6.

46 Cf. Aziz al-Azmeh, *The Emergence of Islam in Late Antiquity: Allah and His People* (Cambridge: Cambridge University Press, 2014), xiii.

47 See Robert G. Hoyland, *In God's Path: The Arab Conquests and the Creation of an Islamic Empire* (Oxford: Oxford University Press, 2015); Hugh Kennedy, *The Great Arab Conquests: How the Spread of Islam Changed the World We Live In* (London: Weidenfeld & Nicolson, 2007).

48 Christopher Tyerman, *God's War: A New History of the Crusades* (Cambridge, Mass.: Belknap Press of Harvard University Press, 2006); Jonathan Riley-Smith, ed., *The Oxford History of the Crusades* (Oxford: Oxford University Press, 2002).

49 Claire L. Adida, David D. Laitin, and Marie-Anne Valfort, *Why Muslim Integration Fails in Christian-Heritage Societies* (Cambridge, Mass.: Harvard University Press, 2016), 126. This is in part due to a "discriminatory equilibrium whereby (1) rooted French exhibit taste-based and statistical discrimination against Muslims and (2) Muslims, perceiving more hostility in France, separate more from the host

society than do their Christian counterparts" (125). This analysis is drawn from their study of France.

50 Adida, Laitin, and Valfort, *Why Muslim Integration Fails*. They claim that "both Muslim immigrants and the host population in France bear joint responsibility for the failure of Muslims not only in France but in other Christian-heritage societies as well" (14). See also Ruud Koopmans, "Religious Fundamentalism and Hostility against Out-Groups: A Comparison of Muslims and Christians in Western Europe," *Journal of Ethnic and Migration Studies* 41, no. 1 (2015): 33–57. For a critical analysis of the current state of integration, see Bassam Tibi, "Warum ich kapituliere," in *Cicero* 13/6 (2016): 115–19. Tibi is the author of the popular work *Euro-Islam: die Lösung eines Zivilisationskonfliktes* (Darmstadt: Wissenschaftliche Buchgesellschaft, 2009).

51 See Leila Ahmed, *Women and Gender in Islam: Historical Roots of a Modern Debate* (New Haven, Conn.: Yale University Press, 1992).

52 On the violent ideology of radical Islam, see Rukmini Callimachi, "Enslaving Young Girls, the Islamic State Builds a Vast System of Rape," *New York Times*, August 14, 2015, A1; see also Cole Bunzel, *From Paper State to Caliphate: The Ideology of the Islamic State*, The Brookings Project on U.S. Relations with the Islamic World, Analysis Paper No. 19 (Washington: Brookings Institution, 2015), https://www.brookings.edu/wp-content/uploads/2016/06/The-ideology-of-the-Islamic-State-1.pdf; V. G. Julie Rajan, *Al Qaeda's Global Crisis: The Islamic State, Takfir and the Genocide of Muslims* (London: Routledge, 2016).

53 Bernard Lewis, *The Political Language of Islam* (Chicago: University of Chicago Press, 1988), 72.

54 See, for example, Katajun Amirpur, *Den Islam neu denken: Der Dschihad für Demokratie, Freiheit und Frauenrechte* (München: Beck, 2013).

55 Francesca Forte, "Ethical Questions in Western Islamic Experience," in *Routledge Handbook of Islam in the West*, ed. Roberto Tottoli (New York: Routledge, 2015), 378–94, here 387.

56 "Erstes Zentrum für Islamische Theologie eingeweiht," *Zeit Online*, January 17, 2012, http:/www.zeit.de/studium/hochschule/2012–01/zentrum-islamische-theologie-2.

57 David J. Collins, ed., *The Cambridge History of Magic and Witchcraft in the West: From Antiquity to the Present* (Cambridge: Cambridge University Press, 2015); Brian A. Pavlac, *Witch Hunts in the Western World: Persecution and Punishment from the Inquisition through the Salem Trials* (Westport, Conn.: Greenwood, 2009).

58 "Egypt's Top Muslim Cleric Denounces 'Hideous' Paris Attacks," *Ahram*, November 14, 2015.

Chapter 7

1 The movement toward dialogue had already begun in the sixteenth century; see Olivier Christin, "Religious Colloquies and Toleration," in *Cambridge History of Christianity*, vol. 6: *Reform and Expansion, 1500–1660*, ed. R. Po-Chia Hsia (Cambridge: Cambridge University Press, 2007), 302–20. See also my "Die Ökumene nach der ökumenischen Bewegung," in *Rationalität im Gespräch. Philosophische und Theologische Perspektiven—Rationality in Conversation: Philosophical and Theological Perspectives*, ed. C. Drobe, A. Kupsch, M. Mühling, P. S. Peterson, and M. Wendte (Leipzig: Evangelische Verlagsanstalt, 2016).

2   *Unitatis redintegratio* (1964), §1, in *Decrees of the Ecumenical Councils*, ed. Norman P. Tanner, vol. 2: *Trent to Vatican II* (Washington, D.C.: Georgetown University Press, 1990).

3   *Unitatis redintegratio*, §1.

4   *Unitatis redintegratio*, §4.

5   "Joint Declaration of Pope Paul VI and the Ecumenical Patriarch Athenagoras I" (December 7, 1965), in *Vatican Council II, Closing Speeches, December 7–8, 1965* (Boston: St. Paul Editions, 1965), 16.

6   "Joint Declaration of Pope Paul VI and the Ecumenical Patriarch Athenagoras I," 17.

7   William G. Rusch and Daniel F. Martensen, eds., *The Leuenberg Agreement and Lutheran-Reformed Relationships: Evaluations by North American and European Theologians* (Minneapolis: Augsburg, 1989).

8   Rusch and Martensen, *Leuenberg Agreement and Lutheran-Reformed Relationships*, §20.

9   Rusch and Martensen, *Leuenberg Agreement and Lutheran-Reformed Relationships*, §28.

10   World Council of Churches, *Baptism, Eucharist, and Ministry*, Faith and Order Paper No. 111 (Geneva: WCC Publications, 1982).

11   World Council of Churches, *Baptism, Eucharist, and Ministry*, §15.

12   World Council of Churches, *Baptism, Eucharist, and Ministry*, §33.

13   The German version was published in "Wechselseitige Taufanerkennung," *Ökumenische Rundschau* 56 (2007): 257. The English translation is from the Evangelical Church in Germany, ekd.de. See also WCC, *One Baptism: Towards Mutual Recognition*, Faith and Order Paper No. 210 (Geneva: WCC Publications, 2011).

14   George Lindbeck, "The Unity We Seek: Setting the Agenda for Ecumenism," *Christian Century* 122, no. 16 (2005): 28–31, here 28.

15   Cf. Yves Congar, *Divided Christendom: A Catholic Study of the Problem of Reunion*, trans. M. A. Bousfield (London: Centenary, 1939).

16   Lindbeck, "Unity We Seek," 28.

17   Lindbeck, "Unity We Seek."

18   Lindbeck, "Unity We Seek."

19   Lindbeck, "Unity We Seek," 29.

20   As cited by Lindbeck, "Unity We Seek," 29. He refers to the institute's collection "Ecumenical People, Programs, Papers."

21   Lindbeck, "Unity We Seek," 29.

22   Lindbeck, "Unity We Seek."

23   Cf. Michael Kinnamon, *Vision of the Ecumenical Movement and How It Has Been Impoverished by Its Friends* (St. Louis, Mo.: Chalice, 2003); Carl E. Braaten and Robert W. Jenson, eds., *In One Body through the Cross: The Princeton Proposal for Christian Unity; A Call to the Churches from an Ecumenical Study Group* (Grand Rapids: Eerdmans, 2003).

24   Lindbeck, "Unity We Seek," 30.

25   Carl E. Braaten and Robert W. Jenson, "To the Churches," in idem, *Princeton Proposal*, 5–7, here 6. The new paradigm is addressed in paragraph 17, including, among other things, a shift from "traditional Christian doctrinal and structural

concerns to interreligious dialogue" (24). The new paradigm shift is also characterized as a turn to "care for the planet" and issues regarding "gender and race." "It is now generally agreed that the classical interests of Faith and Order and Mission and Evangelism have been marginalized in the Council" (25). In the new paradigm, the agenda of "Life and Work" prevailed over that of Faith and Order and Mission and Evangelism (24). Although the authors of the *Princeton Proposal* do not name him, the "new paradigm" came with Konrad Raiser, WCC general secretary from 1993 to 2003. In 1989, before his election, he called for a "paradigm shift" in ecumenism. See Raiser, *Ecumenism in Transition: A Paradigm Shift in the Ecumenical Movement?* (Geneva: WCC Publications, 1991).

26   See "Evangelicals and Catholics Together: The Gift of Salvation," *Christianity Today* 41, no. 14 (1997): 35–38. See also the collection of all the statements in Timothy George and Thomas G. Guarino, eds., *Evangelicals and Catholics Together at Twenty: Vital Statements on Contested Topics* (Grand Rapids: Brazos, 2015).

27   See Lutheran World Federation and the Roman Catholic Church, *Joint Declaration on the Doctrine of Justification* (Grand Rapids: Eerdmans, 2000), §15.

28   Lutheran World Federation and Roman Catholic Church, *Joint Declaration on the Doctrine of Justification*, §40.

29   Lutheran World Federation and Roman Catholic Church, *Joint Declaration on the Doctrine of Justification*, §41.

30   For an account of the history, see John A. Radano, *Lutheran and Catholic Reconciliation on Justification* (Grand Rapids: Eerdmans, 2009), 147ff. See also Pieter de Witte, *Doctrine, Dynamic and Difference: To the Heart of the Lutheran–Roman Catholic Differentiated Consensus on Justification* (London: Bloomsbury, 2013); my review of this book was published in *International Journal for the Study of the Christian Church* 14 (2014): 83–85. See also William G. Rusch, ed., *Justification and the Future of the Ecumenical Movement: The Joint Declaration on the Doctrine of Justification* (Collegeville, Minn.: Liturgical, 2003); Lutherischer Weltbund, *10 Jahre Gemeinsame Erklärung zur Rechtfertigungslehre: Dokumentation der Jubiläumsfeier in Augsburg 2009* (Paderborn: Bonifatius, 2011); Udo Hahn, Friedrich Hauschildt, and Andreas Siemens, eds., *Die gemeinsame Erklärung zur Rechtfertigungslehre: Dokumentation des Entstehungs- und Rezeptionsprozesses* (Göttingen: Vandenhoeck & Ruprecht, 2009).

31   Nicholas Rescher, *Pluralism: Against the Demand for Consensus* (Oxford: Clarendon, 1993).

32   Jürgen Moltmann, *A Broad Place: An Autobiography* (Minneapolis: Fortress, 2007), 86.

33   George Lindbeck in *Postliberal Theology and the Church Catholic: Conversations with George Lindbeck, David Burrell and Stanley Hauerwas*, ed. John Wright (Grand Rapids: Baker Academic, 2012), 120.

34   Lindbeck in *Postliberal Theology and the Church Catholic*, 120. For more on the interrelationship of Judaism and Christianity, see Peter Schäfer, *Anziehung und Abstoßung: Juden und Christen in den ersten Jahrhunderten ihrer Begegnung* [Attraction and Repulsion: Jews and Christians in the First Centuries of their Encounter], ed. Jürgen Kampmann, trans. P. S. Peterson (Tübingen: Mohr Siebeck, 2015).

35   "Was ist und zu welchem Ende betreibt man Konsensökumene?"

36   Michael Kinnamon, *Can a Renewal Movement Be Renewed: Questions for the Future of Ecumenism* (Grand Rapids: Eerdmans, 2014).

37   Bryan R. Wilson, *Religion in Secular Society: A Sociological Comment* (London: Watts, 1966), 125–41; see David M. Thompson, "Ecumenism," in *Cambridge History of Christianity*, vol. 9: *World Christianities, c. 1914–2000*, ed. Hugh McLeod (Cambridge: Cambridge University Press, 2006), 50–70, here 69. See also Elesha J. Coffman, *The Christian Century and the Rise of the Protestant Mainline* (Oxford: Oxford University Press, 2013).

38   Thompson, "Ecumenism," 70.

39   Adelle M. Banks, "Hopes for an 'Ecumenical Spring,'" *Christian Century* 129, no. 7 (2012), 14–15, here 14.

40   S. Wesley Ariarajah, "Achievements and Limits of the World Council of Churches," in *Celebrating a Century of Ecumenism: Exploring the Achievements of International Dialogue; In Commemoration of the Centenary of the 1910 Edinburgh World Missionary Conference*, ed. John A. Radano (Grand Rapids: Eerdmans, 2012), 3–14, here 13–14.

41   A recent example of this is provided by Jordan J. Ballor. In his book from 2010, he challenged the politicization of ecumenism. Ballor, *Ecumenical Babel: Confusing Economic Ideology and the Church's Social Witness* (Grand Rapids: Christian Library, 2010).

42   Steven R. Harmon, *Ecumenism Means You, Too: Ordinary Christians and the Quest for Christian Unity* (Eugene, Ore.: Cascade, 2010).

43   Robert W. Jenson, "Ecumenism's Strange Future," January 17, 2014, http://living church.org/strange-future-of-ecumenism.

44   *Unitatis redintegratio*, §3.

45   Michael Welker, "Die Leuenberger Konkordie, die Leistungskraft des Modells 'Kirchengemeinschaft' und systematisch-theologische Zukunftsaufgaben," in *Kirche in Gemeinschaft—Kirchengemeinschaft?: Impulse der Leuenberger Konkordie für die ökumenische Zukunft*, ed. Michael Weinrich, Ulrich Möller, Vicco von Bülow, and Heike Koch (Neukirchen-Vluyn: Neukirchener Theologie, 2014), 162–66, here 164–65. The conference was held from July 22 to 25, 2013, in the Haus Villigst, near Schwerte in Germany.

46   The "Common Declaration of Pope Francis and the Ecumenical Patriarch Bartholomew I" (May 25, 2014) is accessible at http://w2.vatican.va/content/francesco/en/speeches/2014/may/documents/papa-francesco_20140525_terra-santa-dichiarazione-congiunta.html. See also recent engagement with this theme found in John Panteleimon Manoussakis, *For the Unity of All: Contributions to the Theological Dialogue between East and West* (Eugene, Ore.: Wipf & Stock, 2015). In the foreword of this book, Ecumenical Patriarch Bartholomew I of Constantinople remarks with a view to the dialogue with the Roman Church since the 1960s to today, "The 'dialogue of love' gradually prompted and progressed into the 'dialogue of truth.'"

47   "Common Declaration," §3.

48   "Common Declaration," §4.

49   "Common Declaration," §4.

50   The Pan-Orthodox Council (Orthodox Academy of Crete, June 16–27, 2016) has set a new agenda in discussions about "the Mission of the Orthodox Church in

the Contemporary World, The Orthodox Diaspora, Autonomy and its Manner of Proclamation, The Sacrament of Marriage and its Impediments, The Significance of Fasting and its Application Today, and Relations of the Orthodox Church with the Rest of the Christian World." Communiqué from the Secretariat of the Sacred Synaxis of the Primates of the Orthodox Churches, Orthodox Center of the Ecumenical Patriarchate in Chambésy-Geneva, January 27, 2016.

51 World Council of Churches, *The Church: Towards a Common Vision*, Faith and Order Paper No. 214 (Geneva: WCC Publications, 2013), §10, p. 8.

52 World Council of Churches, "God's Gift and Call to Unity—and Our Commitment," Tenth Assembly, October 30 to November 8, 2013, Busan, Republic of Korea, document no. PRC 01.1, §10.

53 World Council of Churches, "God's Gift and Call to Unity," §11.

54 Harding Meyer, "Einheit in versöhnter Verschiedenheit. Eine ökumenische Zielvorstellung; ihre Absicht, Entstehung und Bedeutung," *Kerygma und Dogma: Zeitschrift für theologische Forschung und kirchliche Lehre* 61 (2015): 83–106.

55 Mark A. Noll and Carolyn Nystrom, *Is the Reformation Over?: An Evangelical Assessment of Contemporary Roman Catholicism* (Grand Rapids: Baker Academic, 2005), 230. The title follows Geoffrey Wainwright, *Is the Reformation Over? Catholics and Protestants at the Turn of the Millennia* (Milwaukee, Wis.: Marquette University Press, 2000). Originally, it was a lecture that followed the discussion about the *Joint Declaration*.

56 Noll and Nystrom, *Is the Reformation Over?*, 251.

57 Noll and Nystrom, *Is the Reformation Over?*, 237.

58 Wainwright, *Is the Reformation Over?*, 27.

59 Hanns Chritof Brennecke, "Papacy, I. Early Church," in *Religion Past and Present*, vol. 9, ed. Hans Dieter Betz et al. (Leiden: Brill, 2011), 489–91, here 489.

60 Brennecke, "Papacy, I. Early Church."

61 Vatican Council II, *Dogmatic Constitution on the Church, Lumen gentium*, §22. Cf. *Acta Apostolicae Sedis* 57 (1965): 26: "Romanus enim Pontifex habet in Ecclesiam, vi muneris sui, Vicarii scilicet Christi et totius Ecclesiae Pastoris, plenam, supremam et universalem potestatem, quam semper libere exercere valet." This was also taken into the *Catechism of the Catholic Church*, pt. 1, sec. 2, chap. 3, art. 9, par. 4, no. 882.

62 Matt 16:18-19: "And I tell you, you are Peter, and on this rock I will build my church, and the gates of Hades will not prevail against it. I will give you the keys of the kingdom of heaven, and whatever you bind on earth will be bound in heaven, and whatever you loose on earth will be loosed in heaven."

63 David L. Turner, *Matthew*, Baker Exegetical Commentary on the New Testament (Grand Rapids: Baker Academic, 2008), 407.

64 Donald A. Hagner, *Matthew 14–28*, Word Biblical Commentary 33B (Dallas, Tex.: Word, 1995), 470.

65 Matthias Konradt, *Das Evangelium nach Matthäus* (Göttingen: Vandenhoeck & Ruprecht, 2015), 262.

66 Gerhard Ludwig Müller, *Katholische Dogmatik* (Freiburg: Herder, 2012), 622: "Wenn die neutestamentlichen Quellen ihrer literarischen Gattung nach auch nicht von einem Nachfolger Petri sprechen und sprechen konnten, so gibt es doch Anhaltspunkte in der frühesten nachapostolischen Tradition, die den Apostolat Petri in besonderer Weise mit der römischen Kirche verbinden."

67 Müller, *Katholische Dogmatik*, 625: "Er kann jederzeit seine ordentliche Vollmacht gegenüber allen Gläubigen und Bischöfen unmittelbar ausüben." Müller's presentation of the Catholic teaching about the papacy is, nevertheless, very learned. He also does his best to emphasize the authority of the council in his interpretation.

68 The possibility of a reformed papacy was addressed above in chap. 3, §3.4, "Scripture, tradition, and the magisterium."

69 *Dogmatic Constitution on Divine Revelation; Dei verbum* (Washington, D.C.: United States Catholic Conference, 1994), §10. Cf. *Acta Apostolicae Sedis* 58 (1966): 817–36.

70 Thomas A. Brady Jr., *German Histories in the Age of Reformations, 1400–1650* (Cambridge: Cambridge University Press, 2009), 420.

71 Thomas Kaufmann, *Geschichte der Reformation* (Frankfurt: Verlag der Weltreligionen, 2009), 719: "In dieser Hinsicht ist die Reformation gescheitert."

72 Wolfhart Pannenberg, *Beiträge zur systematischen Theologie: Kirche und Ökumene* (Göttingen: Vandenhoeck & Ruprecht, 2000), 173: "Die Existenz besonderer evangelischer Kirchen bekundet das Scheitern der Reformation." See also Wolfhart Pannenberg, *Reformation zwischen gestern und morgen* (Gütersloh: Gütersloher Verlagshaus G. Mohn, 1969).

73 Pannenberg, *Reformation zwischen gestern und morgen*, 190: "Vollendung der im 16. Jahrhundert gescheiterten oder zumindest abgebrochenen Reformation der Christenheit."

74 See Emidio Campi, "'Ecclesia semper reformanda' Metamorphosen einer alterwürdigen Formel," in *Zwingliana* 37 (2010): 1–19.

75 Karl Lehmann and Wolfhart Pannenberg, eds., *Condemnations of the Reformation Era: Do They Still Divide?*, trans. Margaret Kohl (Minneapolis: Fortress, 1990); The Lutheran World Federation and Pontifical Council for Promoting Christian Unity, *The Apostolicity of the Church: Study Document of the Lutheran–Roman Catholic Commission on Unity* (Minneapolis: Lutheran University Press, 2006).

76 Lutheran–Roman Catholic Commission on Unity, *From Conflict to Communion: Lutheran-Catholic Common Commemoration of the Reformation in 2017* (Leipzig: Bonifatius, 2013). See also Petra Bosse-Huber, Serge Fornerod, Thies Gundlach, and Gottfried Locher, eds., *500 Jahre Reformation—Bedeutung und Herausforderungen* (Zurich: Theologischer Verlag, 2014).

77 Dorothea Sattler and Volker Leppin, eds., *Reformation 1517–2017: Ökumenische Perspektiven; für den ökumenischen Arbeitskreis evangelischer und katholischer Theologen* (Freiburg im Breisgau: Herder, 2014), 103–4.

78 Sattler and Leppin, *Reformation 1517–2017*, 105.

79 Sattler and Leppin, *Reformation 1517–2017*.

80 The theologians affirm that the Protestants have learned to embrace a new understanding of ordination and a new emphasis on the sacraments. Sattler and Leppin, *Reformation 1517–2017*, 106.

81 Sattler and Leppin, *Reformation 1517–2017*, 107.

82 Sattler and Leppin, *Reformation 1517–2017*, 109.

83 Sattler and Leppin, *Reformation 1517–2017*.

84 Sattler and Leppin, *Reformation 1517–2017*, 111.

85 Sattler and Leppin, *Reformation 1517–2017*, 112.

86 Sattler and Leppin, *Reformation 1517–2017*, 113.

87 *John Wesley*, ed. Albert C. Outler (New York: Oxford University Press, 1964), 66. He had this experience while reading Luther's preface to Romans with a group of Moravians.

88 Bob Scribner, "Germany," in *Reformation in National Context*, ed. Bob Scribner, Roy Porter, and Mikulás Teich (Cambridge: Cambridge University Press, 1994), 4–29, here 4.

89 Ulrich Barth, *Aufgeklärter Protestantismus* (Tübingen: Mohr Siebeck, 2004), 53, 94.

90 Barth, *Aufgeklärter Protestantismus*, 94.

91 Barth, *Aufgeklärter Protestantismus*, 94.

92 *LW* 32:112–13.

93 Karlstadt, "Whether We Should Go Slowly and Avoid Offending the Weak (1524)," in *The Essential Carlstadt: Fifteen Tracts*, ed. and trans. Edward J. Furcha, Classics of the Radical Reformation, vol. 8 (Waterloo: Herald, 1995), 253.

94 See above, chap. 3, §3.4, "Scripture, tradition, and the magisterium."

95 Luther, "Disputation of Martin Luther on the Power and Efficacy of Indulgences," in *LW* 31:29. See *WA* 1.233–38.

96 Karlstadt, "On the Removal of Images and That There Should Be No Beggars among Christians (1522)," in Furcha, *Essential Carlstadt*, 121.

97 Karlstadt, "On the Removal of Images," in Furcha, *Essential Carlstadt*, 125. He also argues for the establishment of a common chest of money to be established by the churches and communities in order to care for the poor.

98 See the essays in *Spurenlese: Wirkungen der Reformation auf Wissenschaft und Bildung, Universität und Schule*, ed. Reformationsgeschichtliche Sozietät der Martin-Luther-Universität Halle-Wittenberg (Leipzig: Evangelische Verlagsanstalt, 2014); Thomas Schlag, "Der Protestantismus hat 'die Religion zweifellos intellektualisiert,'" in *Protestantisches Ethos und moderne Kultur: zur Aktualität von Ernst Troeltschs Protestantismusschrift*, ed. Georg Pfleiderer and Alexander Heit (Zurich: Theologischer Verlag, 2008), 141–53.

99 See Lee Palmer Wandel, "The Reformation and the Visual Arts," in Hsia, *Reform and Expansion*, 345–70; Alexander J. Fisher, "Music and Religious Change," in Hsia, *Reform and Expansion*, 387–405, esp. 387–97; Jochen M. Arnold, Konrad Küster, and Hans Otte, eds., *Singen, Beten, Musizieren: theologische Grundlagen der Kirchenmusik in Nord- und Mitteldeutschland zwischen Reformation und Pietismus (1530–1750)* (Göttingen: V&R unipress, 2014); Christoph Wolff, "Musik aus dem Geist der Reformation: Bibel und Gesangbuch in der Musik Johann Sebastian Bachs," in *Spurenlese: kulturelle Wirkungen der Reformation*, ed. Reformationsgeschichtliche Sozietät der Martin-Luther-Universität Halle-Wittenberg (Leipzig: Evangelische Verlagsanstalt, 2013), 350–62; Jan Harasimowicz, "Protestantismus und Bildende Kunst," in *Spurenlese: kulturelle Wirkungen der Reformation*, 333–47.

100 Vatican Council II, *Dogmatic Constitution on the Church, Lumen gentium*, §10.

101 Sattler and Leppin, *Reformation 1517–2017*, 113.

102 See Landesbischof Dr. Heinrich Bedford-Strohm, Vorsitzender des Rates der Evangelischen Kirche in Deutschland, Open Letter to Reinhard Kardinal Marx, Vorsitzender der Deutschen Bischofskonferenz, May 18, 2015, https://www.ekd.de/download/pm114_briefwechsel_reformationsjubilaeum.pdf.

103 Thomas Söding, "Reformation auf dem Prüfstand: Die ökumenische Debatte vor 2017–aus katholischer Sicht," in *Catholica* 69 (2015): 1–13, here 1. See Thomas

Kaufmann, "Reformationsgedenken in der Frühen Neuzeit: Bemerkungen zum 16. bis 18. Jahrhundert: Johannes Wallmann zum 80. Geburtstag," *Zeitschrift für Theologie und Kirche* 107 (2010): 285–324.

104 Braaten and Jenson, *Princeton Proposal*, §28, p. 32.

105 Pope Francis, *The Light of Faith; Lumenfidei* (Washington, D.C.: United States Conference of Catholic Bishops, 2013), §48.

106 Luther, "Defense and Explanation of All the Articles," in *LW* 32:82.

107 Pacian of Barcelona, Letter 3.2; as cited in *Iberian Fathers*, vol. 3: *Pacian of Barcelona, Orosius of Braga*, trans. Craig L. Hanson (Washington, D.C.: Catholic University of America Press, 1999), 40.

108 Luther, "Eine treue Vermahnung zu allen Christen, sich zu verhüten vor Aufruhr und Empörung" (1522), *WA* 8:685: "Tzum ersten bitt ich, man wolt meynes namen geschweygen und sich nit lut(h)ersch sondern Christen heyssen. [. . .] Nitt alszo, lieben freund, last uns tilgenn die parteysche namen unnd Christen heyssen, des lere wir haben." *LW* 45:70–71. See Scott Hendrix, "Martin Luther, Reformer," in Hsia, *Reform and Expansion*, 16.

109 Luther, "Von dem Papsttum zu Rom," *WA* 6:293; *LW* 39:65. See Hendrix, "Martin Luther, Reformer," in Hsia, *Reform and Expansion 1500–1660*, 10.

110 Katharina Zell, "Ein Brief an die ganze Stadt Straßburg (1557)," in Johann Conrad Füßly, *Beyträge zur Erläuterung der Kirchenreformationsgeschichte des Schweitzerlands, 5. Theil* (Zurich, 1753), 293–94; as cited in Thomas Kaufmann, *Reformatoren* (Göttingen: Vandenhoeck & Ruprecht, 1998), 30.

111 Vatican Council II, *Dogmatic Constitution on the Church, Lumen gentium*, §13. Cf. *Acta Apostolicae Sedis* 57 (1965): 17–18.

112 Sattler and Leppin, *Reformation 1517–2017*, 99 (emphasis in original).

113 See Alberto Ferreiro, ed., *Ancient Christian Commentary on Scripture*, vol. 14: *The Twelve Prophets* (Downers Grove, Ill.: InterVarsity, 2003), 57–82.

114 *Catechetical Lecture*, 27.19. See *Ancient Christian Commentary on Scripture*, 14:76.

115 St. Cyprian, "The Unity of the Catholic Church," chap. 5 in idem, *The Lapsed: The Unity of the Catholic Church*, trans. and annot. Maurice Bévenot (London: Longmans, Green., 1957), 47f.

116 Bévenot, in Cyprian, *Lapsed*, 103n26; emphasis in original.

117 Kinnamon, *Can a Renewal Movement Be Renewed?*, 37. Kinnamon gave the 2013 alumnus of the year address at the University of Chicago Divinity School. It was titled "A Report from the Front Lines of a Renewal Movement under Siege" (May 2, 2013). This issue was recently addressed by the Protestant Church in Germany: Evangelische Kirche in Deutschland, *Ökumene im 21. Jahrhundert, Bedingungen— theologische Grundlegungen—Perspektiven* (Hannover: EKD, 2015), 13ff. It claims that in many cases *"no deeper understanding of ecumenism and ecumenical institutions* has grown in regional churches and parishes" since the movement got going (15; emphasis in original).

118 *WA* 2:280. Translation cited in William G. Naphy, *Documents on the Continental Reformation* (Basingstoke: Macmillan, 1996), 18.

119 Regarding the conversation between Protestant and Orthodox churches, see Tim Grass, "Dialogue between Evangelicals and Orthodox: Past, Present and Future," *Transformation: An International Journal of Holistic Mission Studies* 27 (2010): 186–19; Dorothea Wendebourg, *Reformation und Orthodoxie. Der ökumenische*

Briefwechsel zwischen der Leitung der Württembergischen Kirche und Patriarch Ieremias II. von Konstantinopel in den Jahren 1573–1581 (Göttingen: Vandenhoeck & Ruprecht, 1986); Johannes Panagopoulos, "Luther außerhalb des Luthertums: Orthodoxe Sicht," *Concilium* 12 (1976): 497–501; Daniel Buda, "Wem gehört 2017? Versuch einer orthodoxen Perspektive," *Ökumenische Rundschau* 61 (2012): 70–78. According to Konstantinos Delikostantis, the Orthodox churches have something to learn from the Protestant tradition, especially regarding the theme of Christian freedom: "Der Reformator und das Reformationsjubiläum in orthodoxer Sicht" (paper presented at the Internationales Ökumenisches Seminar titled "Was tun mit 2017? Die ökumenische Herausforderung des Jubiläums," 46, Institut für Ökumenische Forschung, Strasbourg, France, July 4–11, 2012).

120 Pope Francis, Pastoral Visit of His Holiness Pope Francis to Turin, Visit to the Waldensian Temple, Address of the Holy Father, Corso Vittorio Emanuele II, Monday, June 22, 2015; https://w2.vatican.va/content/francesco/en/speeches/2015/june/documents/papa-francesco_20150622_torino-chiesa-valdese.html. Pope Francis draws upon Cyprian's understanding of ecclesial unity. He goes on to say to the Waldensians, "On behalf of the Catholic Church I ask your forgiveness. I ask your forgiveness for unchristian-like and even inhuman attitudes and conduct which, historically, we have had against you. In the name of the Lord Jesus Christ, forgive us!"

121 Pope John Paul II, *Ut unum sint: On Commitment to Ecumenism* (Washington, D.C.: United States Catholic Conference, 1995), §40; *Lumen fidei* also captures this sense: "the light of faith is concretely placed at the service of justice, law and peace." Pope Francis, *The Light of Faith; Lumen fidei*, §51. Pope Benedict XVI has rightly addressed how we need both a deepening of our faith and also a working together for the common good. On September 23, 2011, in an address at the Augustinian monastery in Erfurt, where Luther lived as an Augustinian friar, he spoke about the subject of ecumenism: "This is a key ecumenical task in which we have to help one another: developing a deeper and livelier faith. [...] Through such faith, Christ enters this world of ours, and with him, the living God." Pope Benedict XVI, *Address at the Meeting with the Council of the Evangelical Church of Germany*; Chapter Hall of the Former Augustinian Convent, Erfurt, Friday, September 23, 2011, https://w2.vatican.va/content/benedict-xvi/en/speeches/2011/september/documents/hf_ben-xvi_spe_20110923_evangelical-church-erfurt.html.

122 The importance of goodwill and dialogue was also addressed in *Ut unum sint*: "Each side must presuppose in the other a desire for reconciliation" (§29).

123 Pope Francis, *The Joy of the Gospel; Evangelii gaudium* (Washington, D.C.: United States Conference of Catholic Bishops, 2013), §99.

124 Andreas Bodenstein von Karlstadt, *Centum quinquagintaunum conclusiones de natura, lege et gratia, contra scolasticos et usum comunem*, 26 April 1517, in *Kritische Gesamtausgabe der Schriften und Briefe Andreas Bodensteins von Karlstadt, Teil I (1507–1518)*, ed. Thomas Kaufmann (Wolfenbüttel: Herzog-August-Bibliothek, 2012), thesis 133.

Conclusion

1 On this theme, see Werner G. Jeanrond, *A Theology of Love* (London: T&T Clark, 2010).

2   Cf. Nancy R. Heisey, "Remembering Dirk Willems: Memory and History in the Future of Ecumenical Relationships," *Journal of Ecumenical Studies* 47 (2012): 355–75.

3   Regarding a correct understanding of forgiveness in connection with the righting of wrongs, see Maria Mayo, *The Limits of Forgiveness: Case Studies in the Distortion of a Biblical Ideal* (Minneapolis: Fortress, 2015).

Further Reading

INTRODUCTORY LITERATURE ON THE REFORMATION

Appold, Kenneth G. *The Reformation: A Brief History*. Malden, Mass.: Wiley-Blackwell, 2011.

Cameron, Euan. *The European Reformation*. 2nd ed. Oxford: Oxford University Press, 2012.

Hsia, R. Po-Chia, ed. *Cambridge History of Christianity*. Vol. 6: *Reform and Expansion 1500–1660*. Cambridge: Cambridge University Press, 2007.

MacCulloch, Diarmaid. *The Reformation: A History*. New York: Viking, 2004.

GERMAN:

Kaufmann, Thomas. *Geschichte der Reformation*. Frankfurt: Verlag der Weltreligionen, 2009. Leppin, Volker. *Die Reformation*. Darmstadt: Wissenschaftliche Buchgesellschaft, 2013.

THE HISTORIOGRAPHY OF THE REFORMATION

Dixon, C. Scott. *Contesting the Reformation*. Malden, Mass.: Wiley-Blackwell, 2012.

Opitz, Peter, ed. *The Myth of the Reformation*. Göttingen: Vandenhoeck & Ruprecht, 2013.

GERMAN:

Danz, Christian, and Rochus Leonhardt, eds. *Erinnerte Reformation: Studien zur Luther-Rezeption von der Aufklärung bis zum 20. Jahrhundert.* Berlin: de Gruyter, 2008.

THE REFORMATION AND CATHOLICISM

Eire, Carlos M. N. "The Reformation." In *The Blackwell Companion to Catholicism*, edited by James J. Buckley et al., 63–80. Chichester: Wiley-Blackwell, 2011.

THE "RADICAL REFORMATION"

McLaughlin, R. Emmet. "The Radical Reformation." In Hsia, *Reform and Expansion, 1500–1660*, 37–55.

Williams, George Huntston. *The Radical Reformation.* 3rd ed. Kirksville, Mo.: Truman State University Press, 1992.

THE REFORMATION, JEWS, ANTI-SEMITISM, AND ANTI-JUDAISM

Bell, Dean Phillip, and Stephen G. Burnett, eds. *Jews, Judaism, and the Reformation in Sixteenth-Century Germany.* Leiden: Brill, 2006.

Oberman, Heiko A. *The Roots of Antisemitism in the Age of Renaissance and Reformation.* Trans. James I. Porter. Philadelphia: Fortress, 1984.

THE REFORMATION AND WOMEN

Stjerna, Kirsi Irmeli. *Women and the Reformation.* Malden, Mass.: Blackwell, 2009.

Wiesner-Hanks, Merry. "Women and Religious Change." In Hsia, *Reform and Expansion 1500–1660*, 465–82.

THE REFORMATION AND SOCIAL HISTORY

Benedict, Philip. *Christ's Churches Purely Reformed: A Social History of Calvinism.* New Haven, Conn.: Yale University Press, 2002.

THE REFORMATION AND TOLERANCE

Mout, Nicolette. "Peace without Concord: Religious Toleration in Theory and Practice." In Hsia, *Reform and Expansion, 1500–1660*, 227–43.

THE REFORMATION AND CAPITALISM

Lehmann, Hartmut, and Guenther Roth, eds. *Weber's Protestant Ethic: Origins, Evidence, Contexts.* Cambridge: Cambridge University Press, 1993.

THE REFORMATION, ENCHANTMENT, AND DISENCHANTMENT

Cameron, Euan. *Enchanted Europe: Superstition, Reason, and Religion, 1250–1750.* Oxford: Oxford University Press, 2011.

Scribner, Robert W. "Elements of Popular Belief." In *Handbook of European History, 1400–1600: Late Middle Ages, Renaissance and Reformation,* edited by Thomas A. Brady Jr. et al. Vol. 1: *Structures and Assertions,* 231–62. Leiden: Brill, 1994.

THE REFORMATION AND ECUMENISM

Lehmann, Karl, and Wolfhart Pannenberg, eds. *Condemnations of the Reformation Era: Do They Still Divide?* Trans. Margaret Kohl. Minneapolis: Fortress, 1990.

Lutheran–Roman Catholic Commission on Unity. *From Conflict to Communion: Lutheran-Catholic Common Commemoration of the Reformation in 2017.* Leipzig: Bonifatius, 2013.

Name and Subject Index